"*Head First Rails* continues the tradition of the Head First series, providing useful, real-world information to get you up and going quickly. *Head First Rails* is an excellent book for people learning Rails, as well as those brushing up on the latest features."

— Jeremy Durham, Web Developer

W9-BZC-427

"I wish this book was out when I was getting started with Rails. It would have helped immensely."

— Mike Isman, Web Developer

"I love the Head First Books. They are both educational and entertaining!!"

— LuAnn Mazza

"*Head First Rails* is a great, broad introduction to iterative Web 2.0 development. This book will show you how quick and easy it is to develop robust, next-generation websites."

— Matt Proud, Systems Administrator and Developer

"*Head First Rails* is the book I wish I had when I was first learning Rails. It leads you through the essential things you need to know in a humorous, no-nonsense, manner."

— Eamon Walshe, Agile Coach

Praise for *Head First* Ajax

"Ajax is more than just revisiting existing technologies, making some small changes to your web application and then declaring it Ajax-enabled. Rebecca M. Riordan walks you through all of the steps of building an Ajax application in *Head First Ajax*, and shows you that Ajax is more than 'that little asynchronous part', but a better approach to web design all together."

> — **Anthony T. Holdener III, author of "Ajax: The Definitive Guide"**

"You don't just read Head First books, you *do* Head First books. And it makes all the difference."

> — **Pauline McNamara, Techno-pedagogical Consultant for university eLearning projects, Switzerland**

"The author does an excellent job teaching the various aspects of Ajax, bringing back previous lessons without being repetitive and introducing common problems in a way that helps readers discover the problems themselves. In areas where there still isn't a definitive practice, the reader is exposed to all the options and encouraged to make up his or her own mind."

> — **Elaine Nelson, Website Designer**

"Behind the Ajax eight ball? Get out of the shadows with this book. You'll wrap your mind around the core concepts, and have some fun in the process."

> — **Bear Bibeault, Web Applications Architect**

Other related books from O'Reilly

Learning Rails

Enterprise Rails

The Ruby Programming Language

Ruby Pocket Reference

RESTful Web Services

Other books in O'Reilly's *Head First* series

Head First Java™

Head First Object-Oriented Analysis and Design (OOA&D)

Head First HTML with CSS and XHTML

Head First Design Patterns

Head First Servlets and JSP

Head First EJB

Head First PMP

Head First SQL

Head First Software Development

Head First JavaScript

Head First Ajax

Head First Physics

Head First Statistics

Head First Web Design

Head First PHP & MySQL

Head First Algebra

Head First **Rails**

Wouldn't it be dreamy if there was a book on Rails programming that wasn't just a bunch of theory and shopping cart examples? It's probably just a fantasy...

David Griffiths

O'REILLY®

Beijing • Cambridge • Köln • Sebastopol • Taipei • Tokyo

Head First Rails

by David Griffiths

Published by O'Reilly Media, Inc., 1005 Gravenstein Highway North, Sebastopol, CA 95472.

O'Reilly Media books may be purchased for educational, business, or sales promotional use. Online editions are also available for most titles (*safari.oreilly.com*). For more information, contact our corporate/institutional sales department: (800) 998-9938 or *corporate@oreilly.com*.

Series Creators:	Kathy Sierra, Bert Bates
Series Editor:	Brett D. McLaughlin
Editors:	Brett D. McLaughlin, Louise Barr
Design Editor:	Louise Barr
Cover Designers:	Louise Barr, Steve Fehler
Production Editor:	Brittany Smith
Proofreader:	Matt Proud
Indexer:	Julie Hawks
Page Viewers:	Dawn Griffiths, Friski the Wi-fi Bunny

Printing History:

December 2008: First Edition.

Dawn Griffiths

Friski the Wi-fi bunny

ISBN: 978-0-596-51577-5

[M]

For Dawn, and in memory of my Mother, Joan Beryl Griffiths.

Author of Head First Rails

David Griffiths

David Griffiths began programming at age 12, after watching a documentary on the work of Seymour Papert. At age 15 he wrote an implementation of Papert's computer language LOGO. After studying Pure Mathematics at University, he began writing code for computers and magazine articles for humans and he is currently working as an agile coach in the UK, helping people to create simpler, more valuable software. He spends his free time traveling with his lovely wife, Dawn.

Table of Contents (Summary)

	Intro	xxi
1	Really Rapid Rails: *Getting Started*	1
2	Rails Apps, Made to Order: *Beyond Scaffolding*	45
3	Everything Changes: *Inserting, Updating, and Deleting*	103
4	Truth or Consequences?: *Database Finders*	153
5	Preventing Mistakes: *Validating Your Data*	187
6	Bringing It All Together: *Making Connections*	219
7	Avoiding the Traffic: *Ajax*	263
8	It All Looks Different Now... : *XML and Multiple Representations*	307
9	Taking Things Further: *REST and Ajax*	357
10	Rails in the Real World: *Real-World Applications*	401

Table of Contents (the real thing)

Intro

Your brain on Rails. Here *you* are trying to *learn* something, while here your *brain* is doing you a favor by making sure the learning doesn't *stick*. Your brain's thinking, "Better leave room for more important things, like which wild animals to avoid and whether naked snowboarding is a bad idea." So how *do* you trick your brain into thinking that your life depends on knowing Rails?

Who is this book for?	xxii
We know what you're thinking	xxiii
Metacognition	xxv
Bend your brain into submission	xxvii
Read me	xxviii
The technical review team	xxx
Acknowledgments	xxxi

1

getting started

Really Rapid Rails

Want to get your web app development off to a flying start? Then you need to know **Rails**. Rails is the **coolest** and **quickest development framework** in town, allowing you to develop **fully functional web apps** quicker than you ever thought possible. Getting started is simple; all you need to do is **install Rails**, and start turning the pages. Before you know it, you'll be **miles ahead of the competition**.

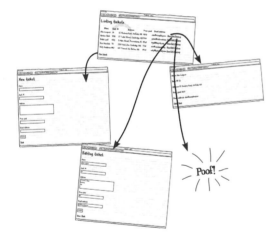

Poof!

The application needs to do lots of things	3
So what things do we need for the app?	4
Rails is for database-centric apps like the ticket sales system	6
You create a new application with the rails command	7
Now you need to add your own code to the default app	9
Scaffolding is generated code	10
There are no tables in the database yet!	14
Create the table by running a migration	15
Sweet! You saved your buddy's job!	19
To modify an app, you need to dig into the app's architecture	20
The 3 parts of your app: model, view, and controller	21
Rails Exposed	22
The 3 types of code are kept in separate folders	25
The files in the view need to be edited	26
Edit the HTML in the view	27
The application needs to store more information now	31
A migration is just a Ruby script	32
Rails can generate migrations	33
Give your migration a "smart" name, and Rails writes your code for you	34
You need to run your migration with rake	35
But changing the database isn't enough	36

beyond scaffolding
Rails apps, made to order

2

So what's really going on with Rails? You've seen how **scaffolding** generates heaps of code and helps you write web applications wicked fast, but what if you want something a little different? In this chapter you'll see how to really *seize control* of your Rails development and take a look underneath the hood of the framework. You'll learn how Rails decides which **code** to run, how **data** is read from the database, and how **web pages** are generated. By the end, you'll be able to publish data the way *you* want.

Scaffolding does way too much	49
Let's start by generating the MeBay model...	50
... and then we'll actually create the table using rake	51
But what about the controller?	52
The view is created with a page template	54
The page template contains HTML	55
A route tells Rails where your web page is	57
The view doesn't have the data to display	64
So what should the page show?	65
The controller sends the ad to the view	66
Rails turned the record into an object	68
The data's in memory, and the web page can see it	69
There's a problem—people can't find the pages they want	73
Routes run in priority order	76
To get data into the view, you will also need code in the controller	78
An index page will need data from all of the records	79
Ad.find(:all) reads the whole table at once	80
The data is returned as an object called an array	81
An array is a numbered sequence of objects	82
Read all of the ads with a for loop	86
We need HTML for each element in the array	87
Rails converts page templates into Ruby code	88
Loops can be added to page templates using scriptlets	89
On each pass of the loop, the page generates one link	90
So what does the generated HTML look like?	91
But there are two page templates... should we change the code of each one?	94
But what about the new static content MeBay sent over?	97

inserting, updating, and deleting

Everything changes

Change is a fact of life—especially for data. So far you've seen how to whip up a quick Rails application with scaffolding, and how to write your own code to publish data from a database. But what if you want users to be able to edit data *your* way? What if scaffolding doesn't do what *you* want? In this chapter, you'll learn how to **insert**, **update**, and **delete** data in exactly the way you want. And while you're doing that, you'll be taken deeper into how Rails *really* works and maybe even learn a little about security along the way.

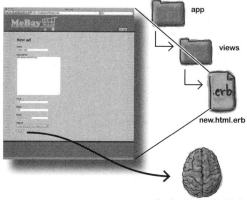

The "create" method in the ads controller

People want to post new ads online   104

You already know how to build an app that publishes data from the database   105

Saving data works just the opposite of reading data   106

You need a form to submit data and an action method to save it   107

Are forms and objects related?   109

Rails can create forms that are associated with model objects   110

The @ad form object has not been created   114

The form object needs to be created before the form is displayed   115

The forms ad object will be created in the new action of the controller   116

Each page template now has a matching controller method   117

The form doesn't send an object back, it sends data back   119

Rails needs to convert the data into an object before it can be saved   120

The controller create method, step-by-step   121

The controller needs to save the record   122

Don't create a new page, use an existing one   128

But how can a controller action display another action's page?   129

Redirects let the controller specify which view is displayed   130

But what if an ad needs to be amended after it's been posted?   133

Updating an ad is just like creating one... only different   134

Instead of creating an ad, you need to find one; instead of saving it, you need to update the ad   135

Restricting access to a function   142

... but now old ads need to be deleted   145

Doing it yourself gave you the power to do more than scaffolding   151

database finders

Truth or consequences?

4

Every decision you make has consequences.

In Rails, knowing how to make **good decisions** can save you both time and effort. In this chapter, we'll look at how **user requirements** affect the choices you make, right from the very **beginning** of your app. Should you use scaffolding and modify the generated code? Should you create things from scratch? Either way, when it comes time to customize your app further, you need to learn about **finders**: *getting at your data* in a way that makes sense to you and serves your **users' needs**.

Keep fit with the Rubyville Health Club	154
The application actually looks pretty close...	157
We're going to fix the scaffolding	158
Design the search function	159
Let's start by building the form	160
Add the search to the interface	163
How do we find client records?	171
We only need those records where client_name = the search string	172
There's a finder for every attribute	173
We need to match either the client name or the trainer name	178
Finders write database queries	179
We need to be able to modify the conditions used in the SQL query	180
Use :conditions to supply SQL	181

Business is really taking off but we're having trouble keeping track of all the personal fitness sessions of our clients. Think you can help?

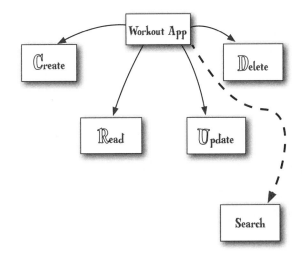

5

validating your data

Preventing mistakes

Everyone makes mistakes... but many of them are preventable!

Even with the very best of intentions, your users will still enter bad data into your web app, **leaving you to deal with the consequences**. But just imagine if there was some way of **preventing mistakes** from happening in the first place. That's where **validators** come in. Keep reading, and we'll show you how to add **clever Rails validation** to your web app so that you can **take control** of what data is allowed in—and what needs to be kept out.

Watch out—there's bad data in the room	188
Validation code goes in the MODEL	190
Rails uses validators for simple validation	191
So how do validators work?	192
Let's check if something is a number	194
Users have been leaving out data on their workout forms	196
How do we check for mandatory fields?	197
Validators are simple and work well	200
Something strange has happened at MeBay	203
The validators work, but they don't display errors	204
If you build your own pages, you need to write your own error message code	207
The controller needs to know if there was an error	208
We still need to display error messages!	212
The MeBay system is looking pretty sweet	214

making connections

Bringing it all together

6

Some things are stronger together than apart.

So far you've had a taste of some of the **key Rails ingredients**. You've created entire web applications and taken what Rails generates and **customized** it for your needs. But out in the real world, **life can be more complex**. Read on... it's time to build some **multi-functional web pages**. Not only that, it's time to deal with **difficult data relationships**, and take control of your data by writing your own **custom validators**.

Coconut Airways need a booking system	220
We need to see flights and seat bookings together	222
Let's look at what the seat scaffolding gives us	223
We need the booking form and seat list on the flight page	224
How can we split a page's content up into separate files?	225
ERb will assemble our pages	229
So how do we create the booking form partial?	230
Now we need to include the partial in the template	231
We need to give the partial a seat!	234
You can pass local variables to a partial	235
We also need a partial for the seat list	242
People are ending up on the wrong flights	244
A relationship connects models together	245
But how do we define the relationship?	247
But some people have too much baggage	249
We need to write our own validation	250
We need the reverse relationship	253
The system's taken off at Coconut Airways	260

> Dude... I booked a flight to a beach party but wound up on a historical tour of an old leper colony!

ajax

Avoiding the traffic

7

People want the best experiences out of life... and their apps.

No matter how good you are at Rails, there are times when traditional web apps just don't cut it. Sometimes users want something that's more **dynamic** and that responds to their every whim. Ajax allows you to build **fast, responsive web apps**, designed to give your users the **best experience the web has to offer**, and Rails comes complete with its own set of Ajax libraries just waiting for you to use. It's time to **quickly and easily add Ajax goodness** to your web app and please even more users than before.

There's a new offer at Coconut Airways	264
Which parts of a page change most?	265
Doesn't the browser always update the entire page?	270
So what ELSE can make a request?	271
First we need to include the Ajax libraries...	272
...then we need to add an Ajax "Refresh" link	273
The browser needs to ask for an update	278
But should we make the browser ask over and over again?	279
You listen to a timer like you listen to a button	280
Ajax Exposed	284
Someone's having trouble with their bachelor party	285
The form needs to make an Ajax request	286
The form needs to be under the control of JavaScript	287
We need to replace the create method	289
So what effect does this code have?	290
There's a problem with the flight bookings	295
We only know how to update one part of the page at a time	296
The controller needs to return JavaScript instead of HTML	297
So what does Rails generate?	301
If you don't say where to put the response, it will be executed	302

Psst...Just give me the seats again.

XML and multiple representations

8

It all looks different now...

You can't please everyone all of the time. Or can you?

So far we've looked at how you can use Rails to quickly and easily develop web apps that **perfectly fit one set of requirements**. But what do you do when **other requirements come along**? What should you do if some people want **basic web pages**, others want a **Google mashup**, and yet more want your app available as an **RSS feed**? In this chapter you'll create **multiple representations** of the same basic data, giving you the **maximum flexibility** with **minimum effort**.

Climbing all over the world	308
The users hate the interface!	309
The data needs to be on a map	310
We need to create a new action	311
The new action seems to work...	312
The new page needs a map... that's the point!	313
So what code do we need?	314
The code will only work for localhost	315
Now we need the map data	316
What do we need to generate?	318
We'll generate XML from the model	319
A model object can generate XML	320
What will the controller code look like	321
Meanwhile, at 20,000 feet...	326
We need to generate XML and HTML	327
XML and HTML are just representations	329
How should we decide which format to use?	330
How does the map page work?	334
The code is ready to go live	336
RSS feeds are just XML	344
We'll create an action called news	345
We have to change the structure of the XML	348
So we'll use a new kind of template: an XML builder	349
Now let's add the feed to the pages	353
On top of the world!	355

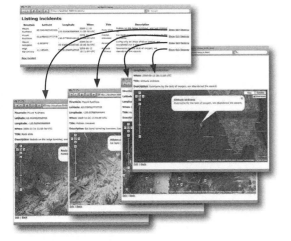

REST and Ajax

Taking things further

It's time to consolidate your mash-up skills.

9

So far you've seen how you can add **Google Maps** to your web apps to clearly show spatial data. But what if you want to **extend the functionality that's already there**? Keep reading, and we'll show you how you can add more **advanced Ajax goodness** to your **mash-ups**. And what's more, you'll learn a bit more about **REST** along the way.

Too many incidents!	358
The map could show more details	359
We can extend the map using Ajax	360
But how do we convert the index page?	361
What will the "show" action need to generate?	362
The new map functionality is a success!	367
We need to create requests using Ajax, too	368
The map partial lets us specify a "new" action	370
How do we prove an incident was saved?	375
The form needs to update the contents of the pop-up's <div>	376
Avalanche!	381
How things works now...	382
We could have an "Edit" link in the pop-up	383
We'll start by modifying the "edit" action	384
And we'll also need a new link on the show page	386
So how do we use the link_to helper?	387
Ajax links to the rescue	391
We're using the wrong route!	393
The HTTP method affects the route that's chosen	394
So what's an HTTP method?	395
Head First Climbers needs you!	398

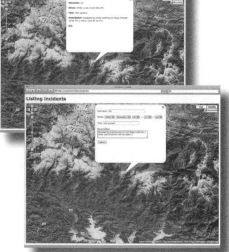

real-world applications

Rails in the real world

10

You've learned a lot about Ruby on Rails.

But to apply your knowledge to **the real world**, there are a number of things you need to think about. How do you connect your application to **another database**? How do you **test** Rails apps? How do you make the most out the Rails and the **Ruby language**? And where do you find out the latest on **what's happening** with Rails? Keep reading, and we'll put you on the inside track that will take your development skills to the next level.

Look! It's a big Ruby "Try this" page	405
Web apps need testing too	406
So what kinds of tests are available?	407
Going live	408
So how do you change the database?	409
What's REST?	410
The web application that went astray	411
Living on the Edge	412
Getting more information	413
A little light reading...	414
Head First books on related topics	415
Leaving town...	417

```
development:
  adapter: sqlite3
  database: db/development.sqlite3
  timeout: 5000
```
SQLite

```
development:
  adapter: oracle
  host: mydatabaseserver
  username: scott
  password: tiger
```
Oracle

```
production:
  adapter: mysql
  database: my_db_name
  username: root
  password:
  host: localhost
```
MySQL

Intro

In this section we answer the burning question:
"So why DID they put that in a Rails book?"

Who is this book for?

If you can answer "yes" to all of these:

 1 Are you **comfortable with HTML**?

 2 Do you have some experience of a computer language like **Java**, **C#** or **PHP**?

 3 Do you want to build **cool stuff** for the web in a **fraction of the time** it used to take?

this book is for you.

Who should probably back away from this book?

If you can answer "yes" to any of these:

 1 Are you someone who **doesn't have any experience with HTML**?

 2 Are you an **accomplished Rails developer looking for a reference book**?

 3 Are you **afraid to try something different**? Would you rather have a root canal than mix stripes with plaid? Do you believe a technical book can't be serious if it anthropomorphizes clients and servers?

If this is the case, don't worry. Go pick up Head First HTML with CSS & XHTML by Elisabeth Freeman and Eric Freeman, and then come back to this book

this book is not for you.

[Note from marketing: this book is for anyone with a credit card.]

We know what you're thinking

"How can *this* be a serious Rails book?"

"What's with all the graphics?"

"Can I actually *learn* it this way?"

Your brain thinks
THIS is important.

We know what your *brain* is thinking

Your brain craves novelty. It's always searching, scanning, *waiting* for something unusual. It was built that way, and it helps you stay alive.

So what does your brain do with all the routine, ordinary, normal things you encounter? Everything it *can* to stop them from interfering with the brain's *real* job—recording things that *matter*. It doesn't bother saving the boring things; they never make it past the "this is obviously not important" filter.

How does your brain *know* what's important? Suppose you're out for a day hike and a tiger jumps in front of you, what happens inside your head and body?

Neurons fire. Emotions crank up. *Chemicals surge.*

And that's how your brain knows...

This must be important! Don't forget it!

But imagine you're at home, or in a library. It's a safe, warm, tiger-free zone. You're studying. Getting ready for an exam. Or trying to learn some tough technical topic your boss thinks will take a week, ten days at the most.

Just one problem. Your brain's trying to do you a big favor. It's trying to make sure that this *obviously* non-important content doesn't clutter up scarce resources. Resources that are better spent storing the really *big* things. Like tigers. Like the danger of fire. Like the winners of the last three seasons of American Idol. And there's no simple way to tell your brain, "Hey brain, thank you very much, but no matter how dull this book is, and how little I'm registering on the emotional Richter scale right now, I really *do* want you to keep this stuff around."

Great. Only 420 more dull, dry, boring pages.

Your brain thinks THIS isn't worth saving.

We think of a "Head First" reader as a <u>learner</u>.

So what does it take to *learn* something? First, you have to *get* it, then make sure you don't *forget* it. It's not about pushing facts into your head. Based on the latest research in cognitive science, neurobiology, and educational psychology, *learning* takes a lot more than text on a page. We know what turns your brain on.

Some of the Head First learning principles:

Make it visual. Images are far more memorable than words alone, and make learning much more effective (up to 89% improvement in recall and transfer studies). It also makes things more understandable. **Put the words within or near the graphics** they relate to, rather than on the bottom or on another page, and learners will be up to *twice* as likely to solve problems related to the content.

Use a conversational and personalized style. In recent studies, students performed up to 40% better on post-learning tests if the content spoke directly to the reader, using a first-person, conversational style rather than taking a formal tone. Tell stories instead of lecturing. Use casual language. Don't take yourself too seriously. Which would *you* pay more attention to: a stimulating dinner party companion, or a lecture?

> Hey, I want to look like him!

index.html.erb   show.html.erb

Get the learner to think more deeply. In other words, unless you actively flex your neurons, nothing much happens in your head. A reader has to be motivated, engaged, curious, and inspired to solve problems, draw conclusions, and generate new knowledge. And for that, you need challenges, exercises, and thought-provoking questions, and activities that involve both sides of the brain and multiple senses.

Test Drive

Get—and keep—the reader's attention. We've all had the "I really want to learn this but I can't stay awake past page one" experience. Your brain pays attention to things that are out of the ordinary, interesting, strange, eye-catching, unexpected. Learning a new, tough, technical topic doesn't have to be boring. Your brain will learn much more quickly if it's not.

> Dude... I booked a flight to a beach party but wound up on a historical tour of an old leper colony!

Touch their emotions. We now know that your ability to remember something is largely dependent on its emotional content. You remember what you care about. You remember when you *feel* something. No, we're not talking heart-wrenching stories about a boy and his dog. We're talking emotions like surprise, curiosity, fun, "what the...?", and the feeling of "I Rule!" that comes when you solve a puzzle, learn something everybody else thinks is hard, or realize you know something that "I'm more technical than thou" Bob from engineering *doesn't*.

Metacognition: thinking about thinking

If you really want to learn, and you want to learn more quickly and more deeply, pay attention to how you pay attention. Think about how you think. Learn how you learn.

I wonder how I can trick my brain into remembering this stuff...

Most of us did not take courses on metacognition or learning theory when we were growing up. We were *expected* to learn, but rarely *taught* to learn.

But we assume that if you're holding this book, you really want to master Rails. And you probably don't want to spend a lot of time. If you want to use what you read in this book, you need to *remember* what you read. And for that, you've got to *understand* it. To get the most from this book, or *any* book or learning experience, take responsibility for your brain. Your brain on *this* content.

The trick is to get your brain to see the new material you're learning as Really Important. Crucial to your well-being. As important as a tiger. Otherwise, you're in for a constant battle, with your brain doing its best to keep the new content from sticking.

So just how *DO* you get your brain to treat Rails like it was a hungry tiger?

There's the slow, tedious way, or the faster, more effective way. The slow way is about sheer repetition. You obviously know that you *are* able to learn and remember even the dullest of topics if you keep pounding the same thing into your brain. With enough repetition, your brain says, "This doesn't *feel* important to him, but he keeps looking at the same thing *over* and *over* and *over*, so I suppose it must be."

The faster way is to do ***anything that increases brain activity,*** especially different *types* of brain activity. The things on the previous page are a big part of the solution, and they're all things that have been proven to help your brain work in your favor. For example, studies show that putting words *within* the pictures they describe (as opposed to somewhere else in the page, like a caption or in the body text) causes your brain to try to makes sense of how the words and picture relate, and this causes more neurons to fire. More neurons firing = more chances for your brain to *get* that this is something worth paying attention to, and possibly recording.

A conversational style helps because people tend to pay more attention when they perceive that they're in a conversation, since they're expected to follow along and hold up their end. The amazing thing is, your brain doesn't necessarily *care* that the "conversation" is between you and a book! On the other hand, if the writing style is formal and dry, your brain perceives it the same way you experience being lectured to while sitting in a roomful of passive attendees. No need to stay awake.

But pictures and conversational style are just the beginning...

Here's what WE did:

We used *pictures*, because your brain is tuned for visuals, not text. As far as your brain's concerned, a picture really *is* worth a thousand words. And when text and pictures work together, we embedded the text *in* the pictures because your brain works more effectively when the text is *within* the thing the text refers to, as opposed to in a caption or buried in the text somewhere.

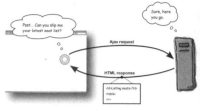

We used *redundancy*, saying the same thing in *different* ways and with different media types, and *multiple senses*, to increase the chance that the content gets coded into more than one area of your brain.

We used concepts and pictures in *unexpected* ways because your brain is tuned for novelty, and we used pictures and ideas with at least *some emotional* content, because your brain is tuned to pay attention to the biochemistry of emotions. That which causes you to *feel* something is more likely to be remembered, even if that feeling is nothing more than a little *humor*, *surprise*, or *interest.*

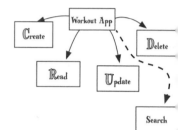

We used a personalized, *conversational style*, because your brain is tuned to pay more attention when it believes you're in a conversation than if it thinks you're passively listening to a presentation. Your brain does this even when you're *reading*.

We included more than 80 *activities*, because your brain is tuned to learn and remember more when you *do* things than when you *read* about things. And we made the exercises challenging-yet-do-able, because that's what most people prefer.

We used *multiple learning styles*, because *you* might prefer step-by-step procedures, while someone else wants to understand the big picture first, and someone else just wants to see an example. But regardless of your own learning preference, *everyone* benefits from seeing the same content represented in multiple ways.

We include content for *both sides of your brain*, because the more of your brain you engage, the more likely you are to learn and remember, and the longer you can stay focused. Since working one side of the brain often means giving the other side a chance to rest, you can be more productive at learning for a longer period of time.

And we included *stories* and exercises that present *more than one point of view,* because your brain is tuned to learn more deeply when it's forced to make evaluations and judgments.

We included *challenges*, with exercises, and by asking *questions* that don't always have a straight answer, because your brain is tuned to learn and remember when it has to *work* at something. Think about it—you can't get your *body* in shape just by *watching* people at the gym. But we did our best to make sure that when you're working hard, it's on the *right* things. That *you're not spending one extra dendrite* processing a hard-to-understand example, or parsing difficult, jargon-laden, or overly terse text.

We used *people*. In stories, examples, pictures, etc., because, well, because *you're* a person. And your brain pays more attention to *people* than it does to *things*.

Here's what YOU can do to bend your brain into submission

So, we did our part. The rest is up to you. These tips are a starting point; listen to your brain and figure out what works for you and what doesn't. Try new things.

Cut this out and stick it on your refrigerator.

- -

① Slow down. The more you understand, the less you have to memorize.

Don't just *read*. Stop and think. When the book asks you a question, don't just skip to the answer. Imagine that someone really *is* asking the question. The more deeply you force your brain to think, the better chance you have of learning and remembering.

② Do the exercises. Write your own notes.

We put them in, but if we did them for you, that would be like having someone else do your workouts for you. And don't just *look* at the exercises. **Use a pencil.** There's plenty of evidence that physical activity *while* learning can increase the learning.

③ Read the "There are No Dumb Questions"

That means all of them. They're not optional sidebars, ***they're part of the core content!*** Don't skip them.

④ Make this the last thing you read before bed. Or at least the last challenging thing.

Part of the learning (especially the transfer to long-term memory) happens *after* you put the book down. Your brain needs time on its own, to do more processing. If you put in something new during that processing time, some of what you just learned will be lost.

⑤ Talk about it. Out loud.

Speaking activates a different part of the brain. If you're trying to understand something, or increase your chance of remembering it later, say it out loud. Better still, try to explain it out loud to someone else. You'll learn more quickly, and you might uncover ideas you hadn't known were there when you were reading about it.

⑥ Drink water. Lots of it.

Your brain works best in a nice bath of fluid. Dehydration (which can happen before you ever feel thirsty) decreases cognitive function.

⑦ Listen to your brain.

Pay attention to whether your brain is getting overloaded. If you find yourself starting to skim the surface or forget what you just read, it's time for a break. Once you go past a certain point, you won't learn faster by trying to shove more in, and you might even hurt the process.

⑧ Feel something.

Your brain needs to know that this *matters*. Get involved with the stories. Make up your own captions for the photos. Groaning over a bad joke is *still* better than feeling nothing at all.

⑨ Practice writing Rails applications!

There's only one way to truly master Rails programming: **program Rails applications**. And that's what you're going to do throughout this book. The best way to understand a subject is by **doing it**. Activity strengthens the neural pathways, so we're going to give you a **lot** of practice: every chapter has apps that we'll build. So don't just skip over them—a lot of learning happens when you build these apps yourself. And don't worry if you make mistakes. Your brain actually learns more quickly from mistakes than it does from successes. Finally, make sure you understand what's going on before moving on to the next part of the book. Each chapter builds on the chapters that come before it.

Read Me

This is a learning experience, not a reference book. We deliberately stripped out everything that might get in the way of learning whatever it is we're working on at that point in the book. And the first time through, you need to begin at the beginning because the book makes assumptions about what you've already seen and learned.

Before you begin this book you will need to get Ruby on Rails installed on your machine.

This is not a *how-to* book, so we don't have any chapters that give you instructions on how to install Ruby on Rails on your computer. It's better to get that kind of information from the web. You will need to install Ruby on Rails version 2.1 or above, as well as SQLite 3. You can find out more from
`http://www.rubyonrails.org/down`

This is not a reference book.

So don't expect to see lots and lots of pages explaining 15 different ways to do something. We want you to **understand** by **doing**, so right from the get-go, we'll give you just enough information to move your learning forward. By the end of the book, you will have a mental framework of how Rails works and what it can do. You will then be able to slot the reference material into your brain much more rapidly and meaningfully than you would have been able to before. Psychologists call this the ability to **chunk** information.

All of the code in this book is available on the Head First site.

We'll present all of the code you'll need as we go along. It's a **good idea** to program along with the book, and it's a **great idea** to play around with the code and make it do your own thing. But sometimes you may want a copy of the code used in each chapter, so we've made it available on the Head First Labs web site. Rails applications are quite self-contained, so there's no reason why you can't have the code that does what the *book says* it should do, alongside your own buffed and pimped out version. You can download the code from

`http://www.headfirstlabs.com/books/hfrails`

We don't fully explain every piece of code.

Rails can generate a lot of code for you, and we don't want you to get bogged down in line-by-line descriptions. We'll describe the important parts that you need to know, and then we'll move on. Don't worry—by the end of the book, all of the pieces should fall into place.

This is a Rails book, not a Ruby book.

Ruby is the language that the Rails framework is written in, and we'll teach you just enough Ruby as we go along. Don't worry—if you have some experience of another programming language like **C#** or **Java**, you'll do just fine. Rails is such a powerful system that you can get a very long way with just a little Ruby knowledge.

The activities are NOT optional.

The exercises and activities are not add-ons; they're part of the core content of the book. Some of them are to help with memory, some are for understanding, and some will help you apply what you've learned. Don't skip the exercises.

The redundancy is intentional and important.

One distinct difference in a Head First book is that we want you to really get it. And we want you to finish the book remembering what you've learned. Most reference books don't have retention and recall as a goal, but this book is about learning, so you'll see some of the same concepts come up more than once.

We don't show all the code all the time.

Our readers tell us that it's frustrating to wade through 10 slightly different versions of the same piece of code, so sometimes we will only show the parts of a script that have changed.

The chapters are skills-based not technology-based.

Each chapter will give you the skills to write more and more **advanced** and **valuable** applications. So we don't have chapters that just deal with talking to databases or designing a pretty interface. Instead, every chapter teaches you a little about the database, a little about the interface, and a little about several other parts of Rails. By the end of each one, you'll be able to say, "Cool—now I can build apps that can do **X**."

The technical review team

Andrew Bryan

Jeremy Durham

Matt Harrington

Mike Isman

LuAnn Mazza

Eamon Walshe

Technical Reviewers:

Andrew Bryan is a software development and business consultant from Auckland, New Zealand. He is currently working for an online media and advertising company in Boston, where he lives with his lovely wife Angie.

Jeremy Durham has been building web applications using Ruby on Rails since early 2005, and has contributed to several Ruby libraries. He lives in Arlington, Massachusetts with his wife and two children.

Matt Harrington is a Northeastern University alumni and has been an avid programmer since age 9.

Mike Isman has been working with Ruby on Rails since he joined the eons.com team early in 2006, before Rails 1.0 was released. While working at Eons, Mike has also written smaller sites in Rails including the Life Expectancy Calculator at livingto100.com. He graduated in 2004 with a degree in Computer Science from the University of Rochester and has been busy doing web development ever since.

LuAnn Mazza is a Computer Analyst from Illinois.

Eamon Walshe is an Agile Coach with Exoftware and a former Distinguished Engineer with IONA Technologies. He is a fan of Rails because it allows developers to concentrate on what matters—delivering real business value, quickly.

Acknowledgments

My editors:

I owe a huge debt of gratitude to my editors, **Brett McLaughlin and Lou Barr**. They were always available for advice and support and whenever I came across a problem that seemed completely insoluble, they were not only able to identify exactly *what* was wrong, but *why* it was wrong and then come up with several ways of fixing it.

Brett McLaughlin

Lou Barr

I owe a very particular thank you to my wife, the author of *Head First Statistics*, **Dawn Griffiths**. This book would simply not have been completed on time had it not been for the immense amount of work she did on the final version.

This book is every bit as much hers as mine.

Dawn Griffiths

The O'Reilly team:

To **Caitrin McCullough** and **Karen Shaner**, who kept track of everything from contracts to web content.

To **Brittany Smith**, the book's Production Editor, for being a powerhouse of practical support.

To **Catherine Nolan**, for patiently guiding me through the first phase of the book.

To **Laurie Petrycki**, for her faith in the book and for allowing me to use her office in Cambridge.

And to **Kathy Sierra** and **Bert Bates,** the creators of the *Head First* Series, whose original vision has transformed the way technical books are written.

And not forgetting:

Brian Hanly, the CEO at *Exoftware*, and **Steve Harvey.** Their unstinting support and kindness made this book possible.

And finally the entire **technical review team** who had to perform an amazing amount of work in a very small amount of time.

I owe you all more than I can ever repay.

Safari® Books Online

When you see a Safari® icon on the cover of your favorite technology book that means the book is available online through the O'Reilly Network Safari Bookshelf.

Safari offers a solution that's better than e-books. It's a virtual library that lets you easily search thousands of top tech books, cut and paste code samples, download chapters, and find quick answers when you need the most accurate, current information. Try it for free at `http://safari.oreilly.com`.

1 getting started

Really Rapid Rails

Just look at the speed of this web app development! They must be using Rails...

Want to get your web app development off to a flying start? Then you need to know **Rails**. Rails is the **coolest** and **quickest development framework** in town, allowing you to develop **fully functional web apps** quicker than you ever thought possible. Getting started is simple; all you need to do is **install Rails**, and start turning the pages. Before you know it, you'll be **miles ahead of the competition**.

Friday, 9 AM

The first email you open is from an old friend in trouble:

Hey - how you doing?

I need a *big* favor! Remember that ticket-sales application I said we were working on? It's not going well. We've been working on it for weeks! The team is having real problems.

Do you think you could create the application for us?

We need a web site that can:

- List all sold tickets
- Create a new ticket sale
- Read and display a single ticket
- Update the details of a sale
- Delete a ticket sale

I know that seems like a lot of functions, but the boss says that it's the minimum set of features they need - and you know he's a tough guy to argue with! Here's the data structure:

Ticket:

name - name of purchaser (string)

seat_id_seq - the seat number e.g. E14 (string)

address - address of purchaser (long string)

price_paid - sales price of ticket (decimal)

email_address - email of purchaser (string)

I've attached sketches of the pages too so you know what we're aiming at.

Oh - and we need all of this for Monday or my butt's on the line. Help!

The system is designed to be used by front-of-house staff in the concert arena. The database will be reset for each concert, so it will only need to record the details for one concert at a time. Think you can help?

The application needs to do lots of things

Here are the sketches of the pages. How do they fit in with the system requirements?

The front page will need to list all of the tickets that have been sold.

There will be a button on the front page that will let you create a new ticket sale.

Next to every ticket on the list there will be a "Show" link that will display the details of a single ticket.

As well as a "Show" link, there will be an "Edit" link that can be used to update the details of a ticket sale.

Finally there will be a "Delete" link to remove a ticket sale.

Poof!

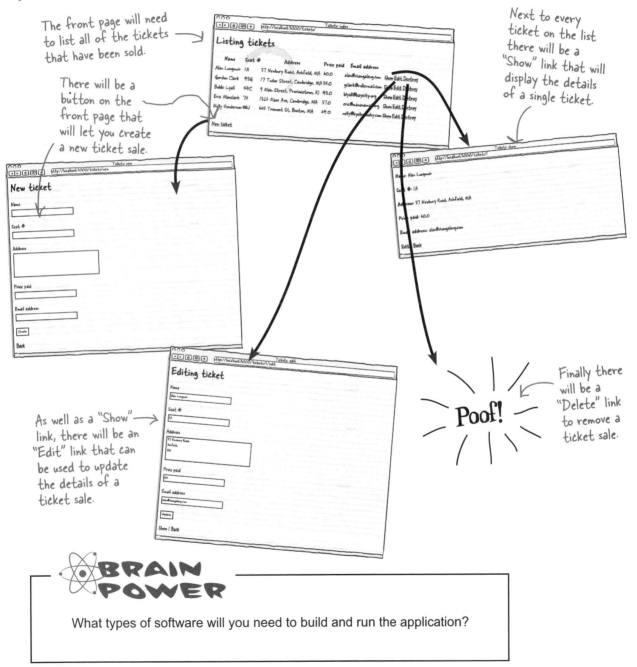

BRAIN POWER

What types of software will you need to build and run the application?

So what things do we need for the app?

There are several things we need to run the application on the
arena's server. We need:

 An application framework.
We need a set of pre-written code to that will form the foundation of
the web application.

 A database system.
We need some sort of database where we can store the data.

 A web server.
We need somewhere to run the web application.

 An object-relational mapping library.
To simplify access to the database, most web applications now use an
O-R mapping library to convert the database records into objects.

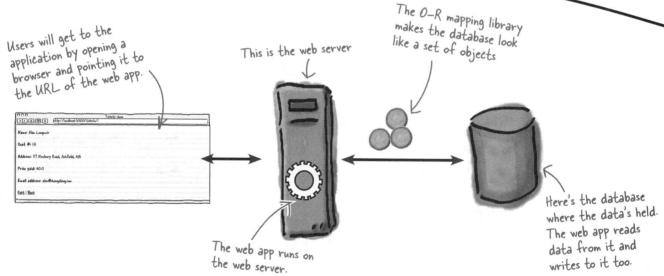

Users will get to the application by opening a browser and pointing it to the URL of the web app.

This is the web server

The O-R mapping library makes the database look like a set of objects

The web app runs on the web server.

Here's the database where the data's held. The web app reads data from it and writes to it too.

So how does Rails help us?

Regardless of what language you code in, you will probably still
need these three things for your deployed application. One of the
great things about Rails is that it contains *all* of the software you
will need—***all bundled in for free***.

Let's see how this works.

Pŏōl Puzzle

There are many features built in to Rails. Your job is to <u>guess</u> which of the features in the pool we need for the web app and then place them in the blank lines below. You won't need all of the features.

① ....

② ....

③ ....

④ ....

Note: each thing from the pool can only be used once!

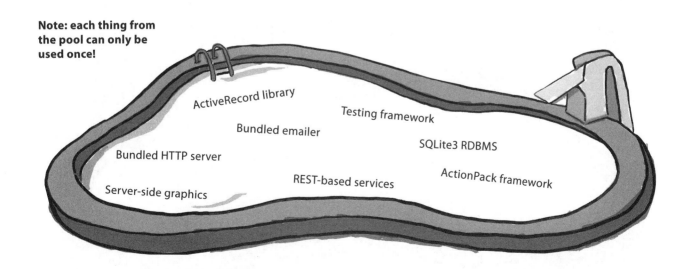

ActiveRecord library

Testing framework

Bundled emailer

SQLite3 RDBMS

Bundled HTTP server

REST-based services

ActionPack framework

Server-side graphics

Rails is for database-centric apps like the ticket sales system

A lot of applications have a database at the heart of them. The main reason these application exists is so that users can access and modify the contents of the database *without* using SQL directly.

So what are the problems that need to be solved when you connect a database to a web application?

Well, the web application will need to allow the user to access and modify data, so Rails includes an **application framework** called the **ActionPack** that will help you generate data-driven, interactive pages.

Secondly, web applications need to be run on a **web server** to display these pages, so Rails comes with one built in.

Thirdly, you need a **database**. Rails creates applications that are configured to work with an integrated **SQLite3** database.

The fourth thing you need is an **object-relational mapping library** and Rails provides one called **ActiveRecord**. This makes your database look like a collection of simple *Ruby objects*.

As well as all this, Rails also includes a pile of **tool scripts** to help you manage the application. So if you are creating a database-centric web application you'll find that

Rails gives you everything you need.

Pool Puzzle Solution

There are many features built in to Rails. Your job is to find the three features in the pool that we need for the web app and place them in the blank lines below. You won't need all of the features.

ActionPack framework
....

Bundled HTTP server
....

⟶ SQLite3 RDBMS
....

ActiveRecord library
....

On some operating systems you need to install this separately from Rails

Rails gives you all of these too, it's just that you don't need them for this web app.

Bundled emailer   Testing framework

Server-side graphics   REST-based services

You create a new application with the r<u>ails</u> command

So how do you get started with Rails?

Creating a new web application is actually really simple in Rails. All you need to do is open up a command prompt or terminal window, and type in **rails tickets**, where tickets is the name of the application you want to create.

Do this!

```
File Edit Window Help RailsRules
> rails tickets
```

↖ Just type "rails tickets" at a command prompt.

So what does this do?

Typing `rails tickets` cleverly generates a web application in a new folder called "tickets". Not only that, within the tickets folder, Rails generates a whole host of other folders and files that form the basic structure of a new application.

This means that you've effectively created an entire basic web application with just one short command.

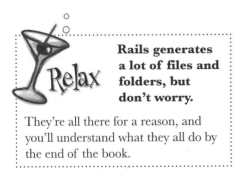

Rails generates a lot of files and folders, but don't worry.

They're all there for a reason, and you'll understand what they all do by the end of the book.

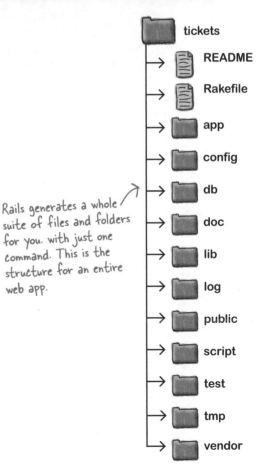

Rails generates a whole suite of files and folders for you, with just one command. This is the structure for an entire web app.

- tickets
  - README
  - Rakefile
  - app
  - config
  - db
  - doc
  - lib
  - log
  - public
  - script
  - test
  - tmp
  - vendor

Test Drive

Because the application you have just created is a *web* application, you will need to start the built-in web server to see it running.

At a command prompt or terminal, change into the tickets folder and type **ruby script/server**.

This is the console. You get to it via a command prompt in Windows or a terminal on either Linux or a Mac.

Go into the folder for the application...

...and start the web server.

```
File  Edit  Window  Help
> cd tickets
> ruby script/server
```

A few messages will appear on the screen that will confirm the web server is running. Now you can see the default home page by opening a browser at:

```
http://localhost:3000/
```

This is the default home page of the web server.

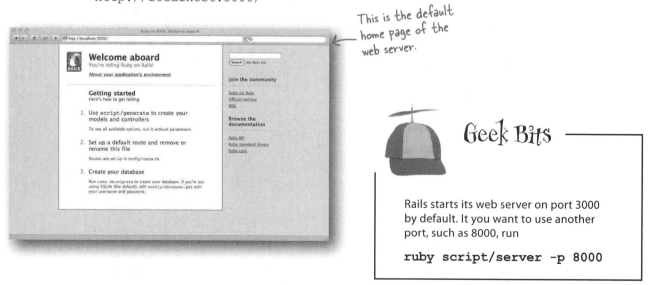

Geek Bits

Rails starts its web server on port 3000 by default. It you want to use another port, such as 8000, run

ruby script/server -p 8000

Now you need to add your own code to the default app

Rails creates the basic structure of your app from the get-go, but you still need to add the code that is specific to what **you** want. Everybody's application is different, but does Rails have any tools or tricks that make it easier for you to create custom code?

Well, actually, it does. Did you notice how Rails created a whole file structure for you, almost as if it knew what you were going to need? That's because Rails apps follow very strong naming conventions.

Rails apps always follow conventions

All Rails applications follow the same basic file structure and use consistent names for things. This makes the application easier to understand, but it also means that the built-in Rails tools will understand how your application works.

So why is that important? Well if the tools know how your app is structured, you can use them to automate a lot of the coding tasks. That way, Rails can use conventions to generate code for you, without you having to configure your web application. In other words, Rails follows *convention over configuration*.

Let's look at one of Rails most powerful tools: scaffolding.

Rails principle:

<u>Convention</u>
Over
<u>Configuration</u>

there are no
Dumb Questions

Q: **You keep talking about Ruby and Rails. What's the difference?**

A: Ruby is a programming language. Rails is a collection of Ruby scripts. So the web server, the ActionPack application framework, and the bundled tool scripts are all just Ruby scripts... and therefore, part of Rails.

Q: **How do I edit the front page of my new web site?**

A: That HTML file in the `public/ index.html` file below the application directory. The public directory contains all the static content for the application.

Q: **What if I want to use a different web server? Can I do that?**

A: It makes sense to use the bundled server while you're developing. If you want to deploy the live version of your application to another web server, you can.

Q: **Does it matter which folder I'm in when I run `ruby script/server`?**

A: Yes, sure does. You need to be in the folder containing your web application

Q: **What is it that compiles my code?**

A: Ruby is an interpreted language, like JavaScript. That means there is no compilation necessary. You can just change your code, and immediately run it.

Scaffolding is GENERATED code

So what does our application need to do? Let's look at that email again:

This is the same email as before.

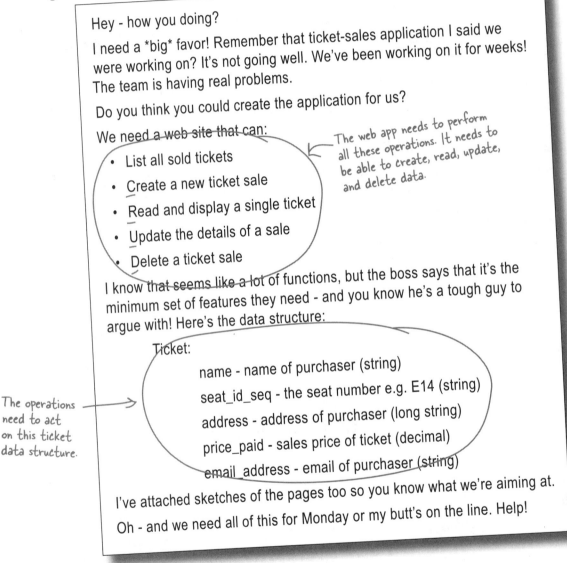

Hey - how you doing?

I need a *big* favor! Remember that ticket-sales application I said we were working on? It's not going well. We've been working on it for weeks! The team is having real problems.

Do you think you could create the application for us?

We need a web site that can:

- List all sold tickets
- Create a new ticket sale
- Read and display a single ticket
- Update the details of a sale
- Delete a ticket sale

The web app needs to perform all these operations. It needs to be able to create, read, update, and delete data.

I know that seems like a lot of functions, but the boss says that it's the minimum set of features they need - and you know he's a tough guy to argue with! Here's the data structure:

Ticket:

name - name of purchaser (string)

seat_id_seq - the seat number e.g. E14 (string)

address - address of purchaser (long string)

price_paid - sales price of ticket (decimal)

email_address - email of purchaser (string)

The operations need to act on this ticket data structure.

I've attached sketches of the pages too so you know what we're aiming at.

Oh - and we need all of this for Monday or my butt's on the line. Help!

So we need to create web pages that allow us to **Create**, **Read**, **Update,** and **Delete** tickets. Because the initial letters of the operations are **C**, **R**, **U,** and **D**, they are known as the **CRUD operations**. These are pretty common operations in database-centric applications—so common that Rails has a way of quickly generating all the code and pages you need. It does all this using **scaffolding**.

Code Magnets

There's a simple command that you can issue from the console to generate the scaffolding code. See if you can arrange the magnets to complete the command.

ruby script/generate *Scaffold* **ticket name:** *string*

seat-id-seq : *string*   *address* : *string*

price-paid : *decimal*   *email-add:* *string*

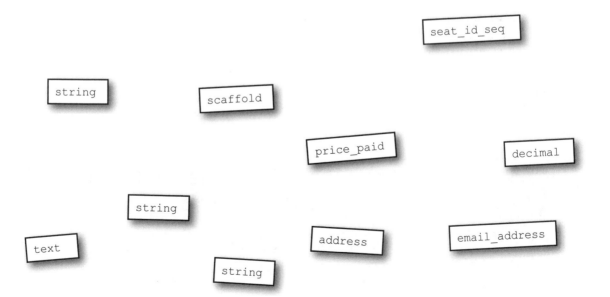

```
seat_id_seq
```

```
string
```

```
scaffold
```

```
price_paid
```

```
decimal
```

```
string
```

```
text
```

```
address
```

```
email_address
```

```
string
```

Code Magnets Solution

There's a simple command that you can issue from the console to generate the scaffolding code. See if you can arrange the magnets to complete the command.

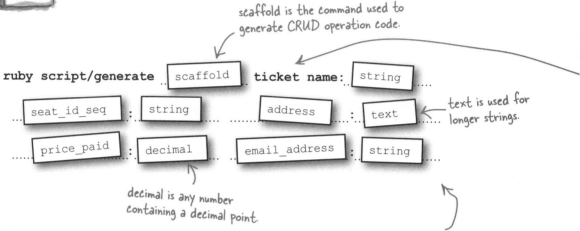

scaffold is the command used to generate CRUD operation code.

```
ruby script/generate    scaffold    ticket name: string
    seat_id_seq : string    address : text
    price_paid : decimal    email_address : string
```

text is used for longer strings.

decimal is any number containing a decimal point.

Remember: this command needs to be entered when you are in the "tickets" directory.

So what does the scaffold command do?

Scaffolding creates code that allows a user to create, read, update, and delete data in the database.

If you have a database-centric web application that needs to create, read, update, and delete data from a database, then scaffolding can save you lots of time and effort.

Type the scaffold command for the ticket table into the console, and let's see what happens:

Do this!

```
File  Edit  Window  Help  CRUD
> ruby script/generate scaffold ticket name:string
seat_id_seq:string address:text price_paid:decimal
email_address:string
```

TEST DRIVE

Now it's time to see if our application is really working. To see the new tickets pages, point your browser to

```
http://localhost:3000/tickets
```

This matches the name given in the scaffold command. See how Rails made it plural?

ActiveRecord::StatementInvalid in Tic

SQLite3::SQLException: no such table: tickets: SELECT * FROM "tickets"

RAILS_ROOT: /Users/davidg/Desktop/chap1-scaffold/tickets

<u>Application Trace</u> | <u>Framework Trace</u> | <u>Full Trace</u>

```
/Library/Ruby/Gems/1.8/gems/activerecord-2.1.2/lib/active_record/connection_ac
/Library/Ruby/Gems/1.8/gems/activerecord-2.1.2/lib/active_record/connection_ac
/Library/Ruby/Gems/1.8/gems/activerecord-2.1.2/lib/active_record/connection_ac
/Library/Ruby/Gems/1.8/gems/activerecord-2.1.2/lib/active_record/connection_ac
/Library/Ruby/Gems/1.8/gems/activerecord-2.1.2/lib/active_record/connection_ac
/Library/Ruby/Gems/1.8/gems/activerecord-2.1.2/lib/active_record/connection_ac
/Library/Ruby/Gems/1.8/gems/activerecord-2.1.2/lib/active_record/connection_ac
/Library/Ruby/Gems/1.8/gems/activerecord-2.1.2/lib/active_record/connection_ac
/Library/Ruby/Gems/1.8/gems/activerecord-2.1.2/lib/active_record/connection_ac
/Library/Ruby/Gems/1.8/gems/activerecord-2.1.2/lib/active_record/base.rb:586:
/Library/Ruby/Gems/1.8/gems/activerecord-2.1.2/lib/active_record/base.rb:1345
/Library/Ruby/Gems/1.8/gems/activerecord-2.1.2/lib/active_record/base.rb:540:
app/controllers/tickets_controller.rb:5:in `index'
/Library/Ruby/Gems/1.8/gems/actionpack-2.1.2/lib/action_controller/base.rb:11
/Library/Ruby/Gems/1.8/gems/actionpack-2.1.2/lib/action_controller/base.rb:11
/Library/Ruby/Gems/gems/action        -2.1.2/lib/action_controller/filters.rb
```

Hmmm... this definitely doesn't look right.

So what went wrong? Even though we generated the scaffold code correctly, there's an error on the web server. All we get are a bunch of error messages being sent back.

BRAIN POWER

Think about the error message you can see in the web browser. Why do you think the application crashed?

There are no tables in the database yet!

The application should have displayed an empty list of sold tickets, but it didn't. **Why not?** It needed to read the list from table called **tickets** in the database, but we haven't created any tables yet.

Should we just connect to the database and create the table? After all—the database is sitting right there in the application. But then, why should we have to? We already told Rails enough information for Rails to create the table for us. Look again at our scaffold command:

Note: the scaffold is "ticket" (singular) and the table will be called "tickets" (plural).

```
File  Edit  Window  Help  DRY
> ruby script/generate scaffold ticket name:string
seat_id_seq:string address:text price_paid:decimal
email_address:string
```

tickets	
name	string
seat_id_seq	string
address	text
price_paid	decimal
email_address	string

We already told Rails the details of the data structure when we ran the scaffold command, and there is an important principle in Rails: ***Don't Repeat Yourself***. If you tell Rails something once, you shouldn't have to say it again.

So how do we get Rails to create the table?

Geek Bits

Rails comes bundled with a database, SQLite3. So where is it?

The database is located within the db folder, in the file development.sqlite3.

Rails principle:

Don't
Repeat
Yourself

You'll hear this principle called DRY when you're talking programming with your buddies.

Create the table by running a <u>migration</u>

When Rails generated the scaffolding, it also generated a small Ruby script called a **migration** to create the table. A migration is a script that alters the structure of the underlying database.

Take a look in the db/migrate folder. You should see a file there called `<timestamp>_create_tickets.rb` where `<timestamp>` is the UTC timestamp of when the file was created. If you open the file in a text editor, it should look something like this:

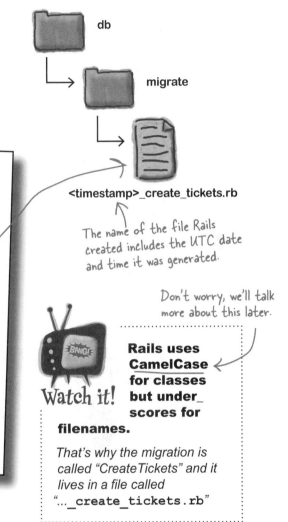

db

migrate

`<timestamp>_create_tickets.rb`

The name of the file Rails created includes the UTC date and time it was generated.

```ruby
class CreateTickets < ActiveRecord::Migration
  def self.up
    create_table :tickets do |t|
      t.string :name
      t.string :seat_id_seq
      t.text :address
      t.decimal :price_paid
      t.string :email_address
      t.timestamps
    end
  end
  def self.down
    drop_table :tickets
  end
end
```

← *Here's the contents of the migration file.*

Don't worry, we'll talk more about this later.

Watch it!

Rails uses CamelCase for classes but under_scores for filenames.

That's why the migration is called "CreateTickets" and it lives in a file called "..._create_tickets.rb"

The migration is a small Ruby script. Instead of running this script directly, you should run this script using another Rails tool called **rake**. To run the migration, type **rake db:migrate** at the command prompt. This runs the migration code and creates the table:

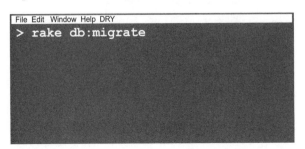

```
File Edit Window Help DRY
> rake db:migrate
```

BRAIN BARBELL

Why does the migration include the date and time in its name?

Test Drive

Make sure you've created your tickets table with the rake command. Then go back to the web browser and refresh this page:

```
http://localhost:3000/tickets
```

The web application works! Within a couple of minutes you should be able to enter a few test records:

These are a few records we added. Go ahead and add some yourself!

Listing tickets

Name	Seat id seq	Address	Price paid	Email address			
Alan Longmuir	1A	37 Newbury Road, Ashfield, MA	60.0	alan@shangalang.com	Show	Edit	Destroy
Gordon Clark	43G	17 Tudor Street, Cambridge, MA	35.0	gclark@rollermail.com	Show	Edit	Destroy
Bobbi Lyall	54C	9 Main Street, Provincetown, RI	43.0	blyall@baycity.org	Show	Edit	Destroy
Eric Manclark	7H	1326 Mass Ave, Cambridge, MA	37.0	eric@mananamail.org	Show	Edit	Destroy
Nelly Henderson	88J	665 Tremont St, Boston, MA	64.0	nelly@byebyebaby.com	Show	Edit	Destroy

New ticket

Wait! No Way! We've only entered a few commands at the console and that's built the **entire** app?

Yes - we've built much more than just a front page. We've built an entire system.

Scaffolding generated a whole set of pages that allow us to create, modify, and delete ticket details. To see how the application hangs together, let's create and edit another record.

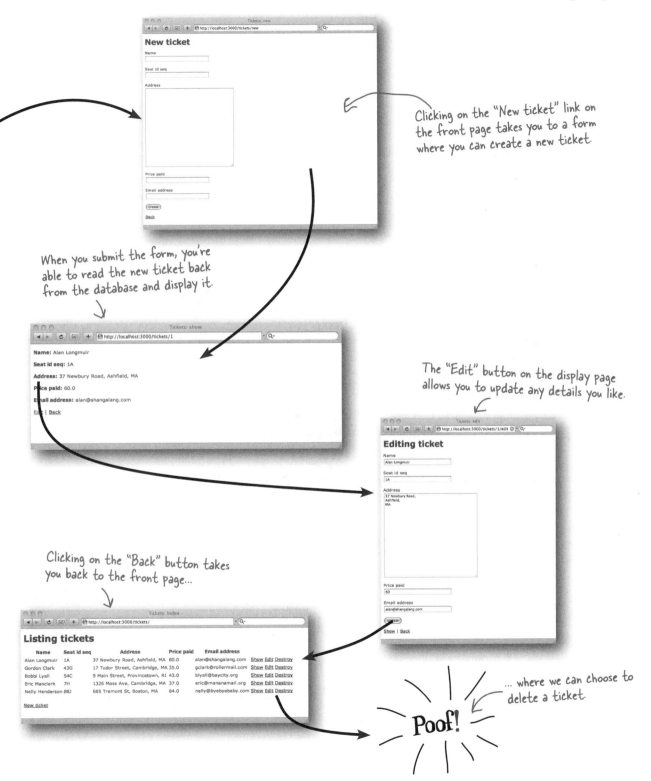

Clicking on the "New ticket" link on the front page takes you to a form where you can create a new ticket.

When you submit the form, you're able to read the new ticket back from the database and display it.

The "Edit" button on the display page allows you to update any details you like.

Clicking on the "Back" button takes you back to the front page...

... where we can choose to delete a ticket.

Poof!

BULLET POINTS

- The command

  ```
  rails <app name>
  ```

  generates a web application for you in folder `<app name>`. Rails also creates the folders and files that form the basic structure of your application.

- Rails comes with a bundled web server. To start the server running, use the command

  ```
  ruby script/server
  ```

  The default home page is at

  ```
  http://localhost:3000/
  ```

- Rails apps follow Convention Over Configuration.

- Create, Read, Update, and Delete operations on a database are known as the CRUD operations.

- Scaffolding generates CRUD code for you. To create scaffolding for "thing" data, run:

  ```
  ruby script/generate scaffold
    thing
  <column name 1>:<column type 1>
  <column name 2>:<column type 2>
  . . .
  ```

- To see your scaffolding, point your browser to URL

  ```
  http://localhost:3000/things
  ```

- Rails apps follow the principle Don't Repeat Yourself.

- A migration is a script that alters the structure of the underlying database. You run a migration using the command

  ```
  rake db:migrate
  ```

there are no Dumb Questions

Q: Some commands start with `rails` and some start with `ruby` and some with `rake`. What's the difference?

A: The `rails` command is used to create a new application. But `ruby` is the Ruby interpreter and it is used to run the tool scripts that are stored in the `scripts` folder. The `ruby` and `rake` commands are used for pretty much everything in Rails.

Q: So what's `rake`?

A: `rake` is the command we used to run the database migration. The name means "Ruby make," and it is used for some of the same kinds of tasks that `make` and `ant` are used for in other languages like C and Java, respectively. When `rake` is given a task to do (like running migrations), it is able to smartly analyze the application and decide which scripts to run. So it's a little smarter than `ruby` and is used for more complicated tasks like modifying the database structure and running tests.

Q: I don't understand the "Convention over Configuration" thing. What's it mean?

A: Many languages give you a lot of options to choose from, like picking options for a new car. If you have a language that has a lot of options available, you need to store the developer's choices somewhere - usually in large XML files. Rails takes a different approach. In Rails things are named consistently and are stored in standardized place. This is called a "conventional" approach - not because it is old-fashioned, but because it follows "conventions" or "standards".

Q: So I can't change how Rails works?

A: You can change pretty much everything in Rails, but if you follow the conventions you will find that you will develop your applications more quickly, and other people will find your code easier to understand.

Sweet! You saved your buddy's job!

Your quick Rails work saved the day for your pal... at least, for the moment. Looks like there's another email to deal with:

Thank you!

It's great to see the application up and running - and you did it so quickly! Rails sounds amazing. The way changes appear as soon as you edit the code. No compile. No deploy. Must be nice.

You really saved my butt on this one.

Just one thing - the labels for seat_id_seq should be something more human-readable, like maybe "Seat #". Do you think you could fix that?

So how can we change the labels?

Rails generated a web app for us very quickly, which saved us a lot of time and effort. But what if we want to make small changes to the appearance of the generated pages, what do we do?

How easy is it to modify the pages that Rails has generated for us?

To modify an app, you need to dig into the app's architecture

Scaffolding just generates code for us. Once the code's been generated, it's up to you to customize that code. And if you look in the app folder, you'll see there's quite a lot of generated code you might want to customize.

So if you need to make a change to the application—like modifying the page labels—where do you begin?

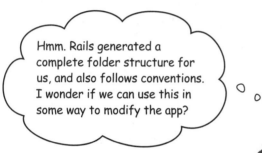

Hmm. Rails generated a complete folder structure for us, and also follows conventions. I wonder if we can use this in some way to modify the app?

Rely on Rail's conventions.

Remember how we said that Rails apps follow conventions over configuration? This will make it easier for us to modify the application. Why? Well, because the code is separated according to it's **function**. That means Ruby scripts that do *similar things* live in *similar places*.

So if you need to change the behavior of your Rails application, you should be able to identify where the code is that needs to be amended, and change the code.

But of course to do that, you need to understand the...

Standard Rails <u>Architecture</u>

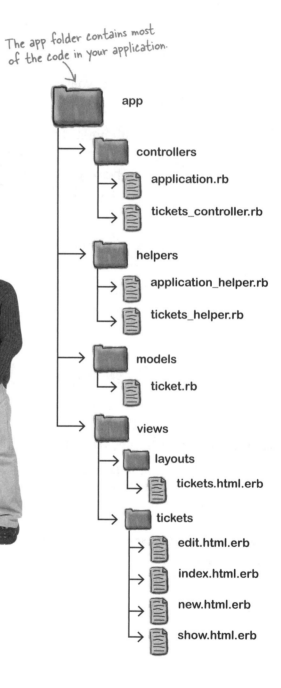

The app folder contains most of the code in your application.

- app
  - controllers
    - application.rb
    - tickets_controller.rb
  - helpers
    - application_helper.rb
    - tickets_helper.rb
  - models
    - ticket.rb
  - views
    - layouts
      - tickets.html.erb
    - tickets
      - edit.html.erb
      - index.html.erb
      - new.html.erb
      - show.html.erb

The 3 parts of your app:
model, view, and controller

Pretty much all of the code in a Rails application falls into one of
three categories:

 Model Code

The model code manages how data is written and read to your database.
Model code **objects** represent things that exist in the system's *problem*
domain—like the **tickets** in the ticket system

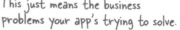
This just means the business
problems your app's trying to solve.

 View Code

The view is the part of the application that is **presented** to the user.
For that reason it is sometimes called the **presentation layer.** For a
web application, the view mostly generates web pages.

③ Controller Code

The controller is the real *brain* of the application. It decides how the user
interacts with the system, controlling what data is accessed from the
model, and which parts of the view will present it.

This is how the different types of code are connected in a Rails application:

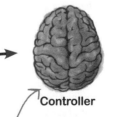

View

The view consists of the
web pages that present the
application to the user.

Controller

The controller is the key decision
maker. It decides what data
needs to be accessed from the
model, and which part of the
view will display that data.

Model

The model emulates the things
in the real world that the
application is managing. In the
ticket sales system, the ticket
objects live in the model

Rails Exposed

This week's interview:
We ask the web's hottest
framework what makes him tick

Head First: Hello Rails, we're so glad you could join us.

Rails: Please - call me Ray. Glad to be here.

Head First: It must be tough to find a break in your hectic schedule.

Rails: I'm busy, sure. With database connections, application logic, and web pages to serve up I don't get a lot of what you'd call "Me time". But it's OK - I have good people.

Head First: One thing I was wondering: if you don't mind me asking, when you create a new application, why are there so many directories?

Rails: What can I say? I'm a helpful guy. Over time I've learned what kinda things people want to do in their applications. I don't like to see people manually creating the same stuff over and over again.

Head First: But isn't it all a little... well... confusing?

Rails: Please. I'm a conventional guy. No surprises. Once you've learned the way I work, you'll find me easy to get along with.

Head First: I hear you don't like to be configured.

Rails: You can configure me if you like, but most people prefer to work the way I like. Convention over configuration. Capiche?

Head First: Oh yes - that's one of your design principles isn't it?

Rails: Yeah - that and Don't Repeat Yourself.

Head First: And what?

Rails: Don't Repeat Yourself?

Head First: And what?

Rails: Don't... Hey, you're a funny guy.

there are no Dumb Questions

Q: **Where should the business logic go in my web app?**

A: Well, it all depends what you mean by "business logic." Some people define the business logic as the rules associated with the management of data. In that case, the business logic lives in the model. Other people define business logic as the rules defining the workflow of the system - such as what features the application has and in what sequence the user accesses them. In that case the "business logic" lives in the

controller. In the rest of the book we will use "model logic" and "application logic" to distinguish these two cases.

Q: **What is the difference between the view and the controller?**

A: The view decides how the application *looks* and the controller decides how it *works*. So the view will define the color of a button on a page and what text appears on it, but the controller will decide what happens when the button is pressed.

Q: **So what code will I write most?**

A: It depends upon the application and the developer. If you find that you are mostly adding code to a particular one of the three app parts, you may want to think carefully whether the next piece of code you are adding is about presentation, interaction, or modeling.

✦ WHAT'S MY PURPOSE?

Match the code description to the part of the app that code goes with.

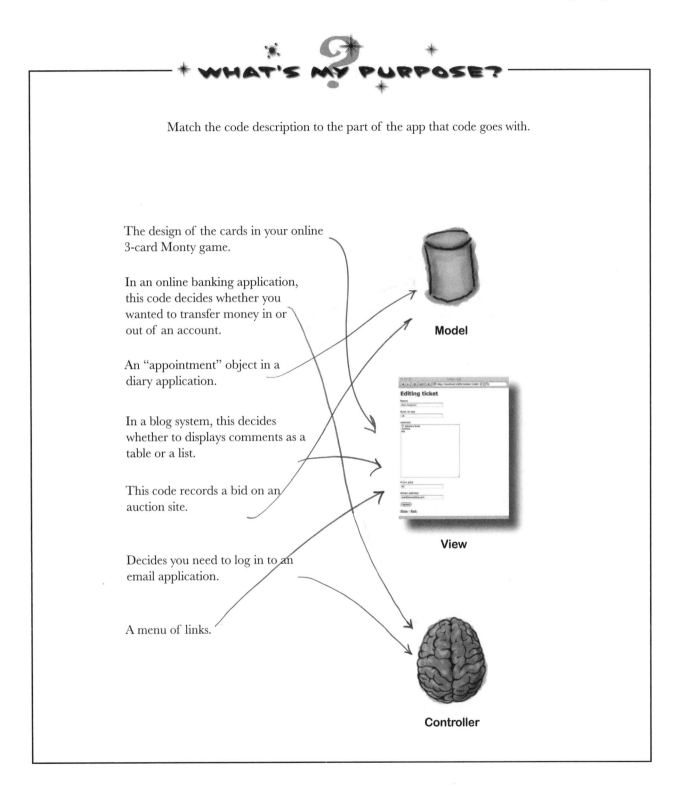

The design of the cards in your online 3-card Monty game.

In an online banking application, this code decides whether you wanted to transfer money in or out of an account.

An "appointment" object in a diary application.

In a blog system, this decides whether to displays comments as a table or a list.

This code records a bid on an auction site.

Decides you need to log in to an email application.

A menu of links.

Model

View

Controller

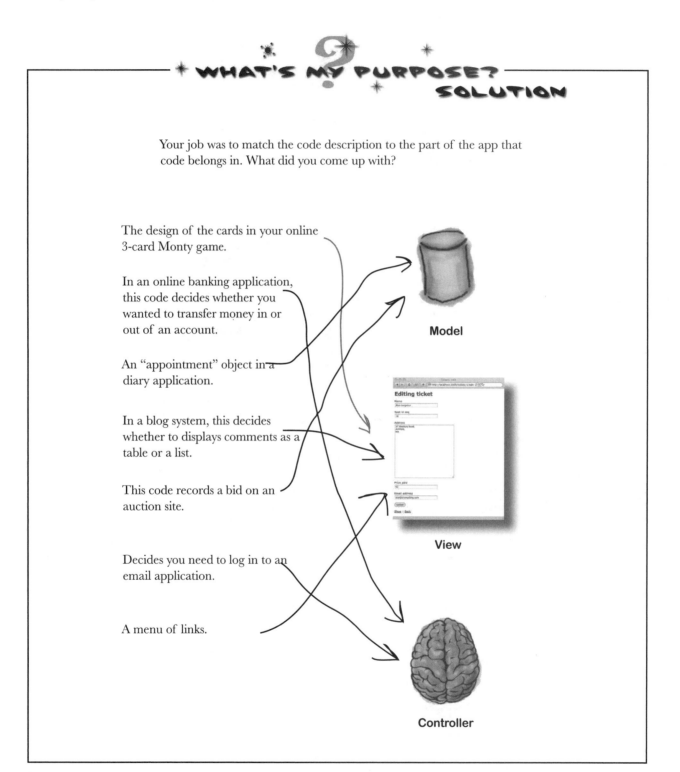

WHAT'S MY PURPOSE?
SOLUTION

Your job was to match the code description to the part of the app that code belongs in. What did you come up with?

The design of the cards in your online 3-card Monty game.

In an online banking application, this code decides whether you wanted to transfer money in or out of an account.

An "appointment" object in a diary application.

In a blog system, this decides whether to displays comments as a table or a list.

This code records a bid on an auction site.

Decides you need to log in to an email application.

A menu of links.

Model

View

Controller

The 3 types of code are kept in SEPARATE folders

So Rails favors convention over configuration and uses the MVC architecture. So what?

How does the MVC architecture help us change the labels on our pages and fix the app? Let's look back at the files that were generated by the scaffolding one more time. Because the code is cleanly separated into three distinct types—model, view, and controller—Rails puts each type in a separate folder.

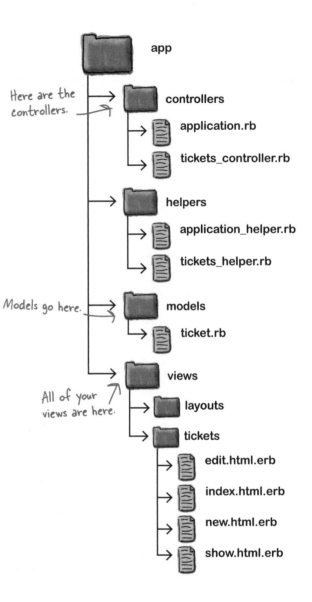

Here are the controllers.

app
→ controllers
→ application.rb
→ tickets_controller.rb
→ helpers
→ application_helper.rb
→ tickets_helper.rb

Models go here.
→ models
→ ticket.rb

→ views
All of your views are here.
→ layouts
→ tickets
→ edit.html.erb
→ index.html.erb
→ new.html.erb
→ show.html.erb

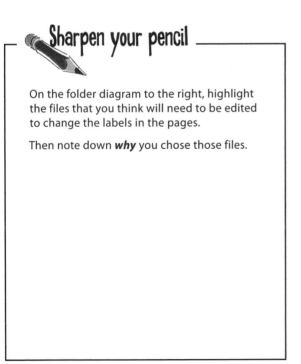

Sharpen your pencil

On the folder diagram to the right, highlight the files that you think will need to be edited to change the labels in the pages.

Then note down *why* you chose those files.

Sharpen your pencil Solution

Your job was to highlight the files that you'll need to edit to change the labels in the pages.

Since we need to change the appearance of the pages, we need to change the underlined word: views. The files we need to update are found in the views folder and have the extension .html.erb.

app

→ controllers

→ helpers

→ models

We don't need to change any of the files in the controllers, helpers or models folders.

→ views

→ layouts

We can change labels in the pages by changing the .html.erb files in the views folder.

→ tickets

→ edit.html.erb

→ index.html.erb

→ new.html.erb

→ show.html.erb

The files in the VIEW need to be edited

If we want to change the labels in web pages, we need to modify view code. And the view code all lives inside the app/views folder.

The view files generate web pages, and are called **page templates**. So what's a page template, and what do those templates contain?

Edit the HTML in the view

So what do the page templates actually look like? Open the four `.html.erb` files in the `views/tickets` folder using a text editor. The contents of the files look an awful lot like HTML.

We want to change the labels for seat_id_seq to Seat #. To do this, search for the text "Seat id seq" in the four files, change it to "Seat #", and then save your changes.

Do this!

> Go into each of the four **.html.erb** files in the **views/tickets** folder, and change the text **Seat id seq** to **Seat #**. This will change the label on the pages to Seat #.

```
<p>
  <b>Name:</b>
  <%=h @ticket.name %>
</p>
<p>
  <b>Seat id seq:</b>
  <%=h @ticket.seat_id_seq %
</p>
<p>
  <b>Address:</b>
  <%=h @ticket.address %>
</p>
```

This is the text you need to change. to Seat # → #

```
<h1>Editing ticket</h1>

<% form_for(@ticket) do |f| %>
  <%= f.error_messages %>
```

Don't forget to add quotes – because it's becoming a string

```
  <p>
    <%= f.label :name %><br />
    <%= f.text_field :name %>
  </p>
  <p>
    <%= f.label :seat_id_seq %><br />
    <%= f.text_field :seat_id_seq %>
  </p>
```

"Seat #"

This symbol will need to be changed to the string "Seat #"

If you edit the labels in your HTML, your changes become immediately visible in your web browser. If you make the changes *now* and refresh, they should be visible *immediately*. Let's take a look next...

there are no Dumb Questions

Q: You called :seat_id_seq a symbol. What's a symbol?

A: A symbol is a little like a string. A string is surrounded with quotes, but a symbol always starts with a colon (:). Symbols are generally used to name things in Rails because they are slightly more efficient in memory. In most cases symbols and strings can be used interchangeably.

TEST DRIVE

Refresh the page at:

```
http://localhost:3000/tickets/
```

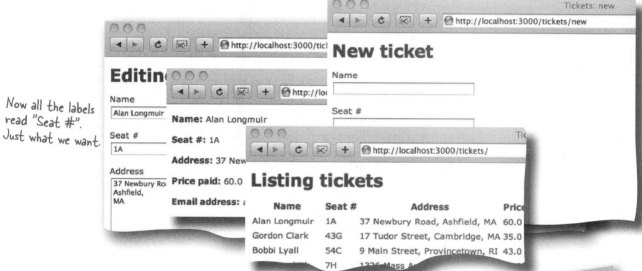

Now all the labels read "Seat #". Just what we want.

Did you notice how quickly the change appeared in your application?

That's because Rails is built with Ruby, and Ruby code doesn't need to be compiled. So the Rails web server can just run your updated source code. But is that really a big deal?

So you've got a lot fewer stages you need to go through to try out code that you change. You don't need to compile your code, for instance, and you don't need to package that code and deploy it anywhere. All you need to do is write your code and run it. The Rails development cycle is pretty quick, and it's quick to make changes to your web app, too.

Development Cycle

Write/amend code

~~Compile the code~~

~~Package the application~~

~~Deploy the application~~

Run it

Repeat

These steps are irrelevant when you're developing in Rails.

Sunday, 8 AM

Two fixes down, but your phone's ringing... what now?

Hey there! Great to hear about how well the application's going. Hey, listen... I thought you ought to know that my boss called and wanted to know where you live. He was really eager to see all of the work that you'd done, but he's still a little worried that it might not be ready for tomorrow morning, so he wants to check today. Thanks for all the work you did. Oh - by the way - did I mention that he wants a contact phone number recording as well as an email address for each ticket? Sorry - slipped my mind.

KNOCK!

KNOCK!

So, **you're** the one responsible for the new application. The first concert bookings are suposed to be available in less than 24 hours, so this app had better be complete or **I'm** going to want to know why...

The application needs to store more information now

Everything was pretty much finished until your friend mentioned that phone numbers need to be recorded. We need more data, so what's that mean for our app?

 We need an extra field displayed on each page.
Fortunately we know how to amend page templates, so this shouldn't be too big of a problem.

We need to add an extra field to the page like this.

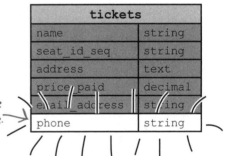

② We need to store an extra column on the database.
We need to store an extra column in our database, but how?

We need to add phone to the tickets table in the database.

tickets	
name	string
seat_id_seq	string
address	text
price_paid	decimal
email_address	string
phone	string

Sharpen your pencil

We need to add a column to the database table. Write down what **type** of script we used before to change the database structure.

....

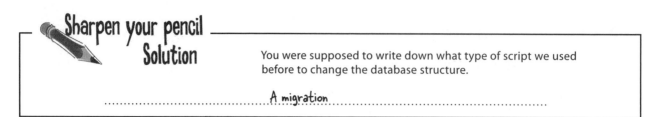

Sharpen your pencil
Solution

You were supposed to write down what type of script we used before to change the database structure.

A migration

A migration is just a Ruby script

So we need a migration to add a column to the table. But what *is* a migration, really? Let's look back at the one that created our tickets table.

```ruby
class CreateTickets < ActiveRecord::Migration
  def self.up
    create_table :tickets do |t|
      t.string :name
      t.string :seat_id_seq
      t.text :address
      t.decimal :price_paid
      t.string :email_address
      t.timestamps
    end
  end
  def self.down
    drop_table :tickets
  end
end
```

We need to create code that's something like this, except instead of creating a table, we need our migration to add a column.

Hello? How are we supposed to write code to change a table? We don't know how!

We need to CREATE code, but that doesn't mean we need to WRITE code.

there are no
Dumb Questions

Q: Some of the code in the migration looks like it is dropping the table. Why is that?

A: Migrations can do a lot more than we are showing here. For example, every migration has the ability to undo itself. That's why the code to create a new table is matched by code that can drop the table. But you don't need to know much about that just yet.

Q: I don't need to understand the code? Isn't it important to understand Ruby's code to master Rails?

A: The more you understand Ruby, the more control you will have over Rails. As we go through the book, you will learn more and more about the Ruby language.

Q: If the migration is just a Ruby script, why do I have to use rake? Why can't I just run the script?

A: Good question. Some Ruby is designed to be run directly and some is not. Migrations are not designed to be run directly. They are meant to be run by rake.

Q: Okay, great - but why?

A: rake is "smarter" than ruby. When you call rake db:migrate you are actually saying to rake, "Make sure all of the migrations have been run". rake may decide not to call the migration if it doesn't need to. Ruby can't make those kinds of decisions by itself.

Q: Can't I just edit my tickets table manually?

A: You could, but it is better to manage your database structure with migrations. When you make your application live, you will need to recreate your data structures in your production database. If you use migrations, then rake will be able to make the data structures in your production database match what you need for your application. If you modify your data structure manually, things can get out of sync pretty easily. Like most things in Rails, if you go along with the conventional way of using Rails, you'll make things easier for yourself.

Rails can generate migrations

Remember when we generated the scaffolding using:

```
ruby script/generate scaffold ticket name:string seat_id_seq:string
address:text price_paid:decimal email_address:string
```

generate is a script to create Ruby code. And the good news is that generate doesn't *just* write scaffolding code. It can also generate migrations.

Now suppose you were to type in this command:

← *Don't actually type this in.*

```
ruby script/generate migration PhoneNumber
```

This would generate a brand new blank migration file. We could then add in the Ruby code to modify the table. The trouble is, we don't know how to write the code to complete the migration.

So what can we do? And what can Rails do for us?

Give your migration a "smart" name, and Rails writes your code for you

You've probably noticed by now that names are really important to Rails. When we created scaffolding called "ticket," Rails made the app visible at http://localhost:3000/tickets and generated a migration to create a table called tickets.

Naming conventions are important in Rails because they save you work. The same is true with how you name migrations. Instead of just giving the new migration any old name, try giving it a name like this:

The important bit is this name here. It takes the form Add...To...

```
File  Edit  Window  Help  NamesMatter
> ruby script/generate migration AddPhoneToTickets phone:string
```

You need to run this command.

So why does the name make any difference?

Rails knows that a migration called Add...To... is probably going to be adding a particular column to a particular table, so instead of just generating a blank migration for you to fill in, **Rails will actually write your migration code for you**.

AddPhoneToTickets

tickets	
name	string
seat_id_seq	string
address	text
price_paid	decimal
email_address	string
phone	string

AddPhoneToTickets adds phone to the ticket table. This is just another convention that Rails uses.

You need to run your migration with <u>rake</u>

Here's the migration that Rails cleverly generates for you.

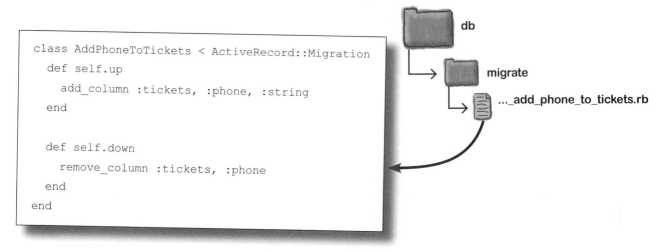

```
class AddPhoneToTickets < ActiveRecord::Migration
  def self.up
    add_column :tickets, :phone, :string
  end

  def self.down
    remove_column :tickets, :phone
  end
end
```

db

migrate

..._add_phone_to_tickets.rb

When we wanted to run a migration before we used the `rake` command:

```
rake db:migrate
```

But can we do that this time? After all, we don't want `rake` to run the first migration again by mistake.

Timestamps tell rake which migrations to run, and in which order

Rails records the latest timestamp of all the migrations it runs. That allows rake to tell which migrations have been run and which haven't. This means that whenever you run `rake db:migrate`, ***Rails will only run the latest migrations***.

Let's put this to the test. Run `rake db:migrate` again to add the phone column to the tickets table.

Do this!

```
> rake db:migrate
```

But changing the database isn't enough

Scaffolding *generates* code—and that's great because it gets you up and running very quickly. But the downside is that once the code has been generated it the **developer's responsibility** to keep the code **up-to-date**.

We just added a phone attribute to the database. But because the forms had already been created by scaffolding, they won't automatically pick-up the new phone field. So we'll have to go back to the page templates and add in references to the phone number:

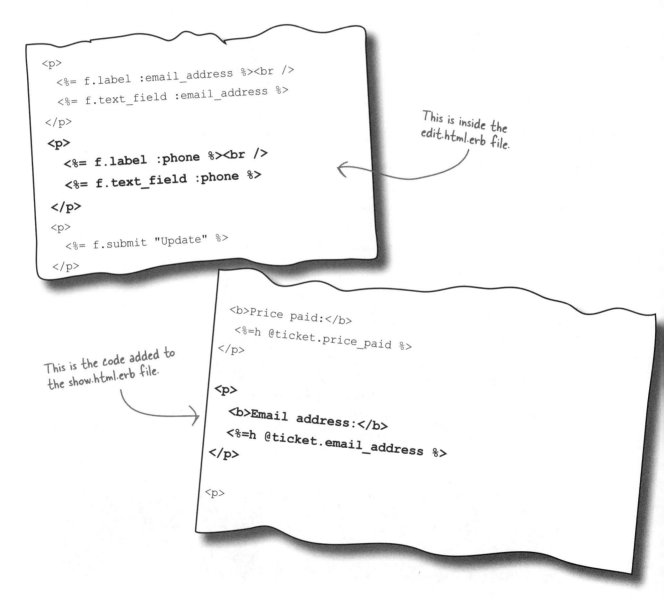

```
<p>
  <%= f.label :email_address %><br />
  <%= f.text_field :email_address %>
</p>
<p>
  <%= f.label :phone %><br />
  <%= f.text_field :phone %>
</p>
<p>
  <%= f.submit "Update" %>
</p>
```

This is inside the edit.html.erb file.

```
  <b>Price paid:</b>
  <%=h @ticket.price_paid %>
</p>

<p>
  <b>Email address:</b>
  <%=h @ticket.email_address %>
</p>

<p>
```

This is the code added to the show.html.erb file.

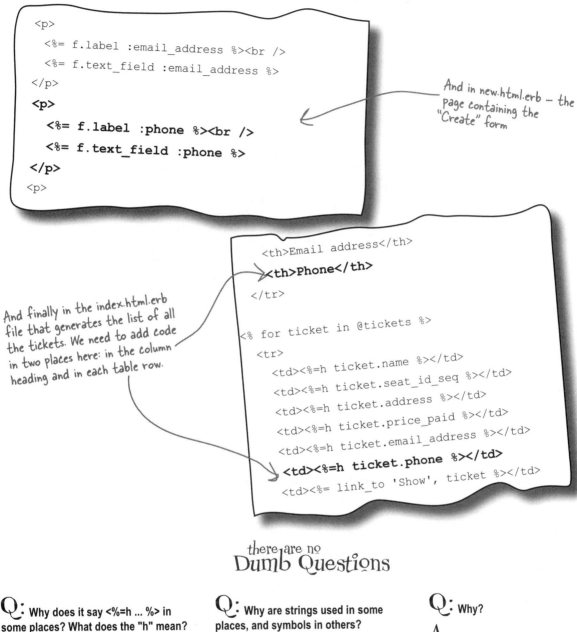

```
<p>
  <%= f.label :email_address %><br />
  <%= f.text_field :email_address %>
</p>
<p>
  <%= f.label :phone %><br />
  <%= f.text_field :phone %>
</p>
<p>
```

And in new.html.erb – the page containing the "Create" form

```
    <th>Email address</th>
    <th>Phone</th>
  </tr>

<% for ticket in @tickets %>
  <tr>
    <td><%=h ticket.name %></td>
    <td><%=h ticket.seat_id_seq %></td>
    <td><%=h ticket.address %></td>
    <td><%=h ticket.price_paid %></td>
    <td><%=h ticket.email_address %></td>
    <td><%=h ticket.phone %></td>
    <td><%= link_to 'Show', ticket %></td>
```

And finally in the index.html.erb file that generates the list of all the tickets. We need to add code in two places here: in the column heading and in each table row.

there are no
Dumb Questions

Q: Why does it say <%=h ... %> in some places? What does the "h" mean?

A: h is a helper method. Helpers are used for things like formatting output. The h helper escapes special characters in the field like "<" and "&". This will prevent anyone from submitting text to the web site that contains JavaScript or other potentially dangerous code.

Q: Why are strings used in some places, and symbols in others?

A: Strings are used in the page templates where a simple piece of text is required. Symbols (the words that begin ":"s) are commonly used in labels.

Q: Why?

A: Symbols are memory efficient and most methods (like f.label) that accept parameters like to have symbols instead of strings. But in most cases, Rails methods let you optionally use strings instead of symbols if they are easier to format.

LONG EXERCISE

The boss is pleased with the way the application is going, and now he wants to record events as well as ticket sales. This is the events data structure:

Event:

artist - the performer (string)

description - short bio (text)

price_low - cheapest tickets (decimal)

price_high - sales price of ticket (decimal)

event_date - when it happens (date)

What command would you enter at the console to create scaffolding for the event data?

$ Ruby Script/generate Scaffold Event artist : String,
dscr :text price :decimal price_high :decimal evend_dt : date

What would you type to create the events table in the database?

rake db:migrate

The boss wants the labels in the pages for price_low to be "Prices from", price_high to be "To", and event_date to be "Date". You will need to edit four templates to make the change. Write the changes for the new.html.erb page template shown here:

```erb
<h1>New event</h1>
<% form_for(@event) do |f| %>
  <%= f.error_messages %>

  <p>
    <%= f.label :artist %><br />
    <%= f.text_field :artist %>
  </p>
  <p>
    <%= f.label :description %><br />
    <%= f.text_area :description %>
  </p>
  <p>
    <%= f.label :price_low %><br />
    <%= f.text_field :price_low %>
  </p>
  <p>
    <%= f.label :price_high %><br />
    <%= f.text_field :price_high %>
  </p>
  <p>
    <%= f.label :event_date %><br />
    <%= f.date_select :event_date %>
  </p>
  <p>
    <%= f.submit "Create" %>
  </p>
<% end %>
<%= link_to 'Back', events_path %>
```

new.html.erb

What are the names of the other three templates in the app/views/events directory that will need changing?

edit.html.erb, show.html.erb, index.html.erb.

Long Exercise
Solution

The boss is pleased with the way the application is going, and now he wants to record events as well as ticket sales. Here's the events data structure:

> Event:
> artist - the performer (string)
> description - short bio (text)
> price_low - cheapest tickets (decimal)
> price_high - sales price of ticket (decimal)
> event_date - when it happens (date)

What command would you enter at the console to create scaffolding for the event data?

ruby script/generate scaffold event artist:string description:text price_low:decimal
price_high:decimal event_date:date

What would you type to create the events table in the database?

rake db:migrate

The boss wants the labels in the pages for price_low to be "Prices from", price_high to be "To", and event_date to be "Date". You will need to edit 4 templates to make the change. Write the changes for the new.html.erb page template shown here:

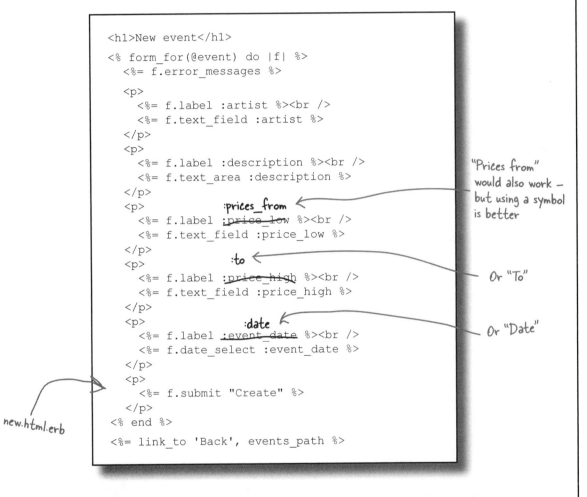

```
<h1>New event</h1>
<% form_for(@event) do |f| %>
  <%= f.error_messages %>
  <p>
    <%= f.label :artist %><br />
    <%= f.text_field :artist %>
  </p>
  <p>
    <%= f.label :description %><br />
    <%= f.text_area :description %>
  </p>
  <p>                     :prices_from ←
    <%= f.label :price_low %><br />
    <%= f.text_field :price_low %>
  </p>
  <p>                     :to ←
    <%= f.label :price_high %><br />
    <%= f.text_field :price_high %>
  </p>
  <p>                    :date ←
    <%= f.label :event_date %><br />
    <%= f.date_select :event_date %>
  </p>
  <p>
    <%= f.submit "Create" %>
  </p>
<% end %>
<%= link_to 'Back', events_path %>
```

"Prices from" would also work — but using a symbol is better

Or "To"

Or "Date"

new.html.erb

What are the names of the other three templates in the app/views/events directory that will need changing?

edit.html.erb, show.html.erb and index.html.erb

TEST DRIVE

The application now has all of the contact information on the tickets pages:

And all of the events information is also recorded:

This looks great! Looks like you've saved the day.

The concert is a sell-out!

The application runs perfectly all week, and the following Friday night, every seat in the arena is sold.

Phew. Those tickets sold out fast... Ready for a little boogy action, guys?

BULLET POINTS

- Rails follows a Model-View-Controller architecture, known as the MVC architecture.

- Rails generates separate folders for the model, view, and controller code.

- Any changes you make to your application can be seen as soon as you save your changes and refresh the pages in your browser. This is because Rails is built with Ruby, and doesn't need to be compiled.

- You can make changes to your table structure using a migration. To generate a migration that adds a column to a table, use the following command:

```
ruby script/generate migration
Add<column>To<table>
 <column>:<data type>
```

- To run a migration, use the command

```
rake db:migrate
```

Tools for your Rails Toolbox

You've got Chapter 1 under your belt, and now you've added the ability to create Rails applications to your toolbox.

Rails Tools

rails app-name

Create an application

ruby script/server

Start the application

ruby script/generate scaffold...

Generate CRUD code for a model

ruby script/generate migration

Generate a migration to alter the database structure

rake db:migrate

Run new migrations on the database

2 beyond scaffolding

Rails apps, made to order

He's going to get a shock when he realizes I've fitted an after-burner.

So what's really going on with Rails? You've seen how **scaffolding** generates heaps of code and helps you write web applications wicked fast, but what if you want something a little different? In this chapter you'll see how to really *seize control* of your Rails development and take a look underneath the hood of the framework. You'll learn how Rails decides which **code** to run, how **data** is read from the database, and how **web pages** are generated. By the end, you'll be able to publish data the way *you* want.

MeBay, Inc. needs your help

MeBay, Inc. is a sales company that helps people sell their unwanted stuff online. They need a new version of their site, and they need **you** to help them out.

To place an ad on the site, the seller calls MeBay on their toll-free number, and gives their seller ID and the details of the item they want to sell. MeBay has their own data entry system, and your application is needed to publish the MeBay ads online.

MeBay will store their ads in a database

All of the ads contain the same types of information, and MeBay wants to store the ads in a database. They'll insert the data into the tables you create when you build the app. They need something like this:

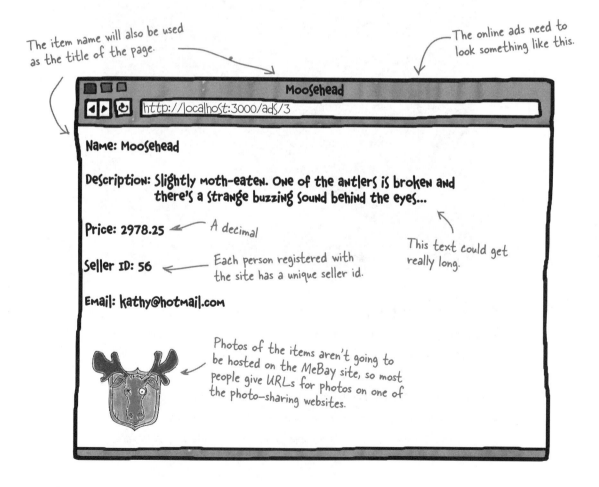

The item name will also be used as the title of the page.

The online ads need to look something like this.

Name: Moosehead

Description: Slightly moth-eaten. One of the antlers is broken and there's a strange buzzing sound behind the eyes...

This text could get really long.

Price: 2978.25 ← A decimal

Seller ID: 56 ← Each person registered with the site has a unique seller id.

Email: kathy@hotmail.com

Photos of the items aren't going to be hosted on the MeBay site, so most people give URLs for photos on one of the photo-sharing websites.

Sharpen your pencil

Suppose you were going to use Rails scaffolding for the website. Fill in the blanks in the architecture diagram below.

First, you'd create a new Rails application called mebay using this command:

$ Rails MeBay

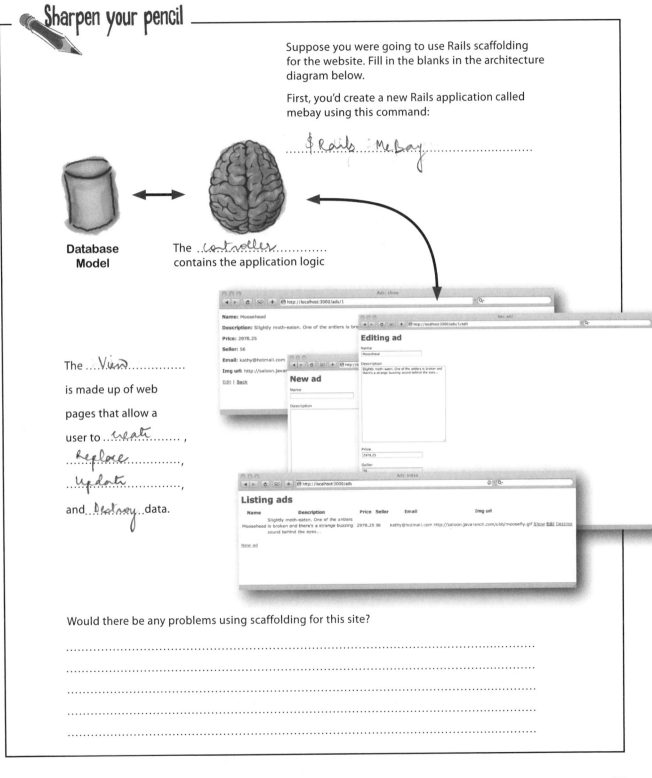

Database Model

The ...Controller... contains the application logic

The ...View... is made up of web pages that allow a user to ...create...., ...Replace...., ...Update...., and ...Destroy...data.

Would there be any problems using scaffolding for this site?

....

....

....

....

....

Sharpen your pencil
Solution

Suppose you were going to use Rails scaffolding for the website. Fill in the blanks in the architecture diagram below.

First, you'd create a new Rails application called mebay using this command:

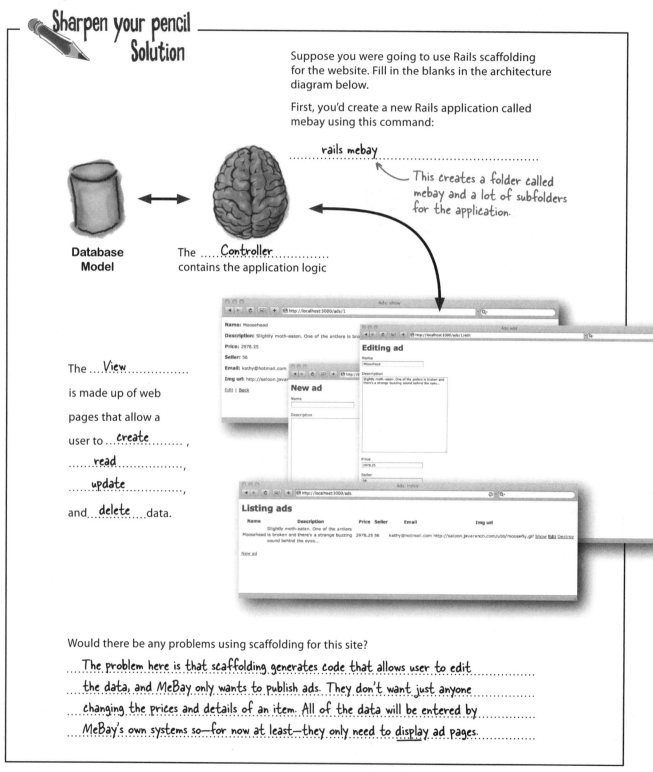

rails mebay

This creates a folder called mebay and a lot of subfolders for the application.

Database Model

The .....**Controller**..... contains the application logic

The ....**View**.... is made up of web pages that allow a user to ...**create**..., ...**read**......, ...**update**......, and...**delete**....data.

Would there be any problems using scaffolding for this site?

The problem here is that scaffolding generates code that allows user to edit the data, and MeBay only wants to publish ads. They don't want just anyone changing the prices and details of an item. All of the data will be entered by MeBay's own systems so—for now at least—they only need to display ad pages.

Scaffolding does <u>WAY</u> too much

MeBay want an application that does *less* than a scaffolded app would. Scaffolding's great, but some applications are so simple that you'll sometimes be better off building your app manually.

So why's that? Well, if you write the code yourself, the application will be **simpler** and **easier** to maintain. The downside to this is that in order to build a Rails web app manually, you need to go ***under the hood*** and understand how Rails really **works**.

Let's start by looking at what code you need to create for MeBay:

To build an app without scaffolding, you need to understand how Rails really works.

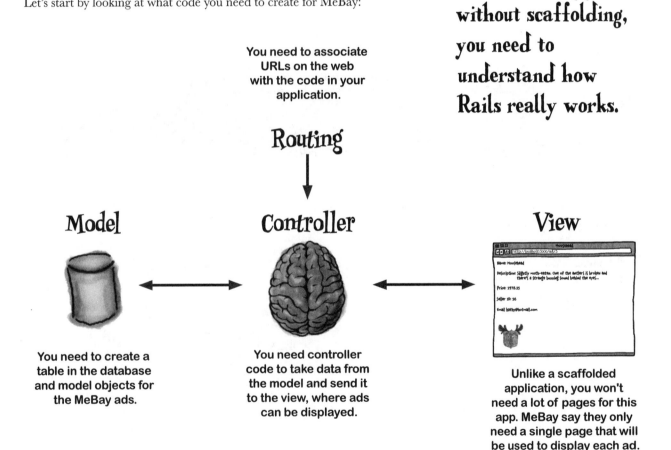

You need to associate URLs on the web with the code in your application.

Routing

Model

You need to create a table in the database and model objects for the MeBay ads.

Controller

You need controller code to take data from the model and send it to the view, where ads can be displayed.

View

Unlike a scaffolded application, you won't need a lot of pages for this app. MeBay say they only need a single page that will be used to display each ad.

So which code will you write first?

Let's start by generating the MeBay model...

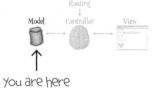

You are here

It's a good idea to begin with creating the **model** code, because the structure of the data in the model affects both the controller and the view.

Creating model code is very similar to creating scaffolding. In fact, the only difference is that you replace the word "scaffold" with the word "model," like this:

Models have singular names — so it's "ad", not "ads".

```
File Edit Window Help AdvertizeMeBaby
> ruby script/generate model ad name:string description:text
price:decimal seller_id:integer email:string img_url:string
```

The model-generator command creates two key scripts within the app and db subfolders:

- the **model class**
  (app/models/ad.rb) and

- the data **migration**
  (db/migrate/..._create_ads.rb).

The migration is a Ruby script that can connect to the database and create a table for the ads. To run this script and create the table, we need to use rake.

This is just like we did in Chapter 1. rake figures out which migrations to run based on timestamps.

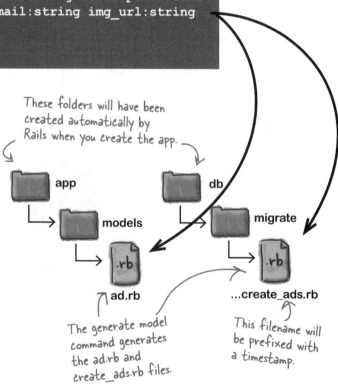

These folders will have been created automatically by Rails when you create the app.

app

db

models

migrate

.rb

.rb

ad.rb

...create_ads.rb

The generate model command generates the ad.rb and create_ads.rb files.

This filename will be prefixed with a timestamp.

... and then we'll actually create the table using rake

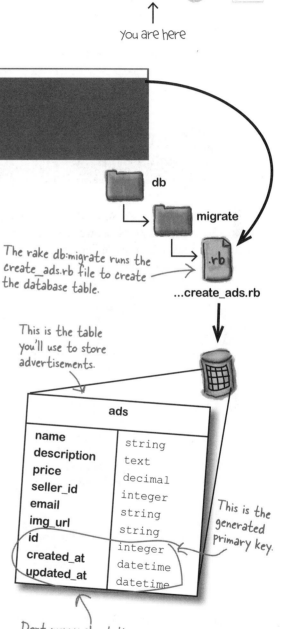

You are here

To create the table, we need to call the migration using the `rake db:migrate` command:

```
File Edit Window Help AdvertizeMeBaby
> rake db:migrate
```

Remember, the `rake db:migrate` command creates a table in the database using the `..._create_ads.rb` script you just created with `model`.

But if you were to look really closely at the table it creates, you'd see a strange thing. Rails creates three extra columns in the table *without being asked*.

These are "magic columns": `id`, `created_at`, and `updated_at`. The `id` column is a generated primary key, and `created_at` and `updated_at` record when the data is entered or updated.

The rake db:migrate runs the create_ads.rb file to create the database table.

...create_ads.rb

This is the table you'll use to store advertisements.

ads	
name	string
description	text
price	decimal
seller_id	integer
email	string
img_url	string
id	integer
created_at	datetime
updated_at	datetime

This is the generated primary key.

Dont worry about these. They are called the three "magic columns" and they get created even though you didn't ask for them.

Do this!

Rake creates a table for you in the database, but what it *doesn't* do is populate that table with data for you to experiment.

You're going to need some data in the table before we get much further. Fortunately, the kind folks at MeBay Inc. have left a copy of their test data for you at the Head First website. Point your browser to `www.headfirstlabs.com/books/hfrails` for a full set of instructions and the data.

Make sure you do this, or you'll hit problems later on.

But what about the controller?

The model isn't a lot of use on its own. You need some code
that uses the data the model produces, and that's the job of the
controller.

Just like scaffolding and the model, controllers have their own
generators. Use the `generate controller` command
below to generate an empty controller class:

Controllers have plural names.

```
File Edit Window Help
> ruby script/generate controller ads
```

This command generates a **class file** for your controller at
app/controllers/ads_controller.rb. If you open
the file with a text editor, you'll find some Ruby code like this:

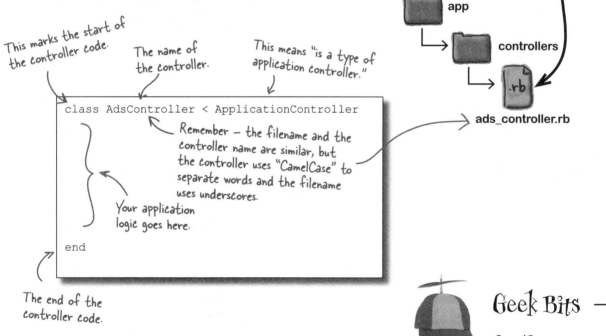

This marks the start of the controller code.

The name of the controller.

This means "is a type of application controller."

```
class AdsController < ApplicationController



end
```

Remember — the filename and the controller name are similar, but the controller uses "CamelCase" to separate words and the filename uses underscores.

Your application logic goes here.

The end of the controller code.

We'll come back to what code needs to be added to this class
in just a few pages... for now, it's just cool that we didn't have
to write any of this Ruby- and Rails-specific syntax.

Geek Bits

CamelCase means
using uppercase
within identifiers that consist of
more than one word to help you
make out the individual words.

app

controllers

.rb

ads_controller.rb

Routing

Model   Controller   View

You are here

there are no
Dumb Questions

Q: Does rake db:migrate always add the magic columns?

A: Yep, it sure does.

Q: Even if the table is created by scaffolding?

A: Yes. If you examined the database table in the previous chapter, you'll see the magic columns in there as well.

Q: Is there any way I can open up the database and examine the tables?

A: Yes - but you'll need a tool. There's a Firefox add-in available called SQLite Manager that will open and read the sqlite3 files used by Rails.

Q: I noticed that in the `generate model` command you used ad, but in the `generate controller` command you used ads. Was that intentional?

A: Yes. In Rails, models all have **singular** names, but controllers and tables are **plural**. This means that when we used the command to generate the model, we gave the singular name of ad, but when we used the command to generate the controller, we gave the plural name ads.

Q: How important is it to get that right?

A: *Very!* Rails relies on these conventions, so it's crucial that you follow them too. If you don't, Rails won't be able to set up your web app for you properly, and some things may not work. Life is much easier if you follow the conventions Rails expects.

Models have singular names but controllers and tables are plural.

We've created the model and controller, now let's move onto the view...

The view is created with a page template

You are here

So what view code do we need to create? The MeBay web app only needs a single page, and this page will be used as a template for all of the ads on the website. For this reason, pages in Rails are often called **page templates** (or simply **templates**).

Web pages are created from templates by Embedded Ruby (called ERb), and this is part of the standard Ruby library. If someone asks for for ad #3, ERb will generate the HTML web page for the ad using the page template and data from the model.

So how does ERb produce web pages?

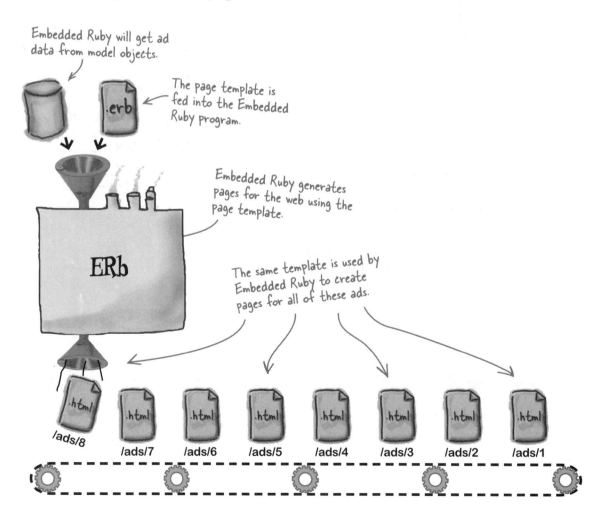

Embedded Ruby will get ad data from model objects.

The page template is fed into the Embedded Ruby program.

Embedded Ruby generates pages for the web using the page template.

ERb

The same template is used by Embedded Ruby to create pages for all of these ads.

/ads/8   /ads/7   /ads/6   /ads/5   /ads/4   /ads/3   /ads/2   /ads/1

The page template contains HTML

When you generated the model and the controller, Rails generated **Ruby** code. The view's a little different though. The application has an HTML interface, so it makes sense that the **view code is written in HTML**, too.

To create the ad template, open up a text editor and create a file called **show.html.erb** and save it in app/views/ads. Here's what you need the contents of show.html.erb to look like:

Do this!

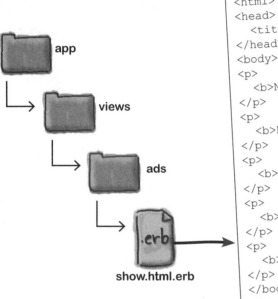

Create file show.html.erb and add this code to the file.

```
<html>
<head>
  <title>     </title>
</head>
<body>
<p>
   <b>Name:</b>
</p>
<p>
   <b>Description:</b>
</p>
<p>
   <b>Price:</b>
</p>
<p>
   <b>Seller Id:</b>
</p>
<p>
   <b>Email:</b>
</p>
</body>
</html>
```

app

views

ads

.erb

show.html.erb

At the moment the template looks pretty blank, but you'll see in a little while how the controller can cleverly insert values into it.

So what does the actual web app look like?

Embedded Ruby (ERb) creates web pages from a template.

Test Drive

Start your server with

```
ruby script/server
```

and point a browser at

```
http://localhost:3000/ads/3
```

What happens?

The web app crashes. So what happened?

We've manually created the bare bones of a web app, but we haven't told Rails how to use the new show.html.erb template.

So how do we do that?

A <u>route</u> tells Rails where your web page is

Rails needs a rule to say which code to run for a given URL. It's one of the very few times where Rails actually needs some **configuration**.

The rules that Rails uses to map URL paths to code are called **routes**. Routes are defined in a Ruby program in `config/routes.rb`, and we need to add a new route for the `show.html.erb` template:

> If someone asks for '/ads/3', I'll use the ad controller and the show template, and set the id parameter to '3'

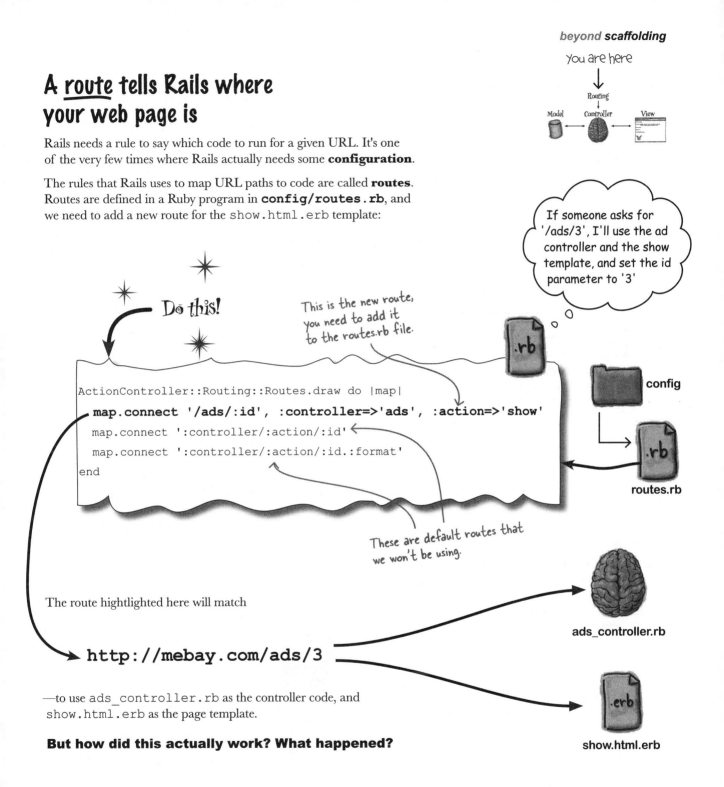

Do this!

This is the new route, you need to add it to the routes.rb file.

```
ActionController::Routing::Routes.draw do |map|
  map.connect '/ads/:id', :controller=>'ads', :action=>'show'
  map.connect ':controller/:action/:id'
  map.connect ':controller/:action/:id.:format'
end
```

These are default routes that we won't be using.

config

routes.rb

The route hightlighted here will match

http://mebay.com/ads/3

ads_controller.rb

—to use `ads_controller.rb` as the controller code, and `show.html.erb` as the page template.

show.html.erb

But how did this actually work? What happened?

Behind the scenes with routes

❶ When Rails receives a request from a browser, it passes the request-path to the routes.rb program to find a matching route.

```
map.connect '/ads/:id',
  :controller=>'ads', :action=>'show'
```

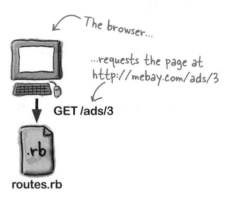

The browser...

...requests the page at http://mebay.com/ads/3

GET /ads/3

.rb

routes.rb

---

❷ If the matching route contains symbols, then the Routing system will create matching parameters in the request parameters table params[...]. By a symbol. we mean a sequence of letters prefixed with a colon (:).

The Routing system sees a sequence of letters prefixed by a colon as a symbol.

```
map.connect '/ads/:id',
  :controller=>'ads', :action=>'show'
```

GET /ads/3

.rb

routes.rb

params[...]

params[:id] = '3'

Name
:name
:description

---

❸ The route can also specify additional parameters that will be inserted into params[...].
:controller and :action are often specified here. Can you think why?

```
map.connect '/ads/:id',
  :controller=>'ads', :action=>'show'
```

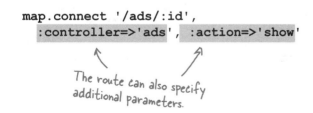

The route can also specify additional parameters.

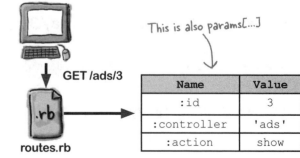

This is also params[...]

GET /ads/3

.rb

routes.rb

Name	Value
:id	3
:controller	'ads'
:action	show

4 Once the routes.rb program has finished, Rails will look at the value of params[:controller] and use it to decide which type of controller object it needs to create.

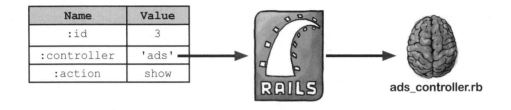

ads_controller.rb

---

5 Once the controller object has been created, Rails will then use the value stored in params[:action], to choose the method within the controller to call.

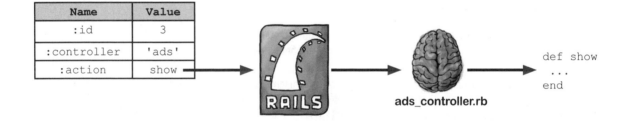

ads_controller.rb

```
def show
  ...
end
```

---

6 Then, when the controller method completes, Rails calls the page template that also matches the params[:action] value. The page template then generates the response which is sent back to the browser.

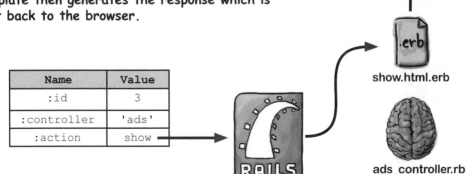

show.html.erb

ads_controller.rb

there are no
Dumb Questions

Q: Wouldn't it be quicker to generate scaffolding and edit that?

A: It depends on the application. MeBay only want a very small amount of functionality. If your application needs to work significantly differently than scaffolding, it will be quicker to just generate the model and controller, and then add your own code.

Q: Does scaffolding generate the model as well?

A: Yes. The scaffolding generator calls the generators for the model and controller. It also creates page templates for the standard create, read, update, and delete operations.

Q: What sort of parameter is :id?

A: It's a request parameter, like the values that are submitted by forms or parameters passed into a URL.

Q: What's a request?

A: A request is what the browser sends to the server whenever you click on a link. It tells the server exactly what path you want.

Q: So what's a response?

A: The response is the content that the server returns to the browser, as well as other information, like the mime-type of the content.

Q: Why does Rails need route configuration? Why not just have standard paths?

A: Rails always prefers convention to configuration, except when the system needs to talk to the outside world. The format of the URLs affects how the outside world sees the application, so Rails lets you configure them.

When you use scaffolding, Rails generates routes for you, but it's still useful to know how routes work in case you need to track down errors or create custom routes, like in this application.

Q: I still don't quite understand when to use camel case. What gives?

A: CamelCase just means using uppercase within identifiers that consist of more than one word. It's called that because the uppercase words look like a camel's humps.

In Rails, the filename and controller names are similar, but the controller uses "CamelCase" to separate words. Filenames use underscores to help you differentiate between a bit of code and a file.

Q: Which gets called first: the controller or the view?

A: The controller always gets called before the view.

Q: Why has the page template got a .html.erb file extension? Isn't it just an HTML file?

A: A template can simply be an HTML file, but templates can also contain extra instructions that will be processed by the Embedded Ruby system. Files that you want Embedded Ruby to process all have ".erb" at the end of their filename.

Q: Why are the templates in a folder called "views/ad" but the controllers are not in "controllers/ad"?

A: Imagine you want to edit an object and also view an object. There will be an "edit" page and a "view" page. But both "edit" and "view" requests will pass through a single controller. So models have a single controller, but potentially several pages. That's why page templates are in their own sub-folder; there may be several of them.

Q: I've heard some people talk about "business objects" and "domain objects". Does Rails have them?

A: Yes, because business objects and domain objects are just other names for model objects.

MeBay's competition already has a Rails application, which is using this set of routes:

```
map.connect '/shows/:title', :controller => 'shows', :action=> 'display'
map.connect '/cats/:name', :controller => 'cats', :action=> 'show'
map.connect '/gadgets/:type', :controller => 'gadgets', :action=> 'show
```

Can you work out which page template file will be used to generate the HTML for each of the given URLs? **Draw a line** to connect the URL to the page template that will be used, then write down the name and value of the parameter that will be extracted from each URL.

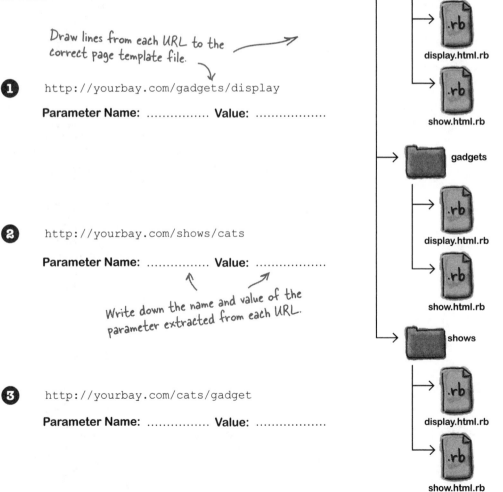

Draw lines from each URL to the correct page template file.

1 http://yourbay.com/gadgets/display

Parameter Name: .... **Value:** ....

2 http://yourbay.com/shows/cats

Parameter Name: .... **Value:** ....

Write down the name and value of the parameter extracted from each URL.

3 http://yourbay.com/cats/gadget

Parameter Name: .... **Value:** ....

WHAT'S MY ROUTE? SOLUTION

MeBay's competition already has a Rails application, which is using this set of routes:

```
map.connect '/shows/:title', :controller => 'shows', :action=> 'display'
map.connect '/cats/:name', :controller => 'cats', :action=> 'show'
map.connect '/gadgets/:type', :controller => 'gadgets', :action=> 'show
```

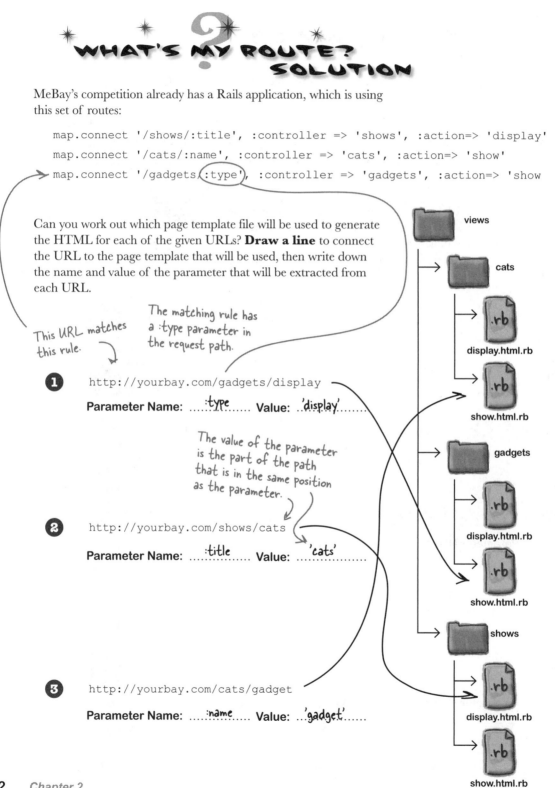

Can you work out which page template file will be used to generate the HTML for each of the given URLs? **Draw a line** to connect the URL to the page template that will be used, then write down the name and value of the parameter that will be extracted from each URL.

This URL matches this rule.

The matching rule has a :type parameter in the request path.

① `http://yourbay.com/gadgets/display`

Parameter Name: ....:type..... Value: ..'display'......

The value of the parameter is the part of the path that is in the same position as the parameter.

② `http://yourbay.com/shows/cats`

Parameter Name: ....:title..... Value: ...'cats'.....

③ `http://yourbay.com/cats/gadget`

Parameter Name: ....:name..... Value: ..'gadget'.....

views

cats
.rb
display.html.rb
.rb
show.html.rb

gadgets
.rb
display.html.rb
.rb
show.html.rb

shows
.rb
display.html.rb
.rb
show.html.rb

Test Drive

Open the browser at a couple of pages:

http://localhost:3000/ads/3 and

http://localhost:3000/ads/5

The pages have no titles.

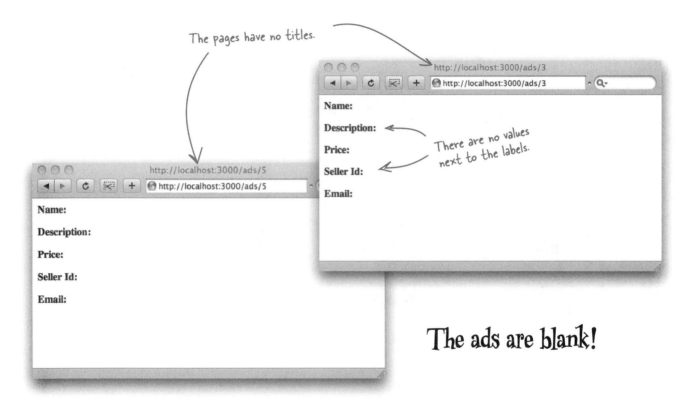

http://localhost:3000/ads/3

Name:

Description: ← There are no values

Price: next to the labels.

Seller Id: ←

Email:

http://localhost:3000/ads/5

Name:

Description:

Price:

Seller Id:

Email:

The ads are blank!

BRAIN POWER

Why is there no detail on the pages? Was it the routing? The model? The view? The controller?

The view doesn't have the data to display

Look back at `show.html.erb`. This file is used to create the pages for each of the ads— and that's exactly what the template has done:

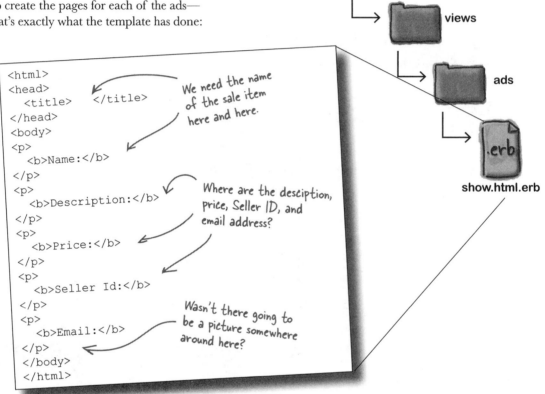

Although we put the main skeletal parts of the HTML in place— the labels, the body and head sections—there were a couple of things that were missed out. We haven't specified:

What data needs to be displayed

or

Where in the page that data needs to be inserted.

So what should the page show?

We need the ad page to display the data for the ad number specified in the URL. As an example, here's the URL for ad #3:

http://localhost:3000/ads/3 ← *We want ad #3 for this URL.*

The database holds...   *...the ads table, and that holds...*   *...the record with id = 3*

id	name	description	price	seller_id	email	img_url
1	Typewriter	Old manual typ...	71.95	54	dhammett@email...	http://www.fot...
2	Football	Some strings f...	74.02	45	marty@googlema...	http://www.dai...
3	Moosehead	Slightly moth-...	2978.25	56	kathy@hotmail....	http://saloon....
4	Desk	Milk desk - go...	4800	123	andy@allmail.c...	http://picasaw...

The first thing you need to do is to tell the model to read the record from the ads table in the database with an id number that's the same as the id number in the URL. If the user asks for the page for ad #3, the model needs to be told to read the record with id = 3.

We need to display the data in the right place

Reading the data's just half the story. Once the model's read the data, it needs to send the data to the view. The view then needs to know where to display the data in each of the pages. Each of the fields in the record needs to be displayed next to the corresponding labels in the web pages. Plus you need to use the value in the img_url column to insert an image of the sales item into the page.

So which part of the system is responsible for asking for the appropriate data from the database and then sending the data to the view?

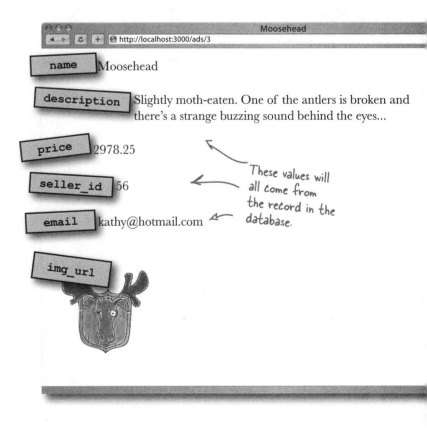

These values will all come from the record in the database.

The controller sends the ad to the view

Let's see what the code in the controller will look like and
how it will work:

1 When the user's browser sends a
request for a page to the application,
Rails calls the routes.rb program to
decide which code needs to run.

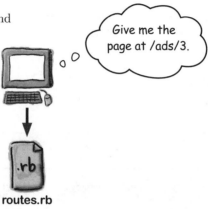

Give me the
page at /ads/3.

routes.rb

---

2 routes.rb examines the path of
the request and decides that the
application needs to carry out
a "show" action using the ads
controller. It also creates an :id
parameter with the value "3" from
the requested path.

routes.rb also creates
:controller and :action
parameters.

routes.rb tells Rails
to create a new ads
controller.

routes.rb

I've created a
parameter called
:id with value "3".

This piece of Ruby code
returns the value of the
:id parameter.

This has the
value 3.

```
params[:id]
```

---

3 The controller sees that the :id
parameter is set to "3", so it
asks the Ad model to find the ad
object with id = 3. The controller
talks to the model using a method
called a "finder".

routes.rb

A "finder"

The controller calls
the method using the
params[:id] value.

```
Ad.find(params[:id])
```

Give me the ad
with an id of 3.

4 The Ad model reads the record from the ads table with id = 3 and sends the result back to the controller.

OK - here's the ad data.

The ads table

routes.rb

The ad data from the Ad model is returned to the controller as the return value of the finder call.

`Ad.find(params[:id])`

---

5 The controller stores the data for ad #3 into memory by assigning it to a variable called @ad. The page template can see the @ad variable and so it will now be able to use the ad data when generating the web page.

Thanks - I'll store the ad data in memory with the name @ad.

Hmmm... someone's selling a Moosehead...

routes.rb

The controller "assigns" the data to a variable called @ad.

id
name
description
price
seller_id
email
img_url

@ad

show.html.erb

`@ad = Ad.find(params[:id])`

Stored in memory with the name @ad

Memory

The page template

This is a controller "method" with a name that matches the name of the action: "show".

```
class AdsController < ApplicationController
  def show
    @ad = Ad.find(params[:id])
  end
end
```

ads_controller.rb

Type in the completed controller code above.

Do this!

/app/controllers/ads_controller.rb

The completed code in **ads_controller.rb** needs to go inside a **method** called **show**—which matches the name of the `:action` parameter created by `routes.rb`

But how exactly does the model read the data from the database, and how will the page template use that data?

Rails turned the record into an object

When Rails reads the record from the database that matches the id in the URL, the data from the record is converted into an **object**. That object's stored in memory and the controller assigns it the name **@ad**.

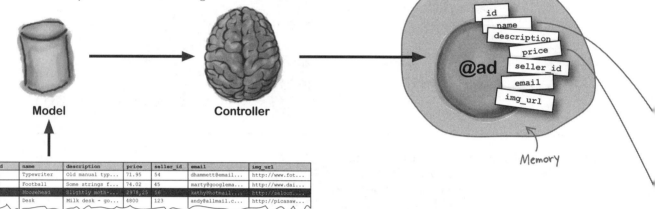

Model   **Controller**

Memory

id	name	description	price	seller_id	email	img_url
1	Typewriter	Old manual typ...	71.95	54	dhammett@email...	http://www.fot...
2	Football	Some strings f...	74.02	45	marty@googlema...	http://www.dai...
3	Moosehead	Slightly moth-...	2978,25	56	kathy@hotmail....	http://saloon....
4	Desk	Milk desk - go...	4800	123	andy@allmail.c...	http://picasaw...

But a record has several fields with data in each one. How does all the data get stored in a single object?

The answer is that an object can have several ***attributes***. An attribute is like a field in a record. It has a **name** and a **value**. So when Rails reads the description value from the record on the database, it stores it in the @ad.description attribute of the @ad object. The same thing for the id, the name, the seller-id, and so on.

In this way, the @ad model object ***exactly matches*** the record in the database. This is useful because **this memory object will be visible to the view code**.

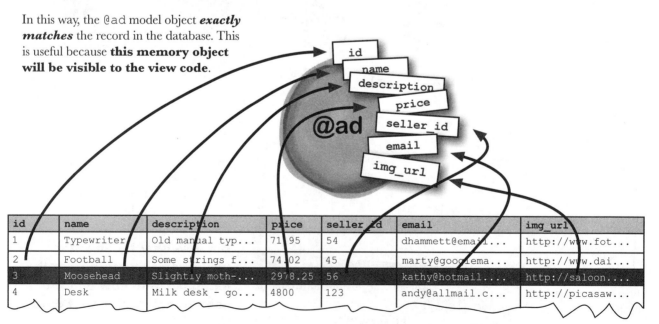

id	name	description	price	seller_id	email	img_url
1	Typewriter	Old manual typ...	71.95	54	dhammett@email...	http://www.fot...
2	Football	Some strings f...	74.02	45	marty@googlema...	http://www.dai...
3	Moosehead	Slightly moth-...	2978.25	56	kathy@hotmail....	http://saloon....
4	Desk	Milk desk - go...	4800	123	andy@allmail.c...	http://picasaw...

The data's in memory, and the web page can see it

The page template (show.html.erb) isn't just sent straight back to the browser. First it gets processed by the **Embedded Ruby** program ERb, and that's why our template had that **.erb** file extension. So let's take a closer look at how ERb reads objects from memory.

ERb reads through the template looking for little pieces of embedded Ruby code called **expressions**. An expression is surrounded by **<%=** and **%>** and ERb will replace the expression with its value. So if it finds:

<%= 1 + 1 %>

somewhere in the web page, Rails will replace this expression with 2 before returning the page to the browser.

But what we *really* want to do is get at the values in the @ad object from memory, like this:

```
<html>
<head>
  <title><%= @ad.name %></title>
</head>
<body>
<p>
  <b>Name:</b><%= @ad.name %>
 </p>
<p>
  <b>Description:</b><%= @ad.description %>
</p>
<p>
  <b>Price:</b><%= @ad.price %>
</p>
<p>
  <b>Seller Id:</b><%= @ad.seller_id %>
</p>
<p>
  <b>Email:</b><%= @ad.email %>
</p>
<p>
  <img src="<%= @ad.img_url %>"/>
</p>
</body>
</html>
```

This ERb template with embedded Ruby will generate the HTML for this page.

> **Moosehead**
> http://localhost:3000/ads/3
>
> **Name:** Moosehead
>
> **Description:** Slightly moth-eaten. One of the antlers is broken and there's a strange buzzing sound behind the eyes...
>
> **Price:** 2978.25
>
> **Seller ID:** 56
>
> **Email:** kathy@hotmail.com

Before sending the page back, Rails replaces all the <%=...%> tags with their object values.

So—does it work?

Test Drive

To try out the system, the folks at MeBay have used their data entry system to insert data into the Rails database.

As soon as the data is stored in the database it becomes available through the web. So if someone requests /ads/1, /ads/2, and so on, they see a page that's been generated by the appropriate data in the database.

MeBay data entry team

Congratulations!

You've just created your first hand-crafted Rails application! Although it took a little longer than using scaffolding, you were in control at every step. What's more, you taken a peek under the hood of Rails and learned about some of the things it does:

BULLET POINTS

- **Routes** tell Rails what code to run when a request is received for a URL

- The controller uses the **id** from the **URL** to read the correct data from the model

- The model reads the database and returns the data as a **Ruby object**

- The controller gives the object a name **in memory** so that it can be found by...

- ...the **page template**, which uses embedded Ruby expressions to insert the data values into the page

---

Pool Puzzle

MeBay want to display information about sellers
at /seller/:id. Complete the controller and
the page template with the code provided.

```
def stats
    ................ = Seller.find(.........................)
end
```

```
<p>
  <b>Number of sales:</b> ................ ................................. ................
</p>
<p>
  <b>Total sales value:</b> ................ ................................. ................
</p>
<p>
  <b>Average price:</b> ................ ................................. ............. ........................ .........
</p>
```

**Note: each snippet
from the pool can only
be used once!**

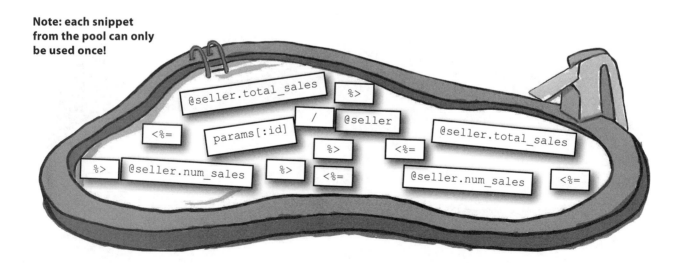

@seller.total_sales   %>

<%=   params[:id]   /   @seller   @seller.total_sales

%>   <%=

%>   @seller.num_sales   %>   <%=   @seller.num_sales   <%=

Pool Puzzle Solution

MeBay want to display information about sellers
at /seller/:id. Complete the controller and
the page template with the code provided.

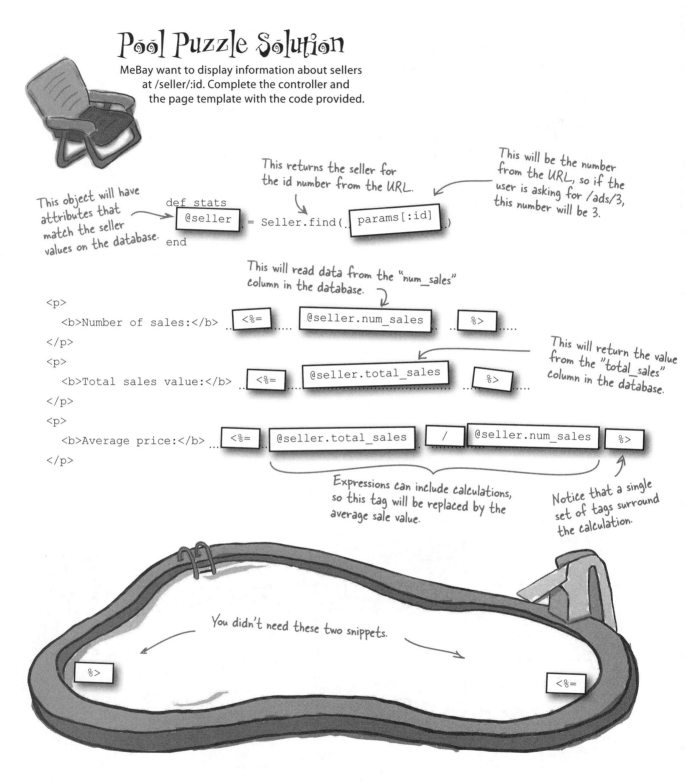

This returns the seller for
the id number from the URL.

This will be the number
from the URL, so if the
user is asking for /ads/3,
this number will be 3.

This object will have
attributes that
match the seller
values on the database.

```
def stats
  @seller = Seller.find( params[:id] )
end
```

This will read data from the "num_sales"
column in the database.

```
<p>
  <b>Number of sales:</b> <%= @seller.num_sales %>
</p>
<p>
  <b>Total sales value:</b> <%= @seller.total_sales %>
</p>
<p>
  <b>Average price:</b> <%= @seller.total_sales / @seller.num_sales %>
</p>
```

This will return the value
from the "total_sales"
column in the database.

Expressions can include calculations,
so this tag will be replaced by the
average sale value.

Notice that a single
set of tags surround
the calculation.

You didn't need these two snippets.

`%>`

`<%=`

There's a problem — people can't find the pages they want

Even though there are pages for every ad in the database, there's no easy way for people to find them.

> If I want to browse through the ads on the site, I have to type in URLs like /ads/1 and /ads/2. That's not exactly user-friendly.

To help people see what ads there are, and help them skip through the ads to find the ones that are interesting to them, the MeBay folks have asked for an **index** page to display links to all of the pages.

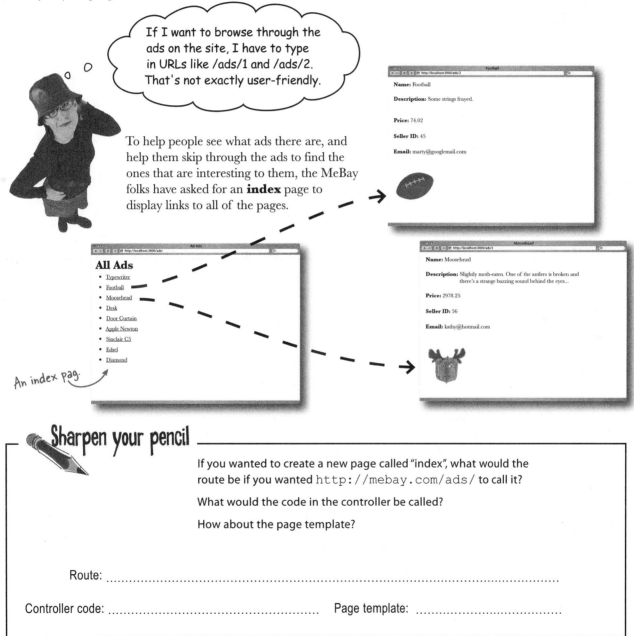

An index pag.

Sharpen your pencil

If you wanted to create a new page called "index", what would the route be if you wanted `http://mebay.com/ads/` to call it?

What would the code in the controller be called?

How about the page template?

Route: ....

Controller code: ....   Page template: ....

Sharpen your pencil
Solution

If you wanted to create a new page called "index", what would the route be if you wanted `http://mebay.com/ads/` to call it?

What would the code in the controller be called?

How about the page template?

Route: _____ map.connect '/ads/', :controller=>'ads', :action=>'index' _____

Controller code: .... index ....   Page template: app/views/ads/index.html.erb

there are no
Dumb Questions

Q: **What is an action?**

A: The action is the *set of operations* that a Rails app carries out in response to a request from a user. The action parameter specifies a name for the action. All of your code (like the method in the controller, and the page template file) uses the action name so that Rails can find them.

Q: **Can I use any database with Rails?**

A: All of the major databases - like SQLite3, MySQL and Oracle - are supported. Plus, most of the time you don't need to write a lot of database-specific code. That way, you can switch between database systems without breaking your application or rewriting a ton of code.

Q: **Languages like Java have primitives as well as objects. Does Ruby or Rails have primitives?**

A: No. There are no primitives in Ruby. Everything you deal with in the Ruby language (including things like numbers and even blocks of code) are objects.

Q: **Isn't a page template just a fancy name for a page?**

A: No. A page template is used to generate pages, but it is not a page itself. Pages are generated from page templates.

Sharpen your pencil (again)

There are now two routes:

```
map.connect '/ads/:id', :controller=>'ads', :action=>'show'
map.connect 'ads/', :controller=>'ads', :action=>'index'
```

Which page would be displayed for each of the URLs?

All Ads
- Typewriter
- Football
- Moosehead
- Desk
- Door Curtain
- Apple Newton
- Sinclair C5
- Edsel
- Diamond

index.html.erb

/ads/3

/ads/something

/ads/

Name: Moosehead

Description: Slightly moth-eaten. One of the antlers is broken and there's a strange buzzing sound behind the eyes...

Price: 2978.25

Seller ID: 56

Email: kathy@hotmail.com

show.html.erb

Is there a problem? If so, how would you fix it?

....

....

Sharpen your pencil (again)
Solution

There are now two routes:

```
map.connect '/ads/:id', :controller=>'ads', :action=>'show'

map.connect 'ads/', :controller=>'ads', :action=>'index'
```

Which page would be displayed for each of the URLs?

All Ads

- Typewriter
- Football
- Moosehead
- Desk
- Door Curtain
- Apple Newton
- Sinclair C5
- Edsel
- Diamond

index.html.erb

/ads/3

/ads/something

/ads/

Name: Moosehead

Description: Slightly moth-eaten. One of the antlers is broken and there's a strange buzzing sound behind the eyes...

Price: 2978.25

Seller ID: 56

Email: kathy@hotmail.com

show.html.erb

Is there a problem? If so, how would you fix it?

The "/ads/" path will match both of the routes, it needs to be changed so it only matches one route.

Routes run in priority order

Both of the routes match the /ads path. Rails avoids any ambiguity by only using the first matching route, so the routes need to be re-ordered to get rid of the confusion.

```
map.connect '/ads/', :controller=>'ads', :action=>'index'

map.connect '/ads/:id', :controller=>'ads', :action=>'show'
```

These are the routes Rails will use. Now you need to complete the code.

Do this!

Add these routes to `config/routes.rb`.

Routing Exposed

This week's interview:
What's life like at Rails' main traffic intersection?

Head First: Ah, Routing. So kind of you to spare us a few moments of your valuable time.

Routing: No, the ads controller.... ads... Yeah, that's the one.

Head First: Routing?

Routing: Woah - stand aside buddy. Request coming through... [Beep... Beep]

Head First: Clearly you have a very busy job. The thing is, although you hold a very important post within a Rails application, some people are unsure what you do.

Routing: Hey - I ain't in this job for the recognition. To direct and to serve. That's me. I'm like a traffic cop, see? A request comes in through that door over there?

Head First: What - the port?

Routing: Yeah. What is it on this server? Port 3000 over there. The request comes in from a web browser, for—I don't know—let's say /donuts/cream.

Head First: Yes?

Routing: But Rails don't know what piece of code to run to provide an answer to that. So he comes to me and I look at /donuts/cream and I check it against this sheet of routes I got here...

Head First: Oh, there's quite a few.

Routing: Yeah. So I go down the list and look for the first route that looks kinda the same as /donuts/cream. I might find... /donuts/:flavor, say.

Head First: That route's pretty similar. But how does that help you direct the request to the correct code?

Routing: Well every request comes in with paperwork for me to fill out. A set of names and values called the request parameters. See?

Head First: Oh yes. Lots of stuff.

Routing: Yeah. All requests have them. params[...] they're called. So I look at the route, and it tells me that every path that matches /donuts/:flavor needs to use the donuts controller, say, with the display action.

Head First: That makes sense.

Routing: So I add more things to the params[...], like params[:controller] with the value donuts and params[:action] with the value display...

Head First: ...and Rails uses that to choose what code to run.

Routing: Exactly! You learn fast, kid! Rails says, "Oh I see. I need to use a donuts controller. Forsooth I shall create one".

Head First: Forsooth?

Routing: Maybe not forsooth. But whatever he says, he knows he needs to create a donuts controller object. And because params[:action] is set to display, once the donuts controller object exists, he calls the display method on it.

Head First: What about the :flavor you mentioned in the route?

Routing: Oh, that. Yeah. Well if the request was for /donuts/cream and that matches /donuts/:flavor, I just add another parameter with param[:flavor] = 'cream'. So I just record what was asked for in case it's important to the code in the controller later on.

Head First: Thanks, Routing it's been a real...

Routing: Hey, stand back a moment! Sorry. It's the nervous guy who always double-clicks his hyperlinks... One at a time! One at a time!

Head First: Thank...

Routing: Don't mention it. Listen, getting a bit busy here now. Why don't you move along and see what happens in the rest of the app. Yeah, just down there on the left... I think there's some new code going into the ads controller...

To get data into the view, you will also need code in the controller

The model's already in place, and there's a route for the new controller code you need. But is there anything else?

Well, yes—you'll need two things. The index page needs separate code in the controller because it's looking at lots of ads, and you'll need a new page to display that in the view.

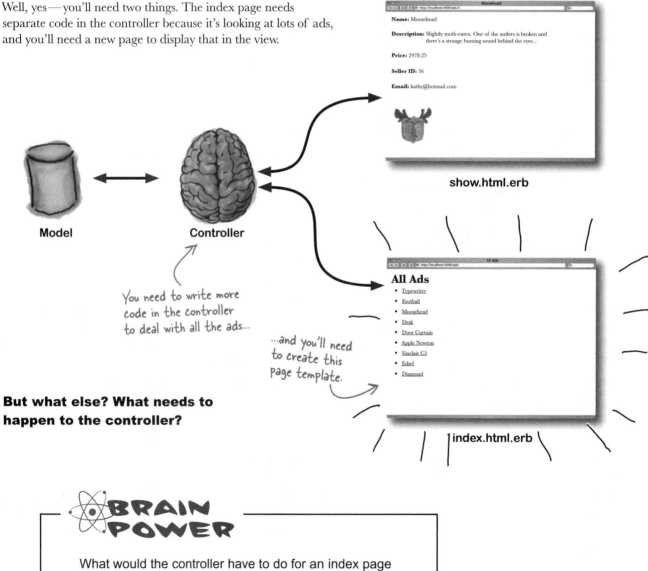

show.html.erb

You need to write more code in the controller to deal with all the ads...

...and you'll need to create this page template.

index.html.erb

But what else? What needs to happen to the controller?

⚛ BRAIN POWER

What would the controller have to do for an index page that it *wouldn't* need to do for an ad page?

An index page will need data from ALL of the records

The ad page only needed data from a single record, but what about the index page? That will need to read data from each of the records in the **entire** ads table. But why?

Look at the design for the index. It needs to create links for **all** of the ads pages, which means it will need to know the name and id number of **every** ad on the system.

But isn't that a problem? So far we've only read single records at a time. Now we need to read a whole bunch of records all at once... in fact, we need *all* of the records.

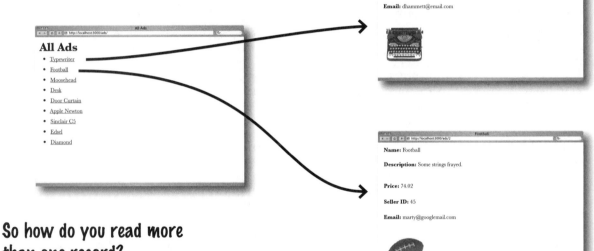

So how do you read more than one record?

The controller is only called **once** before the page is displayed so all of the records need to be read **completely** before the view is called.

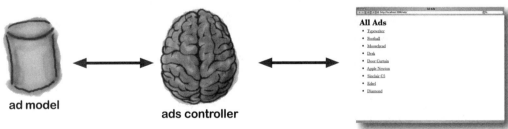

ad model   ads controller   ad index page

How do you think the controller will read the objects from the model and send them to the view?

Ad.find(:all) reads the whole table at once

There's another version of the Ad.find(...) **finder method**, which returns data about every record in the whole ads table:

```
def index
    @ads = Ad.find(:all)
end
```

You need to add this method to the controller

This reads all of the records at once

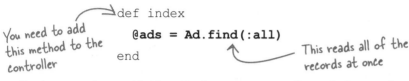
Do this!

Add this method to the controller.

But how can that work? After all, when you were reading a single record, things were fairly simple. You passed the model an id number, and the model returned a single object containing all of the data in the row with the corresponding id.

But now you don't know how many records you're going to read. Won't that mean you need some really *horribly complex* code?

Well, fortunately not. Rails makes reading every record in a table very similar to reading a single object. When you call Ad.find(:all), the model returns a **single object** that contains data for every record in the table. The controller can assign the object to a single variable.

But how can Rails store all of the data for an unknown number of rows inside a single object?

It does this by using a special type of object...

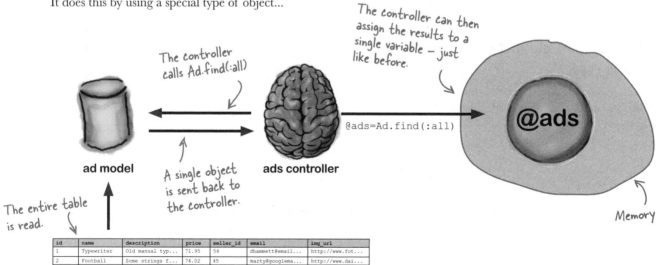

The controller calls Ad.find(:all)

A single object is sent back to the controller.

The entire table is read.

ad model

ads controller

The controller can then assign the results to a single variable — just like before.

@ads=Ad.find(:all)

@ads

Memory

id	name	description	price	seller_id	email	img_url
1	Typewriter	Old manual typ...	71.95	54	dhammett@email...	http://www.fot...
2	Football	Some strings f...	74.02	45	marty@googlema...	http://www.dai...
3	Moosehead	Slightly moth-...	2978.25	56	kathy@hotmail....	http://saloon....
4	Desk	Milk desk – go...	4800	123	andy@allmail.c...	http://picasaw...

The data is returned as an object called an <u>array</u>

Rather than just return an object containing the data from a single record, the find method creates lots of objects — one for each record — and then wraps them up in an object called an *array.*

The `Ad.find(:all)` finder returns a single array object, that in turn contains as many **model objects** as there are **rows** in the database table.

The controller can store the single array object in memory with the name **@ads**. That makes it simpler for the page template, because instead of looking for an unknown number of model objects in memory, the template only needs to know the name of the array, to get access to all of the model objects.

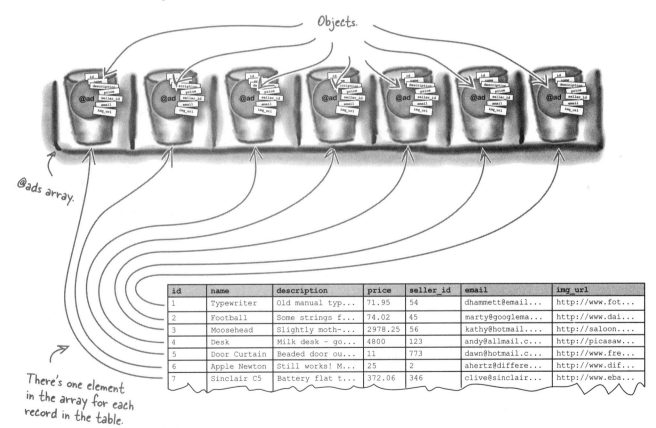

Objects.

@ads array.

There's one element in the array for each record in the table.

id	name	description	price	seller_id	email	img_url
1	Typewriter	Old manual typ...	71.95	54	dhammett@email...	http://www.fot...
2	Football	Some strings f...	74.02	45	marty@googlema...	http://www.dai...
3	Moosehead	Slightly moth-...	2978.25	56	kathy@hotmail....	http://saloon....
4	Desk	Milk desk - go...	4800	123	andy@allmail.c...	http://picasaw...
5	Door Curtain	Beaded door ou...	11	773	dawn@hotmail.c...	http://www.fre...
6	Apple Newton	Still works! M...	25	2	ahertz@differe...	http://www.dif...
7	Sinclair C5	Battery flat t...	372.06	346	clive@sinclair...	http://www.eba...

But how do you get access to the objects, once they're stored in the array?

An array is a numbered sequence of objects

The @ads array stores the model objects in a sequence of numbered slots, beginning with slot 0. The objects that are contained in each of the slots are called the array's *elements*.

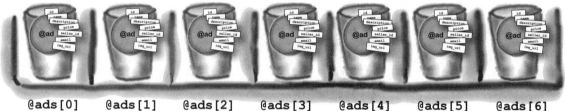

@ads[0]   @ads[1]   @ads[2]   @ads[3]   @ads[4]   @ads[5]   @ads[6]

You can read the individual elements of the array by using the number of the slot that contains the element.

@ads[4]

The object stored in slot 4 of the array is the table row with id = 5.

The slots are always numbered upwards from slot 0, and arrays can be as big as needed, so it doesn't really matter how many records there are on the table, they can all be stored inside a single array object.

Watch it!

Arrays start at index 0

That means the position of each element is its index number plus one. So @ads[0] *contains the first element,* @ads[1] *contains the second, and so on.*

---

there are no Dumb Questions

Q: Why do arrays start at zero instead of 1?

A: It's historical. Most programming languages have arrays, and in most cases their indexes start at zero.

Q: When you put something into an array, does the array keep a separate copy?

A: No. Arrays just keep references to objects stored in memory. It doesn't keep it's own copy of an object, it just remembers where they live.

Q: Is the array really an object?

A: Yes. An array is a full Ruby object.

Q: How big can an array be?

A: There is no limit on the size of an array, so long as it fits in memory.

Exercise

Insert the objects into the page, as if there are just these three rows in the database:

id	name	description	price	seller_id	email	img_url
1	Typewriter	Old manual typ...	71.95	54	dhammett@email...	http://www.fot...
2	Football	Some strings f...	74.02	45	marty@googlema...	http://www.dai...
3	Moosehead	Slightly moth-...	2978.25	56	kathy@hotmail....	http://saloon....

Write your answer here.

Write down what the HTML `index.html.erb` might look like.

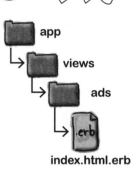

app

views

ads

.erb

index.html.erb

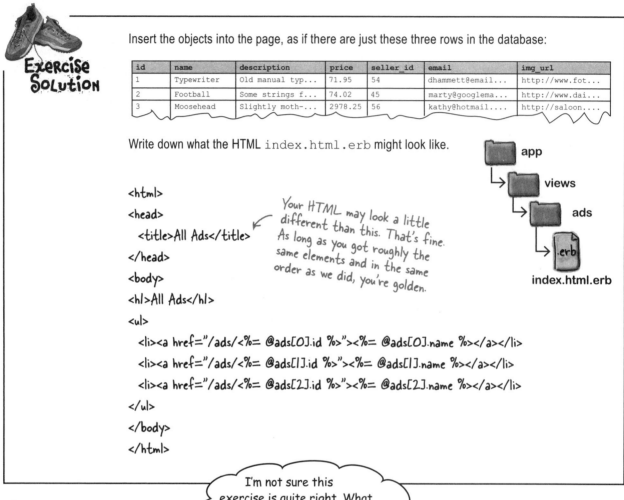

Insert the objects into the page, as if there are just these three rows in the database:

id	name	description	price	seller_id	email	img_url
1	Typewriter	Old manual typ...	71.95	54	dhammett@email...	http://www.fot...
2	Football	Some strings f...	74.02	45	marty@googlema...	http://www.dai...
3	Moosehead	Slightly moth-...	2978.25	56	kathy@hotmail....	http://saloon....

Write down what the HTML `index.html.erb` might look like.

```
<html>
<head>
  <title>All Ads</title>
</head>
<body>
<h1>All Ads</h1>
<ul>
  <li><a href="/ads/<%= @ads[0].id %>"><%= @ads[0].name %></a></li>
  <li><a href="/ads/<%= @ads[1].id %>"><%= @ads[1].name %></a></li>
  <li><a href="/ads/<%= @ads[2].id %>"><%= @ads[2].name %></a></li>
</ul>
</body>
</html>
```

Your HTML may look a little different than this. That's fine. As long as you got roughly the same elements and in the same order as we did, you're golden.

app → views → ads → .erb

index.html.erb

I'm not sure this exercise is quite right. What if there aren't exactly three records in the table?

In practice, you won't know how many ads there are.

The code above will only display 3 ads. But what if there are 4, or 5, or 3,000? You don't want to have to change the template every time an ad is added or removed from the database.

You need some way of writing code that will cope with any number of ads in the database.

Wouldn't it be dreamy if there was some way of handling all the elements in an array regardless of how many there are. But I know it's just a fantasy...

Read <u>all</u> of the ads with a for loop

A Ruby **for** loop lets you run the same piece of Ruby code over and over again. It can be used to read the elements in an array, one at a time, and then run a piece of code on each element.

The piece of code that's run each time is called the **loop body**. The loop body will execute for each element of the array, in sequence, starting with element 0:

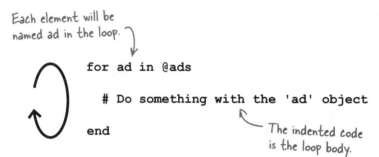

Each element will be named ad in the loop.

```
for ad in @ads

    # Do something with the 'ad' object

end
```

The indented code is the loop body.

In the above code, each time the body runs, the current element in the array is given the name ad. So ad refers to each of the Ad model objects, and inside the loop you can access all of the model objects attributes: the details of the ad, such as the name or the description of the thing being sold.

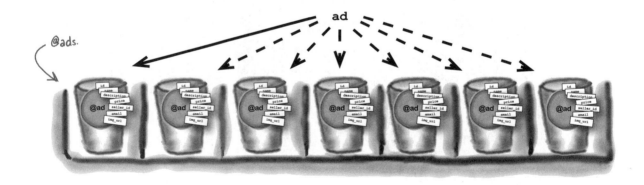

Right now, we need to generate the HTML that will create a link to the ad's web page. But the HTML is generated by the page template. How can we use a for loop with that?

We need HTML for each element in the array

For each ad object in the @ads array, we need to generate a hyperlink in HTML.

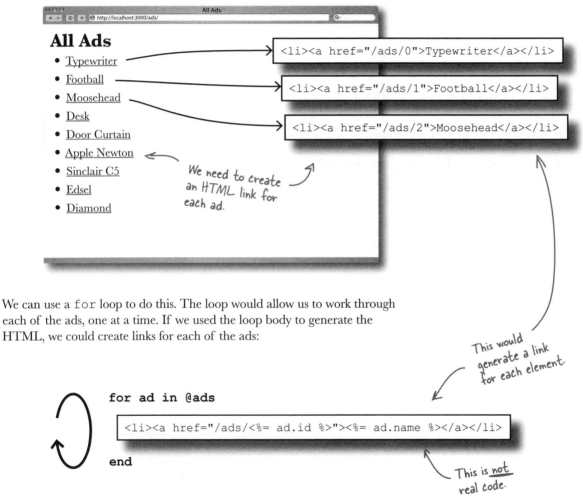

We can use a `for` loop to do this. The loop would allow us to work through each of the ads, one at a time. If we used the loop body to generate the HTML, we could create links for each of the ads:

```
for ad in @ads

    <li><a href="/ads/<%= ad.id %>"><%= ad.name %></a></li>

end
```

This is not real code.

The problem is that we generate web pages by putting Ruby expressions inside page templates. The *HTML* in the page template controls when the *Ruby expressions* are called. But we want to do things *the other way round*. We want a Ruby **for** loop to control when the HTML is generated.

So how can we combine control statements like for loops with page template HTML?

Rails converts page templates into Ruby code

When we wanted to get object values into a page before, we inserted them using `<%=...%>`:

<%=@ad.name%>

ERb (Embedded Ruby) generates a web page from the template by replacing each of the expressions with their values. ERb does this by converting the entire page into Ruby code.

Imagine this was all you had in a page template:

<title><%= @ad.name %></title>

↳ Page template tags.

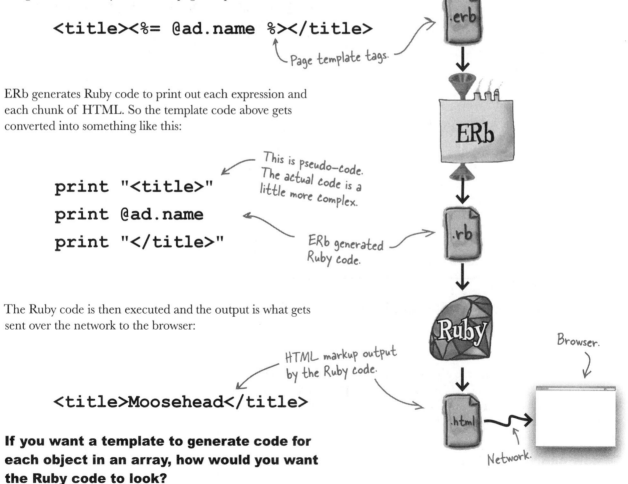

ERb generates Ruby code to print out each expression and each chunk of HTML. So the template code above gets converted into something like this:

print "<title>"
print @ad.name
print "</title>"

This is pseudo-code. The actual code is a little more complex.

ERb generated Ruby code.

The Ruby code is then executed and the output is what gets sent over the network to the browser:

HTML markup output by the Ruby code.

<title>Moosehead</title>

Browser.

Network.

If you want a template to generate code for each object in an array, how would you want the Ruby code to look?

Loops can be added to page templates using <u>scriptlets</u>

Let's forget about page templates for the moment. If you were writing a piece of code to print out HTML for each element in an array, what would that code look like? It might look a little like this:

```
for ad in @ads
  print '<li><a href="'
  print ad.id
  print '">'
  print ad.name
  print '</a></li>'
end
```

The scriptlets and expressions will output this code.

An expression

Object <u>values</u> are inserted with <%= . . .%> But <u>code</u> is inserted with <% . . . %>

A scriptlet

We need to loop through the array and print out HTML and expressions for each element. So far we've only seen ERb generating print commands, but the `for` loop isn't a print command. So how can we pass ERb chunks of Ruby code—like the `for` loop?

The solution is to use **scriptlets**.

A scriplet is a tag containing a piece of Ruby code. Expression tags are surrounded by <%=... %>, but scriptlets are surrounded by <%...%>. Scriptlets don't have the = sign at the start of them.

To see how scriptlets work, let's take a look at a page template to produce the `for` loop code above:

There's no "=" at the start of the scriptlet.

Expressions have "="

```
<% for ad in @ads %>
  <li><a href="/ads/<%= ad.id %>"><%= ad.name %></a></li>
<% end %>
```

There's no "=" at the end of the scriptlet.

This code uses scriptlets for the looping code and expressions where values will be inserted. Let's see what the index page template will look like if we use scriptlets to loop through the @ads array.

On each pass of the loop, the page generates one link

This is the code you'll be using for the `index.html.erb` template:

Do this!

```
<html>
<head>
  <title>All Ads</title>
</head>
<body>
<h1>All Ads</h1>
<ul>
<% for ad in @ads %>
  <li><a href="/ads/<%= ad.id %>"><%= ad.name %></a></li>
<% end %>
</ul>
</body>
</html>
```

When Rails processes the template, the HTML at the top and the bottom of the file will just be output as you'd expect. The interesting part is in the middle of the page. Each pass of the loop will generate an HTML link to the matching ad page.

So what does the generated HTML look like?

Imagine there are just these three ads in the database.

That means the controller will produce an @ads array containing three model objects. When the page template loops through the @ads array it should produce HTML that looks something like this:

```
<html>
<head>
  <title>All Ads</title>
</head>
<body>
<h1>All Ads</h1>
<ul>
  <li><a href="/ads/1">Typewriter</a></li>
  <li><a href="/ads/2">Football</a></li>
  <li><a href="/ads/3">Moosehead</a></li>
</ul>
</body>
</html>
```

So it looks like this will generate just enough HTML for all of the ads in the database. If there are more ads created in the database, a larger @ads array will be produced, and the template should generate a longer piece of HTML.

That's the theory. Now that the route's been created, the controller action's been written, and the index.html.erb template's in place it's time to run the code.

TEST DRIVE

With the route to /ads/ in place, the controller reading all of the records with Ad.find(:all), and the template using a scriptlet to embed a for-loop that reads all of the model objects from the @ads array, it's time to test the new index page.

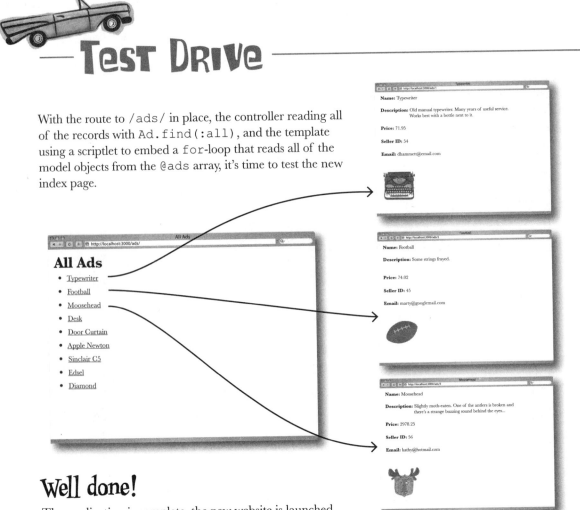

Well done!

The application is complete, the new website is launched... and you did the whole thing **without scaffolding**!

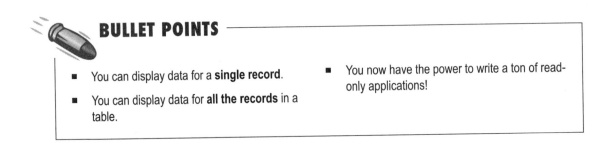

BULLET POINTS

- You can display data for a **single record**.

- You can display data for **all the records** in a table.

- You now have the power to write a ton of read-only applications!

You just got an email from the folks at MeBay...

The functionality of the site now matches exactly what the original spec asked for. Everyone's really pleased. Then, on the morning that the site's due to launch, you get an email:

> Dude!
>
> You did an incredible job with the site. We're really pleased at the way you were able to build it to our exact specification. We'd heard that Rails applications always looked and worked the same!
>
> By the way, here's a design for how the site will look. We think this will be the final look of the application, but if there are any changes, we'll send them through later.
>
> Thanks again for all the hard work :-)

There's a sample web page and a set of stylesheets and images attached to the email. It can't be that hard to change the look of the application, can it?

Download this!

Download the stylesheets and images from:
www.headfirstlabs.com/books/hfrails

BRAIN POWER

You could just modify the page templates so they look like the sample web page from the designer. What's the problem in doing that?

But there are two page templates... should we change the code of each one?

There are two page templates, so if you just change the HTML in both templates to match the MeBay sample page, you'll have **duplicated the code**. Is that really a big deal here? After all, there are only *two* types of web pages in the MeBay site. That's not *so* bad, is it?

The problem is that the application may grow over time and acquire more features and page templates. And what about that comment about the design possibly changing? The more times you duplicate the look, the more places you have to maintain the same HTML. Over time the application could become hard work to maintain.

So what's the answer? Well, the obvious answer is to remove the duplication. Most web sites have a standardized look across most of their pages. They have standard boilerplate HTML surrounding the main content of each page.

So you need some way of defining a **super-template**: one single template that will control how a group of other templates will look.

Rails Principle:
DRY - Don't
Repeat Yourself.

Didn't we say
this already?

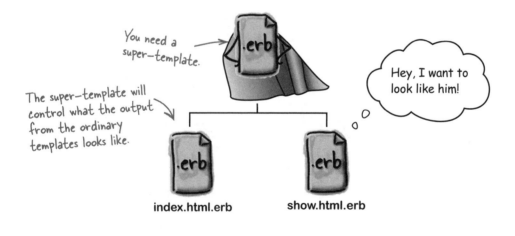

You need a
super-template.

The super-template will
control what the output
from the ordinary
templates looks like.

Hey, I want to
look like him!

index.html.erb   show.html.erb

A layout defines a STANDARD look for a whole set of page templates

Fortunately, just such a super-template exists in Rails, and it's called a *layout*. A layout defines an HTML wrapper for all of the templates belonging to a particular model.

Let's see how it'll work with the new design.

Ready Bake Super-Template Code

This is the example HTML page from the designer after it's been converted into a layout.

```
<!DOCTYPE html PUBLIC "-//W3C//DTD XHTML 1.0 Transitional//EN"
        "http://www.w3.org/TR/xhtml1/DTD/xhtml1-transitional.dtd">
<html xmlns="http://www.w3.org/1999/xhtml">
<head>
    <title>Ads: <%= controller.action_name %></title>
    <%= stylesheet_link_tag 'default.css' %>
</head>
<body>
    <div id="wrapper">
        <div id="header">
            <div>

                <h1>MeBay</h1>
                <ul id="nav">
                    <li><a href="/ads/">All Ads</a></li>
                </ul>
            </div>
        </div>

        <div id="content">
            <%= yield %>
        </div>
        <div id="clearfooter"></div>
    </div>
    <div id="footer"></div>
</body>
</html>
```

You need to put it in the right place by saving it as:

```
app/views/layouts/ads.html.erb
```

That name tells Rails to apply the layout to all of the page templates belonging to the ad model.

We've put in a couple of expressions to specify a stylesheet and give the page a title based upon the current controller name. But much more importantly, the layout contains this tag:

```
<%= yield %>
```

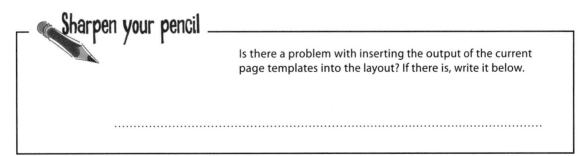

Sharpen your pencil

Is there a problem with inserting the output of the current page templates into the layout? If there is, write it below.

....

Sharpen your pencil
Solution

Is there the problem with inserting the output of the current page templates into the layout? Write it down below:

The page templates contain too much — they already have all of the HTML boilerplate in them.

You need to REMOVE the boilerplate from your page templates

Look at the existing index.html.erb. It already contains HTML boilerplate elements, like the **<head>** and the **<title>**:

```
<html>
<head>
  <title>All Ads</title>
</head>
<body>
<h1>All Ads</h1>
<ul>
<% for ad in @ads %>
  <li><a href="/ads/<%= ad.id %>"><%= ad.name %></a></li>
<% end %>
</ul>
</body>
</html>
```

But now that there's a layout providing the boilerplate, you need to cut down the templates so they display just the main page content:

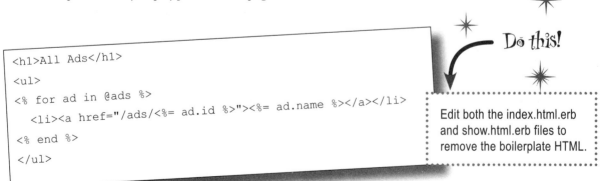

```
<h1>All Ads</h1>
<ul>
<% for ad in @ads %>
  <li><a href="/ads/<%= ad.id %>"><%= ad.name %></a></li>
<% end %>
</ul>
```

Do this!

Edit both the index.html.erb and show.html.erb files to remove the boilerplate HTML.

But what about the new static content MeBay sent over?

So far you've only generated dynamic content from a Rails app. Pretty much everything has been output page templates. But when you're specifying the cosmetics of a site, you often need **static** content like *stylesheets*, *images*, and *JavaScripts*. But how do you include static content in the application?

Rails sets aside a folder just for static files. It's called **public**.

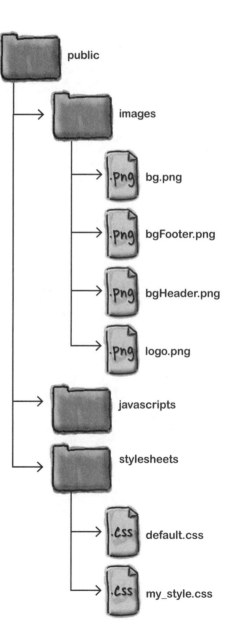

When you create the application, Rails already put quite a few files in the public folder. Remember the first time you started the Rails application and looked at the front page? The files for the standard welcome page all live in the public folder.

Most Rails applications store their images, stylesheets and JavaScripts in **public/images**, **public/stylesheets** and **public/javascripts** respectively.

Once you've saved the extra images and stylesheets from the email, we should be good to go.

TEST DRIVE

Open up a browser and look at:

http://localhost:3000/ads

It's a thing of beauty. My work here is done... for now.

As you browse through the site, the standard look will be applied to all of the pages. And if you add more templates later, or if you modify the HTML in the layout, the application will maintain a consistent look.

Scaffoldless Grid

Fill in the grid with the answers to each of the clues to reveal the mystery word.

Clue for the mystery word:

A reason you would want to manually create an application instead of using scaffolding.

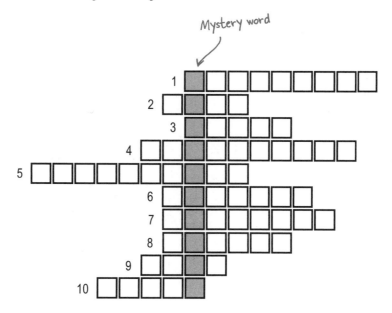

Mystery word

Clues

1. `<% @what.am_i? %>`

2. You could use a page template for this

3. Converts the data from the database into Ruby objects

4. `<%= @what.am_i? %>`

5. Might send data from the model to the view

6. Update the data structure with `rake db:`..................

7. If you are creating a simple application, you might not need this

8. Reads object(s) from a database

9. Every route has a request ....

10. An object containing many objects

Scaffoldless Grid Solution

Fill in the grid with the answers to each of the clues to reveal the mystery word.

Clue for the mystery word:

A reason you would want to manually create an application instead of using scaffolding.

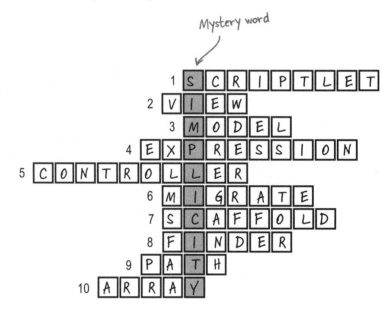

Mystery word

1. S C R I P T L E T
2. V I E W
3. M O D E L
4. E X P R E S S I O N
5. C O N T R O L L E R
6. M I G R A T E
7. S C A F F O L D
8. F I N D E R
9. P A T H
10. A R R A Y

Clues

1. `<% @what.am_i? %>`
2. You could use a page template for this
3. Converts the data from the database into Ruby objects
4. `<%= @what.am_i? %>`
5. Might send data from the model to the view
6. Update the data structure with `rake db:`...................
7. If you are creating a simple application, you might not need this
8. Reads object(s) from a database
9. Every route has a request ....
10. An object containing many objects

Tools for your Rails Toolbox

You've got Chapter 2 under your belt, and now you've added the ability to manually create read-only applications to your toolbox.

Rails Tools

You can generate a model with:

ruby script/generate model...

and a controller with:

ruby script/generate controller...

Ruby Tools

If my_array is a Ruby array, the first element is given by:

my_array[0]

You can loop through all the elements with:

for element in my_array

  # Do stuff with element

end

3 inserting, updating, and deleting

Everything changes

... by the "Ipana Troubadours". Next up: 'If I was your Vampire' by Marilyn Manson...

Change is a fact of life—especially for data. So far you've seen how to whip up a quick Rails application with scaffolding, and how to write your own code to publish data from a database. But what if you want users to be able to edit data *your* way? What if scaffolding doesn't do what *you* want? In this chapter, you'll learn how to **insert**, **update**, and **delete** data in exactly the way you want. And while you're doing that, you'll be taken deeper into how Rails *really* works and maybe even learn a little about security along the way.

People want to post new ads online

People love the MeBay site, but there's a problem. Because MeBay was nervous about people having too much access to the data, sellers have to phone in details of their items to MeBay and *wait* while the system administrators create new ads for the sellers. As the number of people sending in ads has grown, so has the wait time. A lot of people are taking their business to other advertising sites now.

So MeBay has relented. After some discussion, they've decided that people should be allowed to **post their own ads** on the site using a page that looks like this:

Another design sketch from MeBay.

You already know how to build an app that <u>publishes</u> data <u>from</u> the database

The ads only go one way in the current application. The ad records are read from the database by the model, which converts them into ad objects that are then sent to the view by the controller. It works like this:

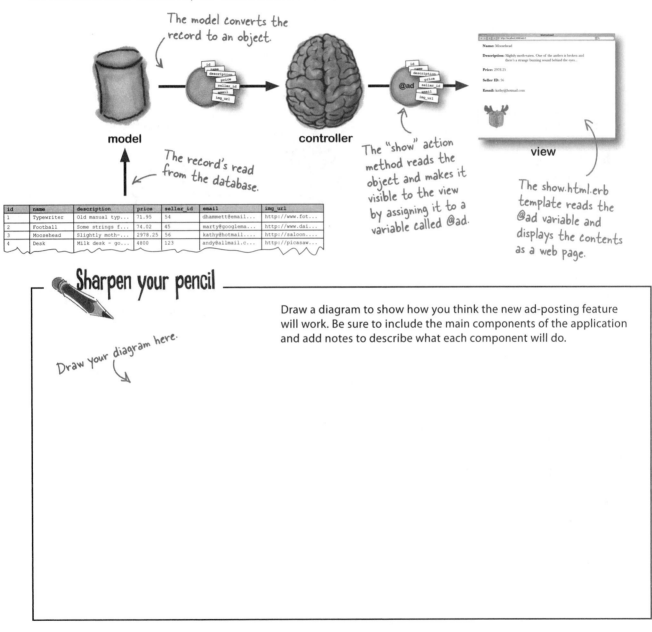

The model converts the record to an object.

model

The record's read from the database.

controller

@ad

The "show" action method reads the object and makes it visible to the view by assigning it to a variable called @ad.

view

The show.html.erb template reads the @ad variable and displays the contents as a web page.

id	name	description	price	seller_id	email	img_url
1	Typewriter	Old manual typ...	71.95	54	dhammett@email...	http://www.fot...
2	Football	Some strings f...	74.02	45	marty@googlema...	http://www.dai...
3	Moosehead	Slightly moth-...	2978.25	56	kathy@hotmail...	http://saloon....
4	Desk	Milk desk - go...	4800	123	andy@allmail.c...	http://picasaw...

Sharpen your pencil

Draw your diagram here.

Draw a diagram to show how you think the new ad-posting feature will work. Be sure to include the main components of the application and add notes to describe what each component will do.

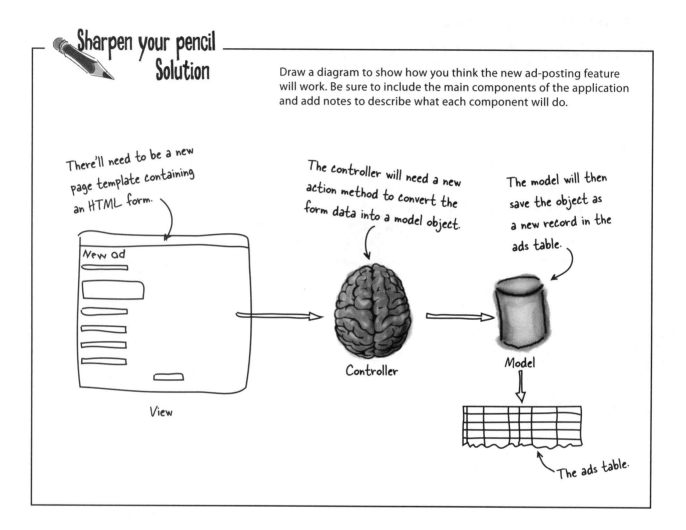

Sharpen your pencil
Solution

Draw a diagram to show how you think the new ad-posting feature will work. Be sure to include the main components of the application and add notes to describe what each component will do.

There'll need to be a new page template containing an HTML form.

The controller will need a new action method to convert the form data into a model object.

The model will then save the object as a new record in the ads table.

New ad

View

Controller

Model

The ads table.

Saving data works just the OPPOSITE of reading data

Saving data to the database is similar to publishing ads from the database, except it works the other way round. Instead of a page template to *display* an ad, you need a page template to **submit** an ad. Instead of a controller action method to send an ad to a page, you need a controller method to read data from a page and turn it into an object. And instead of the model reading a record and converting it into an object, you need the model to convert an object into a new record in the database.

You need a <u>form</u> to submit data and an action <u>method</u> to save it

You need a new page template to create the HTML form. Because it will be used to enter new ads, we'll call this template **new.html.erb**.

The "New ad" page will need to appear at

> http://mebay.com/ads/new

and the form will be submitted to:

> http://mebay.com/ads/create

So we also need to create a new route in **routes.rb**.

Remember, a route is what tells Rails which pieces of code to use to satisfy a request from a browser.

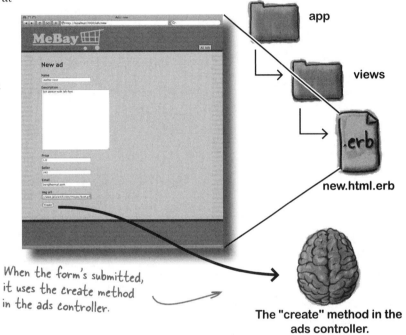

app

views

.erb

new.html.erb

When the form's submitted, it uses the create method in the ads controller.

The "create" method in the ads controller.

Sharpen your pencil

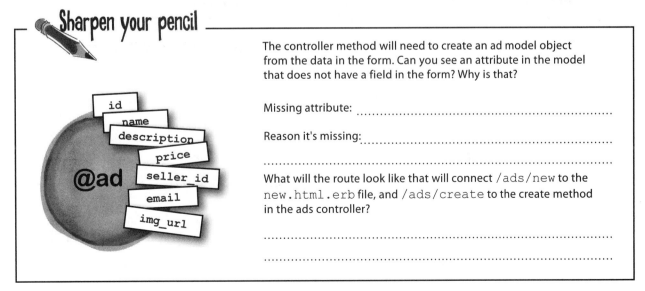

The controller method will need to create an ad model object from the data in the form. Can you see an attribute in the model that does not have a field in the form? Why is that?

Missing attribute: ....

Reason it's missing: ....
....

What will the route look like that will connect /ads/new to the new.html.erb file, and /ads/create to the create method in the ads controller?

....
....

id
name
description
price
@ad
seller_id
email
img_url

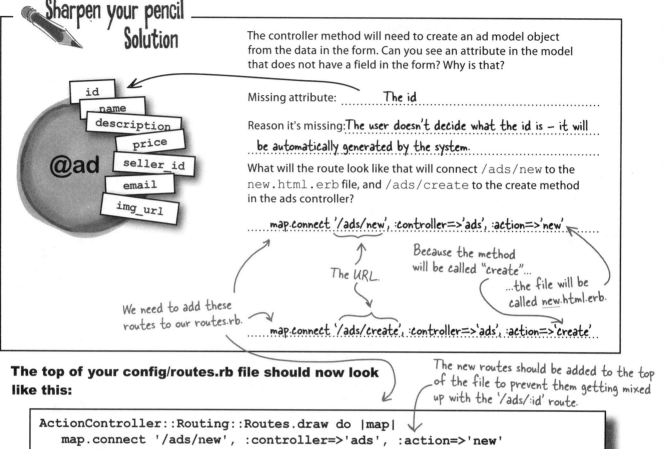

Sharpen your pencil
Solution

The controller method will need to create an ad model object from the data in the form. Can you see an attribute in the model that does not have a field in the form? Why is that?

id
name
description
price
@ad   seller_id
email
img_url

Missing attribute: .... The id ....

Reason it's missing: The user doesn't decide what the id is — it will
be automatically generated by the system.

What will the route look like that will connect /ads/new to the new.html.erb file, and /ads/create to the create method in the ads controller?

.... map.connect '/ads/new', :controller=>'ads', :action=>'new'

Because the method
will be called "create"...
The URL.   ...the file will be
called new.html.erb.

We need to add these
routes to our routes.rb.

.... map.connect '/ads/create', :controller=>'ads', :action=>'create'

The top of your config/routes.rb file should now look like this:

The new routes should be added to the top
of the file to prevent them getting mixed
up with the '/ads/:id' route.

```
ActionController::Routing::Routes.draw do |map|
   map.connect '/ads/new', :controller=>'ads', :action=>'new'
   map.connect '/ads/create', :controller=>'ads', :action=>'create'
   map.connect '/ads/', :controller=>'ads', :action=>'index'
   map.connect '/ads/:id', :controller=>'ads', :action=>'show'
```

It looks like forms and objects carry a lot of the same kinds of information. I wonder if there's some deeper relationship between a form and an object?

There are close relationships between many parts of a Rails application.

After all, the model contains the data for the application, the view allows the user to access that data, and the controller provides the logical glue that connects everything together.

But is there some special relationship between a form and a model?

Are forms and objects related?

Apart from the generated id, the fields in the form match the attributes of an ad object.

There's no match in the form for the id.

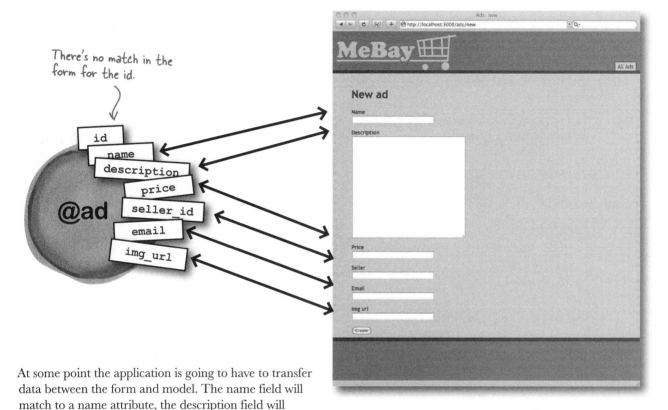

At some point the application is going to have to transfer data between the form and model. The name field will match to a name attribute, the description field will match to a description attribute and so on.

What if the model creates objects with default values in the attributes? Should the code that generates the default values in the form duplicate the model code?

After all, when the data in the form is received by the controller, should the form treat the fields as individual values? Or should all of the field values be associated together, like the attributes of an object?

Could Rails make use of the relationship between form fields and a model object when creating a form?

Rails can create forms that are associated with model objects

Rails can use a model object to help create a form. That means two things:

 The values in the form fields will be set to the values stored in the attributes of the @ad object. This doesn't make a lot of difference to the ad form because new ads are blank.

 The form fields will be given names that explicitly associate those fields with a model object.

So how can a name associate a field with an object? Let's look at what it would mean for the ad form. This is the HTML that will be generated for a form that's based on an Ad object:

This would be generated by show.html.erb

```
<b>Name</b><br />
<input id="ad_name" name="ad[name]" type="text" />
<b>Description</b><br />
<textarea id="ad_description" name="ad[description]"></textarea>
<b>Price</b><br />
<input id="ad_price" name="ad[price]" type="text" />
<b>Seller</b><br />
<input id="ad_seller_id" name="ad[seller_id]" type="text" />
<b>Email</b><br />
<input id="ad_email" name="ad[email]" type="text" />
<b>Img url</b><br />
<input id="ad_img_url" name="ad[img_url]" type="text" />
```

id
name
description
price
@ad → seller_id
email
img_url

BRAIN BARBELL

Comparing the field names and their matching attributes, how do you think Rails will present the form data to the controller?

You have a few pages to think about this...

Field names	Object attributes
ad[name]	name
ad[description]	description
ad[price]	price
ad[seller_id]	seller_id
ad[email]	email
ad[img_url]	img_url

Form Object Magnets

It's time to write the new.html.erb page template.
The `<% form for %>` tag is used to generate a form
using a form object. Complete the fields in the form using
the magnets below:

No boilerplate HTML...
we're still using a
super-template.

> `<h1>New ad</h1>`

Form tags are <u>scriptlets</u> so don't use
`=` in them. Just use `<%` and `%>`.

`<% form_for(@ad, :url=>{:action=>'create'}) do |f| %>`

The action that the form
will be submitted to.

The object
the form is
based on.

`<p><b>Name</b><br /><%= f.text_field :name %></p>`

Form fields are generated
with <u>expressions</u> like this.

`<p><b>Description</b><br /><%= ...................... ...................... %></p>`

`<p><b>Price</b><br /><%= ...................... ................ %>`

`</p>`

`<p><b>Seller</b><br /><%= ...................... ...................... %></p>`

`<p><b>Email</b><br /><%= ...................... ................ %></p>`

`<p><b>Img url</b><br /><%= ...................... ................ %></p>`

`<p><%= ................ ................ %></p>`

`<% end %>`

`f.text_area`

`f.text_field`

`:email`

`f.text_field`

`:img_url`

`f.text_field`

`:price`

`"Create"`

`f.text_field`

`:description`

`f.submit`

`:seller_id`

Form Object Magnets Solution

It's time to write the new.html.erb page template.

The `<% form for %>` tag is used to generate a form using a form object. Complete the fields in the form using the magnets below:

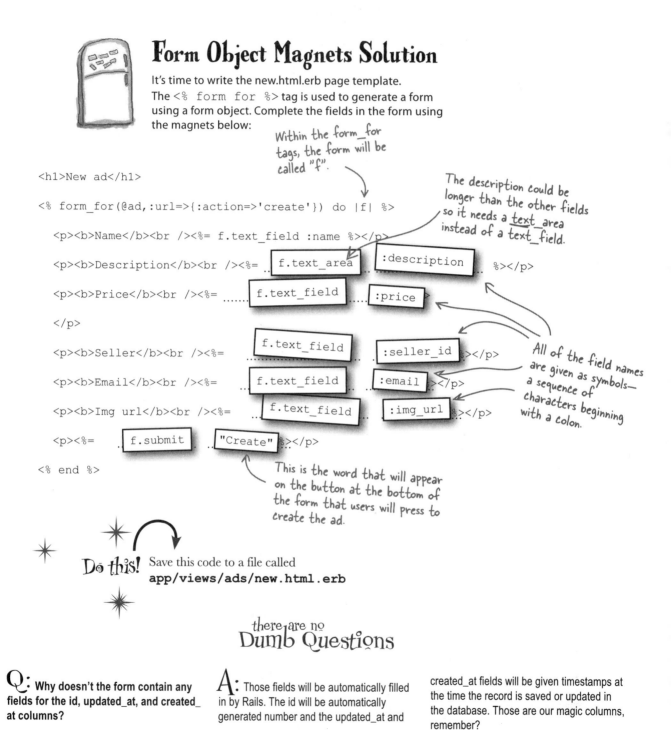

Within the form_for tags, the form will be called "f".

The description could be longer than the other fields so it needs a text_area *instead of a* text_field.

```
<h1>New ad</h1>

<% form_for(@ad, :url=>{:action=>'create'}) do |f| %>

  <p><b>Name</b><br /><%= f.text_field :name %></p>

  <p><b>Description</b><br /><%= f.text_area :description %></p>

  <p><b>Price</b><br /><%= f.text_field :price

  </p>

  <p><b>Seller</b><br /><%= f.text_field :seller_id %></p>

  <p><b>Email</b><br /><%= f.text_field :email %></p>

  <p><b>Img url</b><br /><%= f.text_field :img_url %></p>

  <p><%= f.submit "Create" %></p>

<% end %>
```

All of the field names are given as symbols— a sequence of characters beginning with a colon.

This is the word that will appear on the button at the bottom of the form that users will press to create the ad.

Do this! Save this code to a file called
app/views/ads/new.html.erb

there are no Dumb Questions

Q: Why doesn't the form contain any fields for the id, updated_at, and created_at columns?

A: Those fields will be automatically filled in by Rails. The id will be automatically generated number and the updated_at and created_at fields will be given timestamps at the time the record is saved or updated in the database. Those are our magic columns, remember?

Test Drive

The page template for the "new" form is in place and it should generate HTML in the same way that we generated the "show" pages. There's also a route in place that connect the "/ads/new" path to the "new" template. So let's see if it works by going to:

```
http://localhost:3000/ads/new
```

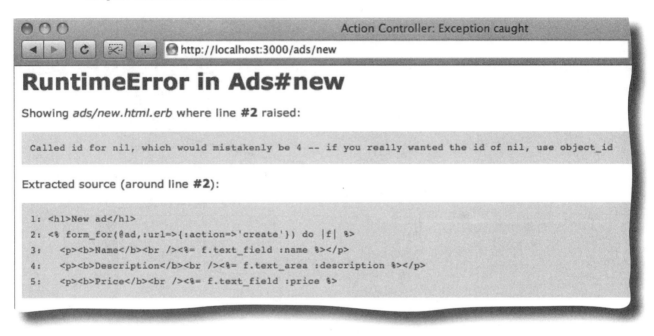

Action Controller: Exception caught

http://localhost:3000/ads/new

RuntimeError in Ads#new

Showing *ads/new.html.erb* where line **#2** raised:

```
Called id for nil, which would mistakenly be 4 -- if you really wanted the id of nil, use object_id
```

Extracted source (around line **#2**):

```
1:  <h1>New ad</h1>
2:  <% form_for(@ad,:url=>{:action=>'create'}) do |f| %>
3:    <p><b>Name</b><br /><%= f.text_field :name %></p>
4:    <p><b>Description</b><br /><%= f.text_area :description %></p>
5:    <p><b>Price</b><br /><%= f.text_field :price %>
```

The page crashed!

BRAIN POWER

Something's gone awry with the form page. Look at the error message that was produced and see if you can work out what went wrong.

The @ad form object has not been created

The problem is caused by the @ad object. By default, a variable like @ad is set to a special value called **nil**, which means **no value**. If @ad is set to nil, instead of being set to an Ad object, it won't have attributes like **@ad.name**, **@ad.description**, and so on.

If @ad doesn't have attributes, does that cause a problem for the form?

You bet! The form is based on the @ad object, and the form accesses each of the object's attributes to generate the initial values of the fields in the form. But as soon as the first attribute is called, nil is returned, and that causes an error.

So how can we avoid this problem?

> Rails creates the @ad variable with a default value of nil, or no value. So there are no other attributes avaialble, like @ad.name.

@ad = nil

```
<h1>New ad</h1>
<% form_for(@ad, :url=>{:action=>'create'}) do |f| %>
  <p><b>Name</b><br /><%= f.text_field :name %></p>
  <p><b>Description</b><br /><%= f.text_area :description %></p>
  <p><b>Price</b><br /><%= f.text_field :price %></p>
  <p><b>Seller</b><br /><%= f.text_field :seller_id %></p>
  <p><b>Email</b><br /><%= f.text_field :email %></p>
  <p><b>Img url</b><br /><%= f.text_field :img_url %></p>
  <p><%= f.submit "Create" %></p>
<% end %>
```

> The initial value of each of the fields will access the matching attribute on @ad. But because @ad is set to nil, this causes an error.

The form object needs to be created <u>before</u> the form is displayed

When the page with the form is generated, the initial values of each of the form fields will come from one of the attributes of the associated object.

Can you think what the problem is with that?

The problem is that before the form can be generated, the new ad object *needs to already exist*. Of course, until the user completes the details of the ad, the object won't be saved to the database—but even so, the object needs to be created *before* the page template is called.

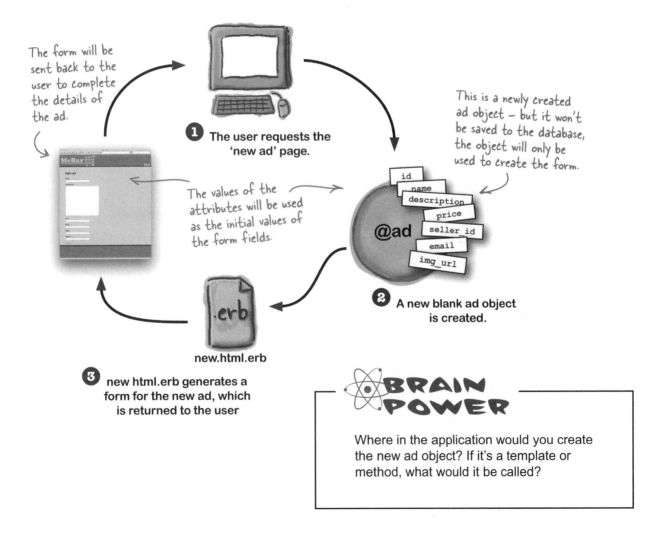

The form will be sent back to the user to complete the details of the ad.

① The user requests the 'new ad' page.

This is a newly created ad object – but it won't be saved to the database, the object will only be used to create the form.

The values of the attributes will be used as the initial values of the form fields.

id
name
description
price
seller_id
email
img_url

@ad

② A new blank ad object is created.

new.html.erb

③ new html.erb generates a form for the new ad, which is returned to the user

The forms ad object will be created in the <u>new</u> action of the controller

❶ **The forms ad object needs to be created before the new.html.erb page template is run.**
If you create the object in a controller method called `new`, this will be run *before* the `new.html.erb` template is called.

The browser requests
`http://mebay.com/ads/new`

The "new" method in the ads controller is called.

If you create a method called "new" in the controller, the method will be called by Rails <u>before</u> calling the new.html.erb template.

```
def new
  ...
end
```

---

❷ **So how do you create a new ad object?**
`Ad.new` returns a new object that you can assign to the `@ad` variable. The new object won't be saved automatically to the database, but you only need it in memory where it can be used to generate the HTML form.

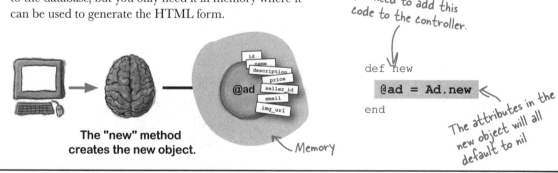

The "new" method creates the new object.

— Memory

You need to add this code to the controller.

```
def new
  @ad = Ad.new
end
```

The attributes in the new object will all default to nil

---

❸ **Now that the object is assigned to the @ad variable in memory, new.html.erb will be able to use it to generate the HTML form within the /ads/new web page.**

No errors

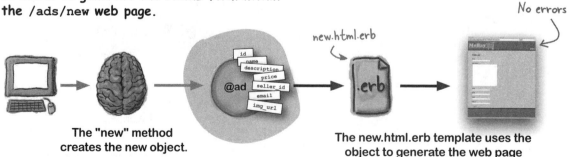

The "new" method creates the new object.

new.html.erb

The new.html.erb template uses the object to generate the web page

Each page template now has a matching controller method

The ads controller now has one method for each of the page template files. Rails will always call the controller method before generating a page from the page template.

It's the **combination** of a controller method and a page template that make up an **action**. That's why the action name appears in the name of the controller method *and* in name of the page template file.

An action is a controller method and a page template.

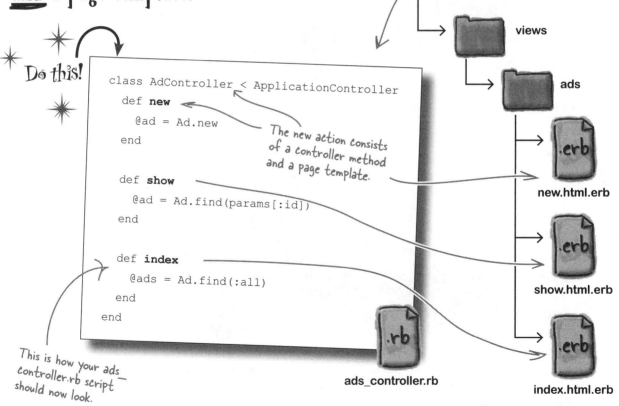

Do this!

```ruby
class AdController < ApplicationController
  def new
    @ad = Ad.new
  end

  def show
    @ad = Ad.find(params[:id])
  end

  def index
    @ads = Ad.find(:all)
  end
end
```

The new action consists of a controller method and a page template.

This is how your ads_controller.rb script should now look.

ads_controller.rb

app
controllers
.rb
ads_controller.rb
views
ads
.erb
new.html.erb
.erb
show.html.erb
.erb
index.html.erb

Now you have the controller creating the new ad object before the new.html.erb page template runs, it's time to see if the code works.

Test Drive

With the controller code in place, it's time to try the application again by opening a browser at:

```
http://localhost:3000/ads/new
```

Now enter some data:

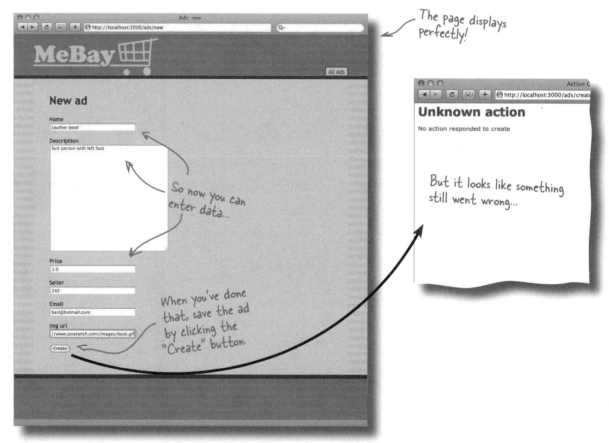

The page displays perfectly!

So now you can enter data...

When you've done that, save the ad by clicking the "Create" button.

But it looks like something still went wrong...

The form page displays perfectly, but when you enter some data and submit the form, Rails returns an error telling you that you haven't written a create action. The create action? That was the action you decided would receive the ad from the form.

What will this action need to do? It'll read the data from the form and use it to create a new ad.

But what does the form send back to the application?

The form doesn't send an object back, it sends DATA back

The form was generated using an Ad object. But what exactly does the form send back to the server when the form's submitted?

Because the form uses HTTP, it can't send the form object over the network. Instead it sends data.

But how is the data FORMATTED?

Think back to how routing works. When a request arrives, Rails sends the details of the request to the routing system, which inserts values into a data structure called params[...], with values for the action and the controller.

The params[...] data structure wasn't created just for routing. It can also be used to store any data submitted to the application by a web form.

A form's fields are recorded in the params[...] table along with the name :ad. Then, the value of the :ad variable is actually *another* table of values, a table that maps a field *name* to a field *value*:

Actually the data structure is more properly called a Hash, or an Associative Array.

The params "hash" table.

This is the answer to the Brain Barbell exercise a few pages back.

Name	Value		
:controller	'ads'		
:action	'create'		
:ad	**Name**	**Value**	
	:name	Leather boot	
	:description	Suit person with left foot	
	:price	1.0	
	:seller_id	242	
	:email	bert@hotmail.com	
	:img_url	http://www.javaranch.com/images/boot.gif	

The value of the :ad parameter is another hash table.

The value of the :ad variable is the params[:ad] table.

But what happens to this data when the controller receives it? And how can we actually USE this data?

Rails needs to convert the data into an object before it can be saved

Rails can only use objects to talk to the database, so before an ad can be saved to the database, you need to find some way to convert the form data into an Ad object.

The model can create objects from raw form data

How do you do that? Well, remember when you created a new blank Ad object to use with the form?

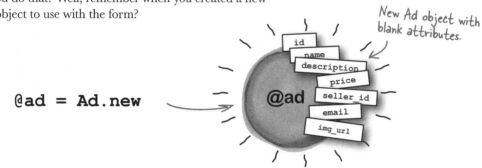

New Ad object with blank attributes.

$$@ad = Ad.new$$

The `Ad.new` method can also be called with a set of hash table of values that will be used to initialize the attributes of the new Ad object. And the form data just happens to be contained in a hash object:

$$@ad = Ad.new(params[:ad])$$

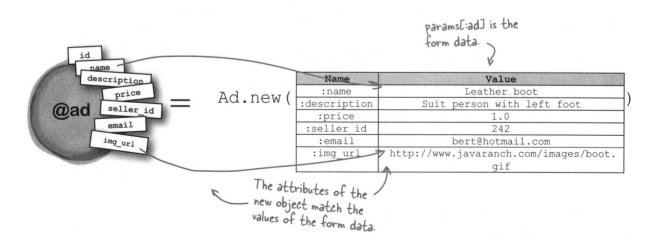

params[:ad] is the form data.

Name	Value
:name	Leather boot
:description	Suit person with left foot
:price	1.0
:seller id	242
:email	bert@hotmail.com
:img url	http://www.javaranch.com/images/boot.gif

The attributes of the new object match the values of the form data.

The controller create method, step-by-step

1 Rails sends the form data to the controller using the `params[...]` hash.

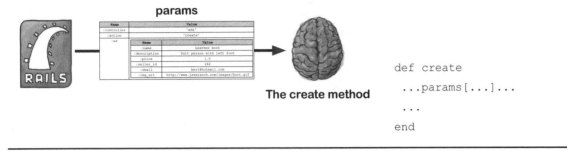

params

Name	Value
:controller	'ads'
:action	'create'
:ad	

Name	Value
:name	Leather boot
:description	Suit person with left foot
:price	1.0
:seller_id	242
:email	bert@hotmail.com
:img_url	http://www.javaranch.com/images/boot.gif

The create method

```
def create
  ...params[...]...
  ...
end
```

2 The controller can read the raw form data by looking at `params[:ad]`. It can then send this value to `Ad.new(...)` to construct a new Ad object.

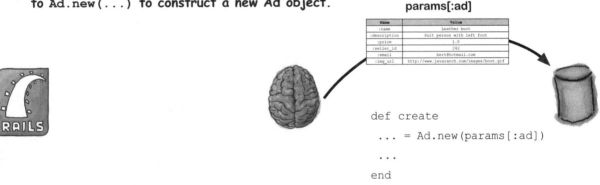

params[:ad]

Name	Value
:name	Leather boot
:description	Suit person with left foot
:price	1.0
:seller_id	242
:email	bert@hotmail.com
:img_url	http://www.javaranch.com/images/boot.gif

```
def create
  ... = Ad.new(params[:ad])
  ...
end
```

3 The Ad object that is returned by `Ad.new(...)` has attributes that match the values in the form fields.

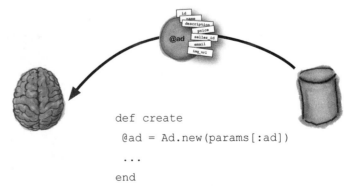

```
def create
  @ad = Ad.new(params[:ad])
  ...
end
```

The controller needs to save the record

The whole reason for converting the form data into an object was so you could save it.

How do you do that? With

        @ad.save

When save is called on the model object, Rails inspects the attributes and generates a SQL <u>insert</u> statement to update the database:

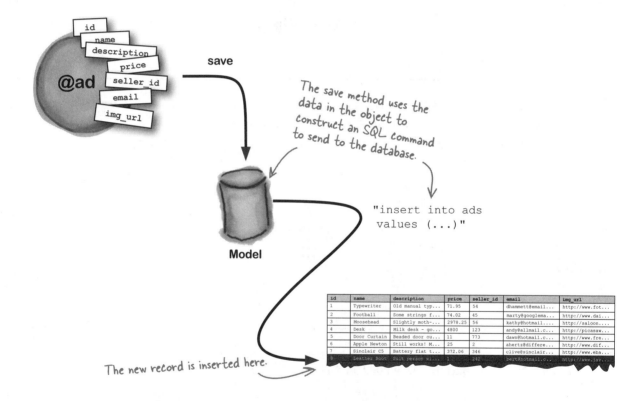

The save method uses the data in the object to construct an SQL command to send to the database.

"insert into ads
values (...)"

The new record is inserted here.

With the save in place, the controller's create method is complete:

```
def create
      @ad=Ad.new(params[:ad])
      @ad.save
end
```

Test Drive

Update your controller's create method, and try out the updated ad creation form. When you click Create, an error page is sent back complaining about a missing template:

○ ○ ○   Action Controller: Exception caught

◄ ► | ⟳ | ✂ | + | ⊕ http://localhost:3000/ads/create   ⊙ ⌐ Q⌐

Template is missing

Missing template ads/create.html.erb in view path
/Users/davidg/mebay/app/views

Sharpen your pencil

1. Was the record you created saved?

....

2. What do you need to do to fix this new error?

....

....

....

Sharpen your pencil
Solution

1. Was the record you created saved?

   ...The data was saved and so the new ad was created...

2. What do you need to do to fix this new error?

   ...There was no template available to generate a response to...
   ...confirm the record was saved – so a create.html.erb page...
   ...needs to be created....

Rails was complaining because it had no way of generating a RESPONSE to your request

HTTP works using *pairs* of requests and responses. For every request, there's got to be a response.

When the controller's create method completed, a new record was created successfully. Then Rails needed to generate a response page, so it looked for the page template that matched the current action. The current action was `create` so it looked for `create.html.erb`. But that template doesn't exist!

So we need to write a create.html.erb page template. But what should the template have in it?

Exercise

Create a `create.html.erb` file to tell users that the record has been created and provide a link to the new record.

Page telling users they successfully created an ad and a link to the newly created ad.

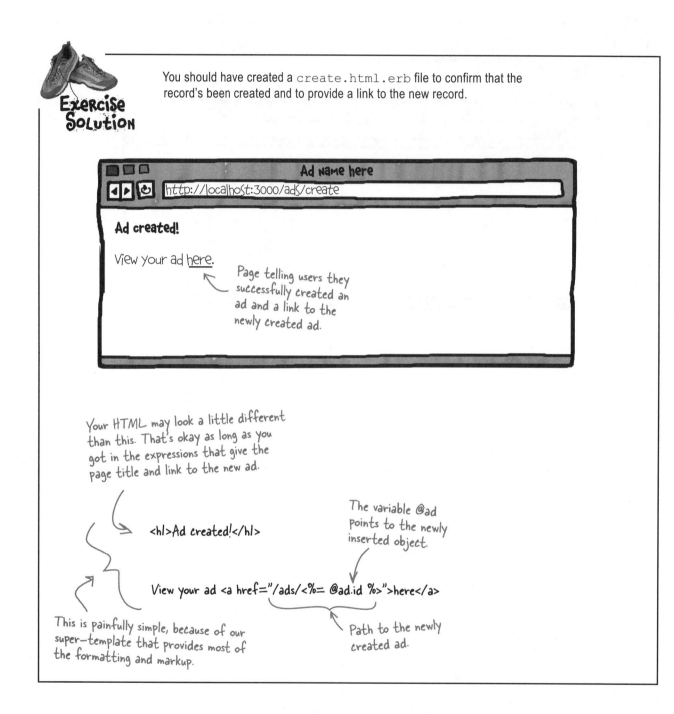

Exercise Solution

You should have created a `create.html.erb` file to confirm that the record's been created and to provide a link to the new record.

Ad name here

http://localhost:3000/ads/create

Ad created!

View your ad here.

Page telling users they successfully created an ad and a link to the newly created ad.

Your HTML may look a little different than this. That's okay as long as you got in the expressions that give the page title and link to the new ad.

```
<h1>Ad created!</h1>
```

The variable @ad points to the newly inserted object.

```
View your ad <a href="/ads/<%= @ad.id %>">here</a>
```

This is painfully simple, because of our super-template that provides most of the formatting and markup.

Path to the newly created ad.

TEST DRIVE

Now that you have the create.html.erb page template in place, it's time to try out the application.

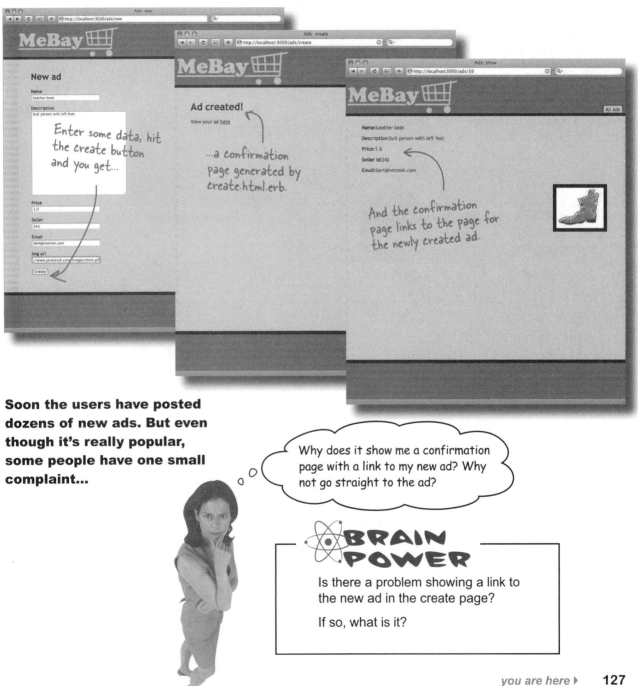

Enter some data, hit the create button and you get...

...a confirmation page generated by create.html.erb.

And the confirmation page links to the page for the newly created ad.

Soon the users have posted dozens of new ads. But even though it's really popular, some people have one small complaint...

Why does it show me a confirmation page with a link to my new ad? Why not go straight to the ad?

BRAIN POWER

Is there a problem showing a link to the new ad in the create page?

If so, what is it?

Don't create a new page, use an existing one

The users don't want to see the intervening confirmation page generated by create.html.erb. They just want to go straight to their ad. So what do you do?

You could edit the create.html.erb page template so that it displays all of the new ad's details, right? After all, the @ad variable is visible from the page template and it contains all of the details of the new ad.

But that would be a bad idea. Why? Because that would mean that the **create**.html.erb page would be exactly the same as the **show**.html.erb page template you use to display each ad.

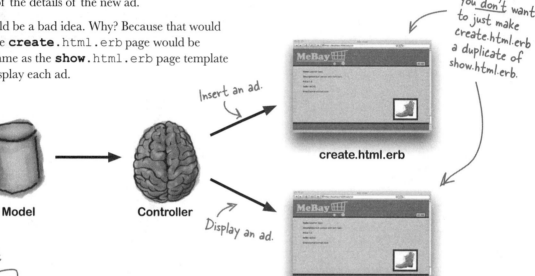

Model   **Controller**

Insert an ad.

Display an ad.

create.html.erb

show.html.erb

You don't want to just make create.html.erb a duplicate of show.html.erb.

Think DRY: Don't Repeat Yourself.

That's **duplication**, and it would mean you had more code to maintain in the future. It would be much better if the create action in the controller can choose to *display* the show.html.erb page.

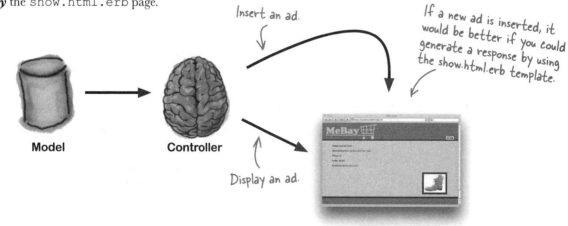

Model   **Controller**

Insert an ad.

Display an ad.

show.html.erb

If a new ad is inserted, it would be better if you could generate a response by using the show.html.erb template.

But how can a controller action display ANOTHER action's page?

A **controller method** works together with a template to form an action. In all of the examples you've seen so far, both the controller method and the page template have been exclusively used for one action.

That's why the controller methods and the page templates have included the action name somehow. When you were performing a show action, you used the show method in the ad controller and the show.html.erb page template.

And we still want to use a controller method and a page template to complete the action, but now we want to be able to *choose* which page template gets called with the controller.

A controller action is a controller method _and_ a page template.

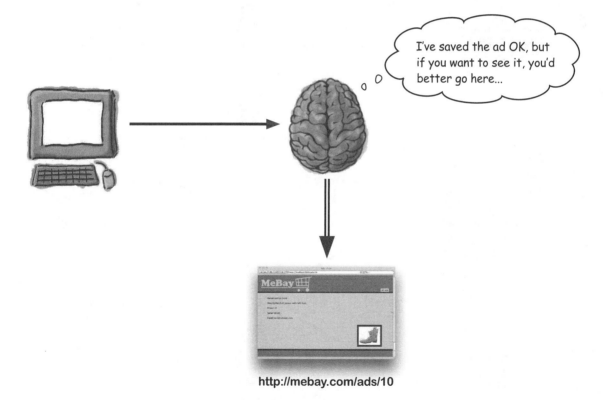

I've saved the ad OK, but if you want to see it, you'd better go here...

http://mebay.com/ads/10

We need a way for the controller to say that the output is found at a different URL.

Redirects let the controller specify which view is displayed

A **redirect** is a special kind of response from the Rails application to the browser. A redirect tells the browser to go to a *different* URL for output. So even though the browser sent the form data to /ads/create, a redirect sends the browser to ads/17 (for example, if 17 is the id number of the new ad).

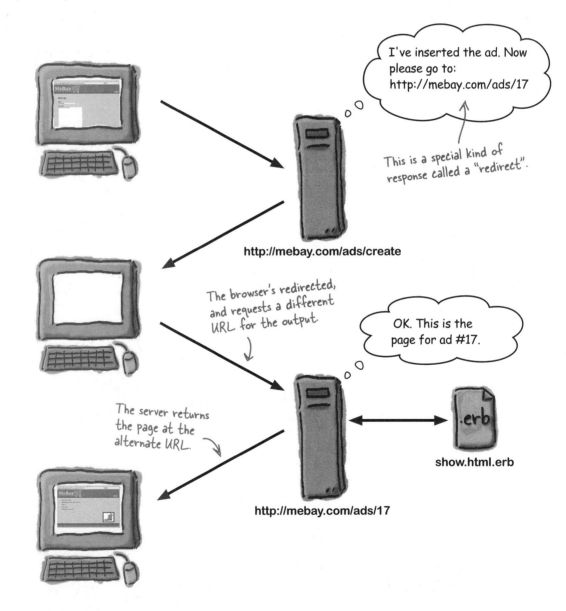

Sharpen your pencil

The <u>redirect</u> command will forward the browser to the URL of the new ad. Fill in the URL:

```
def create
  @ad = Ad.new(params[:ad])
  @ad.save
  redirect_to "/........../#{...............}"
end
```

there are no
Dumb Questions

Q: You said that a redirect is a special type of response. Is it really a response?

A: Yes. There are several types of responses. Ordinarily, a response contains information for the browser to display, but other responses—like redirects—contain special instructions for the browser. A redirect is a special instruction that tells a browser to go to a different URL.

Q: So if a browser is redirected, does the URL in it's address bar change?

A: You got it. Even though the browser made a request for a particular URL, the address bar will update to show the URL the browser ended up at.

Q: If I make a mistake in my code, could I redirect the browser in some sort of infinite loop of redirects?

A: No, because browsers have limits about the number of redirects they will follow. If your code sent continual redirects, the browser would get bored, stop following the redirects, and display an error message.

Q: If I set @ad to an object and then redirect to a different URL, will the new URL see my @ad object?

A: Good question! No, it won't. Once you've redirected to another address, none of the variables assigned by your controller will be visible at that new address.

Q: Can I redirect to an address outside my application?

A: Sure. A redirect is simply a command to the browser to go to a specified URL. If you want to redirect to an external website, go for it.

Q: When would I want to do a redirect?

A: You might do a redirect in order to re-use a page that displays information. That's why you're redirecting in the MeBay application. But it's also a good idea to redirect after you've made an amendment to the database.

Q: Why's that?

A: It's a good idea to split actions into two categories: **update** actions and **display** actions. An update action will change what's on the database and then redirect to a display action. That way, if someone enters a record, then clicks refresh on the next page, they will only be refreshing a display page, and not reinserting the record.

Q: What do #{ } mean in the redirect string?

A: Ruby strings can include Ruby expressions—like Ruby names. By placing them between #{ } you're telling Ruby to replace the expression with its value.

Q: params[...] looks a little like an array. Is it?

A: params is designed to work like an "associative array"—otherwise known as a "hash". A hash is a special type of array that can be indexed by things other than numbers.

Sharpen your pencil
Solution

The redirect command will forward the browser to the URL of the new ad. Fill in the URL:

```
def create
  @ad = Ad.new(params[:ad])
  @ad.save
  redirect_to "/  ads  /#{  @ad.id  }"
end
```

A #-symbol and {} inserts the value of a variable into a string.

TEST DRIVE

Go ahead and update your controller. Now it's time to see if our redirect sends users to their newly created ads:

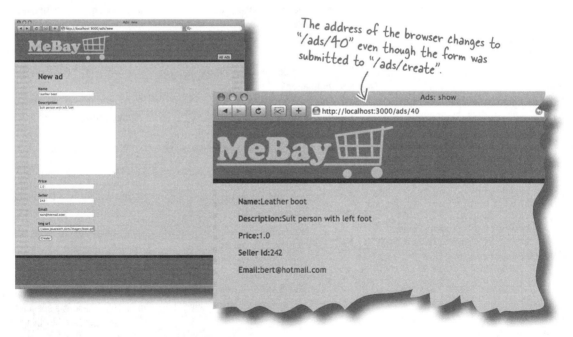

The address of the browser changes to "/ads/40" even though the form was submitted to "/ads/create".

When a new ad is created the browser automatically jumps to the new page.

But what if an ad needs to be amended <u>after</u> it's been posted?

Some users have made mistakes in their ad creations, and want to make changes to their ads. So they want more than just display and creation forms. Users now want to be able to **edit** their ads.

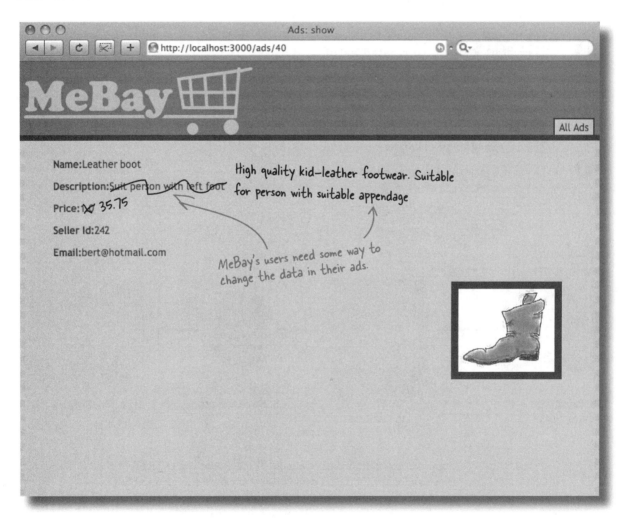

This means the system need to allow <u>updates</u> as well as <u>inserts</u>. Will that be difficult to do?

Updating an ad is just like creating one... only different

Even though the system can't currently edit ads, will it be a lot of work to add an editing feature?

Think for a moment about the sequence the system goes through to insert an ad into the system:

1 A new blank ad object gets **created** and this is used to generate the ad **input** form.

2 The form is sent to the user, who **updates** the field values and submits the form back to the application

3 The data fields are converted back into an Ad object, which is **saved** to the database.

4 The user is forwarded to a page displaying the **new** ad.

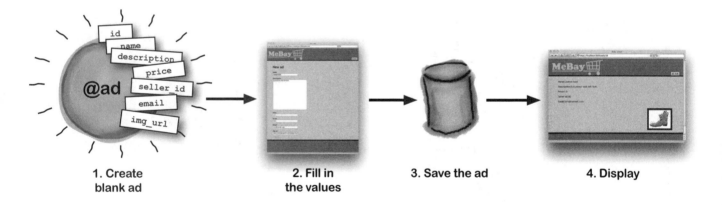

1. Create blank ad

2. Fill in the values

3. Save the ad

4. Display

Suppose you want to change a page. What would you expect to see? Maybe a form with the ad details that you can re-submit and have the changes saved, which is kind of the same sequence you used to create ads. Let's look at the change sequence in more detail...

Instead of creating an ad, you need to find one; instead of saving it, you need to update the ad

When someone edits an ad, they'll use a form just like before. The user will change the details and the ad data will be saved. So just how similar is the change sequence to the creation sequence?

1 An existing ad is **read** from the database, and this ad will be used to generate the **change** form.

2 The form is sent to the user, who updates the field values and submits the form back to the application.

3 The data fields are converted back into an Ad object, which is used to **update** the database.

4 The user is forwarded to a page displaying the **updated** ad.

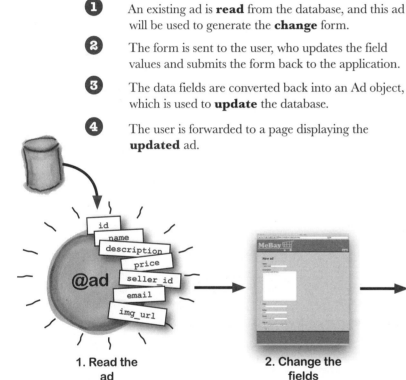

1. Read the ad

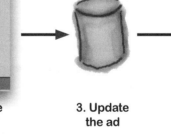

2. Change the fields

3. Update the ad

4. Display

You can see that the sequence between the two operations barely differs at all. In the **creation** sequence, a *new* ad object is *created* and *saved* to the database. In the **change** sequence an *existing* ad is *read*, *updated*, and *saved* to the database.

So you need to make sure you take the differences between the two operations into account. You'll need to keep track of things like the ad id number in the change sequence.

Do you think you could add an edit feature to the application as it stands?

🥿 **Long Exercise**

Add an edit link on each `show` page to a URL (like `ads/17/edit`) that calls a new **edit** action to look up the ad and display it in a form.

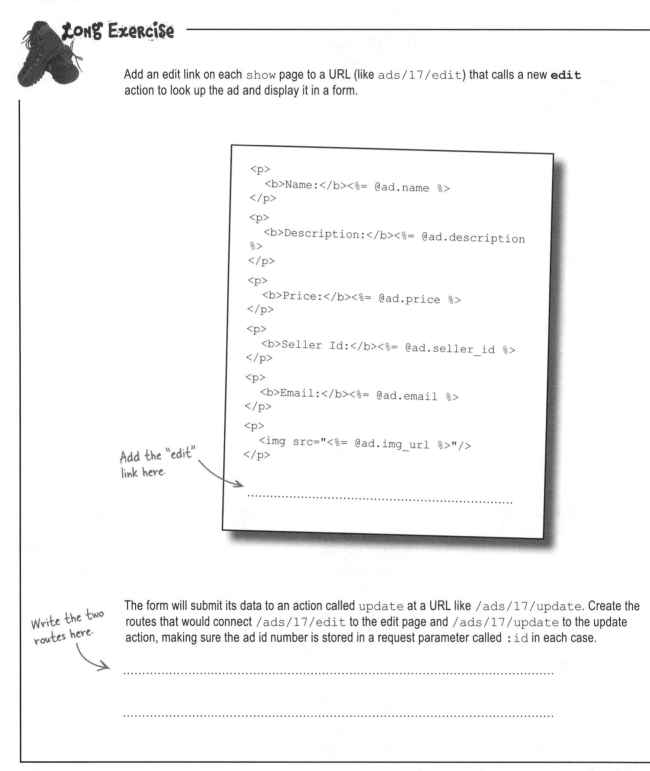

```
<p>
  <b>Name:</b><%= @ad.name %>
</p>
<p>
  <b>Description:</b><%= @ad.description
%>
</p>
<p>
  <b>Price:</b><%= @ad.price %>
</p>
<p>
  <b>Seller Id:</b><%= @ad.seller_id %>
</p>
<p>
  <b>Email:</b><%= @ad.email %>
</p>
<p>
  <img src="<%= @ad.img_url %>"/>
</p>
```

Add the "edit" link here.

....

Write the two routes here.

The form will submit its data to an action called `update` at a URL like `/ads/17/update`. Create the routes that would connect `/ads/17/edit` to the edit page and `/ads/17/update` to the update action, making sure the ad id number is stored in a request parameter called `:id` in each case.

....

....

Now create a new page template, `edit.html.erb`, to allow the user to edit the ad details. It's similar to `new.html.erb` except it displays the ad's name in the page heading and it will use the 'update' action instead of the 'create' action.

Write the edit.html.erb code here.

You'll need two action methods in the ad controller to provide data to the editing form and also to update the ad in the database. The `edit` method will provide data to the edit form, and the `update` method will update the database. Given that:

Write down the hash data structure containing the field values submitted from the form here.

```
@ad.update_attributes(........................)
```

—will update the `@ad` object on the database, write the code for the `edit` and **update** methods of the ad controller below:

Write the edit method here.

....

....

....

....

....

Write the update method here.

....

....

....

....

Long Exercise Solution

Your job was to add an edit link on each `show` page to a URL (like `ads/17/edit`) that calls a new **edit** action to look up the ad and display it in a form.

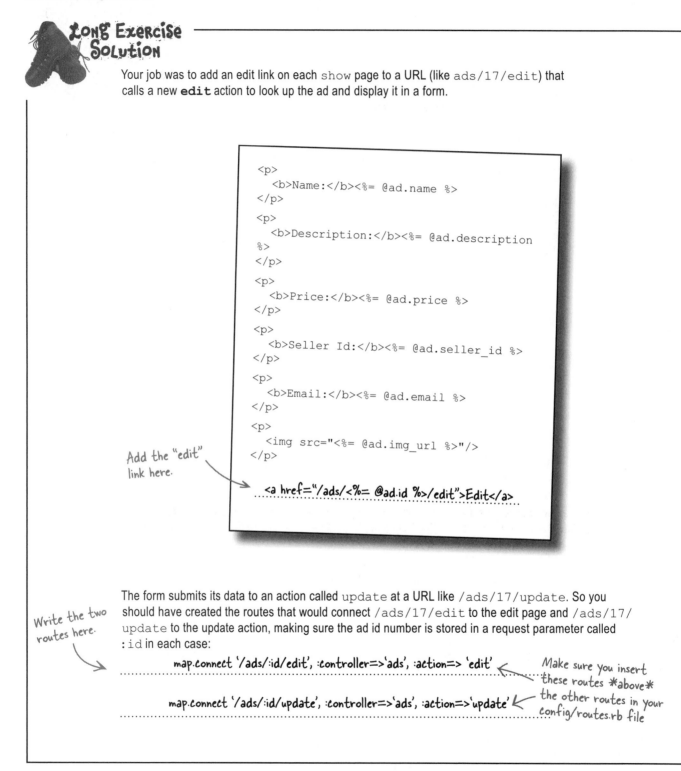

```
<p>
  <b>Name:</b><%= @ad.name %>
</p>
<p>
  <b>Description:</b><%= @ad.description
%>
</p>
<p>
  <b>Price:</b><%= @ad.price %>
</p>
<p>
  <b>Seller Id:</b><%= @ad.seller_id %>
</p>
<p>
  <b>Email:</b><%= @ad.email %>
</p>
<p>
  <img src="<%= @ad.img_url %>"/>
</p>
```

Add the "edit"
link here.

```
<a href="/ads/<%= @ad.id %>/edit">Edit</a>
```

The form submits its data to an action called `update` at a URL like `/ads/17/update`. So you should have created the routes that would connect `/ads/17/edit` to the edit page and `/ads/17/update` to the update action, making sure the ad id number is stored in a request parameter called `:id` in each case:

Write the two
routes here.

```
map.connect '/ads/:id/edit', :controller=>'ads', :action=> 'edit'

map.connect '/ads/:id/update', :controller=>'ads', :action=>'update'
```

Make sure you insert these routes *above* the other routes in your config/routes.rb file

Your job was to create a new page template `edit.html.erb` to allow the user to edit the ad details. It's similar to `new.html.erb` except it displays the ad's name in the page heading and it will use the 'update' action instead of the 'create' action:

```erb
<h1>Editing <%= @ad.name %></h1>
<% form_for(@ad,:url=>{:action=>'update'}) do |f| %>
  <p><b>Name</b><br /><%= f.text_field :name %></p>
  <p><b>Description</b><br /><%= f.text_area :description %></p>
  <p><b>Price</b><br /><%= f.text_field :price %></p>
  <p><b>Seller</b><br /><%= f.text_field :seller_id %></p>
  <p><b>Email</b><br /><%= f.text_field :email %></p>
  <p><b>Img url</b><br /><%= f.text_field :img_url %></p>
  <p><%= f.submit "Update" %></p>
<% end %>
```

Don't worry if you didn't get everything right in this exercise. It was a pretty tough one. But read through the answers and check that you understand what's going on.

You need two action methods in the ad controller to provide data to the editing form and also to update the ad on the database. The `edit` method provides data to the edit form, and the `update` method updates the database. So given that:

```ruby
@ad.update_attributes( params[:ad] )
```

—updates the `@ad` object on the database, you wrote the code for the `edit` and **update** methods of the ad controller:

```ruby
def edit
  @ad = Ad.find(params[:id])
end
```

```ruby
def update
  @ad = Ad.find(params[:id])
  @ad.update_attributes(params[:ad])
  redirect_to "/ads/#{@ad.id}"
end
```

Test Drive

The edit.html.erb page template is in place, as well as the routes and the additional methods in the ad controller. So now it's time to test the new editing feature:

> When their ad displays, a seller can click on the "Edit" link and open up the editing page generated by edit.html.erb.

The seller selects their ad from the index list.

Once a seller's in the edit page, they can amend the details of their ad, then hit the "Update" button.

The seller's ad is updated and displayed.

The code's in place and the editing feature works. So we're done... right?

Wait! No fair. When we started to create this app, you said we couldn't use scaffolding because it allowed people to do too much. Now that's exactly what people can do! How do we know that people will only edit their *own* ads? What's to stop someone from messing with somebody else's ad?

BRAIN POWER

What could be done to the editing feature so that ads can be changed, but *not* vandalized?

Restricting access to a function

The application can now *create* and *update* data. But that means <u>anyone</u> who can create an ad can update **all** ads. And that's a problem.

The MeBay owners want anyone to be able to create ads, but they don't want *everybody else* to be able to change the ad once it's been posted.

Wily hacker

RAILS

Controller
update
method

The ad's creator

One way of preventing just anyone changing ads is to protect the update function with a username and password.

The guys at MeBay have decided that only *system administrators* will be able to change ads. So they want the new update functionality secured with an admin **username** and **password**.

Fortunately, Rails makes it really easy to drop security right in. We're going to use a special kind of web security called **HTTP Authentication**. This is the kind of security that pops up a dialog box and asks for a *username* and *password* when someone tries to enter a secure area of a web site.

Ready Bake Sign-In Code

To add login security to the application, you need to add **two** pieces of code to the ad controller: a **login method** that checks a username and password, and a **filter** that calls the login method whenever certain methods in the controller are accessed:

This is the controller with the login code added.

This is the filter.

```
class AdController < ApplicationController
  before_filter :check_logged_in, :only => [:edit, :update]
  def new
    @ad = Ad.new
  end
  def create
    @ad = Ad.new(params[:ad])
    @ad.save
    redirect_to "/ads/#{@ad.id}"
  end
  def edit
    @ad = Ad.find(params[:id])
  end
  def update
    @ad = Ad.find(params[:id])
    @ad.update_attributes(params[:ad])
    redirect_to "/ads/#{@ad.id}"
  end
  def show
    @ad = Ad.find(params[:id])
  end
  def index
    @ads = Ad.find(:all)
  end
  private
  def check_logged_in
    authenticate_or_request_with_http_basic("Ads") do |username, password|
      username == "admin" && password == "t4k3th3r3dpi11"
    end
  end
end
```

You will only ask people to login if they try to access the "edit" or "update" methods.

The filter calls the check_logged_in method if someone tries to access the "edit" or "update" methods.

This is the name of the secured area of the web site – the "domain".

The username

The password

TEST DRIVE

Now that the security code is in place, it's time to open up your browser and try to edit an ad.

When the "edit" link is clicked the username and password dialog appears.

> Busted... I can't crack this fiendishly hard password.

The MeBay administrator

Only users with the correct username and password can enter.

Now only people who know the admin username and password can edit ads on the site. Nobody else can get at the edit page *or* the update function.

Is it important to secure both the page **and** the update function? The edit page should be off limits to prevent people accidentally accessing it and wasting their time entering data. Not only that, but the update function (the code that does the actual database update) also needs to be secure in case a hacker tries to access it directly without using the edit form.

You've manually built a system that can create, read, and update ads... and is secure!

... but now old ads need to be deleted

The site is up and running, and everything's going great, but after not too long there's a problem: even after stuff gets sold, the ads stay there.

Dude, I already sold both copies of my "Lawn Mower Man" DVDs, so why am I still getting requests for it? Is there no way to take my ad down?

MeBay *could* use their own data entry systems to remove ads from the site, but they were so impressed by how simple the change function was, they'd like you to add a delete function to the website.

The feature will only be available to MeBay administrators, so they want the same security that was applied to the change functionality. Also, because there's been a ton of spam as well as some spoof ads posted onto the site, they'd like to make the delete function easily available from the index page. That way they can remove inappropriate content with a single click.

Let's look at what we need to do...

Long Exercise

Update `index.html.erb` to add a delete link next to each ad. If the ad has `id = 17`, then link to `/ads/17/delete`.

```
h1>All Ads</h1>
<ul>
<% for ad in @ads %>
   <li><a href="/ads/<%= ad.id %>"><%= ad.name %></a>
   [<a href="                                        ">Delete</a>]</li>
<% end %>
</ul>
```
....

↑

Add the link here.

Create a route that will connect paths like `/ads/17/delete` to an action called `destroy` in the ad controller. Remember to record the id number as a request parameter.

....

↑

Write the route here.

Complete the ad controller code to delete an ad and send the user's browser back to the index listing all the remaining ads.

To do this you will need to use a method we have not seen yet—the "destroy" method. This will delete an ad object from the database.

```
class AdController < ApplicationController
  before_filter :check_logged_in, :only => [:edit, :update, .........................]
  def new
    @ad = Ad.new
  end
  def create
    @ad = Ad.new(params[:ad])
    @ad.save
    redirect_to "/ads/#{@ad.id}"
  end
  def edit
    @ad = Ad.find(params[:id])
  end
  def update
    @ad = Ad.find(params[:id])
    @ad.update_attributes(params[:ad])
    redirect_to "/ads/#{@ad.id}"
  end
  def show
    @ad = Ad.find(params[:id])
  end
  def index
    @ads = Ad.find(:all)
  end

  .......................................
      ...........................................................
      @ad.destroy
      ...........................................................
  .......................................
  private
  def check_logged_in
    authenticate_or_request_with_http_basic("Ads") do |username, password|
      username == "admin" && password == "t4k3th3r3dpi11"
    end
  end
end
```

This will delete the @ad object from the database.

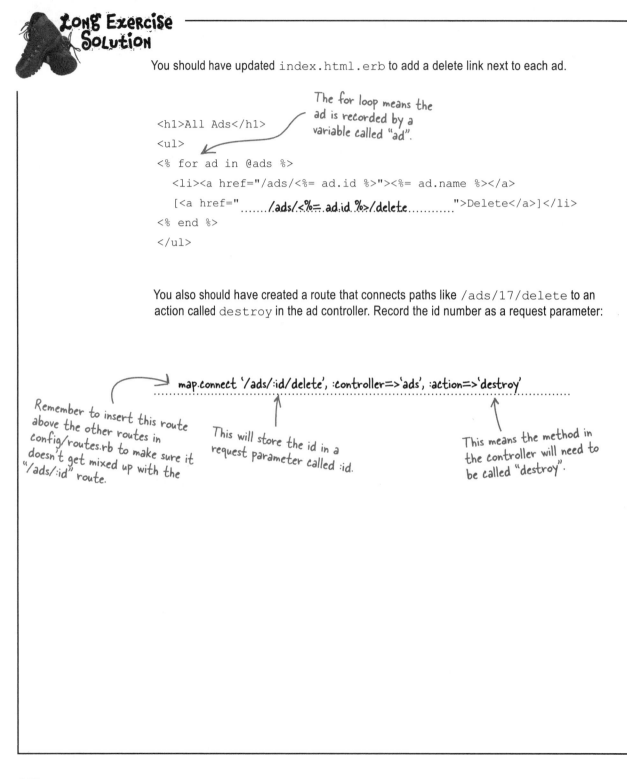

Long Exercise Solution

You should have updated `index.html.erb` to add a delete link next to each ad.

```
<h1>All Ads</h1>
<ul>
<% for ad in @ads %>
   <li><a href="/ads/<%= ad.id %>"><%= ad.name %></a>
   [<a href="........../ads/<%=.ad.id.%>/.delete............">Delete</a>]</li>
<% end %>
</ul>
```

The for loop means the ad is recorded by a variable called "ad".

You also should have created a route that connects paths like `/ads/17/delete` to an action called `destroy` in the ad controller. Record the id number as a request parameter:

```
map.connect '/ads/:id/delete', :controller=>'ads', :action=>'destroy'
```

Remember to insert this route above the other routes in config/routes.rb to make sure it doesn't get mixed up with the "/ads/:id" route.

This will store the id in a request parameter called :id.

This means the method in the controller will need to be called "destroy".

Your job here was to complete the ad controller code to delete an ad and send the user's browser back to the index listing all the remaining ads:

```ruby
class AdController < ApplicationController
  before_filter :check_logged_in, :only => [:edit, :update, :destroy ]

  def new
    @ad = Ad.new
  end

  def create
    @ad = Ad.new(params[:ad])
    @ad.save
    redirect_to "/ads/#{@ad.id}"
  end

  def edit
    @ad = Ad.find(params[:id])
  end

  def update
    @ad = Ad.find(params[:id])
    @ad.update_attributes(params[:ad])
    redirect_to "/ads/#{@ad.id}"
  end

  def show
    @ad = Ad.find(params[:id])
  end

  def index
    @ads = Ad.find(:all)
  end

  def destroy
    @ad = Ad.find(params[:id])
    @ad.destroy
    redirect_to '/ads/'
  end

  private
  def check_logged_in
    authenticate_or_request_with_http_basic("Ads") do |username, password|
      username == "admin" && password == "t4k3th3r3dpill"
    end
  end
end
```

This will make sure people have to give a username and password if they try to delete an ad

You need to read the ad object from the database using the id given in the path to the action...

...then you need to redirect the browser back to the index page.

Test Drive

The destroy action means users can delete ads from the site with a single click. It uses the same security as the amend feature, so before anyone can delete an ad, they must first prove that they're an administrator.

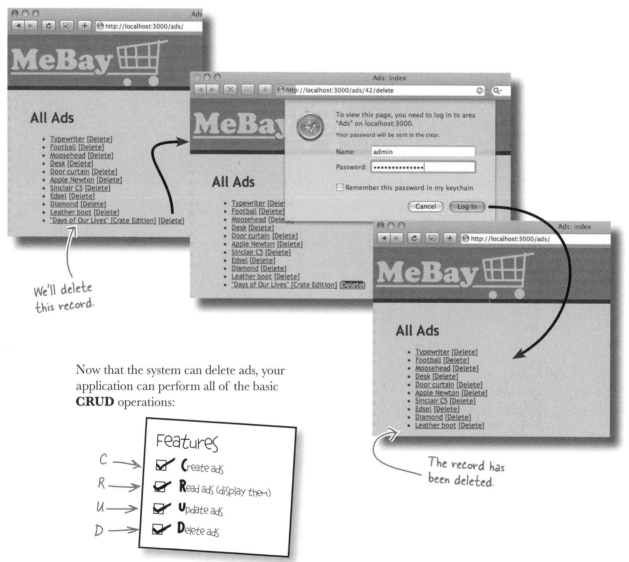

We'll delete this record.

The record has been deleted.

Now that the system can delete ads, your application can perform all of the basic **CRUD** operations:

Features

C ——→ ☑ **C**reate ads

R ——→ ☑ **R**ead ads (display them)

U ——→ ☑ **U**pdate ads

D ——→ ☑ **D**elete ads

But then, so could scaffolding... so why write your own code?

Doing it yourself gave you the power to do more than scaffolding

You can **choose** what functions are available.

You can **add** additional features like security.

And now you **understand** how to create code that inserts, updates and deletes data, you'll be able to amend the code that scaffolding generates.

Tools for your Rails Toolbox

You've got Chapter 3 under your belt, and now you've added the ability to manually create applications that can insert, update and delete data.

Rails Tools

@ad.save saves a model objects

@ad.update_attributes updates a model object

redirect_to lets the controller send the browser to a different URL

http_authentication makes adding security a breeze

Ruby Tools

params[...] is a *hash*, which is like an array indexed by *name*

nil is a special default object that means "no value"

Inside Rails, calling methods on a nil object causes errors

"#{" and "}" can insert expressions into strings like "1 + 1 = #{1+1}"

4 database finders

Truth or consequences?

I told you that old woman wouldn't give up her marble loaf...

Every decision you make has consequences.

In Rails, knowing how to make **good decisions** can save you both time and effort. In this chapter, we'll look at how **user requirements** affect the choices you make, right from the very **beginning** of your app. Should you use scaffolding and modify the generated code? Should you create things from scratch? Either way, when it comes time to customize your app further, you need to learn about **finders**: *getting at your data* in a way that makes sense to you and serves your **users' needs**.

Keep fit with the Rubyville Health Club

The Rubyville Health Club prides itself on its ability to find the perfect class for everyone, and recently they've launched a new personal trainer service. Demand for the service is high... so high that the trainers are having trouble keeping track of all their clients. The trainers need you to build an application for them, and fast.

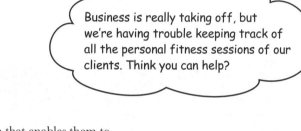

Business is really taking off, but we're having trouble keeping track of all the personal fitness sessions of our clients. Think you can help?

The personal trainers need a web application that enables them to quickly and easily manage the workouts for <u>each</u> of their customers. To start with, they need something that lists basic workout details for each client and allows them to add, update and delete records. Here's a sketch of the main page:

```
ClientWorkouts: find
http://localhost:3000/client_workouts/find/
```

Listing client workouts for Lenny Goldberg ←

Lenny is just one of the clients using the personal trainer service.

Trainer	Duration mins	Date of workout	Paid amount			
Clint	30	2009-07-14 09:14:00 UTC	25.0	Show	Edit	Destroy
Brad	30	2009-07-19 09:13:00 UTC	25.0	Show	Edit	Destroy
Sven	90	2009-08-02 09:13:00 UTC	75.0	Show	Edit	Destroy
Marshall	15	2009-09-29 13:15:00 UTC	15.0	Show	Edit	Destroy
Clint	30	2009-10-01 09:11:00 UTC	25.0	Show	Edit	Destroy
Sara	30	2009-10-05 19:00:00 UTC	25.0	Show	Edit	Destroy

← These are all Lenny's workouts.

New client_workout

Exercise

Let's start the application by scaffolding a set of pages for this model:

client_workouts

Column	Type
client_name	string
trainer	string
duration_mins	integer
date_of_workout	date
paid_amount	decimal

What should the scaffold command be? Write your answer below. Go ahead and run this command, too:

....

....

Write your answer here.

Now, look again at what the trainers want to do with the application, and write down any differences between what the application **needs to do** and what the application actually **does** based on the scaffolded version you just created:

....

....

....

....

....

....

....

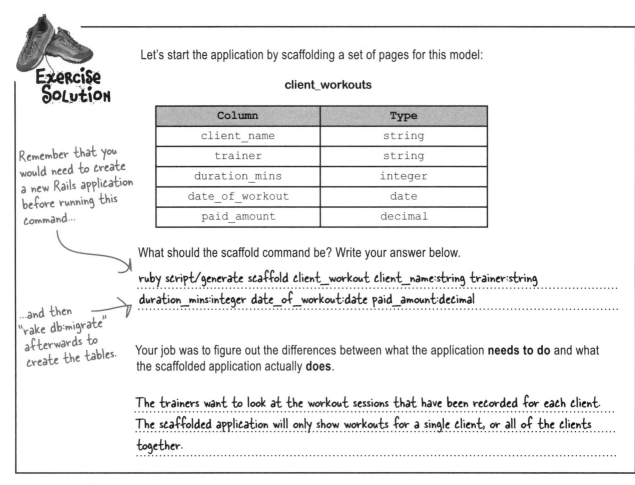

Exercise Solution

Remember that you would need to create a new Rails application before running this command...

...and then "rake db:migrate" afterwards to create the tables.

Let's start the application by scaffolding a set of pages for this model:

client_workouts

Column	Type
client_name	string
trainer	string
duration_mins	integer
date_of_workout	date
paid_amount	decimal

What should the scaffold command be? Write your answer below.

ruby script/generate scaffold client_workout client_name:string trainer:string duration_mins:integer date_of_workout:date paid_amount:decimal

Your job was to figure out the differences between what the application **needs to do** and what the scaffolded application actually **does**.

The trainers want to look at the workout sessions that have been recorded for each client.

The scaffolded application will only show workouts for a single client, or all of the clients together.

The scaffolding isn't right—but do we write our own code or fix the scaffolding?

The scaffolded application doesn't do exactly what we need. We've seen before that it's easier to create **simple** applications manually, without using scaffolding at all. But another approach is to create a scaffolded app, and then either **change** or **add to** the code Rails generates.

So what should we do here?

TEST DRIVE

If you haven't already, use scaffolding to create the training app. Then we can compare that to what the trainers want, and see how close we are.

The application actually looks pretty close...

There is one part of the generated code that looks *kind of* similar to the page that the trainers want. The index page lists a set of data that is almost the same as what the trainers have asked for:

This is what the trainers want to see...

```
ClientWorkouts: find
http://localhost:3000/client_workouts/find/
```

Listing client workouts for Lenny Goldberg

Trainer	Duration mins	Date
Clint	30	2009-07-
Brad	30	2009-07-
Sven	90	2009-08-
Marshall	15	2009-09-
Clint	30	2009-10-
Sara	30	2009-10-

New client_workout

...and this is the index page of the scaffolded application.

```
ClientWorkouts: index
http://localhost:3000/client_workouts
```

Listing client_workouts

Client name	Trainer	Duration mins	Date of workout	Paid amount		
Kirk Stigwood	Clint	60	2009-10-05	50.0	Show	Edit
Lenny Goldberg	Clint	30	2009-07-14	25.0	Show	Edit
Lenny Goldberg	Brad	30	2009-07-19	25.0	Show	Edit
Lenny Goldberg	Sven	90	2009-08-02	75.0	Show	Edit
Lenny Goldberg	Marshall	15	2009-09-29	15.0	Show	Edit
Lenny Goldberg	Clint	30	2009-10-01	25.0	Show	Edit
Lenny Goldberg	Sara	30	2009-10-05	25.0	Show	Edit

New client_workout

Not only does the generated page look similar to what we need, we know that a scaffolded application will give us all of the usual operations on the client workout data. In other words, a scaffolded application will, by default, allow us to create, read, update and delete records.

So, in this case, is it better to **fix the scaffold** and make the changes we need, or **start from scratch**, like we did for MeBay?

Should we start from scratch...

...or should we fix the scaffold?

We're going to fix the scaffolding

When we created the MeBay application, we decided not to use scaffolding. The reason for this was that the clients originally wanted something so simple that it was easier to create the application from scratch. They wanted a lot less functionality than scaffolding provides.

This time around, we need access to *all* of the CRUD operations, plus we need to find the workout sessions for an ***individual client***. As we need more functionality, we can do most of the work using scaffolding as the basis of the application, and then we can add to the generated code.

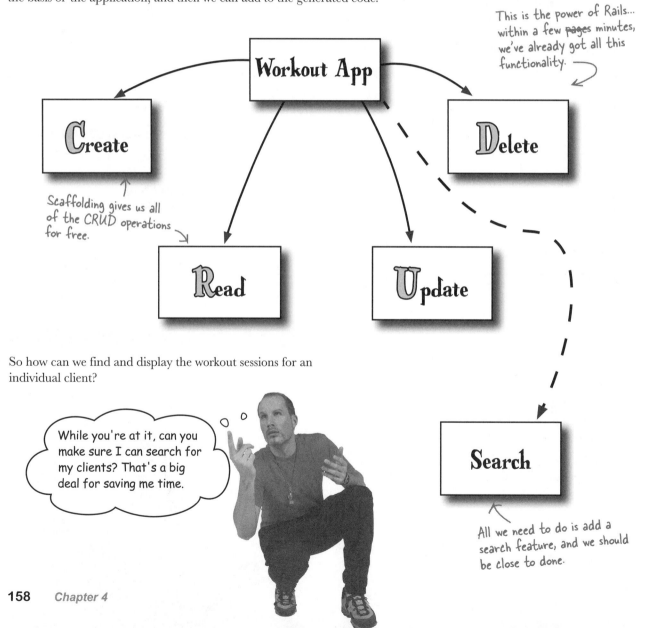

This is the power of Rails... within a few ~~pages~~ minutes, we've already got all this functionality.

Scaffolding gives us all of the CRUD operations for free.

So how can we find and display the workout sessions for an individual client?

While you're at it, can you make sure I can search for my clients? That's a big deal for saving me time.

All we need to do is add a search feature, and we should be close to done.

Design the search function

Here's what the search function should look like:

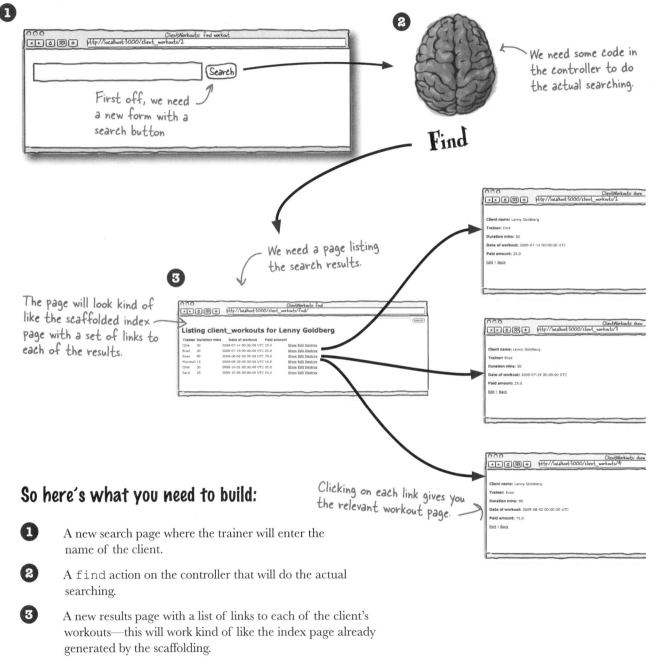

First off, we need a new form with a search button

We need some code in the controller to do the actual searching.

Find

We need a page listing the search results.

The page will look kind of like the scaffolded index page with a set of links to each of the results.

Clicking on each link gives you the relevant workout page.

So here's what you need to build:

1. A new search page where the trainer will enter the name of the client.

2. A `find` action on the controller that will do the actual searching.

3. A new results page with a list of links to each of the client's workouts—this will work kind of like the index page already generated by the scaffolding.

So where should we start?

Let's start by building the form

We have a few new components to create, so let's start with the user interface. That way we'll be able to get some early feedback from the trainers. Here's what the search form trainers will use to find clients should look like:

You've built pages with forms before. Can you see anything different about this one?

Take a look at the other forms we just generated for the application, the create and edit forms. They have fields that match the fields of the ClientWorkout model objects. The difference this time is there's no model object that matches the search form. So how do we create a form when there's no model to base the form on?

The search will need a new kind of form

We need to create a form *without* using a model object, but the `form_for` helper we've been using requires needs a model object to work. So what do we do?

Fortunately there is another helper tag that creates model-free forms—just what we need in this situation.

Search Form Magnets

You'll need to create a search page template. Trouble is— after working out the main part of the code on the fridge door somebody slammed the door and the magnets all fell off!

Fortunately the code for a non-model form is pretty similar to a model form.

Can you figure out what the code should look like?

```
<% ............................................................. %>

<%= ........................................................ %>

<%= ................................................. %>

<% .................. %>
```

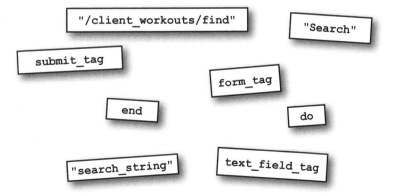

```
"/client_workouts/find"        "Search"

submit_tag
                        form_tag

        end                              do


    "search_string"        text_field_tag
```

Search Form Magnets Solution

Your job was to take the magnets and assemble them into code to create a search form, without requiring a corresponding model.

Did you figure out what the code should look like?

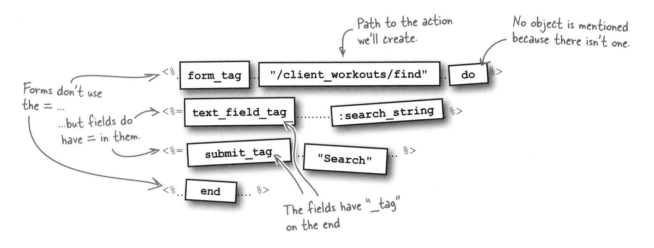

Path to the action we'll create.

No object is mentioned because there isn't one.

```
<% form_tag "/client_workouts/find" do %>
<%= text_field_tag :search_string %>
<%= submit_tag "Search" %>
<% end %>
```

Forms don't use the = ...

...but fields do have = in them.

The fields have "_tag" on the end

there are no Dumb Questions

Q: I don't get why we can't just use scaffolding on its own. Doesn't that give us everything?

A: Scaffolding only provides basic Create, Read, Update, and Delete operations. Most applications will need functions that go beyond basic CRUD functionality.

Q: Why didn't we use scaffolding for the MeBay application?

A: We didn't use scaffolding for MeBay because we originally only needed a basic read-only application. For really simple applications it can be easier and more efficient to create your application manually.

Q: Could we still have generated the application using scaffolding, and then removed the operations we didn't want?

A: Yes, we could have done that. You will probably start most applications using scaffolding. Only in cases where you need very little functionality, or where the functionality is very different from scaffolding, will you want to create an app manually.

Q: So sometimes it's best to start from scratch, and other times it's best to fix the scaffolding. Which option should I use when? How can I decide what's best?

A: Go for scaffolding if you're going to use most of the CRUD operations, create, read,

update, and delete. Ask yourself: which will be quicker—creating the code manually, or stripping out the unused scaffolding code?

Q: What is a model form?

A: A **model form** is a form bound to a model object. When that sort of form is displayed, the field values will come from the attributes of a model object.

Q: And a non-model form?

A: That's a form that isn't bound to a model object. A non-model form is used for a set of individual field values and they are mostly used for things like search forms or other data that won't be saved to the database.

Add the search to the interface

Now that we have the code for the search form, we should probably create a brand new page template for it.

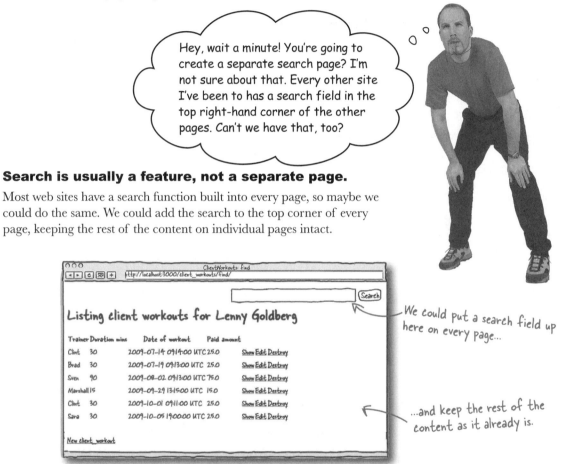

Hey, wait a minute! You're going to create a separate search page? I'm not sure about that. Every other site I've been to has a search field in the top right-hand corner of the other pages. Can't we have that, too?

Search is usually a feature, not a separate page.

Most web sites have a search function built into every page, so maybe we could do the same. We could add the search to the top corner of every page, keeping the rest of the content on individual pages intact.

We could put a search field up here on every page...

...and keep the rest of the content as it already is.

Adding code to every page will mean there's a lot of duplicated code to be maintained, but what if we could add the new search code just to a single file?

Sharpen your pencil

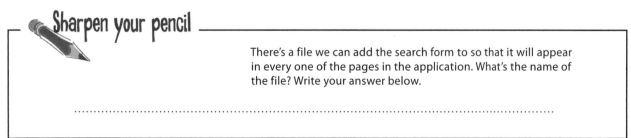

There's a file we can add the search form to so that it will appear in every one of the pages in the application. What's the name of the file? Write your answer below.

....

Sharpen your pencil
Solution

There's a file we can add the search form to so that it will appear in every one of the pages in the application. What's the name of the file? Write your answer below.

Did you remember layouts? They contain markup that every page template will include. →

app/views/layouts/client_workouts.html.erb

Ready Bake Code

This is the code you need to save in the **app/views/layouts/client_workouts.html.erb** layout file.

This is a layout file so it lives in app/views/layouts.

Download the file from: www.headfirstlabs.com/books/rails

```
<!DOCTYPE html PUBLIC "-//W3C//DTD XHTML 1.0 Transitional//EN"
        "http://www.w3.org/TR/xhtml1/DTD/xhtml1-transitional.dtd">

<html xmlns="http://www.w3.org/1999/xhtml" xml:lang="en" lang="en">
<head>
  <meta http-equiv="content-type" content="text/html;charset=UTF-8" />
  <title>ClientWorkouts: <%= controller.action_name %></title>
  <%= stylesheet_link_tag 'scaffold' %>
</head>
<body>


<span style="text-align: right">
  <% form_tag "/client_workouts/find" do %>
    <%= text_field_tag :search_string %>
    <%= submit_tag "Search" %>
  <% end %>
</span>


<p style="color: green"><%= flash[:notice] %></p>


<%= yield  %>


</body>
</html>
```

This adds the stylesheet from public/stylesheets/scaffold.css.

This is our new code for the search form.

This can be used for sending messages to the page. Don't worry about this yet.

TEST DRIVE

Change your app's layout to include the search functionality. If you refresh each of the pages in your application, the search field should appear in the top-right corner.

Our freshly-added search field appears on each of the pages like this.

But how do we get access to the contents of the search field? Here's the HTML that was generated within each page to produce the search form:

```
<form action="/client_workouts/find" method="post">
  <input id="search_string" name="search_string" type="text" />
  <input name="commit" type="submit" value="Search" />
</form>
```

Sharpen your pencil

Given that you know what the HTML for the form will look like, what expression do you think you will be able to use within the controller code to get access to the contents of the search field? Write your answer below:

....

Sharpen your pencil
Solution

Given that you know what the HTML for the form will look like, what expression do you think you will be able to use within the controller code to get access to the contents of the search field? Write your answer below:

params[:search_string]

params["search_string"] would also work, but it's better style to use a symbol.

So are the form parameters structured differently?

The **form_for** helper we used in the previous chapter creates a **model form**—that is, an HTML form based upon the attributes of a model object. When a model form is submitted, Rails knows that you are probably going to want to turn the field values back into a model object. For example, when the scaffolded *Edit* form (which is created with form_for) is submitted, it structures its parameters like this:

This is the contents of params[...] (the request parameters) sent by the client workout form.

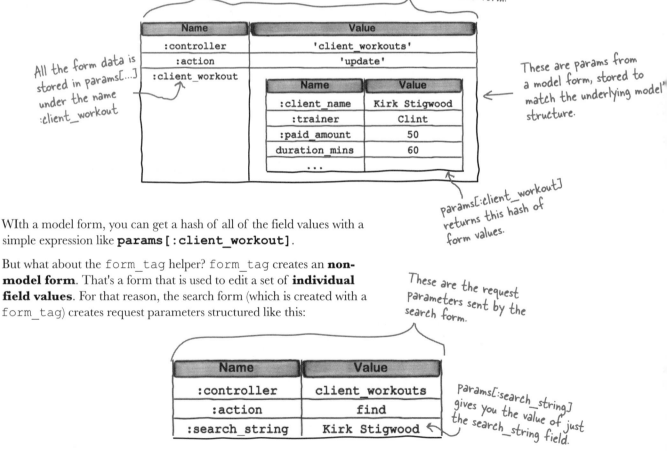

All the form data is stored in params[...] under the name :client_workout

These are params from a model form, stored to match the underlying model structure.

params[:client_workout] returns this hash of form values.

WIth a model form, you can get a hash of all of the field values with a simple expression like **params[:client_workout]**.

But what about the form_tag helper? form_tag creates an **non-model form**. That's a form that is used to edit a set of **individual field values**. For that reason, the search form (which is created with a form_tag) creates request parameters structured like this:

These are the request parameters sent by the search form.

params[:search_string] gives you the value of just the search_string field.

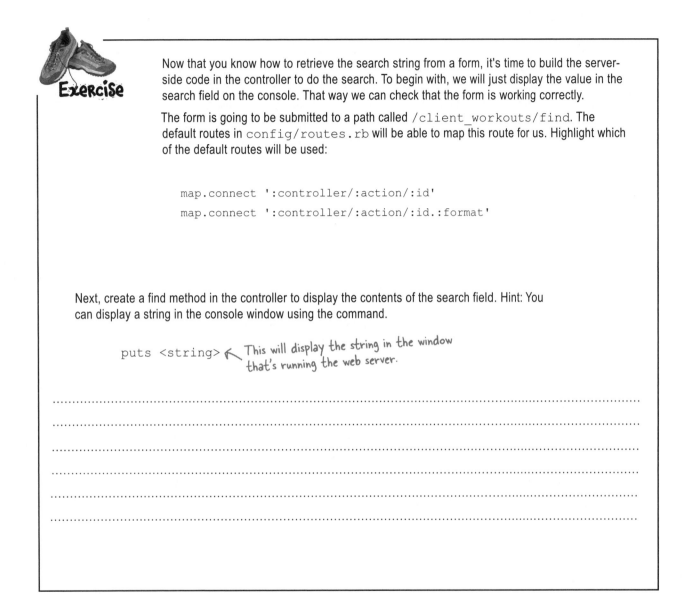

Now that you know how to retrieve the search string from a form, it's time to build the server-side code in the controller to do the search. To begin with, we will just display the value in the search field on the console. That way we can check that the form is working correctly.

The form is going to be submitted to a path called `/client_workouts/find`. The default routes in `config/routes.rb` will be able to map this route for us. Highlight which of the default routes will be used:

```
map.connect ':controller/:action/:id'
map.connect ':controller/:action/:id.:format'
```

Next, create a find method in the controller to display the contents of the search field. Hint: You can display a string in the console window using the command.

```
puts <string>
```
← This will display the string in the window that's running the web server.

Exercise Solution

Now that you know how to retrieve the search string from the form, let's start to build the server-side code in the controller to do the search. To begin with, we will just display the value in the search field on the console. That way we can check that the form is working correctly.

The form is going to be submitted to a path called `/client_workouts/find`. The default routes in `config/routes.rb` will be able to map this route for us. Highlight which of the default routes will be used:

We don't need to create a route – this default one will be used →

```
map.connect ':controller/:action/:id'
map.connect ':controller/:action/:id.:format'
```

Next, create a find method in the controller to display the contents of the search field. Hint: You can display a string in the console window using the command

```
puts <string>
```

← *This will display the string in the window that's running the web server.*

All we need to do is write out the correct parameter name.

```
def find
  puts params[:search_string]
end
```

TEST DRIVE

Let's try the code out. In any of the pages in the application, enter some search text and click the "Search" button.

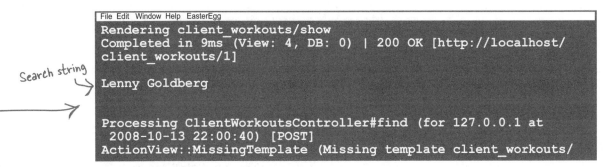

This is what happens when you press the search button.

Don't worry if you get an error when you press the search button. It's simply because we haven't created a search results page template yet. The interesting output will be in the console where you are running your web server. Somewhere amidst a set of errors about the missing results template, you should see this:

```
File  Edit  Window  Help  EasterEgg
Rendering client_workouts/show
Completed in 9ms (View: 4, DB: 0) | 200 OK [http://localhost/
client_workouts/1]

Lenny Goldberg


Processing ClientWorkoutsController#find (for 127.0.0.1 at
  2008-10-13 22:00:40) [POST]
ActionView::MissingTemplate (Missing template client_workouts/
```

Search string

So we've created a search form on each page, and we have some code on the server that can read the string the user is searching form.

Now we need to actually do the searching.

BULLET POINTS

- Applications often need to do more than create, read, update, and delete records.

- You will need to design your own page sequences sometimes—and the easiest way to start is by considering the user's point of view, and how they'll use your application.

- If you need a form that doesn't match a model object, use `form_tag` instead of `form_for`.

- You need to use `_tag` fields with a `form_tag` form.

- `params[:field_name]` will give you the value of the field called :field_name in a non-model form.

- `puts "A string"` will output a string to the console.

there are no Dumb Questions

Q: When would I use a form_tag instead of a form_for?

A: Use `form_tag` if your form is going to be editing data that is not stored in a model object. We used a `form_tag` for the search form because there was no model object to with a single `search_string` attribute.

Q: Why are form_for and form_tag helpers surrounded by <% ... %> instead of <%= ... %>?

A: The form helpers are used with scriptlets (<%...%>) instead of expressions (<%=...%>) because they do more than simply generate HTML. Remember that we used scriptlets for `for` loops? That's because a `for` loop controls the contents of the code in its loop body. In a similar way, forms "control" the HTML generation of the field helpers they contain.

Q: That sounds sort of complicated...

A: That's OK—you don't have to understand it all right now. If you just remember to use `form_for` and `form_tag` with scriptlets, everything will work fine.

Q: Can I still read the individual fields in a form_for model form?

A: Yes. The form fields for the client_workout forms can be retrieved with `params[:client_workout]`—and this is just another hash. So to get the value of the 'trainer' field you would just use `params[:client_workout][:trainer]`.

Q: We used a default route for the "find" action. Couldn't we have used those before?

A: No. The routes that we used before didn't match the default routes closely enough.

Q: How do I know when I need to create a custom route?

A: If you type `rake routes` at the command line, you will see all of the routes available in your application. If none of them match, or if there's a route that matches the wrong action, then you need to add a custom route.

How do we find client records?

So do we have a problem reading the records for a particular client?
When we've read records so far, we've done it by returning a single
record, or by finding all the records in a table. But what's different
this time?

1 ## Reading a single record

We can read a
single record using
the value in the id
column. We know
that this technique
returns just one
record because the
id number is unique
for each record.

2 ## Reading all the records

If instead of passing
the id number, we pass
the special symbol
:all; then the model
will return an array with
all of the records in the
underlying table.

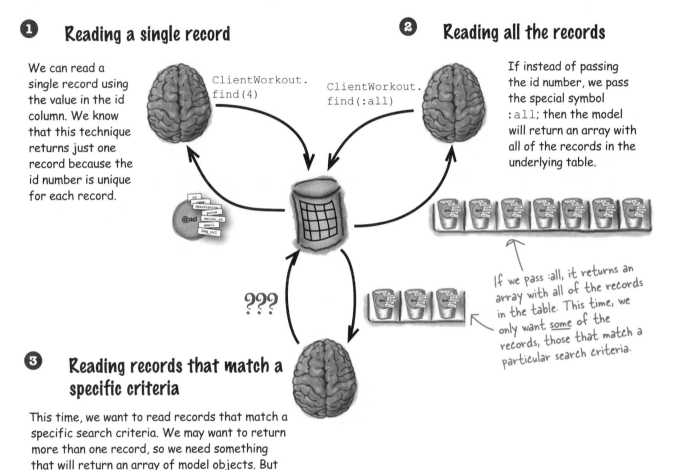

```
ClientWorkout.
find(4)
```

```
ClientWorkout.
find(:all)
```

???

If we pass :all, it returns an
array with all of the records
in the table. This time, we
only want <u>some</u> of the
records, those that match a
particular search criteria.

3 ## Reading records that match a specific criteria

This time, we want to read records that match a
specific search criteria. We may want to return
more than one record, so we need something
that will return an array of model objects. But
we **don't** want a model object for every record—
only those that match the search criteria.

BRAIN POWER

Think about the data in the underlying database table. What does it mean for a
record in the table to match the search criteria? Is there something that would be
true for matching records and false for the rest?

We only need those records where client_name = the search string

The trainers want to search for all of the workouts for a particular customer. The model will need a simple test that will be true for matching records and false for the rest. Something like this:

Is ClientWorkout.client_name = params[:search_string] ?

This is what was entered in the search field.

If the model can apply that test to each of the records in the table, it will find all of the matching records in the table:

id	client_name	trainer	duration_mins	date_of_workout	paid_amount	created_at	updated_at
1	Kirk Stigwood	Clint	60	2009-10-05	50	2008-10-05 20:...	2008-10-05 20:...
2	Lenny Goldberg	Clint	30	2009-07-14	25	2008-10-06 09:...	2008-10-06 09:...
3	Lenny Goldberg	Brad	30	2009-07-19	25	2008-10-06 09:...	2008-10-06 09:...
4	Lenny Goldberg	Sven	90	2009-08-02	75	2008-10-06 09:...	2008-10-06 09:...
5	Lenny Goldberg	Marshall	15	2009-09-29	15	2008-10-06 09:...	2008-10-06 09:...
6	Lenny Goldberg	Clint	30	2009-10-01	25	2008-10-06 09:...	2008-10-06 09:...
7	Lenny Goldberg	Sara	30	2009-10-05	25	2008-10-05 20:...	2008-10-05 20:...

In general terms, then, we need a finder that can find all records that have a particular value in a particular column in the table.

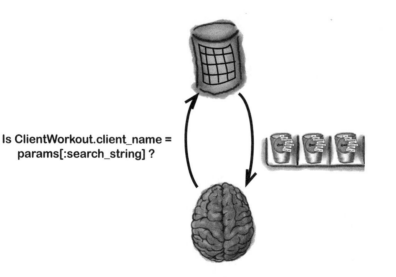

Is ClientWorkout.client_name = params[:search_string] ?

There's a finder for <u>every</u> attribute

Lots of applications need to find all of the records with a certain value in a database column, so Rails makes that really easy to do.

But how? The model code has a finder for each of it's attributes. You don't need to add these finders yourself—Rails provides them. So the ClientWorkout model has finders for the client name, the workout duration, and so on. And each of these finders returns an array containing all of the matching ClientWorkout objects.

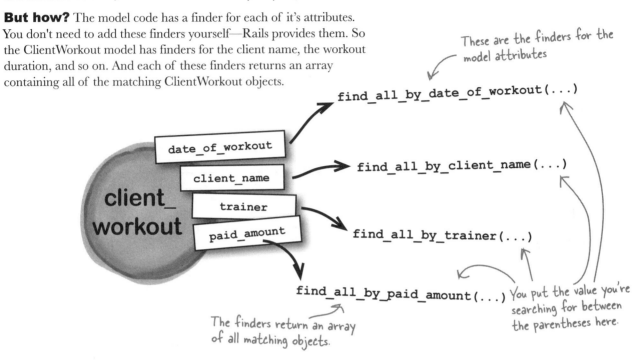

These are the finders for the model attributes

```
find_all_by_date_of_workout(...)

find_all_by_client_name(...)

find_all_by_trainer(...)

find_all_by_paid_amount(...)
```

You put the value you're searching for between the parentheses here.

The finders return an array of all matching objects.

Remember that an attribute in a model object maps to a database column in the underlying table. So each of these finders can be used to find all of the records with a particular value in a particular column.

✏️ Sharpen your pencil

Complete the code for the find method.

```
def find
  @client_workouts = ....................................................................................
end
```

Sharpen your pencil
Solution   Complete the code for the find method.

> We're looking for client names,
> so we use this finder

```
def find
  @client_workouts = ClientWorkout.find_all_by_client_name(params[:search_string])
end
```

> This is the name the user
> entered in the search field.

So what's next?

We now have code that will find all of the records that match the search,
so now we need to display the results back to the user. But how?

**We need to create a find.html.erb page to display
the search results.**

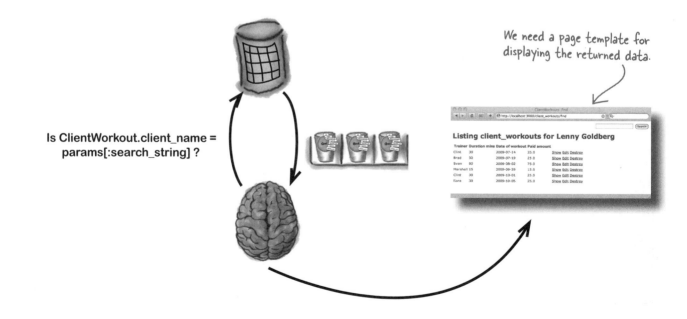

We need a page template for
displaying the returned data.

Is ClientWorkout.client_name =
params[:search_string] ?

Exercise

Create a page template for the find method to display the list of workouts displaying:

```
<Trainer name> <Workout duration> <Date of the workout> <Amount paid>
```

Hint: The index page scaffolding already generated is similar to what you need to produce.

....
....
....
....
....
....
....
....
....
....
....
....
....
....
....
....
....
....
....
....
....
....
....
....

ExerciSe SolutioN

Create a page template for the find method to display the list of work outs displaying:

```
<Trainer name> <Workout duration> <Date of the workout> <Amount paid>
```

Hint: The index page is similar to what you need to produce.

Don't worry if your answer is slightly different.

```erb
<h1>Listing client_workouts for <%= params[:search_string] %></h1>

<table>
  <tr>
    <th>Trainer</th>
    <th>Duration mins</th>
    <th>Date of workout</th>
    <th>Paid amount</th>
  </tr>

<% for client_workout in @client_workouts %>
  <tr>
    <td><%=h client_workout.trainer %></td>
    <td><%=h client_workout.duration_mins %></td>
    <td><%=h client_workout.date_of_workout %></td>
    <td><%=h client_workout.paid_amount %></td>
    <td><%= link_to 'Show', client_workout %></td>
    <td><%= link_to 'Edit', edit_client_workout_path(client_workout) %></td>
    <td><%= link_to 'Destroy', client_workout, :confirm => 'Are you sure?', :method => :delete %></td>
  </tr>
<% end %>
</table>
```

there are no Dumb Questions

Q: Could we have re-used index.html.erb for this?

A: The client name is missing from this template, so it isn't quite the same as the index.html.erb template. But it is always a good idea to reuse code where you can... it just wouldn't have worked out in this case.

TEST DRIVE

The search function should work great now. Let's check it out...

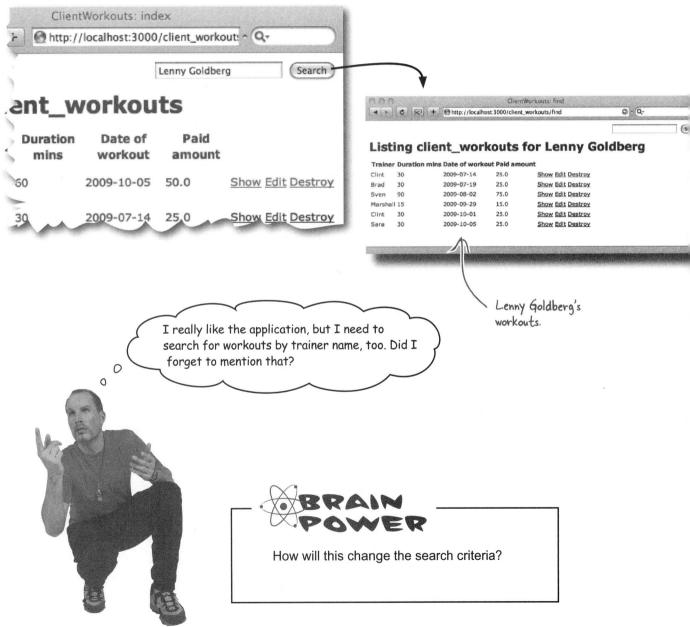

Lenny Goldberg's workouts.

> I really like the application, but I need to search for workouts by trainer name, too. Did I forget to mention that?

BRAIN POWER

How will this change the search criteria?

We need to match <u>either</u> the client name <u>OR</u> the trainer name

The search works by finding all the records with a particular client name. But if the search will also need to find trainers by name, then the logical test it will apply to each record will need to be a little more complicated. Instead of

```
client_name = params[:search_string]
```

the criteria now needs to be:

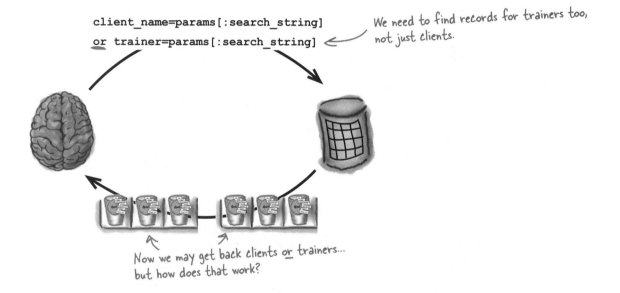

```
client_name=params[:search_string]
or trainer=params[:search_string]
```

We need to find records for trainers too, not just clients.

Now we may get back clients <u>or</u> trainers... but how does that work?

Can you see a problem here?

There's a finder for each of the attributes in the model object. And each of these finders has a simple test that it applies to the records in the database, checking a single column in the database against a given value. But the test is more complex now, so is there some way to specify the test that the finder applies to the database records?

Finders Up Close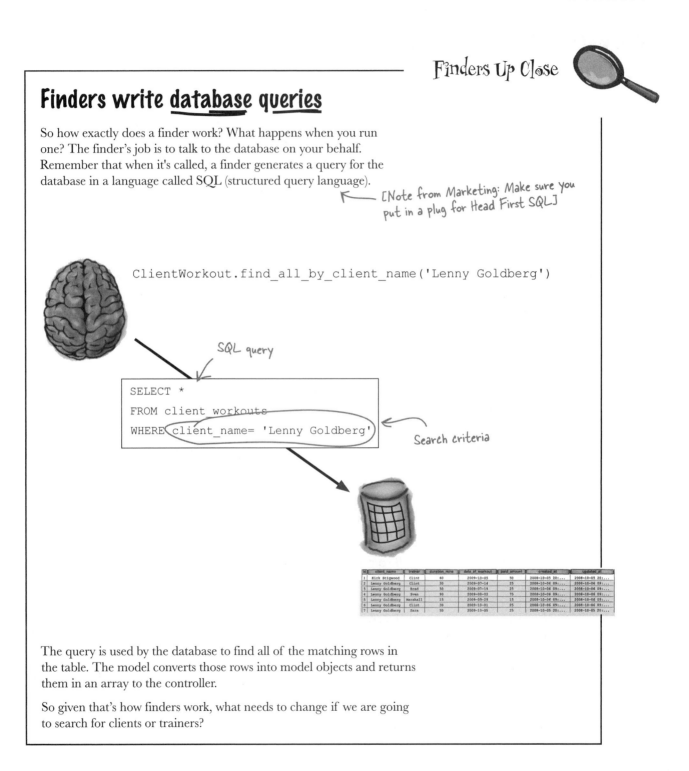

Finders write database queries

So how exactly does a finder work? What happens when you run one? The finder's job is to talk to the database on your behalf. Remember that when it's called, a finder generates a query for the database in a language called SQL (structured query language).

[Note from Marketing: Make sure you put in a plug for Head First SQL]

```
ClientWorkout.find_all_by_client_name('Lenny Goldberg')
```

SQL query

```
SELECT *
FROM client_workouts
WHERE client_name= 'Lenny Goldberg'
```

Search criteria

id	client_name	trainer	duration_mins	date_of_workout	paid_amount	created_at	updated_at
1	Kirk Stigwood	Clint	40	2009-10-05	50	2008-10-05 20:...	2008-10-05 20:...
2	Lenny Goldberg	Clint	30	2009-07-14	25	2008-10-06 09:...	2008-10-06 09:...
3	Lenny Goldberg	Brad	30	2009-07-19	25	2008-10-06 09:...	2008-10-06 09:...
4	Lenny Goldberg	Sven	90	2009-08-02	75	2008-10-06 09:...	2008-10-06 09:...
5	Lenny Goldberg	Marshall	15	2009-09-28	15	2008-10-06 09:...	2008-10-06 09:...
6	Lenny Goldberg	Clint	30	2009-10-01	25	2008-10-06 09:...	2008-10-06 09:...
7	Lenny Goldberg	Sara	30	2009-10-05	25	2008-10-05 20:...	2008-10-05 20:...

The query is used by the database to find all of the matching rows in the table. The model converts those rows into model objects and returns them in an array to the controller.

So given that's how finders work, what needs to change if we are going to search for clients or trainers?

We need to be able to modify the conditions used in the SQL query

We need some way of telling the model to generate a SQL query that looks something like this:

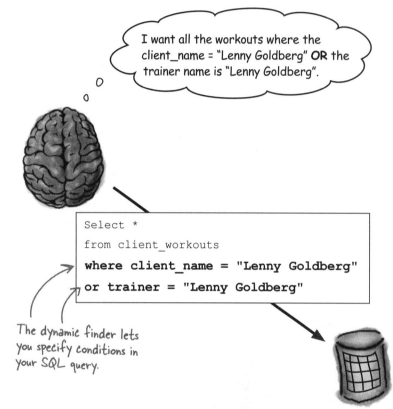

I want all the workouts where the client_name = "Lenny Goldberg" **OR** the trainer name is "Lenny Goldberg".

```
Select *
from client_workouts
where client_name = "Lenny Goldberg"
or trainer = "Lenny Goldberg"
```

The dynamic finder lets you specify conditions in your SQL query.

But the conditions in the SQL query are generated by the finder method. We are able to pass in strings to the finder (like "Lenny Goldberg") but so far we have not done anything to modify the actual structure of the conditions that become part of the SQL sent to the database.

Will being able to modify the SQL query parameters actually be that big a deal? Well—yes, it will. Finders that look for matching values in particular attributes are useful—but specifying the SQL conditions lets you do so much more. It lets you override the default behavior of a finder, and get complete control over the data that is accessed by the model. That's just what we need here, too: more control over the SQL query.

So how do we modify those conditions?

Use :conditions to supply SQL

The finders that are generated for each of the attributes are simple and easy to use, but the trouble is they're not very flexible. You often need to make more complex queries on the database.

For that reason, all finders allow you to pass a named parameter called `:conditions` containing extra conditions to be added to the SQL that the finder generates.

Here's one way in which this could work with the trainer/client search:

```
@client_workouts = ClientWorkout.find(:all,
:conditions=>["client_name = 'Lenny Goldberg' OR trainer = 'Lenny Goldberg'"])
```

The condition parameter is set to an array

This version of the finder will return all of the records that have a trainer or client called 'Lenny Goldberg', but can you see what the problem is? What if we want to search for someone ***other than*** Lenny? What we *really* want is to search for whatever is recorded in the `params[:search_string]`. But how?

Fortunately, Rails has a way of doing just that. It allows you to parameterize the conditions like this:

```
@client_workouts = ClientWorkout.find(:all,
:conditions=>["client_name = ? OR trainer = ?",
params[:search_string], params[:search_string]])
```

Instead of searching for Lenny Goldberg, we can search using whatever's in params[:search_string]. The ? gets replaced by that value.

The ?s in the first string in the conditions array are replaced in sequence with the values that follow. This means that the finder will now be able to generate the correct SQL statement for whatever is in the search parameter. The relevant records are returned for whoever the trainer searches for.

Because Rails inserts these parameter values into the SQL for us, it will do it safely and avoid a type security attack called "SQL Injection."

So how well does this work?

Test Drive

Update your finder code, and reload your application.

I really like this search!

If I search for a client, I get their workouts.

ClientWorkouts: find

http://localhost:3000/client_workouts/find

[Search]

Listing client_workouts for Lenny Goldberg

Trainer	Duration mins	Date of workout	Paid amount			
Clint	30	2009-07-14	25.0	Show	Edit	Destroy
Brad	30	2009-07-19	25.0	Show	Edit	Destroy
Sven	90	2009-08-02	75.0	Show	Edit	Destroy
Marshall	15	2009-09-29	15.0	Show	Edit	Destroy
Clint	30	2009-10-01	25.0	Show	Edit	Destroy
Sara	30	2009-10-05	25.0	Show	Edit	Destroy

If I search for me, I find the workouts I ran.

ClientWorkouts: find

http://localhost:3000/client_workouts/find

[Search]

Listing client_workouts for Clint

Trainer	Duration mins	Date of workout	Paid amount			
Clint	60	2009-10-05	50.0	Show	Edit	Destroy
Clint	30	2009-07-14	25.0	Show	Edit	Destroy
Clint	30	2009-10-01	25.0	Show	Edit	Destroy

The Fitness Club has started to record all of the games played on their outdoor baseball field. Match up the database finders with how they might be used.

Finder

Purpose

```
BaseballGame.find(:all,
:conditions=>[
'month_no > ? and month_no < ?',
9, 3])
```

Games played out of season

```
BaseballGame.find(:all,
:conditions=>[
'month_no > ? or month_no < ?',
3, 9])
```

Actually this query will never return anything, so it won't be used

```
BaseballGame.find(:all,
:conditions=>[
'month_no > ? and month_no < ?',
3, 9])
```

Games played in season

```
BaseballGame.find(:all,
:conditions=>[
'month_no > ? or month_no < ?',
9, 3])
```

This query just returns everything, so it won't be used either

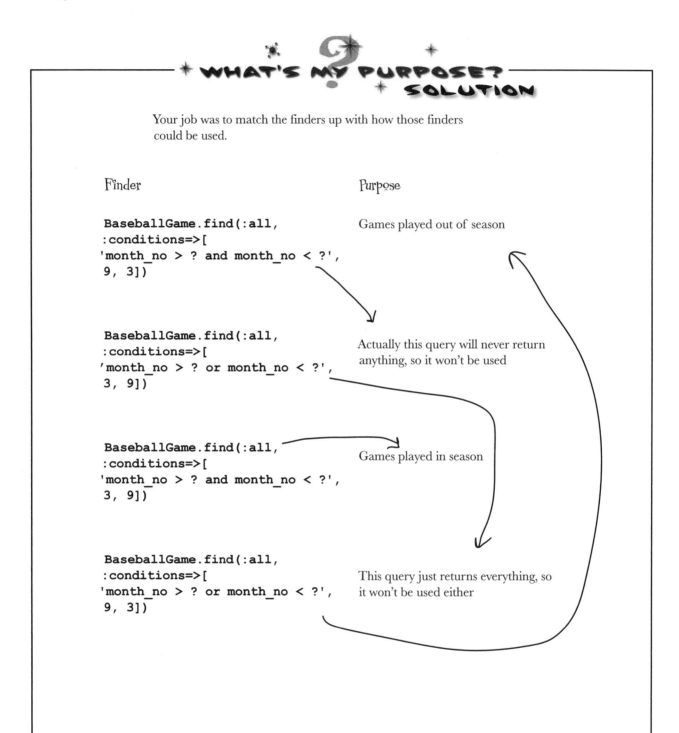

Then there's a knock at the door...

Just as you're demonstrating the system there's a knock at the door.
It's some of the guys from the body building club.

Hey, what's the deal here?
Somebody's saying we haven't paid, and
they're not letting us into the gym! So
you're the one to talk to about that?

Can you say 'roid rage,
anyone? Better help
these guys out...

**It seems like there's been a problem with the
data entered into the system... get ready for the
next chapter, where we'll dig deeper into the
bodybuilding problem.**

Tools for your Rails Toolbox

You've got Chapter 4 under your belt, and now you've added the ability to choose whether to use scaffolding and how to smartly select the correct data for your application.

Rails Tools

find(:all, :conditions=>[...]) allows you to specify the SQL used to select records from the database.

form_tag generates simple forms that are not bound to model objects.

Ruby Tools

puts <string> displays a string on the console (the one running the web server)

5 validating your data

Preventing mistakes

Everyone makes mistakes... but many of them are preventable!

Even with the very best of intentions, your users will still enter bad data into your web app, **leaving you to deal with the consequences**. But just imagine if there was some way of **preventing mistakes** from happening in the first place. That's where **validators** come in. Keep reading, and we'll show you how to add **clever Rails validation** to your web app so that you can **take control** of what data is allowed in—and what needs to be kept out.

Watch out—there's bad data in the room

Everything seemed to be going so well with the personal trainers' web app, at least until the body builders showed up. The body builders say they've paid their gym dues, and have the receipts to prove it, but their payments aren't showing up on the system.

> I don't get it. I entered a paid amount of $50 and clicked save, but it's just showing up as 0.0.

So what went wrong?

Clicking on the save button should have saved the data into the database, but something went wrong. Instead of saving the amount paid as **$50**, the amount got saved as **0.0**. But how? Let's take a look at the chain of events that occurred.

1 A trainer enters "$50" into the paid field in the view, and then clicks on the save button. A value of "$50" is passed to the controller.

2 The controller receives a value of "$50" for the amount paid, and it passes this along to the model.

3 The model receives the value "$50," but there's a problem. Since the value contains a $ symbol, the model can't convert it to a number. It saves the value 0.0 to the database instead.

> You say paid_amount has a value of "$50"? I'll tell the model.

> "$50" isn't a number, so I'll save it as 0.0.

The problem was caused by the trainer entering the wrong sort of data in the web page, and we need to prevent this happening again. We need to write code to validate the form data before it's written to the database—*but where should validation code go?*

> Look guys, it's obvious. The form is in the view, so the validation should be in the view too.

Laura thinks the model.

Mark thinks the controller.

Bob thinks the view.

Mark: Why does it matter where the validation is?

Bob: We fix the problem where it happens. The error happens in the form, so that's where it should be fixed.

Mark: No - look. Just put a check in the controller. The controller calls the save and update methods. We can just make the controller able to decide whether or not to save the object.

Bob: But the problem occurs in the form.

Laura: I'm not sure. Isn't the problem really in the model?

Mark: The model's just data. Most of the code we write is in the controller.

Laura: I thought the model was more than just data. Can't we put code in there, too?

Mark: But the clever logic is all in the *controller*.

Bob: No - it's easier than that. You just put a JavaScript check in the form's markup.

Mark: What if the user's switched JavaScript off in their browser?

Bob: Hey, come on, *nobody* switches JavaScript off anymore.

Laura: But how can you rely on that? Particularly when it's obvious where the code should go.

Mark: The controller.

Laura: The model.

Sharpen your pencil

Where do you think the validation should go? Why? Write your answer below.

....

....

....

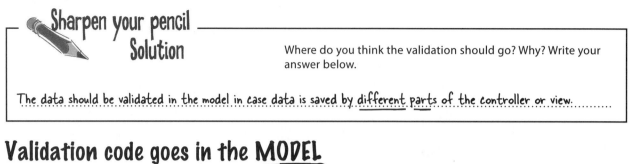

Sharpen your pencil
Solution

Where do you think the validation should go? Why? Write your answer below.

The data should be validated in the model in case data is saved by <u>different parts</u> of the controller or view.

Validation code goes in the <u>MODEL</u>

The trouble with putting validation code in the view or the controller is that two separate bits of code might try to save values to the database. If we have insert and edit methods in the controller, for instance, both of these need validation. If the validation is centralized in the model, it doesn't matter how data gets stored—validation on that data will still occur.

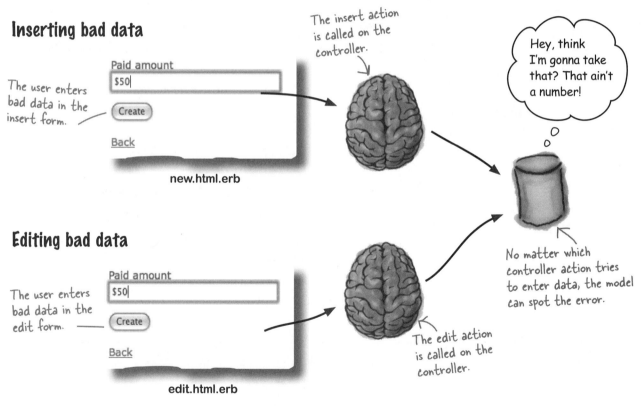

Inserting bad data

The user enters bad data in the insert form.

Paid amount
$50|
Create
Back

new.html.erb

The insert action is called on the controller.

Hey, think I'm gonna take that? That ain't a number!

Editing bad data

The user enters bad data in the edit form.

Paid amount
$50|
Create
Back

edit.html.erb

The edit action is called on the controller.

No matter which controller action tries to enter data, the model can spot the error.

In general, it's a good idea to ***validate in the model***. And after all, that's one of the reasons that we *have* a model layer. The model isn't just data. The reason we wrap the database in a layer of code is so that we can add the kind of smarts—like validation—that a database on its own doesn't provide. So how exactly do we add validation to the model?

Rails uses <u>validators</u> for simple validation

Every system needs to perform some kind of check on the data that gets entered into it, and sometimes the checking code can be long and complicated.

So what can Rails do to help? After all, the checks you need to make are pretty customized, aren't they? Well - yes and no. The set of validation rules for **your** data will probably be unique to your system. But the individual rules themselves will probably be checking for a small set of typical errors, like **missing data**, or data in the **wrong format**, or data of the **wrong type**.

That's why Rails comes with a set of built-in standard checks called **validators**. A validator is a Ruby object that looks at the data people have entered and performs a simple check on it. When does it do the check? Whenever someone tries to save or update the data in the database.

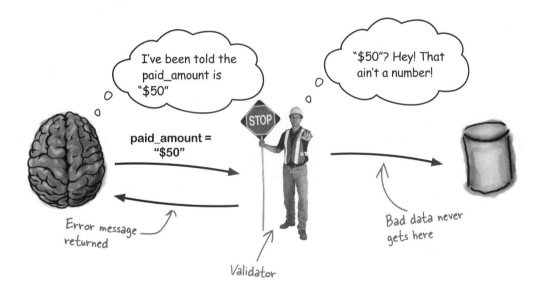

Validators are a quick and effective way of improving the quality of your data. They will help you filter what is and isn't allowed into your database. And in the cases where the data is bad, they will even provide a set of error messages to help the user diagnose what went wrong.

But how do validators work?

So how do validators work?

Let's follow a ClientWorkout as it goes through a validation sequence.

 The user submits the details of a ClientWorkout.
The problem is, the `paid_amount` field contains "$50" rather than "50", and "$50" can't be converted to a numeric value.

> **Paid amount**
>
> `$50|`
>
> (Create)
>
> Back

 The controller converts the form data into a ClientWorkout model object.
The model object stores a copy of the form data, and it uses that to generate the values of its attributes. If you ask the object for the value of its `paid_amount` attribute, it tries to convert the "$50" to a number, but can't, so the controller says the `paid_amount` is 0.0.

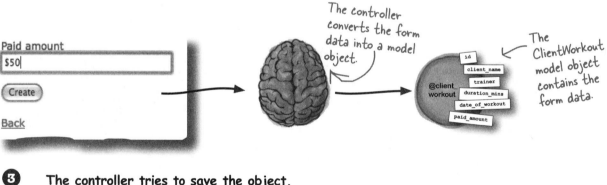

The controller converts the form data into a model object.

The ClientWorkout model object contains the form data.

③ **The controller tries to save the object.**
The controller asks the model object to save itself. Ordinarily the object would save a record of itself to the database with a `paid_amount` value of 0.0. But if there's a validator on the model, then things are a little different...

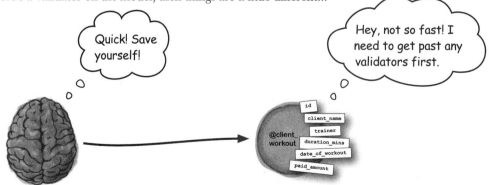

Quick! Save yourself!

Hey, not so fast! I need to get past any validators first.

4 **The model object runs its validator(s).**

When the model object is asked to insert or update a record to the database, it first runs its validators. The validators check the values in the underlying form data stored inside the ClientWorkout object. Our `paid_amount` validator records an error because "$50" is not numeric.

5 **The model object decides whether it's OK to save the record.**

Only after the validator has run will the model object decide if it can save the record to the database. How does it decide? It looks to see if any errors have been created. The `paid_amount` validator failed so the model skips saving a record and tells the controller that something went wrong.

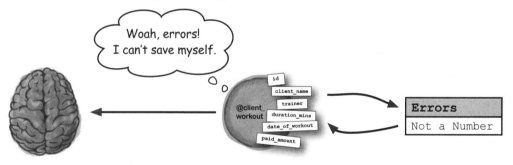

6 **The controller returns the user to the form.**

The code in the controller knows that something went wrong, so it returns the user to the form page so that the errors can be corrected.

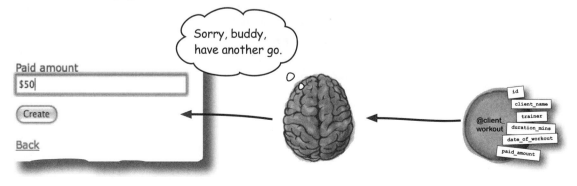

Let's check if something is a number

We'll check the `paid_amount` field with a validator called
validates_numericality_of. The validator will belong to a model
object, so we need to add it to the model code in **client_workout.rb**:

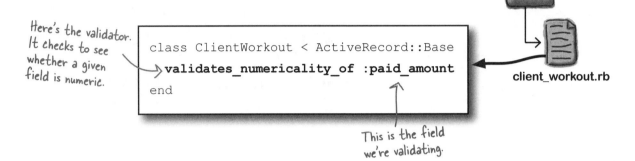

Here's the validator.
It checks to see
whether a given
field is numeric.

```
class ClientWorkout < ActiveRecord::Base
  validates_numericality_of :paid_amount
end
```

This is the field
we're validating.

app

models

client_workout.rb

This will create an *instance* of the validator for each `ClientWorkout`
object.

The validator needs the name of the attribute it's going to check. Like
pretty much all names in Ruby, the attribute name is given as a *symbol*:
:paid_amount.

Remember that a *symbol* is a little like a **string**. Symbols always begin with
a colon (`:`) and are generally used to refer to the names of things, like the
names of fields and attributes.

So how will this all actually work in our app? Let's say the controller has a
ClientWorkout model object called **@client_workout**.

Whenever the controller calls **@client_workout.save** or
@client_workout.update_attributes, the model object will run
the `validates_numericality_of` validator.

If the original form data inside the model object has "$50" recorded
against the `paid_amount` field, the validator will generate an error. Rails
will spot the error and abort the database update.

That's the theory. Let's see if this all works.

Test Drive

Now that the validator's in place, let's try the page out. Here's what happens now when we try to insert a record with bad data in the `paid_amount` field:

Here's the New page with an amount of $50 entered in the paid_amount field.

> **ClientWorkouts: new**
> http://localhost:3000/client_workouts/new
>
> **New client_workout**
> Client name
> Lenny Goldberg
> Trainer
> Horst
> Duration mins
> 30
> Date of workout
> 2009 / November / 7
> Paid amount
> $50
> (Create)
> Back

> **ClientWorkouts: create**
> http://localhost:3000/client_workouts
>
> # New client_workout
>
> **1 error prohibited this client workout from being saved**
>
> There were problems with the following fields:
>
> - Paid amount is not a number
>
> Client name
> Lenny Goldberg

The "$50" value is not numeric, so an error message is generated, the workout is not saved to the database, and the user is returned to the form to correct the error.

So what about the Edit page? Does the validator work there too? It should, because the model will call exactly the same validator when someone tries to update a record on the database.

This time let's try with the Edit page.

> **ClientWorkouts: edit**
> http://localhost:3000/client_workouts/4/edit
>
> **Editing client_workout**
> Client name
> Lenny Goldberg
> Trainer
> Clint
> Duration mins
> 30
> Date of workout
> 2009 / November / 10
> Paid amount
> $50
> (Update)
> Show | Back

> **ClientWorkouts: update**
> http://localhost:3000/client_workouts/4
>
> # Editing client_workout
>
> **1 error prohibited this client workout from being saved**
>
> There were problems with the following fields:
>
> - Paid amount is not a number
>
> Client name
> Lenny Goldberg

> That cleared up the issue with client's dues, but I've had some other problems too...

Talk about high maintenance clients...

Users have been leaving out data on their workout forms

Some people are have been leaving fields blank. For example, one of the trainers has been forgetting to enter his own name on some of the workouts he's entered. Later on, when he searches for all of his own workouts, he can't find the ones where he left his name off.

This is what you get when you search for Steve's workouts... but the new David Ferrie one is missing.

Steve adds a client's workout, for David Ferrie...

Steve keeps forgetting to enter his name.

...but now the workout's gone missing.

And not only does the trainer's name need to completed, but the client's name as well. Lenny Goldberg had a couple of sessions where his name wasn't recorded. Lenny normally gets billed at the end of the month, so when they searched for his training sessions to find which ones didn't have payments, they couldn't find them. The personal trainers just can't afford for this to happen!

So can validators help?

So far, we've only used a validator to check and see if an input value is numeric. But there's a whole family of validators that can do anything from checking that a value is in a list, to whether a value is unique in a particular column in a table.

How do we check for mandatory fields?

There's a validator we can use to check for values in mandatory fields. The validator that does this is **validates_presence_of**:

validates_presence_of :field_name

The name of the mandatory field goes here.

Here's the code with the validators in place:

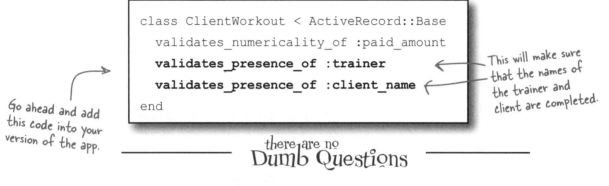

```
class ClientWorkout < ActiveRecord::Base
  validates_numericality_of :paid_amount
  validates_presence_of :trainer
  validates_presence_of :client_name
end
```

This will make sure that the names of the trainer and client are completed.

Go ahead and add this code into your version of the app.

there are no Dumb Questions

Q: If a validator fails, does the model object run the other validators anyway?

A: Good question: yes. Even though the model object will know after the first failure that it will be able to abort the save operation, the model still runs the other validators before telling the controller about any failures.

Q: Why's that?

A: Imagine you have made several errors on a form. By running all of the validators, the model objects ensures that you see *all* of the error messages, so that you can fix all of the errors before resubmitting the form. If you only ever saw the first error, you may have to re-submit the form several times.

Q: Why does the model object keep a copy of the form data? Why doesn't it just store the values from the form in ordinary attributes?

A: The model object needs to run validators on the original strings submitted from the form. If, say, it stored the `paid_amount` value in a numeric attribute, it would have to convert the value to something like 0.0. That would hide the fact that there had been a problem.

Q: So when I ask a ClientWorkout object for @client_workout.paid_amount, isn't that returning a proper attribute value?

A: What the `@client_workout` object will do is look at the value of the submitted form-field ("$50") and then return a numeric version of that. It will do that each time you ask for `@client_workout.paid_amount`

Q: So is that why it saves "$50" to the database as 0.0 ?

A: Yes. If there are no validators, the model constructs a SQL INSERT or UPDATE statement from the attribute-value of the

model object. When it looks at the value of `@client_workout.paid_amount`, the value is 0.0, and that's what gets sent to the database.

Q: Can I ask the model object to skip validation?

A: Yes. If you call `@client_workout.save(false)` it will save the object without running the validators.

Q: Can I change the error messages?

A: Yes - you can provide your own error messages as an extra string: `validates_presence_of :trainer, "Where's your name?"`

Q: How do the error messages get displayed?

A: There is a tag in the form called `f.error_messages`. We'll find out more about the process later on.

Test Drive

Let's fire up a browser and try to enter some bad data into the New form.
Hopefully, our new validator code will catch any problems.

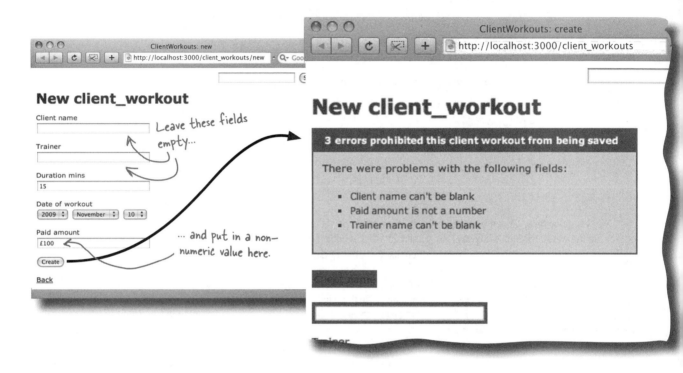

New client_workout

Client name

Leave these fields empty...

Trainer

Duration mins

15

Date of workout

2009 ⬦ November ⬦ 10 ⬦

Paid amount

£100

... and put in a non-numeric value here.

(Create)

Back

New client_workout

3 errors prohibited this client workout from being saved

There were problems with the following fields:

- Client name can't be blank
- Paid amount is not a number
- Trainer name can't be blank

This is great, it looks like you've fixed our bad data problems. Thanks!

✳ WHAT'S MY PURPOSE? ✳

We only needed to check a couple things for this system, but let's see what other validators are available. See if you can work out what validators were used for what purpose:

```
validates_length_of :field1,
  :maximum=>32
```

Check that a credit card # looks like a credit card #

```
validates_format_of :field1,
:with=>/regular expression/
```

Check that a mass-mailing will not go to the same person twice

```
validates_uniqueness_of :field1
```

Did they spell the muscle group correctly?

```
validates_inclusion_of :field1,
:in=>[val1, val2, ..., valn]
```

Check that a username fits into a database column

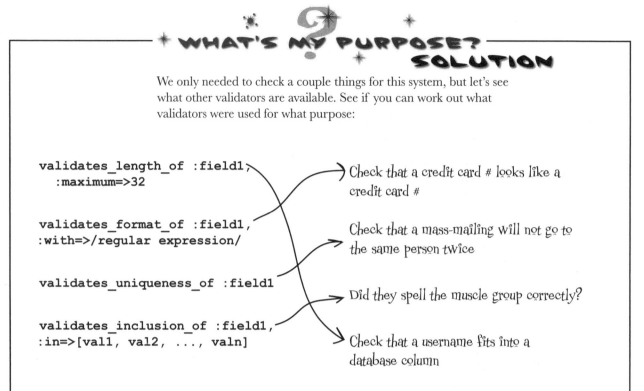

WHAT'S MY PURPOSE? SOLUTION

We only needed to check a couple things for this system, but let's see what other validators are available. See if you can work out what validators were used for what purpose:

```
validates_length_of :field1,
   :maximum=>32
```

Check that a credit card # looks like a credit card #

```
validates_format_of :field1,
:with=>/regular expression/
```

Check that a mass-mailing will not go to the same person twice

```
validates_uniqueness_of :field1
```

Did they spell the muscle group correctly?

```
validates_inclusion_of :field1,
:in=>[val1, val2, ..., valn]
```

Check that a username fits into a database column

Validators are simple and work well

The data quality is now much higher, and workout data has stopped mysteriously vanishing. The accountant is happy because she has a record of all the clients who haven't paid and the body builders no longer have to worry about their payments going missing.

We smoothed over the problems with the body builders and because you fixed the problem so quickly, we avoided any new issues arising. Good job!

BULLET POINTS

- Validators are defined on the **model**.

- Validators check form data which is stored in the **model object**.

- Validators run *before* database inserts or updates.

- A model object may have **several validators**.

- The model object will run **all validators** each time.

- The **controller** should check if the save or update was successful.

- The user will be returned to the form if there are **errors**.

- There are **many validators** available.

Everything was going so well until...

Hi - this is Sarah from MeBay. Can you give us a call? We started to add validators to your code and they don't seem to be working.

Something strange has happened at MeBay

The folks at MeBay heard about your work with validators so they tried
adding them to the code you'd written for them.

But they didn't get such a good result...

What happened to the ad for
my stuff, baby? I spent a long time
crafting it then... boom! No complaints,
no errors, no nothing. But my work
disappeared into cyberspace and I
ain't seen it since!

Wow... can you say
unsatisfied customer?

All MeBay did was add validators to check that all the fields on new
adds were completed, and that the numeric and email fields were
correctly formatted.

Let's look at what's happening in more detail...

The validators work, but they don't display errors

Someone entered an ad with a blank price to see what's wrong with the validators.

This is the Ad model on the MeBay application, with its new validators.

1 An ad is created without a price.

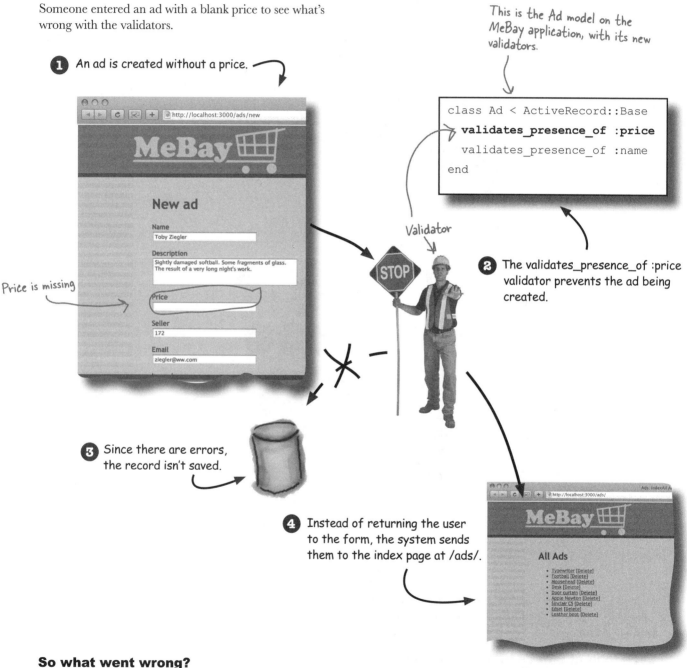

```
class Ad < ActiveRecord::Base
  validates_presence_of :price
  validates_presence_of :name
end
```

Validator

2 The validates_presence_of :price validator prevents the ad being created.

Price is missing

3 Since there are errors, the record isn't saved.

4 Instead of returning the user to the form, the system sends them to the index page at /ads/.

So what went wrong?

Sharpen your pencil

1. If an ad is correctly entered, the next page a person sees is the new ad's page. Why did Rails display the index page at /ads/ instead of the New ad page with errors?

....

....

....

....

....

....

....

....

2. The validators worked correctly on the health club application. Why do you think they didn't work on MeBay?

....

....

....

....

....

....

....

....

Sharpen your pencil
Solution

1. If an ad is correctly entered, the next page a person sees is the new ad's page. Why did Rails display the index page at /ads/ instead?

A record's ID is blank until it's saved. Normally the app redirects to
/ads/<id>
Because the ad wasn't saved, the user got redirected to:
/ads/<blank>

2. The validators worked correctly on the health club application. Why do you think they didn't work on MeBay?

The health club app was created with scaffolding but the MeBay app was created manually.
Scaffolding code checks for errors and displays them... but our custom code doesn't!

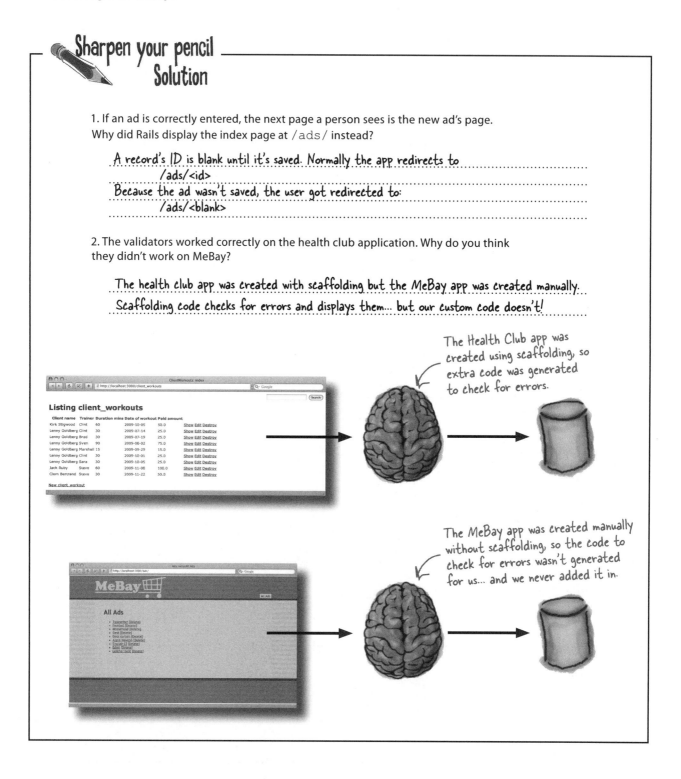

The Health Club app was created using scaffolding, so extra code was generated to check for errors.

The MeBay app was created manually without scaffolding, so the code to check for errors wasn't generated for us... and we never added it in.

If you build your own pages, you need to write your own error message code

When you scaffold part of an application, Rails generates the code you need to handle errors. But if you are creating code manually, you're pretty much on your own. So we need to change the MeBay code to handle errors.

The code will need to do two things:

1 If an error occurs, the system needs to redisplay the page where the error occurred.

Hmm, looks like you've got some errors here.

Errors? We'd better redisplay the page so they can be fixed.

2 The form page will need to display all of the errors that were generated by the validators.

If there are errors, the page needs to show error messages.

So what's the first thing the application needs to do?

The controller needs to know if there was an error

If the user enters bad data into a form, Rails needs to send the user back to the form with the error. Page flow like this is handled by the controller. Remember that the controller is in charge of what data is read and written and which pages are displayed.

What does the controller code need to do to handle errors in the MeBay application? Here's what the app currently does when a new ad is submitted:

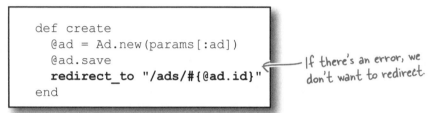

```
def create
  @ad = Ad.new(params[:ad])
  @ad.save
  redirect_to "/ads/#{@ad.id}"
end
```
If there's an error, we don't want to redirect.

The code will always do the same thing—try to save the ad to the database and then go to a page to display the data. It doesn't currently matter if the save *fails*... and that's a big problem

But **how do we tell** if the save method has failed? Well, in Ruby every command has a **return value**. If there's a problem saving an ad, the @ad.save command will return **false**. We can use the return value of @ad.save to determine whether we should **redisplay the page**... or display the saved ad.

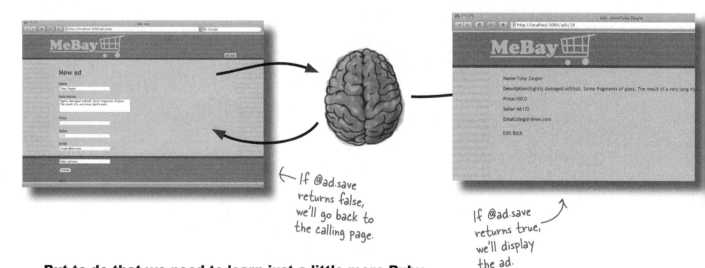

If @ad.save returns false, we'll go back to the calling page.

If @ad.save returns true, we'll display the ad.

But to do that we need to learn just a little more Ruby...

Pool Puzzle

The code you need to correct the page flow is given here. It uses a Ruby language feature we've not met yet—the `if` statement. Your job is to take code snippets from the pool and construct the code needed to correct the page flow.

If the save works, then redirect to display the new ad.

```
if       ........................
         ........................  ........................  ........................
         ........................
         ........................  ........................  ........................
         ........................
```

If it fails, then redisplay the "ad/new" template.

Note: each thing from the pool can only be used once!

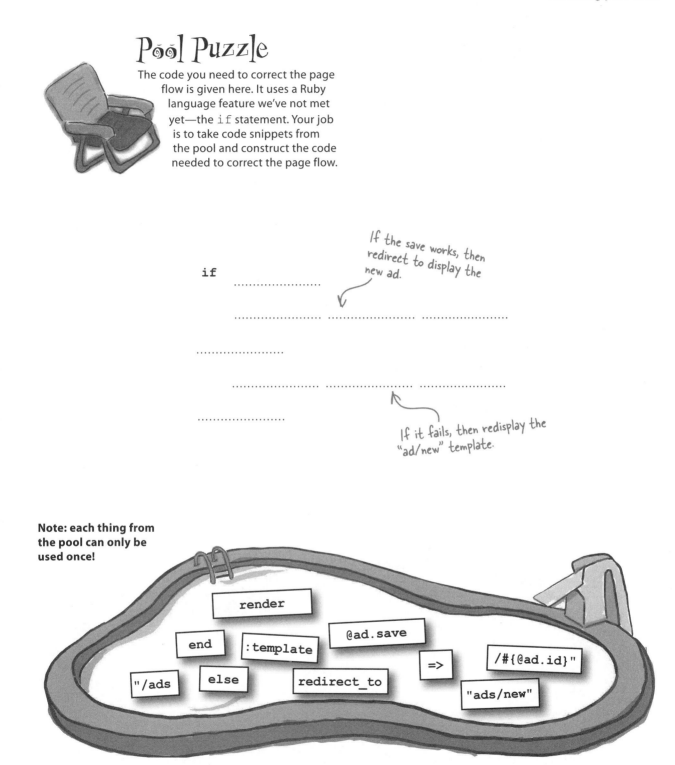

```
render
end        :template        @ad.save
"/ads      else        redirect_to        =>        /#{@ad.id}"
                                           "ads/new"
```

Pool Puzzle Solution

The code you need to correct the page flow is given here. It uses a Ruby language feature we've not met yet—the `if` statement. Your job is to take code snippets from the pool and construct the code needed to correct the page flow.

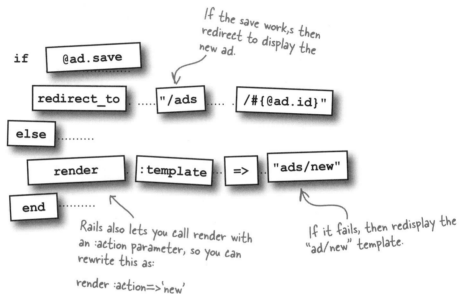

If the save works, then redirect to display the new ad.

```
if      @ad.save

        redirect_to ...... "/ads ..... ./#{@ad.id}"

    else .........

        render    :template .. => .. "ads/new"

    end .........
```

Rails also lets you call render with an :action parameter, so you can rewrite this as:

`render :action=>'new'`

If it fails, then redisplay the "ad/new" template.

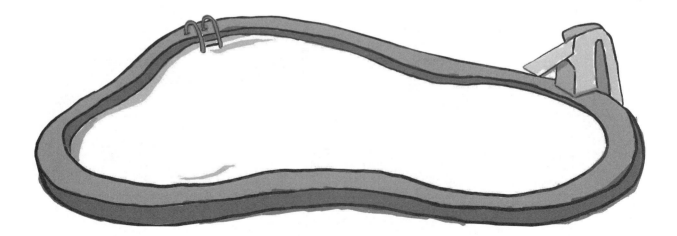

TEST DRIVE

Update your MeBay code to include some custom page control. Now what happens now if we miss putting a value in the price field?

You may want to re-download MeBay from the Head First Labs website to get all their updates.

We're returned to the same form, but no errors are displayed.

Now when the validators run, the controller spots there's a problem with the form data and redisplays the form, so the user can correct the problem. The model doesn't save the record, and the controller is now working correctly.

Except... Isn't there something missing?

We still need to display error messages!

It's good that the app redisplays the form—but **then what**?

To fix form problems, a user needs to know **what went wrong**. They need *error messages* that show them:

1 Which **fields** had a problem

2 Exactly what those **problems** were

Every time one of the validators *fails*, it stores an error message in the **model**. But we want to display the error messages in the **view**. That means the messages need to be transferred from the model to the view.

Which part of the **interface** is tightly bound to a model object?

The form! And the form object has a special method that can generate an error block. That method is called **error_messages**:

app

views

ads

new.html.erb

The error messages are generated by a method of the form object called error_messages.

```
<h1>New ad</h1>
<% form_for(@ad, :url=>{:action=>'create'}) do |f| %>
<%= f.error_messages %>
  <p><b>Name</b><br /><%= f.text_field :name %></p>
  <p><b>Description</b><br /><%= f.text_area :description %></p>
  <p><b>Price</b><br /><%= f.text_field :price %></p>
  <p><b>Seller</b><br /><%= f.text_field :seller_id %></p>
  <p><b>Email</b><br /><%= f.text_field :email %></p>
  <p><b>Img url</b><br /><%= f.text_field :img_url %></p>
  <p><%= f.submit "Create" %></p>
<% end %>
```

Test Drive

The folks at MeBay are now much happier. The validations keep their data clean and the users can now see straight away what the problems are and how to fix them.

> This time around, we're returned to the same form, and errors are displayed. ☺

It's time to release the new version of the code to the public and see what they think about it.

The MeBay system is looking pretty sweet

Now that the system is reporting errors correctly, the folks at MeBay are adding more and more validators. The controller checks for the errors and reports back any problems. Before long the data in the system has really great quality, and the number of errors drops dramatically.

This code is totally tripendicular! Now if I make an error, it lets me know straightaway, baby!

There's just one more thing to do. The validators prevent any major data problems, but the errors are only displayed when a **new** ad is posted.

But errors still aren't reported when ads are <u>edited</u> . . .

Exercise

This is the code that runs when the "edit" page is submitted.

```
def update
  @ad = Ad.find(params[:id])
  @ad.update_attributes(params[:ad])
  redirect_to "/ads/#{@ad.id}"
end
```

Returns true if the update worked.

Rewrite it to respond to errors correctly.

....

....

....

....

....

....

....

....

Write down the name of the file that needs error message display code.

....

This is the code that runs when the "edit" page is submitted.

Exercise Solution

```
def update
  @ad = Ad.find(params[:id])
  @ad.update_attributes(params[:ad])
  redirect_to "/ads/#{@ad.id}"
end
```

Returns true if the update worked.

Rewrite it to respond to errors correctly.

```
def update
  @ad = Ad.find(params[:id])
  if @ad.update_attributes(params[:ad])
    redirect_to "/ads/#{@ad.id}"
  else
    render :template=>"/ads/edit"
  end
end
```

Or you could use:
render :action=>:edit

Write down the name of the file that needs error message display code.

app/views/ads/edit.html.erb

```
<h1>Editing <%= @ad.name %></h1>
<% form_for(@ad,:url=>{:action=>'update'}) do |f| %>
  <%= f.error_messages %>
  <p><b>Name</b><br /><%= f.text_field :name %></p>
```

Tools for your Rails Toolbox

You've got Chapter 5 under your belt, and now you've added the ability to use validators.

Rails Tools

validates_length_of :fieldl, :maximum=>32 checks the field is no longer than 32 characters

validates_format_of :fieldl, :with=>/regular expression/ checks that the field matches the regular expression

validates_uniqueness_of :fieldl checks that no other record in the table has the same value for fieldl

validates_inclusion_of :fieldl, :in=>[vall, val2, ..., valn] checks that the field has one of the given values

f.error_messages displays errors within a form

The save and update_attributes methods on model objects return true if they work, and false if they don't

render :template=>"a/template" renders output using the app/views/a/template.html.erb file

render :action=>'new' renders the template for the new action

6 making connections

Bringing it all together

Take a bunch of fine ingredients, mix them all together, and you'll end up with something that tastes just swell.

Some things are stronger together than apart.

So far you've had a taste of some of the **key Rails ingredients**. You've created entire web applications and taken what Rails generates and **customized** it for your needs. But out in the real world, **life can be more complex**. Read on... it's time to build some **multi-functional web pages**. Not only that, it's time to deal with **difficult data relationships** and take control of your data by writing your own **custom validators**.

Coconut Airways need a booking system

There's no better way of traveling between islands than by seaplane, and Coconut Airways has an entire fleet. They offer scenic tours, excursions, and a handy shuttle service between all the local islands. Their service is proving popular with tourists and locals alike.

Demand for their flights is sky-high, and they need an online reservation system to help them. The system needs to manage flight and seat bookings. Here's the data they need to store:

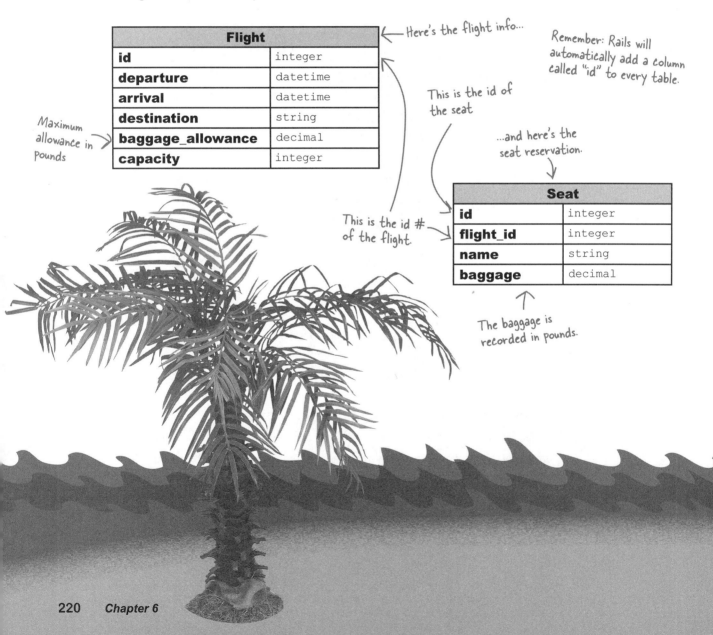

Flight	
id	integer
departure	datetime
arrival	datetime
destination	string
baggage_allowance	decimal
capacity	integer

← Here's the flight info...

Remember: Rails will automatically add a column called "id" to every table.

Maximum allowance in Pounds

This is the id of the seat

...and here's the seat reservation.

Seat	
id	integer
flight_id	integer
name	string
baggage	decimal

This is the id # of the flight.

The baggage is recorded in pounds.

Sharpen your pencil

What are the instructions to:

1. Create an app called `coconut`?

....
....
....

2. Scaffold the flight data?

....
....
....

3. Scaffold the seat booking data?

....
....
....

4. What's the problem with just scaffolding the flight and seat data?

....
....
....

Sharpen your pencil
Solution

What are the instructions to:

1. Create an app called coconut?

    rails coconut

    You don't need to mention the "id" columns in the scaffold. They'll be added automatically.

2. Scaffold the flight data?

    ruby script/generate scaffold flight departure:datetime arrival:datetime

    destination:string baggage_allowance:decimal capacity:integer

    Remember: you'll need to use rake db:migrate to create the tables!

3. Scaffold the seat booking data?

    ruby script/generate scaffold seat flight_id:integer name:string baggage:decimal

4. What's the problem with just scaffolding the flight and seat data?

    Scaffolding the flight and seat data generates one set of pages for the flights and another for the seats. It doesn't combine the two.

We need to see flights and seat bookings <u>together</u>

If we simply create scaffolding and don't customize the app, it will be hard to use. In order to book a seat on a flight, the user will have to look up the id of the flight from its URL:

To book a seat on a flight, the user has to look up the flight id.

Here's the flight page. →

Flights: show
http://localhost:3000/flights/1

Departure: 2009-11-11 11:30:00 UTC

Arrival: 2009-11-11 12:15:00 UTC

Destination: St Cuthberts Island

Baggage allowance: 30.0

Capacity: 12

Edit | Back

http://localhost:3000/seats/new

New seat

Flight

Name

Baggage

Create

Back

We need to display a flight <u>together</u> with its seat bookings.

Let's look at what the seat scaffolding gives us

We need the flight page to look something like this:

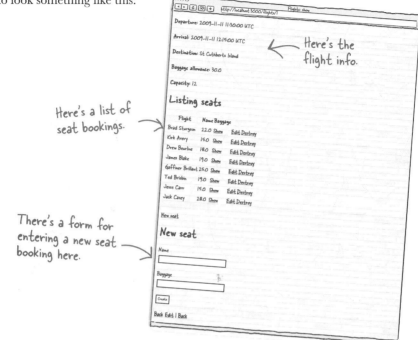

Here's the flight info.

Here's a list of seat bookings.

There's a form for entering a new seat booking here.

Let's see how this compares with the seat pages generated by the scaffolding:

index.html.erb

show.html.erb

edit.html.erb

new.html.erb

Can any of these help us generate the flight page?

We need the booking form and seat list on the flight page

Two of the generated pages look pretty similar to what we need on the flight page, the seat list and the booking form. The middle section of the flight page looks like the seat list, and the booking form looks like the end section:

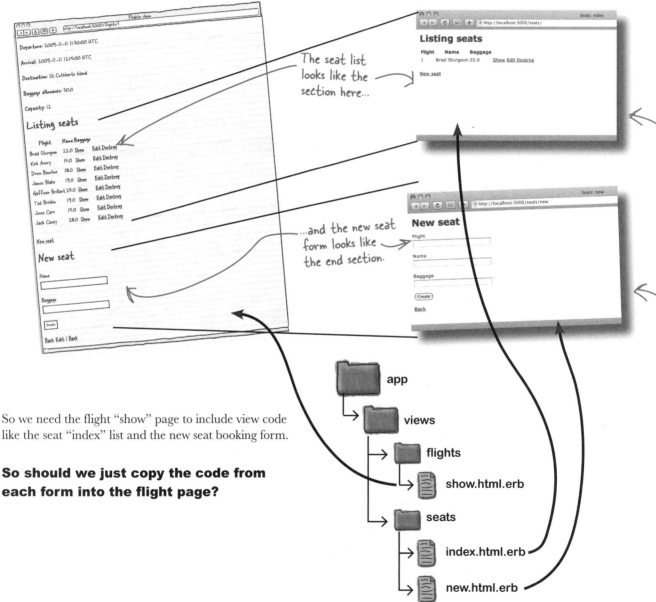

The seat list looks like the section here...

...and the new seat form looks like the end section.

So we need the flight "show" page to include view code like the seat "index" list and the new seat booking form.

So should we just copy the code from each form into the flight page?

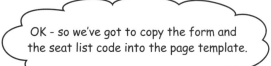

OK - so we've got to copy the form and the seat list code into the page template.

Mark: Woah - wait a minute. How much code is that?

Laura: I dunno. We need the code in the page, though. It's in the design.

Mark: I know we need the seat list and the booking form to *appear* in the page. But does that mean we have to have the code in there?

Laura: Why - what's the problem with that code?

Mark: The seat list and the booking form are doing significantly different things. Can't we break them apart somehow?

Bob: Break them apart? You mean into separate files?

Mark: Yes. That way we could have one file that displays a list of seats, one that displays the booking, and then include or call each page from the main page.

Laura: Oh - like separation of concerns.

Bob: What's that?

Laura: Separation of concerns. It means you get one piece of code to do just one thing. Makes it easier to track down bugs.

Bob: Sure, sounds great... but how do you actually do that?

We can use partials for the new seat and seat list parts of the page.

How can we split a page's content up into separate files?

If we can split a page into separate files, it will make things more manageable. But how do we do that?

Rails lets us store fragments of pages into separate files called **partial page templates** or—more simply—**partials**. A partial is like a sub-routine that outputs a small part of a page. In our case we can use two partials: one for the seat list and another to add a new seat booking.

Partials are simply embedded Ruby files, just like templates. The only difference is that, unlike templates, partials have names that begin with an underscore (_).

ERb Files Up Close

We now have three kinds of Embedded Ruby (ERb) file: **templates**, **layouts**, and **partials**. But what's the difference between the three, and how does each type of ERb fit in with the other types?

You can assemble a web page with ERb files in the same way that you'd use a pile of ingredients to assemble a burger.

A layout wraps the whole thing in a standard bun.

A template provides the main content.

The partials are like the lettuce and tomatoes, separate ingredients included by the template.

Layouts

A **layout** gives a set of web pages a consistent look, mostly by providing standard pieces of HTML that go at the top and bottom of each page, kind of like a bun wrapping a burger. By default, all the pages associated with a given controller will share the same layout.

Templates

A **template** is the main content of the web page, like the filling in the burger. A template is associated with an action. So there's a template to show the flight details, and another for the "New flight" form.

Partials

A template might call separate **partials** to build a page's main content. Partials are like the sub-ingredients of a burger, like the tomato or the lettuce. Partials allow you to break up a complex template into smaller parts. They also allow you to separate out common content, like menus and navigation bars. Partials can be used by templates, but also by layouts.

A bunch of ERb files, in full costume, are playing a party game, "Who am I?" They'll give you a clue — you try to guess who they are based on what they say. Assume they always tell the truth about themselves. Fill in the blanks to the right to identify the attendees.

Tonight's attendees:

Any of the charming types of ERb files you've seen so far just might show up!

Who am I?

Type of ERb File

I contain the navigation menu.   _____

I include the title that appears in the browser window.   _____

I display a form if someone needs to create a new object.   _____

I display a contact email and a copyright message.   _____

I give a set of pages a standard looking navigation bar.   _____

A bunch of ERb files, in full costume, are playing a party game, "Who am I?" They'll give you a clue — you try to guess who they are based on what they say. Assume they always tell the truth about themselves. Fill in the blanks to the right to identify the attendees.

Tonight's attendees:

Any of the charming types of ERb files you've seen so far just might show up!

Who am I?

Type of ERb File

This is a page fragment that could be used in several places.

I contain the navigation menu.

_____partial_____

That whole HTML <title/> section will be handled by a layout.

I include the title that appears in the browser window.

_____layout_____

Templates are used with individual actions, like "new".

I display a form if someone needs to create a new object.

_____template_____

This is a partial because it's a page fragment, but it will probably be called by a layout.

I display a contact email and a copyright message.

_____partial_____

I give a set of pages a standard looking navigation bar.

_____layout_____

A layout controls the look of several pages, even though it will probably call the navigation bar in from a separate partial.

ERb will ASSEMBLE our pages

We need to create partials for the booking form and the seat list, and then Embedded Ruby can process the flight page and call the partials each time the render expression is reached.

← This allows a separation of concerns: we have separate components dealing with booking and seats, and those components are combined for the user when needed.

> ## To Do
> ☐ Create a booking form partial
> ☐ Add the booking form to the page
> ☐ Create a seat list partial
> ☐ Add the seat list to the page

ERb will assemble our flight page out of the template show.html. erb, the booking form partial, and the seat list partial.

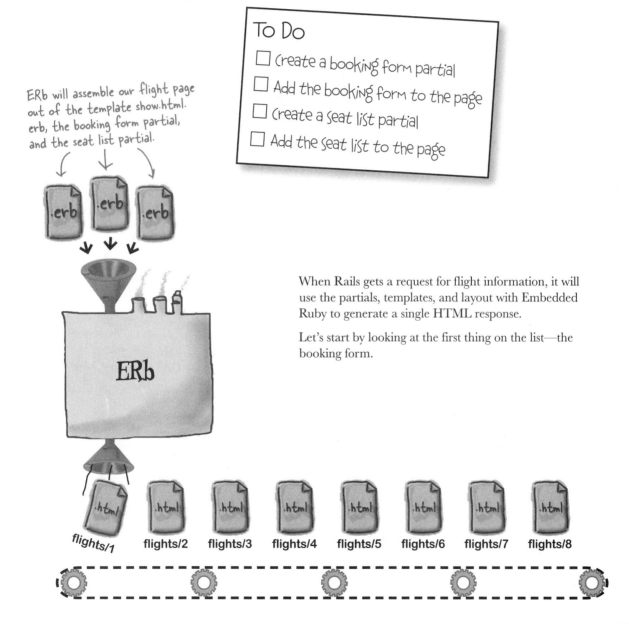

When Rails gets a request for flight information, it will use the partials, templates, and layout with Embedded Ruby to generate a single HTML response.

Let's start by looking at the first thing on the list—the booking form.

flights/1 flights/2 flights/3 flights/4 flights/5 flights/6 flights/7 flights/8

So how do we create the booking form partial?

Partials are just another kind of ERb file, so they contain the **same kinds of tags** that templates contain. Here's the content of our `_new_seat.html.erb` partial. It contains exactly the same code as the new seat page, which means that all we have to do is copy `app/views/seats/new.html.erb` and save it as `app/views/flights/_new_seat.html.erb`:

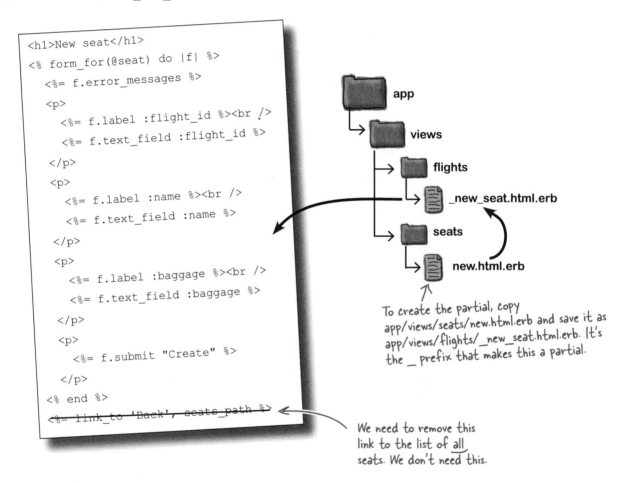

```
<h1>New seat</h1>
<% form_for(@seat) do |f| %>
  <%= f.error_messages %>
  <p>
    <%= f.label :flight_id %><br />
    <%= f.text_field :flight_id %>
  </p>
  <p>
    <%= f.label :name %><br />
    <%= f.text_field :name %>
  </p>
  <p>
    <%= f.label :baggage %><br />
    <%= f.text_field :baggage %>
  </p>
  <p>
    <%= f.submit "Create" %>
  </p>
<% end %>
<%= link_to 'Back', seats_path %>
```

app
 └─ views
     ├─ flights
     │   └─ _new_seat.html.erb
     └─ seats
         └─ new.html.erb

To create the partial, copy app/views/seats/new.html.erb and save it as app/views/flights/_new_seat.html.erb. It's the _ prefix that makes this a partial.

We need to remove this link to the list of all seats. We don't need this.

We could have left the partial in the "seats" folder, but we move it into the "flights" folder to make it slightly easier to call. It's also really important that the partial begins with the _ character. The _ character is used by Rails to distinguish partials from page templates.

Now we need to include the partial in the template

Creating the partial is only half the job. We now need to modify the flight show.html.erb page template to ***include*** the partial in its output. Partials, like templates, are really just pieces of Ruby code disguised to look like HTML. And in the same way that one piece of Ruby code can call another, the template can easily *call* the partial.

So how do you call a partial? By adding a `render` command to the flight page:

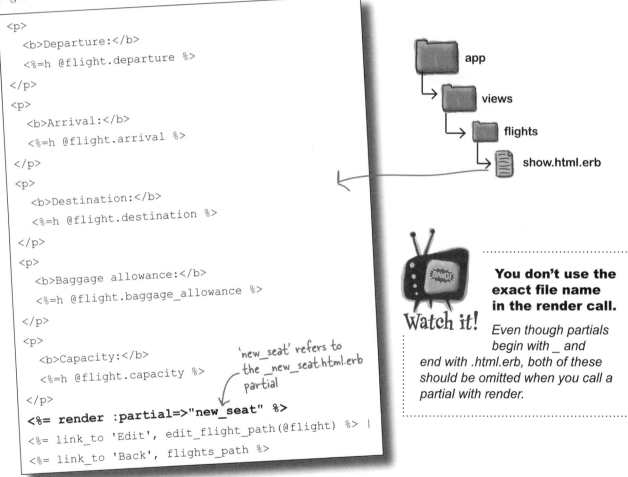

```
<p>
  <b>Departure:</b>
  <%=h @flight.departure %>
</p>
<p>
  <b>Arrival:</b>
  <%=h @flight.arrival %>
</p>
<p>
  <b>Destination:</b>
  <%=h @flight.destination %>
</p>
<p>
  <b>Baggage allowance:</b>
  <%=h @flight.baggage_allowance %>
</p>
<p>
  <b>Capacity:</b>
  <%=h @flight.capacity %>
</p>
<%= render :partial=>"new_seat" %>
<%= link_to 'Edit', edit_flight_path(@flight) %> |
<%= link_to 'Back', flights_path %>
```

'new_seat' refers to the _new_seat.html.erb partial

app
views
flights
show.html.erb

Watch it!

You don't use the exact file name in the render call.

Even though partials begin with _ and end with .html.erb, both of these should be omitted when you call a partial with render.

The render call tell Embedded Ruby to process the partial and include its output at that point in the file.

The partial should now appear in the flight page.

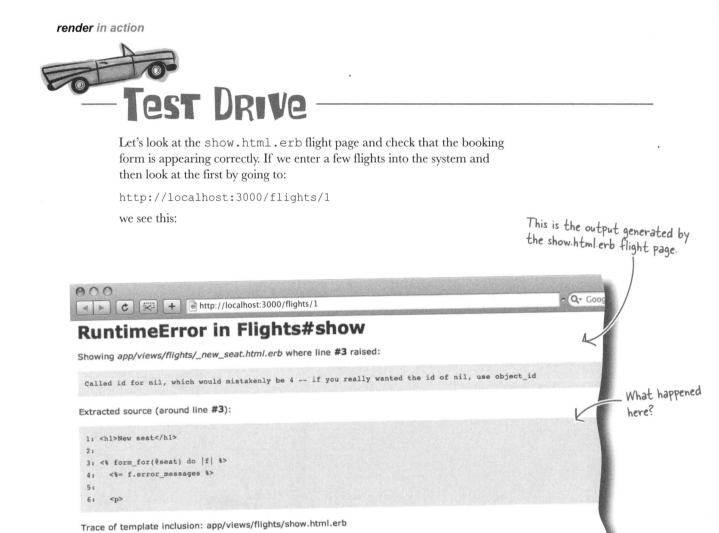

Test Drive

Let's look at the `show.html.erb` flight page and check that the booking form is appearing correctly. If we enter a few flights into the system and then look at the first by going to:

```
http://localhost:3000/flights/1
```

we see this:

> This is the output generated by the show.html.erb flight page.

RuntimeError in Flights#show

Showing *app/views/flights/_new_seat.html.erb* where line **#3** raised:

Called id for nil, which would mistakenly be 4 -- if you really wanted the id of nil, use object_id

> What happened here?

Extracted source (around line **#3**):

```
1: <h1>New seat</h1>
2:
3: <% form_for(@seat) do |f| %>
4:    <%= f.error_messages %>
5:
6:    <p>
```

Trace of template inclusion: app/views/flights/show.html.erb

RAILS_ROOT: /Users/davidg/data/writing/books/hfror/code/chap6-master_detail/coconut1

Application Trace | Framework Trace | Full Trace

```
vendor/rails/actionpack/lib/action_controller/record_identifier.rb:76:in `dom_id'
vendor/rails/actionpack/lib/action_view/hel...              ...in `dom_id'
```

A strange error has occurred. The flight page was working before we inserted the partial, so what went wrong?

BRAIN POWER

Looking at the errors generated in the test drive and the code from the partial, can you figure out what caused the crash?

```
<h1>New seat</h1>
<% form_for(@seat) do |f| %>
  <%= f.error_messages %>
  <p>
    <%= f.label :flight_id %><br />
    <%= f.text_field :flight_id %>
  </p>
  <p>
    <%= f.label :name %><br />
    <%= f.text_field :name %>
  </p>
  <p>
    <%= f.label :baggage %><br />
    <%= f.text_field :baggage %>
  </p>
  <p>
    <%= f.submit "Create" %>
  </p>
<% end %>
```

app
→ views
→ flights
→ _new_seat.html.erb

We need to give the partial a seat!

The problem is caused because the ERb code contains a reference to the @seat variable. So why is this a problem?

This file used to be a page template associated with the SeatsController. The SeatsController initialized the @seat instance variable like this:

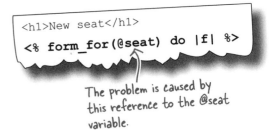

The problem is caused by this reference to the @seat variable.

$$@seat = Seat.new$$

But now the file has become a partial that is going to be used by the FlightsController, and that controller has no @seat instance variable. So we need to change @seat into a local variable called seat:

Instead of using the @seat variable, we can use the local variable seat instead.

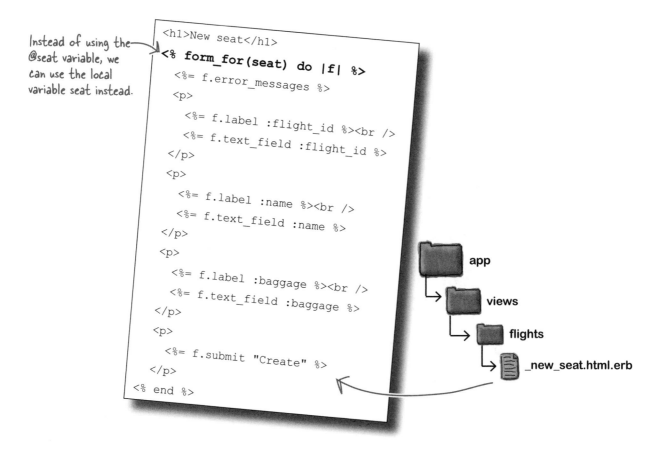

```erb
<h1>New seat</h1>
<% form_for(seat) do |f| %>
  <%= f.error_messages %>
  <p>
    <%= f.label :flight_id %><br />
    <%= f.text_field :flight_id %>
  </p>
  <p>
    <%= f.label :name %><br />
    <%= f.text_field :name %>
  </p>
  <p>
    <%= f.label :baggage %><br />
    <%= f.text_field :baggage %>
  </p>
  <p>
    <%= f.submit "Create" %>
  </p>
<% end %>
```

app
views
flights
_new_seat.html.erb

seat is called a **local variable** because nothing outside the partial can read or write to it. But if that's the case, then how do we pass the partial a value for the seat variable?

You can pass local variables to a partial

Partials and templates work a lot like Ruby methods or functions. When a template renders a partial, it's a little like one function calling another function.

And since a partial's like a function, you can pass in parameters like this:

```
<%= render :partial=>"new_seat", :locals=>{:seat=>_____} %>
```

Value for the local seat variable goes here.

This will call the _new_seat.html.erb partial.

This is a hash of local variables that we are passing to the partial.

There's a single local in the hash that will set the value of the 'seat' variable.

The render method can accept a hash called `locals`. Within the hash, you can include a set of values indexed by a variable name. Like pretty much everywhere in Rails, names are expressed as **symbols**.

But what value should we pass in for `seat`? Let's look at what value the original SeatsController used:

```
def new
  @seat = Seat.new
```

This needs to replace the call to the partial in app/views/flights/show.html.erb.

Because the form is being used to initialize a seat, we just need to pass the form a freshly created `Seat` object:

```
<%= render :partial=>"new_seat", :locals=>{:seat=>Seat.new} %>
```

So has this fixed the problem with the flight page?

there are no
Dumb Questions

Q: Do I have to make the partial use a local variable?

A: No. Partials can see all the same instance variables (the variables beginning with @) that page templates can see. But it is good practice to use local variables in partials.

Q: Why?

A: It makes the partial less dependent upon other code. Page templates are intimately dependent upon the controller, so it's OK for them to look at controller instance variables. But partials are *not* so closely tied to controllers. Many applications use *shared* partials, which are partials used by *more than one* controller. If partials only use local variables, you will find them easier to manage.

TEST DRIVE

With the seat object correctly initialized, the previous crash should be avoided. Let's try refreshing a flight page:

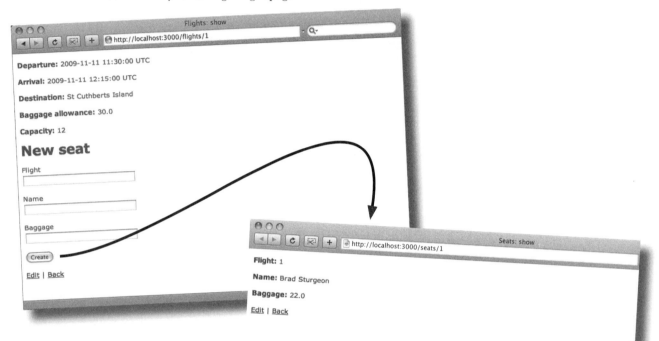

To Do
- ☑ Create a booking form partial
- ☑ Add the booking form to the page
- ☐ Create a seat list partial
- ☐ Add the seat list to the page

This time the form renders correctly. We've got a local seat variable, so no problems with that anymore.

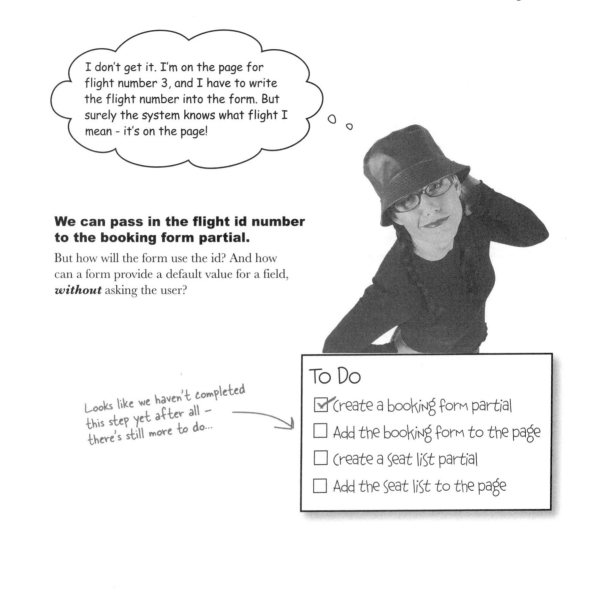

I don't get it. I'm on the page for flight number 3, and I have to write the flight number into the form. But surely the system knows what flight I mean - it's on the page!

We can pass in the flight id number to the booking form partial.

But how will the form use the id? And how can a form provide a default value for a field, *without* asking the user?

Looks like we haven't completed this step yet after all – there's still more to do...

To Do
- ☑ Create a booking form partial
- ☐ Add the booking form to the page
- ☐ Create a seat list partial
- ☐ Add the seat list to the page

Sharpen your pencil

You can specify the flight number when you create the Seat object. Add the code you need in the `flights/show.html.erb` file:

```
<%= render :partial=>"new_seat", :locals=>{:seat=>Seat.new(..................................)} %>
```

Sharpen your pencil Solution

You can specify the flight number when you create the Seat object.
Add the code you need in the `flights/show.html.erb` file:

This is flight.id
with a point "."

```
<%= render :partial=>"new_seat", :locals=>{:seat=>Seat.new(....:flight_id=>@flight.id.....)} %>
```

This code is from
app/views/flights/show.html.erb.

This is flight_id with
an underscore "_"

We can pass in hashed-values to set
the initial values of the model object.

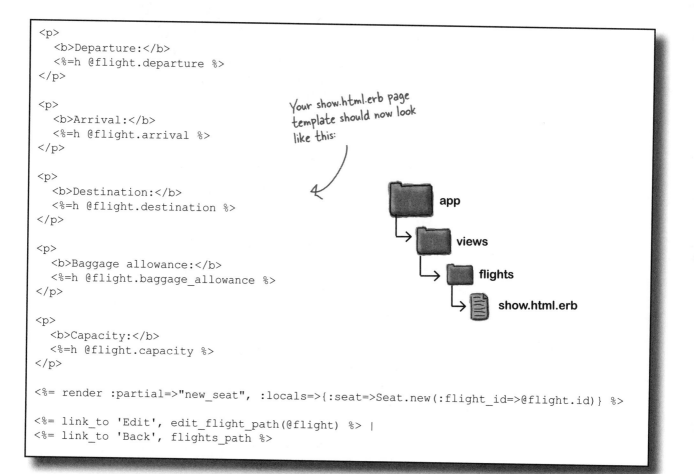

```
<p>
  <b>Departure:</b>
  <%=h @flight.departure %>
</p>

<p>
  <b>Arrival:</b>
  <%=h @flight.arrival %>
</p>

<p>
  <b>Destination:</b>
  <%=h @flight.destination %>
</p>

<p>
  <b>Baggage allowance:</b>
  <%=h @flight.baggage_allowance %>
</p>

<p>
  <b>Capacity:</b>
  <%=h @flight.capacity %>
</p>

<%= render :partial=>"new_seat", :locals=>{:seat=>Seat.new(:flight_id=>@flight.id)} %>

<%= link_to 'Edit', edit_flight_path(@flight) %> |
<%= link_to 'Back', flights_path %>
```

Your show.html.erb page
template should now look
like this:

app
→ views
→ flights
→ show.html.erb

Pool Puzzle

User shouldn't have to enter a flight number, so we need to store the flight number with a hidden field. Can you assemble the pieces of code to do that?

We've taken the old flight_id field away.

```
<h1>New seat</h1>
<% form_for(seat) do |f| %>
  <%= f.error_messages %>
```

The code for the hidden field needs to go right here. ....

```
  <p>
    <%= f.label :name %><br />
    <%= f.text_field :name %>
  </p>
  <p>
    <%= f.label :baggage %><br />
    <%= f.text_field :baggage %>
  </p>
  <p>
    <%= f.submit "Create" %>
  </p>
<% end %>
```

This is
app/views/flights/_new_seat.html.erb

Note: each thing from the pool can only be used once - and you might not need all of them!

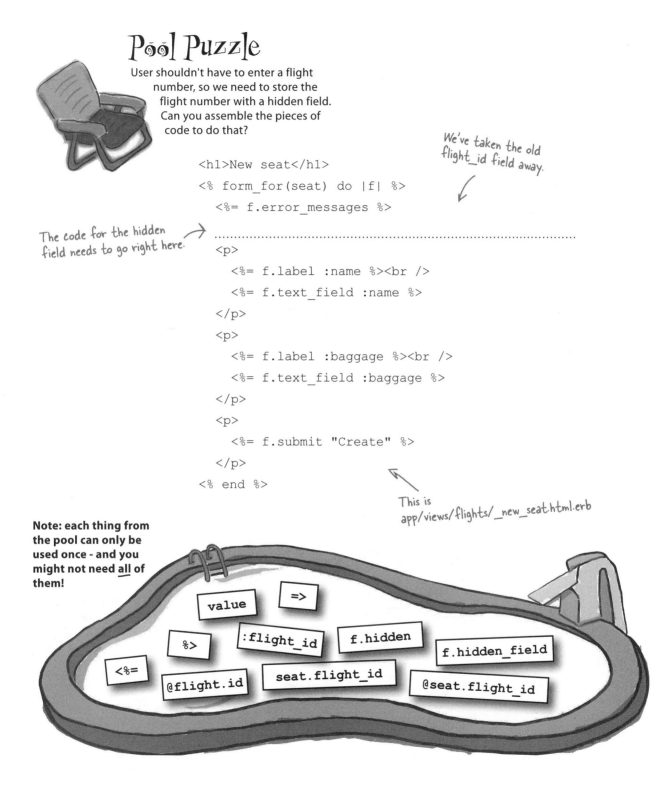

Pool pieces: value, =>, %>, :flight_id, f.hidden, <%=, f.hidden_field, @flight.id, seat.flight_id, @seat.flight_id

Pool Puzzle Solution

We no longer need to enter the flight
number so we need to store the
flight number with a hidden field.
Can you assemble the pieces of
code to do that?

The seat object already has the flight
id so we don't need to pass it in.

```erb
<h1>New seat</h1>
<% form_for(seat) do |f| %>
  <%= f.error_messages %>
  <%= f.hidden_field :flight_id %>
  <p>
    <%= f.label :name %><br />
    <%= f.text_field :name %>
  </p>
  <p>
    <%= f.label :baggage %><br />
    <%= f.text_field :baggage %>
  </p>
  <p>
    <%= f.submit "Create" %>
  </p>
<% end %>
```

Bound fields always
end in "_field".

This is
app/views/flights/_new_seat.html.erb

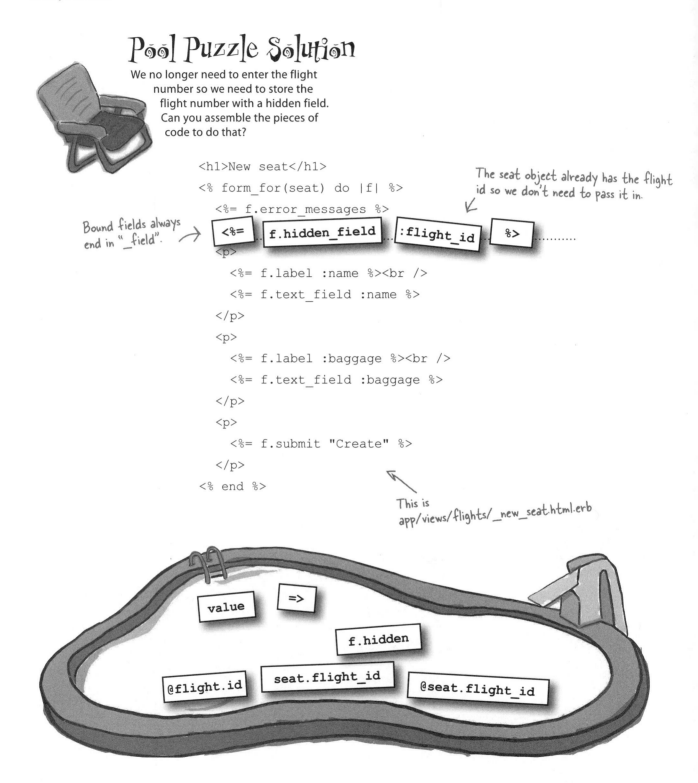

value   =>

f.hidden

@flight.id   seat.flight_id   @seat.flight_id

TEST DRIVE

Now when we go to a flight page, the flight number field has disappeared from the form... just like we wanted.

http://localhost:3000/flights/1

Departure: 2009-11-11 11:30:00 UTC

Arrival: 2009-11-11 12:15:00 UTC

Destination: St Cuthberts Island

Baggage allowance: 30.0

Capacity: 12

New seat

You no longer need to supply the flight id number.

Name

Baggage

(Create)

Edit | Back

The new seat booking has picked up the correct flight number.

http://localhost:3000/seats/1

Flight: 1

Name: Brad Sturgeon

Baggage: 22.0

Edit | Back

The form works!

The flight number is now automatically picked up from the flight object. So what's next?

To Do

☑ Create a booking form partial

☑ Add the booking form to the page

☐ Create a seat list partial   ← *Next we need to create a seat list partial.*

☐ Add the seat list to the page

We also need a partial for the seat list

This is the bottom part of the file — above it are the table headings and the title.

We can convert the seat "index" list in more or less the same way that we converted the booking form—by copying the original seat template file to a partial file. Let's call this new partial `_seat_list.html`:

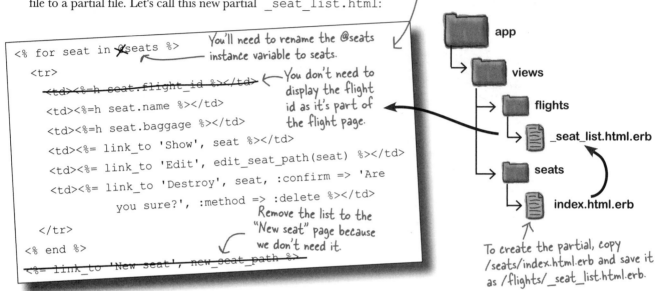

```erb
<% for seat in @seats %>
  <tr>
    <td><%=h seat.flight_id %></td>
    <td><%=h seat.name %></td>
    <td><%=h seat.baggage %></td>
    <td><%= link_to 'Show', seat %></td>
    <td><%= link_to 'Edit', edit_seat_path(seat) %></td>
    <td><%= link_to 'Destroy', seat, :confirm => 'Are
             you sure?', :method => :delete %></td>
  </tr>
<% end %>
<%= link_to 'New seat', new_seat_path %>
```

You'll need to rename the @seats instance variable to seats.

You don't need to display the flight id as it's part of the flight page.

Remove the list to the "New seat" page because we don't need it.

app
→ views
  → flights
    → _seat_list.html.erb
  → seats
    → index.html.erb

To create the partial, copy /seats/index.html.erb and save it as /flights/_seat_list.html.erb.

But the seat-list partial needs an array of seats

The seats "index" page displayed the contents of a SeatsController instance variable called `@seats`. The SeatsController created the instance variable just prior to `index.html.erb` was displayed. But what about now? We copied the `index.html.erb` template to a partial that will be displayed after running the FlightsController... so there's no `@seats` instance variable containing an array of seats.

That means we need to provide the new `_seat_list.html.erb` partial with an array of seats. So what value should we provide for the array of seats? This is how the SeatsController initialized `@seats`:

```ruby
def index
  @seats = Seat.find(:all)
```

So, for now, let's call the seat list like this and see how it works:

```erb
<%= render :partial=>"seat_list", :locals=>{:seats=>Seat.find(:all)} %>
```

We'll add this call to app/views/flights/show.html.erb

We'll pass this as the value for the seats array.

Will this work? Let's see...

Test Drive

Make all these changes, add the new partial, and try the app out.

All of the page sections are now in place.

This part was generated by the _new_seat.html.erb partial.

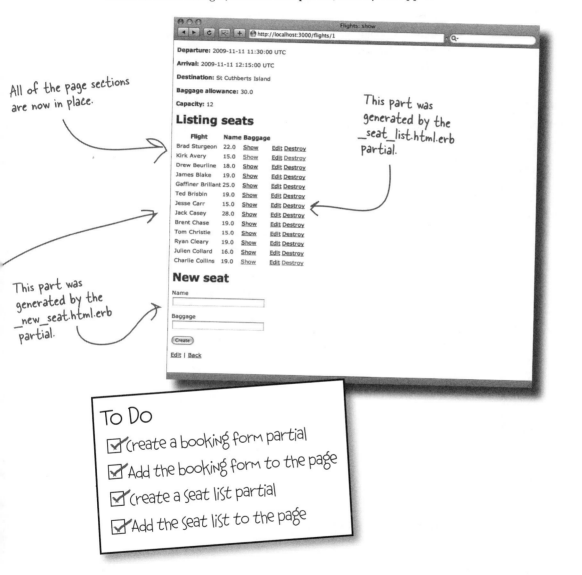

This part was generated by the _seat_list.html.erb partial.

To Do

☑ Create a booking form partial

☑ Add the booking form to the page

☑ Create a seat list partial

☑ Add the seat list to the page

The form *looks* like it's working. **Let's see what the users think.**

People are ending up on the wrong flights

Everyone thinks the system looks great, so the system goes live. Unfortunately, it doesn't takes long before someone spots a problem...

> Dude... I booked a flight to a beach party but wound up on a historical tour of an old leper colony!

So what happened?

The flight page is displaying *all* the seat bookings for *all* the flights!

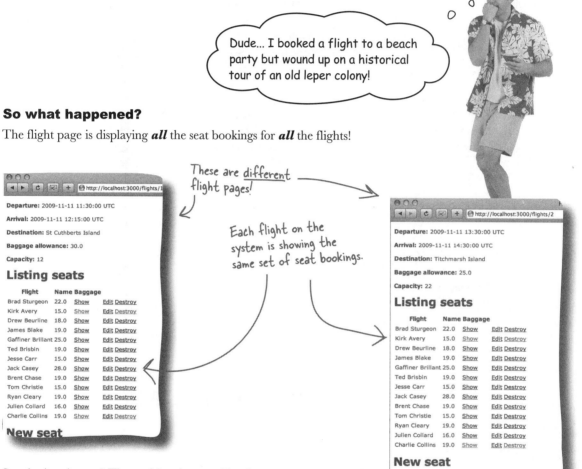

These are different flight pages!

Each flight on the system is showing the same set of seat bookings.

So what's going on? The problem is caused by the render command, which calls the seat list partial. Remember, we called the partial like this:

```
<%= render :partial=>"seat_list",
        :locals=>{:seats=>Seat.find(:all)} %>
```

This displays the list of all seats in the database. That was fine when the seat list was the index page for the seat data... but now that we're displaying the data against the flight, we need to *restrict* the seats so that only seats belonging to the current flight are displayed.

We could fix the finder... but it would be better to create a ***relationship***.

A relationship connects models together

You'll often find that certain model objects are often used together, like flights and seat bookings. You may need to use data from one type—like the flight id—to find the related objects in the other type, like the seats booked on the flight.

You could just use finders to read the related objects. For example, if you had a flight object called `@flight`, you could find the related seat objects like this:

— Returns an array of seat objects.

```
Seat.find_all_by_flight_id(@flight.id)
```

But it's actually easier to ***connect*** the two models together with a **relationship**:

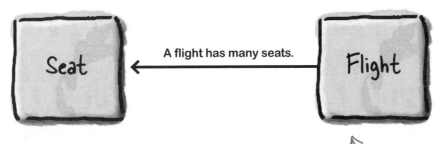

A flight has many seats.

Seat ← Flight

These are now connected at the model level... you don't need to write code to handle this relationship now.

A **relationship** makes objects of one type of object appear to be *attributes* of another type of object. For example, if we create a relationship on the flight model that connects to the seat model, we can refer to the seats associated with a flight like this:

```
@flight.seats
```

This will return the exact same thing as the finder above, but defining a relationship between two models will simplify your code and reduce the chances that you will make a mistake by repeatedly defining finders to jump from one model to another. It will also make your code a lot easier to read.

Sounds good. So how do relationships work?

Relationships Up Close

A relationship will join the data in the seat and flight tables by matching the data in the `seat.flight_id` and `flight.id` columns:

Names are IMPORTANT in Rails.

seat.flight_id matches flight.id

id	departure	arrival	destination	baggage_allowa...	capacity	created_at	updated_at
1	2009-11-11 11:...	2009-11-11 12:...	St Cuthberts I...	30	12	2008-11-11 11:...	2008-11-11 11:...
2	2009-11-11 13:...	2009-11-11 14:...	Titchmarsh Isl...	25	22	2008-11-11 12:...	2008-11-11 12:...
3	2009-11-11 08:...	2009-11-11 09:...	St Augustine L...	8	4	2008-11-11 12:...	2008-11-11 12:...

id	flight_id	name	baggage	created_at	updated_at
1	1	Brad Sturgeon	22	2008-11-11 11:...	2008-11-11 11:...
2	1	Kirk Avery	15	2008-11-11 12:...	2008-11-11 12:...
3	1	Drew Beurline	18	2008-11-11 12:...	2008-11-11 12:...
4	1	James Blake	19	2008-11-11 12:...	2008-11-11 12:...
5	1	Gaffiner Brill...	25	2008-11-11 12:...	2008-11-11 12:...
6	1	Ted Brisbin	19	2008-11-11 12:...	2008-11-11 12:...
7	1	Jesse Carr	15	2008-11-11 12:...	2008-11-11 12:...
8	1	Jack Casey	28	2008-11-11 12:...	2008-11-11 12:...
9	2	Brent Chase	19	2008-11-11 12:...	2008-11-11 12:...
10	2	Tom Christie	15	2008-11-11 12:...	2008-11-11 12:...
11	2	Ryan Cleary	19	2008-11-11 12:...	2008-11-11 12:...
12	2	Julien Collard	16	2008-11-11 12:...	2008-11-11 12:...
13	2	Charlie Collins	19	2008-11-11 12:...	2008-11-11 12:...

For the relationship to work, the field in the seats table **must** be called **`flight_id`**, and the field **must** be an *integer*. ← *That's because the matching id column in the flights table has to connect with this.*

With a relationship in place, it means that when Rails sees this:

```
@flights.seats
```

← *This looks like an attribute, but it's really a relationship between two tables.*

It will treat it like this:

```
Seat.find_all_for_flight_id(@flight.id)
```

But how do we define the relationship?

We are going to give the Flight model an extra attribute called `seats`, so it makes sense that the Flight model code is the place where we define the relationship:

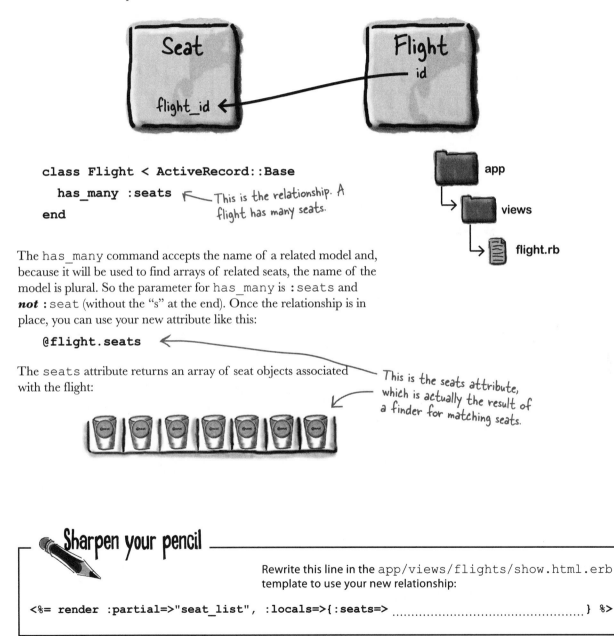

```
class Flight < ActiveRecord::Base
    has_many :seats        This is the relationship. A
end                        flight has many seats.
```

app

views

flight.rb

The `has_many` command accepts the name of a related model and, because it will be used to find arrays of related seats, the name of the model is plural. So the parameter for `has_many` is `:seats` and **not** `:seat` (without the "s" at the end). Once the relationship is in place, you can use your new attribute like this:

`@flight.seats`

The `seats` attribute returns an array of seat objects associated with the flight:

This is the seats attribute, which is actually the result of a finder for matching seats.

Sharpen your pencil

Rewrite this line in the `app/views/flights/show.html.erb` template to use your new relationship:

```
<%= render :partial=>"seat_list", :locals=>{:seats=> ............................................... } %>
```

Sharpen your pencil
Solution

Rewrite this line in the `app/views/flights/show.html.erb` template to use your new relationship:

```
<%= render :partial=>"seat_list", :locals=>{:seats=> @flight.seats } %>
```

TEST DRIVE

Make all these changes, and reload! The flight pages now only show the seats allocated to the given flight. So when we look at flights number 1 and number 3, they now have different seat lists:

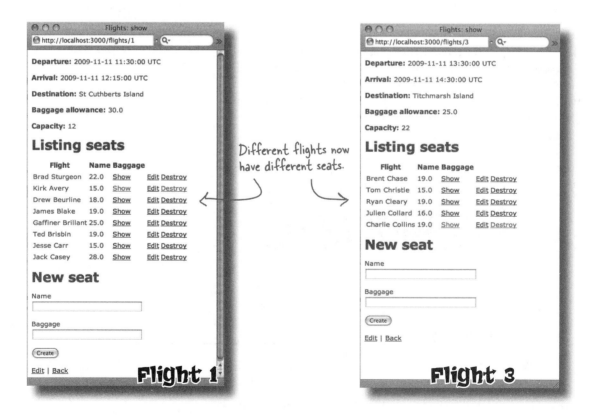

Different flights now have different seats.

But some people have too much baggage

Now there's a problem with the baggage on the flights. Some people are arriving at the airport carrying too much stuff—way more than the allowance for their flight. The flight data records the maximum baggage allowance, but a lot of the passengers are unhappy because they told the airline how much baggage they were bringing with them when they entered the seat booking, and the system didn't complain. The system needs to be modified to prevent people reserving seats with too much baggage... before they show up with a booked seat.

```
000                                          Flights: show
◀ ▶  C  ⊠  +  ⊕ http://localhost:3000/flights/2                              Q-

Departure: 2009-11-11 13:30:00 UTC

Arrival: 2009-11-11 14:30:00 UTC

Destination: Titchmarsh Island

Baggage allowance: 25.0

Capacity: 22

Listing seats

   Flight      Name Baggage
Brent Chase    19.0   Show     Edit Destroy
Tom Christie   15.0   Show     Edit Destroy
Ryan Cleary    19.0   Show     Edit Destroy
Julien Collard 16.0   Show     Edit Destroy
Charlie Collins 19.0  Show     Edit Destroy

New seat
Name
Sam Seaborn

Baggage
110

(Create)

Edit | Back
```

Someone is trying to travel with way more baggage than the allowance.

Sharpen your pencil

We check data in Rails with a validator. Which of the following validators do you think you should use to stop people reserving seats with too much baggage?

☐ None. We'll have to write our own.

☐ validates_length_of

☐ validates_format_of

☐ validates_uniqueness_of

☐ validates_inclusion_of

We check data in Rails with a validator. Which of the following validators do you think we should use to stop people reserving seats with too much baggage?

☑ None. We'll have to write our own.

☐ validates_length_of

☐ validates_format_of

☐ validates_uniqueness_of

☐ validates_inclusion_of

We need to write our OWN validation

Rails comes with a set of built-in validators that can perform a lot of basic tests, like whether data is entered or if it is correctly formatted. But sometimes you will need to check something that isn't covered by the basic validators.

In the case of baggage, Rails doesn't come with a `validates_too_much_baggage` validator. There's not a maximum value validator, either. So we need to write out own validator.

If you create a method in the Seat code called `validate`, that method will **always** be called by the model object just before things get saved or updated to the database:

Here's another case where naming in Rails is really important. By using a certain name – validate, Rails knows what to do with your method.

```
class Seat < ActiveRecord::Base

  def validate
    if name == flight_id
      errors.add_to_base("Your name is the same as your flight number")
    end
  end

end
```

The `errors.add_to_base(...)` command inserts a message into the list of errors. If there's an error message created, the save or update operation is aborted and the user should be sent back to the form to correct the problem.

Exercise

Write a custom validator to check that a flight booking has baggage under the limit for the flight.

....
....
....
....
....
....
....
....
....
....

Write a custom validator to check that a flight booking has baggage under the limit for the flight

Exercise Solution

Find the baggage allowance from the flight object. You can read the flight object using a finder and the flight id.

```
class Seat < ActiveRecord::Base
  def validate
    if baggage > Flight.find(flight_id).baggage_allowance
      errors.add_to_base("You have too much baggage")
    end
  end
end
```

> We're using a finder to look up the flight object from the seat. Is there a way we can use relationships for that?

Prefer relationships over manual finders.

Instead of using finders to look up the related flight object, you can define a ***relationship*** between seats and flights. But the question is, what sort of relationship do we need?

When we created a relationship before, we gave the Flight model a new attribute called `seats`:

```
@flight.seats
```

But what do we need this time? Before, we had a Flight object and we wanted to know what the related seats were. The difference is that now we're checking a seat object, and to do that we need to know about the related flight. So what sort of relationship do we need this time around?

We need the <u>REVERSE</u> relationship

This time we need a relationship that's the *opposite way* around to the one we had before. Given a particular seat object, we need to get the related flight:

We want to have an attribute on seats like this:

```
@seat.flight
```

This time, we're going <u>from</u> Seat <u>to</u> Flight... and we just want one record, the flight for a given seat.

We want to know which flight a seat belongs to. And each seat will have only one flight. How do you think that will be coded?

Rails Magnets

To get related flights from a seat object, you need to add code to a model. But which model and what code? Use the magnets below to fill in the gaps.

The relationship will be defined on the .... model, and it will be a command that looks like this:

....

The if condition in the above model that uses the relationship looks like this:

if ....

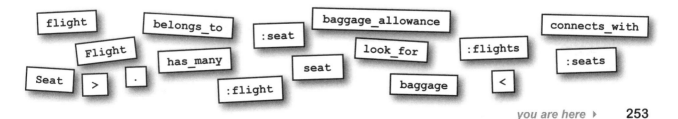

Rails Magnets Solution

To get related flights from a seat object, you need to add code to a model. But which model and what code? Use the magnets below to fill in the gaps.

The relationship will be defined on the ┄┄ Seat ┄┄ model, and it will be a command that looks like this:

┄┄ belongs_to :flight ┄┄

The if condition in the above model that uses the relationship looks like this:

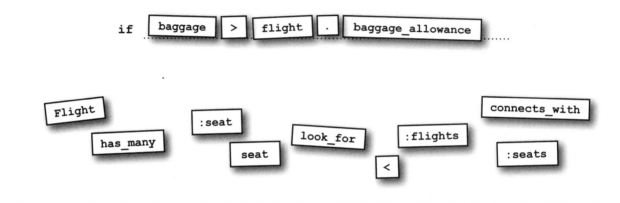

```
if ┄ baggage > flight . baggage_allowance ┄
```

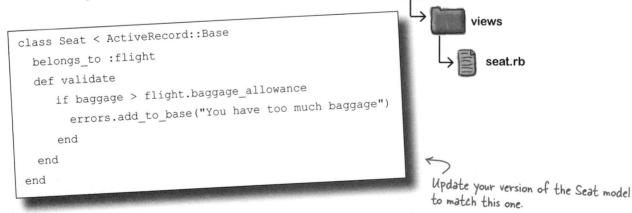

So what does the Seat model look like now?

Let's make the changes to the Seat model:

```ruby
class Seat < ActiveRecord::Base
  belongs_to :flight
  def validate
    if baggage > flight.baggage_allowance
      errors.add_to_base("You have too much baggage")
    end
  end
end
```

app
→ **views**
→ **seat.rb**

Update your version of the Seat model to match this one.

TEST DRIVE

So what happens if you try to reserve a seat with baggage in excess of the allowance for the flight now? Try it out and see...

The validator and relationship combine to take care of the baggage problem.

Departure: 2009-11-11 13:30:00 UTC

Arrival: 2009-11-11 14:30:00 UTC

Destination: Titchmarsh Island

Baggage allowance: 25.0

Capacity: 22

Listing seats

Flight	Name	Baggage			
Brent Chase	19.0	Show	Edit	Destroy
Tom Christie	15.0	Show	Edit	Destroy
Ryan Cleary	19.0	Show	Edit	Destroy
Julien Collard	16.0	Show	Edit	Destroy
Charlie Collins	19.0	Show	Edit	Destroy

New seat

Name
Sam Seaborn

Baggage
110

(Create)

Edit | Back

New seat

1 error prohibited this seat from being saved

There were problems with the following fields:

* You have too much baggage

Flight
2

Name
Sam Seaborn

Baggage
110

(Create)

Back

Woah. Looks like we better leave the rum behind...

BULLET POINTS

- Breaking your page into **partials** will make it easier to maintain.
- Partials, templates, and layouts are the three types of **Embedded Ruby** files.
- Partials are used to generate **fragments** of pages.
- Templates create the **main content** of a page.
- Layouts are used to create standard **HTML wrappers** for pages.
- Partials can be **called by** templates or layouts.
- Partials can be given **local variables**.
- Partials must begin with _ and end with `.html.erb`
- You call a partial using the `render` function.
- **Relationships** make it easier to find connected data in other models.
- Relationships work like **finders**.
- `has_many` attributes return arrays.
- `belongs_to` attributes return single objects.
- You can create custom validation by adding a method to your model called `validate`.

there are no Dumb Questions

Q: Do I really have to break my page into partials?

A: You don't have to, but a larger number of smaller files is usually easier to maintain.

Q: Why's that?

A: If there's a bug, it will be easier to locate broken code in lots of smaller files.

Q: Why else would I want partials?

A: For reuse. If you have a standard menu or contact section, you can reuse it between different templates and layouts.

Q: How do I call a partial from a layout?

A: Using the `render` method, just like you would from a partial.

Q: So do relationships cause table joins using key fields?

A: Yes. By default, relationships work by connecting the id field of one table with another field ending `_id` in the other table. That's why `id` on the flight table connects with `flight_id` on the seat table.

Q: So it matters that the seat table column is called flight_id?

A: Yes. If you didn't use that name, Rails wouldn't know to build the relationship.

Q: Did it matter what data type flight_id was?

A: Good question. It needs to be an integer, because that's what Rails uses for id fields.

Exercise

Extend the custom validator to also check that flights are not booked beyond their seat capacity.

[Hint: All arrays have a method called size that returns the number of elements in the array.]

```
class Seat < ActiveRecord::Base
  belongs_to :flight
  def validate
    if baggage > flight.baggage_allowance
      errors.add_to_base("You have too much baggage")
    end
    ........................................

      ...............................................

    ...
  end
end
```

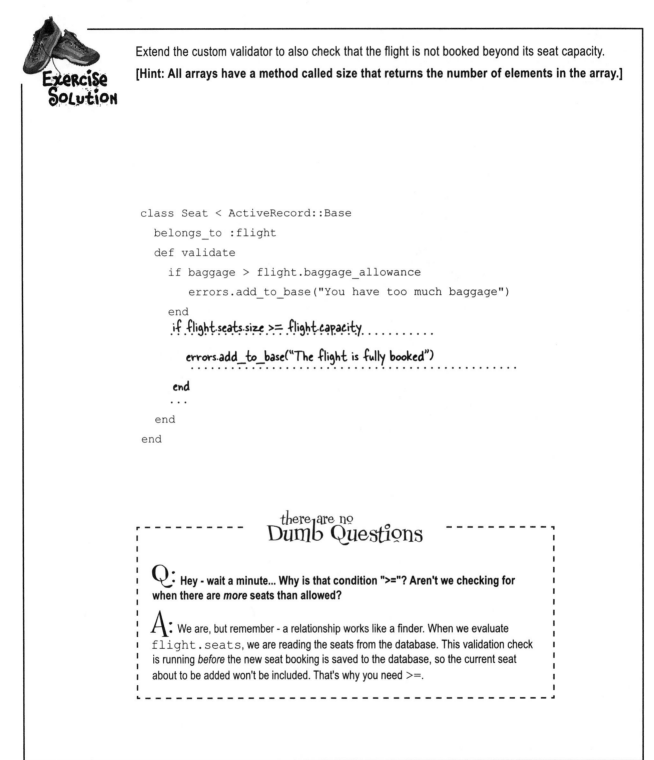

EXERCISE
SOLUTION

Extend the custom validator to also check that the flight is not booked beyond its seat capacity.

[Hint: All arrays have a method called size that returns the number of elements in the array.]

```ruby
class Seat < ActiveRecord::Base
  belongs_to :flight
  def validate
    if baggage > flight.baggage_allowance
        errors.add_to_base("You have too much baggage")
    end
    if flight.seats.size >= flight.capacity

        errors.add_to_base("The flight is fully booked")

    end
    ...
  end
end
```

there are no
Dumb Questions

Q: Hey - wait a minute... Why is that condition ">="? Aren't we checking for when there are *more* seats than allowed?

A: We are, but remember - a relationship works like a finder. When we evaluate `flight.seats`, we are reading the seats from the database. This validation check is running *before* the new seat booking is saved to the database, so the current seat about to be added won't be included. That's why you need >=.

TEST DRIVE

Make all the changes from the previous pages, and check out the app again.

The page now lists the correct seats for the flight. But what happens if someone tries to book a seat on a full flight?

The system's taken off at Coconut Airways

Life's pretty good at the airline. Tourists and locals find it a breeze to use the system. The planes don't get overloaded with baggage or get overbooked. In fact, the staff are using the time they saved a little more productively...

Tools for your Rails Toolbox

You've got Chapter 6 under your belt, and now you've added the ability to make the most of your connections.

Rails Tools

render :partial=>"name" displays _name.html.erb

Pass a variable to a partial with

render :partial=>"name", :locals=>{:var1=>"val1"}

Custom validation code is in a model method called validate

errors.add_to_base(...) creates an error message

belongs_to defines a relationship from an object to its parent

has_many is the reverse relationship

7 ajax

Avoiding the traffic

She's fast, responsive, and has a dynamic personality.

People want the best experiences out of life... and their apps.

No matter how good you are at Rails, there are times when traditional web apps just don't cut it. Sometimes users want something that's more **dynamic** and that responds to their every whim. Ajax allows you to build **fast, responsive web apps**, designed to give your users the **best experience the web has to offer**, and Rails comes complete with its own set of Ajax libraries just waiting for you to use. It's time to **quickly and easily add Ajax goodness** to your web app and please even more users than before.

There's a new offer at Coconut Airways

Coconut Airways has introduced a new promotional offer: the last three seats on every flight are on sale at half price!

But there's a problem. Obviously, everyone wants to grab the final three seats, and so in the last hour or two before the check-in closes, customers are continually hitting the reload buttons on their browser, in the hope of getting a cheap flight. Unfortunately, the increase in traffic is putting enormous pressure on the Coconut Airways server.

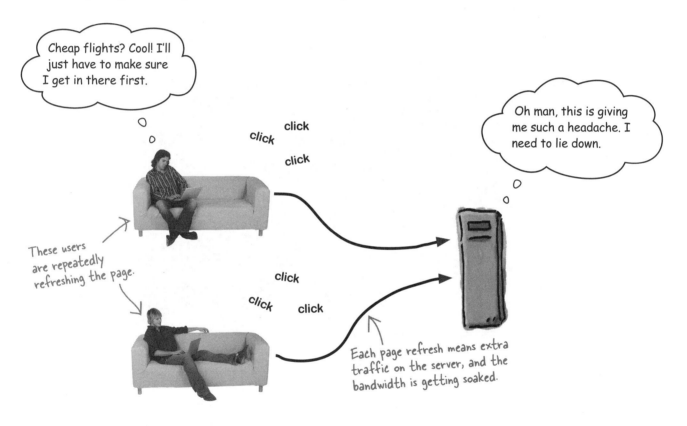

The extra requests are causing the Coconut Airways site to slow down. There are so many people requesting info on the flights that are close to departure, that other users are having problems getting through to the web site to book seats on their flights. Coconut Airways needs you to take another look at the application and see if there is some way of reducing the amount of traffic that's flooding into the web server.

Which parts of a page change most?

The majority of the network traffic is coming in to the flight details page—that, after all, is the one that lists the seat bookings on the flight. This is the page generated by the template at `app/views/flights/show.html.erb` and the `_seat_list.html.erb` and `_new_seat.html.erb` partials. There are three major sections to the page:

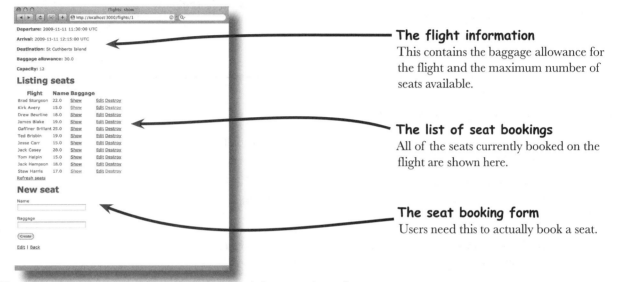

The flight information
This contains the baggage allowance for the flight and the maximum number of seats available.

The list of seat bookings
All of the seats currently booked on the flight are shown here.

The seat booking form
Users need this to actually book a seat.

Whenever a user presses the reload button on their browser, the entire page is requested from the server. This means that the server needs to generate the page again from the template and the partials, and the entire thing has to be wrapped in the flight layout. Now, if there are just one or two requests going on at one time, this really isn't going to cause a problem, but the server is being overwhelmed by the amount of processing it has to do.

Is there some way we can reduce the load on the server?

Sharpen your pencil

Here's how the pages are assembled by the server. Highlight which of the Embedded Ruby files you think is generating the updated information that the user is interested in.

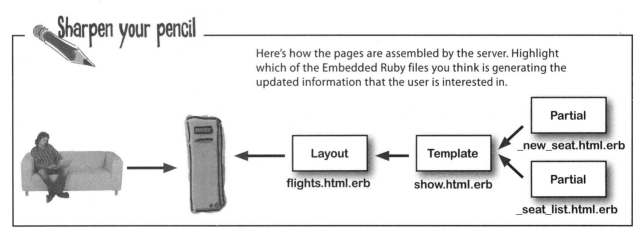

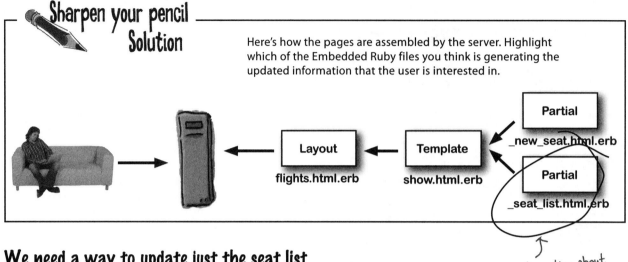

Sharpen your pencil
Solution

Here's how the pages are assembled by the server. Highlight which of the Embedded Ruby files you think is generating the updated information that the user is interested in.

The latest information about reservations is generated by the seat list partial.

We need a way to update just the seat list

When people refresh the page, most of it doesn't change. The only part that is ever likely to be different is the section displaying seat bookings.

So what actually happens when a user clicks the reload button on their browser? Well, "Reload" tells a browser to request the entire page again, and that's because the entire page is the only thing that's available. The application doesn't currently allow a browser to request anything smaller. It may be the case that the only interesting part of the page is the list of booked seats, but the browser can *only* get the seat list by requesting the entire page.

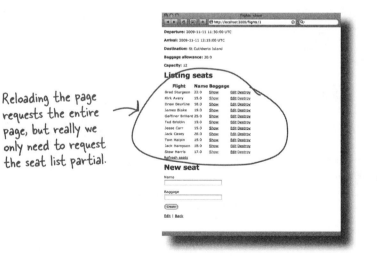

Reloading the page requests the entire page, but really we only need to request the seat list partial.

The first thing we need to do, then, is modify the application so that the interesting part of the web page—the list of seats—is available by a separate request. We need to allow a browser to request a *particular* URL that will generate *just* the seat list.

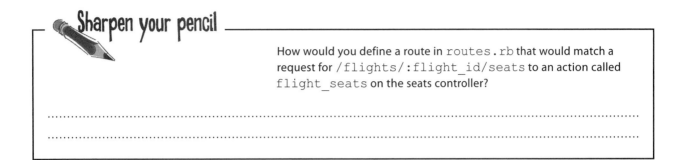

Sharpen your pencil

How would you define a route in `routes.rb` that would match a request for `/flights/:flight_id/seats` to an action called `flight_seats` on the seats controller?

....

....

Code Magnets

Complete the `flight_seats` method in the seats controller:

```
def flight_seats

    ............... = ...............(params[ ............... ])

    ............... ............... => ...............  , :locals=>{:seats=> ............... }

end
```

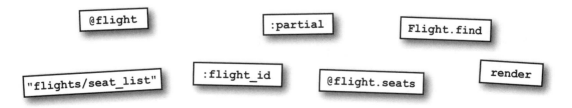

@flight

:partial

Flight.find

"flights/seat_list"

:flight_id

@flight.seats

render

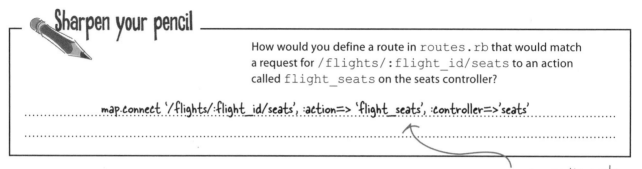

Sharpen your pencil

How would you define a route in `routes.rb` that would match a request for `/flights/:flight_id/seats` to an action called `flight_seats` on the seats controller?

..........map.connect '/flights/:flight_id/seats', :action=> 'flight_seats', :controller=>'seats'..........
....

Remember to add this route *above* the existing routes in config/routes.rb.

Code Magnets Solution

Complete the `flight_seats` method in the seats controller:

```
def flight_seats
    @flight = Flight.find (params[ :flight_id ])
    render :partial => "flights/seat_list" , :locals=>{:seats=> @flight.seats }
end
```

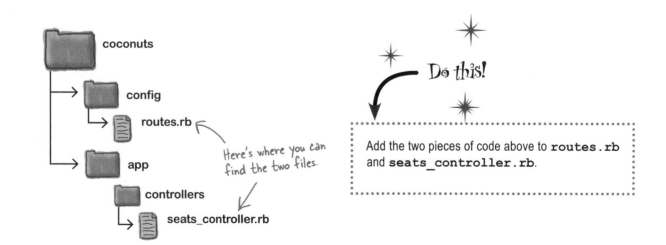

coconuts

config

routes.rb

Here's where you can find the two files.

app

controllers

seats_controller.rb

Do this!

Add the two pieces of code above to **routes.rb** and **seats_controller.rb**.

Test Drive

Imagine there are seats already booked on the flight with `id = 2`. If we go to:

`http://localhost:3000/flights/2/seats`

what should we see?

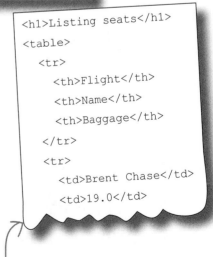

The route that we created should map `/flights/2/seats` to the `flight_seats action` and the `seats` controller, as well as create a new request parameter called `flight_id = 2`. The controller looks up flight number 2 from the database and then generates some HTML from the `seat_list` partial and return it to the browser.

Take a look at the HTML that the controller generates over on the right. What do you notice?

The HTML that gets returned isn't actually a full web page, it's just a web page ***fragment***. But what are we going to do with that? We can't just request users look at this page instead of going to the flight page, as that won't look very good. After all, at some point, the users will want to place a booking for a seat, so we want the users to remain on the flight page anyway.

Somehow we need to get the browser to request this page fragment and then use it to update the list of seats on the page.

But how?

```
<h1>Listing seats</h1>
<table>
  <tr>
    <th>Flight</th>
    <th>Name</th>
    <th>Baggage</th>
  </tr>
  <tr>
    <td>Brent Chase</td>
    <td>19.0</td>
```

Here's the page fragment that the controller generates from the seat_list partial.

Doesn't the browser <u>always</u> update the <u>entire</u> page?

At the moment when the user hits the "reload" button, the browser requests the ***entire*** web page:

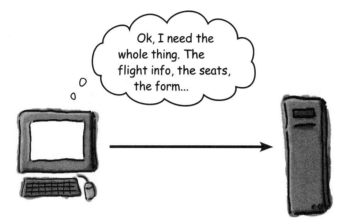

The bad news is ***that's all the browser will ever do***. Full requests are hardwired into the browser's brain. The "reload" button means "reload the entire page," so that's exactly what happens... no matter what

But why?

Under the hood, browsers only work with entire web pages. There's nothing in HTML that allows a browser to request just a part of a page... it's the all or nothing. It doesn't matter that we've now got a fragment of the page publicly available. There's no way that the browser on its own can ask for, and use, a page fragment.

So how do we get around the problem?

Fortunately for us, there's a trick we can use to get the browser to update just a part of a page. The trick is:

We get something OTHER than the browser to make the request.

So what ELSE can make a request?

Living inside the brain of every browser is a **JavaScript engine**. JavaScript allows you to modify the normal operation of the browser. JavaScript can dynamically change the appearance of a web page, it can update the contents of the HTML that is displayed, and it can respond to events within the page, such as when buttons are pressed. Most importantly, JavaScript can also ***make requests*** independent of the browser.

But what does **independent** really mean here? It's true that JavaScript can tell a browser to go to another page, but it can also do something much more subtle. In the background, JavaScript can quietly make requests to a web server and read the contents of whatever the server sends back. And all this can happen *without taking the browser to a different URL*. JavaScript could make dozens, or even hundreds, of background requests, and you wouldn't notice a thing. The browser would look like it was just displaying a page.

The reason why this is so important is that JavaScript can make a **background request**, or **asynchronous request**, asking for the latest version of the seat list. When the page fragment is returned, JavaScript can use the fragment to update the section of the page displaying the list of booked seats.

Psst...Just give me the seats again.

We can use JavaScript instead of the browser to make the request. That way we won't need to reload the entire page, and the web page will seem a lot more responsive.

We need to paste the new page fragment onto the page in the same position as the old seat list

Using JavaScript to update the current page is called **Ajax**, and Rails comes with a lot of Ajax support built right in. But how do we use it?

First we need to include the Ajax libraries...

But how do we get JavaScript in the browser to make asynchronous requests? That kind of processing is likely to be quite complex. The truth is that there is a very large amount of JavaScript code that needs to run inside the browser to make Ajax requests. The code will not only need to handle all of the details of the request processing, but it will also need to do it in a way that is compatible with all the major browsers. That would be a nightmare to create and debug, so most Ajax applications use standard JavaScript libraries to make life easier. Rails comes with one such library built in called **Prototype**.

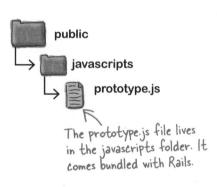

The prototype.js file lives in the javascripts folder. It comes bundled with Rails.

The Prototype library lives in a file named `prototype.js` in the javascripts folder. But even though the library is included in the application code, it's not automatically included in the web pages that are generated by an application. To make sure that Prototype is available to the browser, you need to include a reference to it in your layouts:

```erb
<!DOCTYPE html PUBLIC "-//W3C//DTD XHTML 1.0 Transitional//EN"
        "http://www.w3.org/TR/xhtml1/DTD/xhtml1-transitional.dtd">
<html xmlns="http://www.w3.org/1999/xhtml" xml:lang="en" lang="en">
<head>
  <meta http-equiv="content-type" content="text/html;charset=UTF-8" />
  <title>Flights: <%= controller.action_name %></title>
  <%= stylesheet_link_tag 'scaffold' %>
  <%= javascript_include_tag 'prototype' %>
</head>
<body>
<p style="color: green"><%= flash[:notice] %></p>
<%= yield %>
</body>
</html>
```

← This line here makes sure that the Prototype Ajax library is available to web browsers.

The `javascript_include_tag` helper makes sure the browser downloads the Prototype library from the correct URL.

app
views
layouts
flights.html.erb

Once you've got the Ajax library installed in your web pages, you're ready to create some custom Ajax code.

...then we need to add an Ajax "Refresh" link

The Ajax library makes it easier to make asynchronous requests to the server, but what the library *won't* do is write the custom Ajax code for you. So what custom code do we need?

The network problem is caused by users hitting the reload button on their browsers, which is making the system slower for them and for other users. We can get around this is by giving the users a link in the web page labeled "Refresh." This link will just update the seat bookings on the page, and because it's downloading less HTML, it will be faster for the user than the browser's "Reload." It will also reduce the load on the server, making life easier for other customers, too.

So how will the "Refresh" link work? Ajax is run entirely by JavaScript, so we need the link to generate a JavaScript event. The link's event will call the Prototype library and tell it to make a request for the latest `seat_list` section of the page. When the HTML is returned from the browser, JavaScript will dynamically replace the seats on the page with the new HTML.

So what should the code look like?

Sharpen your pencil

This is the code to add a JavaScript link to the Flight `show.html.erb` template. Write down what you think each part of the code does.

```
<div id="seats">  ←..............................................................
<%= render :partial=>"seat_list", :locals=>{:seats=>@flight.seats} %>
</div>

<%= link_to_remote(  ←..............................................................
   "Refresh seats",  ←..............................................................
   :url=>"/flights/#{@flight.id}/seats", ←.......................................
   :method=>"get",  ←..............................................................
   :update=>"seats") %>←..............................................................

<%= render :partial=>"new_seat", :locals=>{:seat=>
       Seat.new(:flight_id=>@flight.id)} %>
```

Sharpen your pencil
Solution

This is the code to add a JavaScript link to the Flight `show.html.erb` template. Write down what you think each part of the code does.

```
<div id="seats">←—— We're naming the part of the page that's changing.
<%= render :partial=>"seat_list", :locals=>{:seats=>@flight.seats} %>
</div>

<%= link_to_remote( ←—— Create a JavaScript button to update the seats.
    "Refresh seats",←——This is caption for the button.
    :url=>"/flights/#{@flight.id}/seats", ←——The URL where the new seat list will come from.
    :method=>"get", ←——This means we are just reading, not updating data.
    :update=>"seats") %>←——This is the id of the part of the page we're updating.

<%= render :partial=>"new_seat", :locals=>{:seat=>
        Seat.new(:flight_id=>@flight.id)} %>
```

When Embedded Ruby processes the `show.html.erb` template, it generates an HTML link that calls the Ajax libraries when it's clicked:

This helper generates this HTML.

The link calls the Prototype Ajax library on its onclick event.

```
</div>

<a href="#" onclick="new Ajax.Updater('seats', '/flights/1/
seats', {asynchronous:true, evalScripts:true, method:'get',
parameters:'authenticity_token=' + encodeURIComponent('7cb578
0328778ef35ee9d26689784bba0d562170')}); return false;">Refresh
seats</a>

<h1>New seat</h1>
```

there are no
Dumb Questions

Q: What's an asynchronous request?

A: An asynchronous request is a request that runs in the *background*. Asynchronous requests are generated by JavaScript.

Q: So how does that differ from normal requests?

A: Normal requests are generated when a person clicks on a link or types in a URL. Asynchronous requests are generated by JavaScript in response to an event.

Q: Does reloading the page really use up that much bandwidth?

A: It can if large amounts of HTML are required for the rest of the page. Also, the browser may attempt to reload images on the page, which can also take up a significant amount of bandwidth. Plus some parts of the page may take a lot of processing to create. Ajax allows you to leave those parts of the page to remain unchanged, reducing the load on the server.

Q: Do I need to know JavaScript in order to write Ajax code?

A: Rails will generate Ajax code for you, so you don't need to learn JavaScript. If you know JavaScript, however, you will have greater control over how the Ajax calls are made, and be better able to understand how your application works.

Q: The generated JavaScript creates a parameter called "authenticity-token". What's that for?

A: An **authenticity token** is used by Rails to ensure that a request comes from a Rails-generated page. Without the authenticity token, Rails will reject the request.

Q: How does that token work?

A: It's a value generated by Rails. The presence of the value in a request show that a request is from a page that Rails created and not from some third-party application that is trying to access your system.

Q: You say that Ajax requests are sent out by JavaScript instead of the browser, but isn't JavaScript just part of the browser?

A: Yes, but the JavaScript engine can make requests that are not part of the normal browsing sequence—and that's the point. Ajax requests allow you to update parts of a page without making full page requests and without modifying the browser page history.

Q: Why did we use the javascript_include_tag helper instead of just entering the HTML to load the JavaScript?

A: If you want to write HTML for yourself, straight HTML will work, but Rails developers tend to use helpers whenever possible. Helpers are usually a little shorter than the literal HTML, and they also fill in some application specific configuration for you. For example, the javascript_include_tag will fill in the path to the standard javascript path: "/javascripts/...". .

Q: That doesn't sound like that big of a deal.

A: The helper also adds a random number to the end of the JavaScript location.

Q: What use is that?

A: It means that if someone refreshes the page in the browser, the browser will also download a new copy of the JavaScript library. That way, if you change anything in the library, the browser will always request the latest version.

TEST DRIVE

Now that the JavaScript button is in place, it's time to see how the application's looking. Reload your app and try things out.

① The first user goes to the flight page to book a seat.
He sees details of the flight as well as the list of seats already booked and a booking form. Sitting between the seat list and booking form is the new Ajax button.

```
000                    Flights: show
◀ ▶ ℃ ⊠ +  ⊕ http://localhost:3000/flights/2        Q▾

  Flight      Name Baggage
Brent Chase    19.0   Show        Edit Destroy
Tom Christie   15.0   Show        Edit Destroy
Ryan Cleary    19.0   Show        Edit Destroy
Julien Collard 16.0   Show        Edit Destroy
Charlie Collins 19.0  Show        Edit Destroy

Refresh seats

New seat

Name
[                    ]

Baggage
[                    ]

( Create )

Edit | Back
```

② A second user visits the page and books a seat.
When the form is submitted her page is refreshed and she sees her new booking. So will everyone who now goes to the page. But what about the first user?

```
000                    Flights: show
◀ ▶ ℃ ⊠ +  ⊕ http://localhost:3000/flights/2        Q▾

  Flight      Name Baggage
Brent Chase    19.0   Show        Edit Destroy
Tom Christie   15.0   Show        Edit Destroy
Ryan Cleary    19.0   Show        Edit Destroy
Julien Collard 16.0   Show        Edit Destroy
Charlie Collins 19.0  Show        Edit Destroy

Refresh seats

New seat

Name
[Jesse James Garrett ]

Baggage
[12|                 ]

( Create )

Edit | Back
```

③ **The first user can see the new booking by hitting the refresh button.**

The button fires off a JavaScript event that will call the Ajax library and refresh the seat list, showing the new booking.

Flights: show

http://localhost:3000/flights/2

Flight	Name	Baggage			
Brent Chase	19.0		Show	Edit	Destroy
Tom Christie	15.0		Show	Edit	Destroy
Ryan Cleary	19.0		Show	Edit	Destroy
Julien Collard	16.0		Show	Edit	Destroy
Charlie Collins	19.0		Show	Edit	Destroy
Jesse James Garrett	12.0		Show	Edit	Destroy

Refresh seats

New seat

Name

Baggage

(Create)

But why do I have to click refresh to see the changes? Can't the system update the page automatically?

The system works great, but a few users are wondering why they have to sit there repeatedly clicking a button just to see if there are new bookings. It would be much more convenient if the page could somehow discover when there are new bookings automatically.

But is that possible?

The browser needs to ask for an update

But there's a problem with automatically updating the page, and it comes from the way that the web works.

In a perfect world, the web application would be able to tell the user whenever the list of booked seats changes. Unfortunately, web servers don't work like that. They only speak when they're spoken to.

You want me to just **give** you things? If you don't ask, you don't get...

The server will only send a **response** if it gets a **request**. If the server has new information that it wants to let the browser know about, it can't do anything. It has to wait for the browser to *ask* for the new information.

That means if we want the browser to automatically be told whenever the seat list changes, we're going to be disappointed. Instead we need the browser to just keep asking. And asking. And asking...

The browser sends requests to the server...

Gimme the seats.

Here they are.

Gimme the seats.

Here they are.

Gimme the seats.

Here they are.

... and the server sends back responses.

But SHOULD we make the browser ask over and over again?

Think back to the way the Ajax refresh link works. When someone clicks on it, the link generates a JavaScript event, which in turn calls the Prototype library, asking it download a new version of the seat list.

The key point is that whole thing begins with an *event*, something that happens outside of JavaScript.

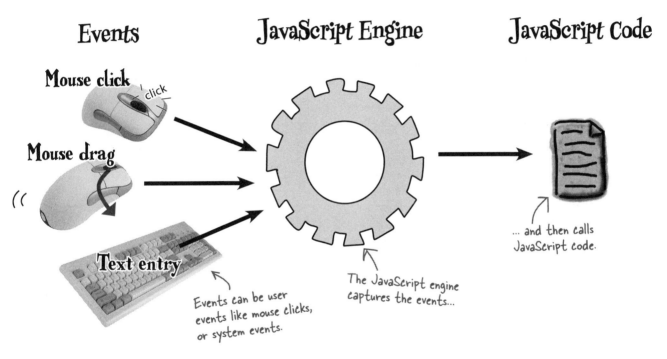

Events

Mouse click

click

Mouse drag

((

Text entry

Events can be user events like mouse clicks, or system events.

JavaScript Engine

The JavaScript engine captures the events...

JavaScript Code

... and then calls JavaScript code.

A piece of JavaScript can register itself with an event, meaning that when the event occurs, the JavaScript runs.

In our situation, we need to run the same piece of JavaScript over and over again. So what kind of event can do that? Well, it won't be an event generated by a human action. Instead, we need to register JavaScript with a **timer** event.

A timer is a system event that occurs at regular intervals, usually every few seconds. We need to create a timer, then register the "Update the seat list" JavaScript with it.

Fortunately, Rails can help us.

You listen to a timer like you listen to a button

The only real difference between running a piece of Ajax code when a button is pressed and running it over and over again every few seconds, really just comes down to exactly what kind of event you are listening to.

For that reason, the Ruby code we place into the page template is actually quite similar to the code we used to create the JavaScript button:

A helper to create JavaScript to listen to a timer

```
<%= periodically_call_remote(
    :url=>"_____",
    :method=>"get",
    :update=>"_____",
    :frequency=>"____") %>
```

The URL where the new seat list will come from

This means we're just reading, not updating data.

This is the id of the part of the page we're updating.

The number of seconds between timer events

This code will create JavaScript to make a request for a new seat list every few seconds. It will then update the specified part of the page with the HTML that's returned by the server. The only real difference between this helper and the code that created the JavaScript button is:

 The button needs caption text.

 The timer needs to be given a frequency.

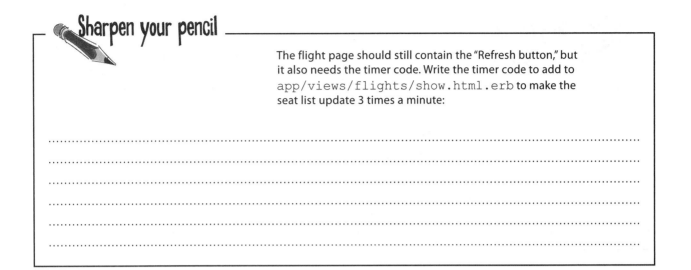

Sharpen your pencil

The flight page should still contain the "Refresh button," but it also needs the timer code. Write the timer code to add to `app/views/flights/show.html.erb` to make the seat list update 3 times a minute:

....

....

....

....

....

....

there are no
Dumb Questions

Q: Is there really no way that the browser can be contacted by the server?

A: The browser could maintain an open connection with the server but that would require a large number of connections for even mimimally popular applications. Polling the server is a much more popular approach.

Q: Is the frequency of a timer always in seconds?

A: Yes, the frequency is always in seconds. It might seem odd that it's called frequency because it doesn't give the frequency (how many times it fires a minute). Instead it gives the "period", which is the amount of time *between* firings.

Q: What's the default frequency?

A: By default, the frequency is 10 seconds.

Q: Where does the id of the part of the page come from?

A: Each tag in HTML can be given an id. That's a unique reference to mark a part of a web page. Usually Ajax apps wrap some part of the page in a <div> tag with an id. That allows you to give an id to a single tag, or to a group of HTML tags all at once.

clicked refresh or timed events?

Sharpen your pencil
Solution

The flight page should still contain the "Refresh button," but it also needs the timer code. Write the timer code to add to app/views/flights/show.html.erb to make the seat list update 3 times a minute:

```
<%= periodically_call_remote(
  :url=>"/flights/#{@flight.id}/seats",
  :method=>"get",
  :update=>"seats",
  :frequency=>"20") %>
```

Your show.html.erb template should contain code looking like this:

```
  <%=h @flight.baggage_allowance %>
</p>
<p>
  <b>Capacity:</b>
  <%=h @flight.capacity %>
</p>
<div id="seats">
<%= render :partial=>"seat_list", :locals=>{:seats=>@flight.seats} %>
</div>
<%= link_to_remote
    "Refresh seats", :url=>"/flights/#{@flight.id}/seats",
    :method=>"get", :update=>"seats" %>
<%= periodically_call_remote(
    :url=>"/flights/#{@flight.id}/seats",
    :method=>"get", :update=>"seats", :frequency=>"20") %>
<%= render :partial=>"new_seat", :locals=>{:seat=>Seat.new(:flight_id=>@flight.id)} %>
```

This is the bottom part of the show.html.erb file.

Now the timer code has been added, the system should automatically update the list of seat bookings without the user doing anything to refresh the page.

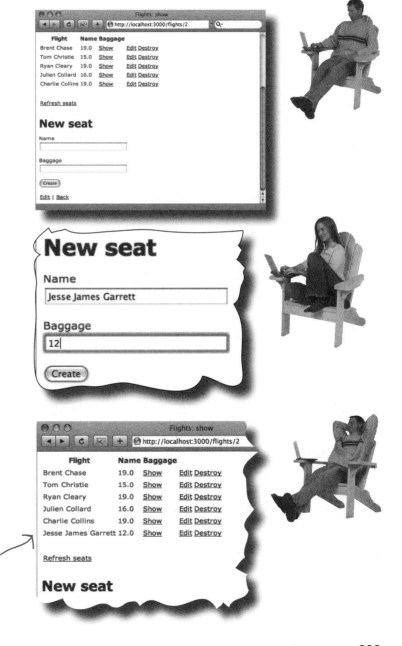

1 The first user goes to the flight page to book a seat.
He sees details of the flight.

2 While he's booking the seat, a second user visits the page.
She quickly books a seat on the flight and submits the data.

3 The first user automatically sees the new booking.
Even though the first user doesn't touch the keyboard, the page automatically updates the seat list within 20 seconds.

New booking automatically appears.

Ajax Exposed

This week's interview:
Getting Up To Speed With Ajax.

Head First: Hello, Ajax, and welcome. It's good of you...

Ajax: My pleasure.

Head First: ...to be interviewed today.

Ajax: Oh, I interrupted you.

Head First: That's quite...

Ajax: I do that a lot. I'm sorry. I can be a little—you know—hyper.

Head First: You're a busy technology?

Ajax: See that? I just updated the data table! What - technology? I'm not technology. I'm a way of life, baby! Or at least a way of writing web apps.

Head First: How do you mean?

Ajax: Well, Rails, JavaScript, Prototype—those dudes are software. Nothin' wrong with that. It's cool, but I'm way beyond that. Prototype is just a support library for me.

Head First: So what are you?

Ajax: I'm a design technique. If you make asynchronous JavaScript requests to update a web page, you're using me.

Head First: Asynchronous? That means your requests...

Ajax: ... interrupt the normal browser stuff, yeah. The requests happen in the background while the user sits on the page.

Head First: And almost anything can trigger Ajax requests?

Ajax: Oh yeah. XHRs can be generated by almost anything—any kind of JavaScript event.

Head First: I'm sorry—XH...?

Ajax: XHRs. Sorry, XHRs are my little Ajax request buddies. "XML HTTP Requests" is the proper name.

Head First: Now you say you're not software, but people do install Ajax libraries, don't they?

Ajax: You can write your own code from the ground up, but sure, most people use Ajax libraries, like the Protoype library. Libraries handle creating requests and dealing with the stuff that comes back.

Head First: And what sort of data is returned by an Ajax request?

Ajax: Whatever floats your boat, baby. Page fragments in HTML. Data in XML or JavaScript format. Even JavaScript itself.

Head First: I see. Tell me more, JavaScript...

Ajax: What's that little buddy? Hey, sorry dude—gotta go.

Head First: Excuse me?

Ajax: Someone just hit a JavaScript button. I got an on-click event with my name on it. Catch you later...

Head First: Ajax, thank...

Ajax: Don't mention it.

Someone's having trouble with their bachelor party

I need to book 19 seats for my bachelor party. But I have to keep hitting the "Back" key to return to the flight page!

At the moment, when you book a seat, the browser submits a form to the server, and a page displaying the booked seat is then returned to the browser. But what if someone needs to book a whole set of seats? In this case, they have to press the "Back" key on the browser to return to the flight page to book another seat... and get another confirmation, and then hit Back again...

So far we've written code that can update the list of seats without going to a new page. Can we do something similar if a seat is booked? If the form could somehow send the booking to the server and then update the list of seats, it would mean that the user could remain on the same page. If they needed to make another booking, they're already on the correct page to enable them to do that.

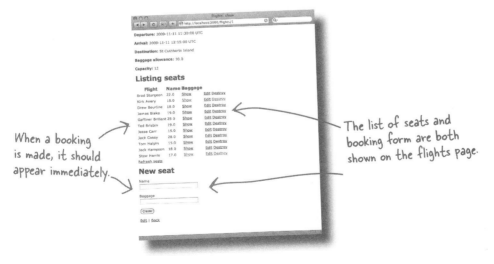

When a booking is made, it should appear immediately.

The list of seats and booking form are both shown on the flights page.

The form needs to make an Ajax request

If we let the browser submit the form we know that we'll be sent to another page. It's just like the problem we had when the user hit the browser "Reload" button—it's built-in browser behavior that we can't modify.

So what do we do? We need to use a different kind of form. Instead of using a standard HTTP form, we need to use a JavaScript form and use that to make a request.

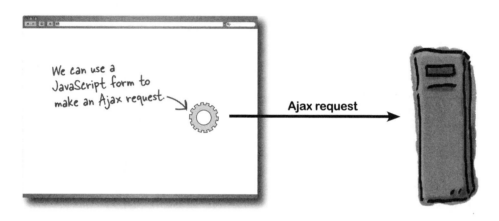

We can use a JavaScript form to make an Ajax request.

Ajax request

Instead of simply asking the browser to submit the form data, we need the submit button to generate a JavaScript event that will submit the form data using an Ajax request. So why is that so important? It means that the act of booking the seat *won't* cause the browser to switch to another page.

The form needs to be under the CONTROL of JavaScript

So we need to convert the form from a simple HTTP form into one that generates JavaScript events and dynamically updates the current page rather than moving the browser to a different URL. Here is the contents of the booking form partial:

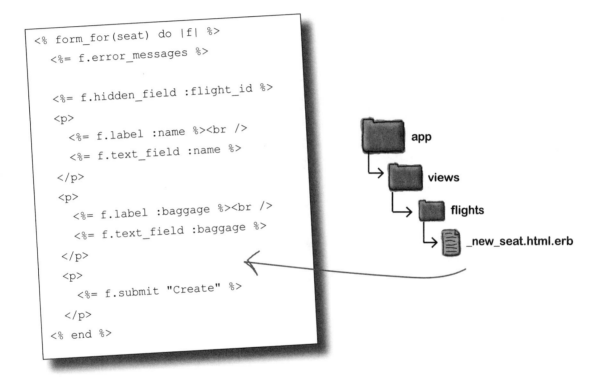

```
<% form_for(seat) do |f| %>
  <%= f.error_messages %>

  <%= f.hidden_field :flight_id %>
  <p>
    <%= f.label :name %><br />
    <%= f.text_field :name %>
  </p>
  <p>
    <%= f.label :baggage %><br />
    <%= f.text_field :baggage %>
  </p>
  <p>
    <%= f.submit "Create" %>
  </p>
<% end %>
```

app
views
flights
_new_seat.html.erb

But how do we make this the form work in this completely different way? We need to change this:

```
<% form_for(seat) do |f| %>
```

to this:

```
<% remote_form_for(seat, :update=>'seats' ) do |f| %>
```

It's a fairly small change, but behind the scenes the form will work in a very different way...

TEST DRIVE

When a user goes to a flight page (http://localhost:3000/flights/2),
the booking form looks exactly as it did before:

But, of course, behind the scenes the HTML is very
different. So what happens when a new seat is booked?

Where did our list of seat bookings go??????

Something's not quite right. Look in your
database... the seat was booked correctly, but the
flight page becomes corrupted. Why?

We've changed the code in the view, but the
controller code—the code on the server—is still
doing the same thing it did before; it sends back
HTML with details of the newly booked seat.
What we need is a new version of the seat list

Let's fix the controller code.

We need to replace the create method

The existing `create` method in the seats controller looks like this:

```
def create
    @seat = Seat.new(params[:seat])
    respond_to do |format|
      if @seat.save
        flash[:notice] = 'Seat was successfully created.'
        format.html { redirect_to(@seat) }
        format.xml  { render :xml => @seat, :status => :created,
                        :location => @seat }

      else
        format.html { render :action => "new" }
        format.xml  { render :xml => @seat.errors,
                        :status => :unprocessable_entity }

      end
    end
end
```

— Don't worry if you don't get what all this code is doing; we'll be replacing it soon anyway.

We need to replace this with code that creates a Seat object, saves the object to the database, and then renders a new copy of the seat list. But what should this code look like?

app

controllers

seats_controller.rb

✏️ **Sharpen your pencil**

Write a new `create` method that will always create a Seat object based on the form data, ask the new object to save itself to the database, and render the contents of the `seat_list` partial.

....

....

....

....

....

```
Sharpen your pencil
           Solution
```

Write a new `create` method that will always create a Seat object based on the form data, ask the new object to save itself to the database, and render the contents of the `seat_list` partial.

Create a seat object
exactly as you did
before.

This allows you to
render the seat list ──→
for all of the seats
on the flight.

```
.def create..............................................................
⌐ @seat = Seat.new(params[:seat])...............................
  @seat.save ⟵ Don't bother checking if the save is successful.
──→.render :partial=>'flights/seat_list', :locals=>{:seats=>@seat.flight.seats}.....
..end..............................................................
```

So what effect does this code have?

The new create method means that when the Ajax form submits a new booking, it should receive a new copy of the seat list from the server:

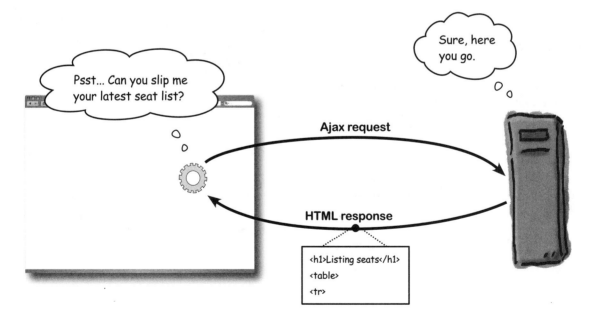

Psst... Can you slip me your latest seat list?

Sure, here you go.

Ajax request

HTML response

```
<h1>Listing seats</h1>
<table>
<tr>
```

Test Drive

Suppose a user goes to a flight page and submits a new booking request:

The system works! Now when a booking is made, the browser stays on the same page and the new booking record appears immediately.

That's awesome! Now I can get to booking the other 18 seats I need.

BULLET POINTS

- JavaScript can make **background requests** to a server.

- JavaScript can use the HTML returned to update only **part of a page**.

- Updating the page using background requests is called **Ajax**.

- The requests are called **XML HTTP Requests** (XHRs).

- JavaScript can be run when **events** occur.

- Events can be the result of **user actions** (like mouse clicks) or **system events** (like timers).

- If you don't want a form to move the browser to a new page, you need to convert it to an **Ajax form**.

- To make a form an Ajax form, you need to change `form_for` to `remote_form_for`.

- The **controller code** that handles the form request can send back HTML to update the page.

- If you give the form an `:update` parameter, it will know where in a page to put returned HTML.

there are no Dumb Questions

Q: How come we only need to amend the form helpers and not all of the fields in the form?

A: The fields in the form stay the same because they just contain data fields as they did before. The only real difference between an Ajax form and a "normal" HTML form, is that the onsubmit event for an Ajax form calls the Prototype libraries instead of submitting the form. Everything else remains the same.

Q: I saw elsewhere that Ajax forms are generated by "form_remote_for". Is that different?

A: No - form_remote_for is just an alias for remote_form_for. They will both do exactly the same thing.

Q: What if I need to convert an unbound form_tag?

A: There is an Ajax form_remote_tag that can be used as a replacement.

Q: I don't get it. The *form* can replace HTML in the *page*???

A: Not quite. The form calls a JavaScript function to make an Ajax request. It is the JavaScript function that replaces the HTML in the page.

Q: When the server receives the form request will it still look the same?

A: The request will be the same as if it had been sent from an HTML form. Prototype will construct the request so that will appear to be a perfectly normal HTTP request.

Q: What HTTP method does the Ajax form use?

A: Just like an HTML form, the Ajax form uses the POST method by default.

Q: But I can change the method, right?

A: You can change the HTTP method by providing a :method=> parameter in the helper.

A bunch of members of the Ajax Club, in full costume, are playing a party game, "Who am I?" They'll give you a clue, and you'll try to guess who they are based on what they say. Assume they always tell the truth about themselves. Fill in the blanks to the right to identify the attendees.

Tonight's attendees:

Any of the charming Ajax buddies you've seen so far just might show up!

Name

I am a library that Rails uses to generate Ajax requests from a browser.

....

I am a language that runs inside the browser.

....

I am a request used in Ajax apps, and my friends call me XHR.

....

I am an event, but I'm not a user event.

....

I am used to generate an Ajax form based on an object.

....

I can call browser code that is registered with me.

....

A bunch of members of the Ajax Club, in full costume, are playing a party game, "Who am I?" They'll give you a clue, and you'll try to guess who they are based on what they say. Assume they always tell the truth about themselves. Fill in the blanks to the right to identify the attendees.

Tonight's attendees:

Any of the charming Ajax buddies you've seen so far just might show up!

Who am I?

Name

I am a library that Rails uses to generate Ajax requests from a browser.

.... Prototype ....

I am a language that runs inside the browser.

.... JavaScript ....

I am a request used in Ajax apps, and my friends call me XHR.

...XML Http Request...

I am an event, but I'm not a user event.

.... System event ....

I am used to generate an Ajax form based on an object.

.... remote_form_for ....

I can call browser code that is registered with me.

.... Event ....

There's a problem with the flight bookings

The bachelor party organizer was booking his bachelor party trip when he hit a problem. There was plenty of space on the flight when he started booking seats, but then...

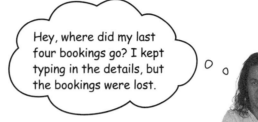

Hey, where did my last four bookings go? I kept typing in the details, but the bookings were lost.

Someone else was booking seats at the same time.

While the Ajax form can book seats OK, our simplified controller code doesn't check if there's an error, and it doesn't check to see if the flight's already been booked up.

So what do we need to do? As well as displaying the latest version of the seat list, the controller code somehow need to update the notices section of the page to say whether or not the booking was successful.

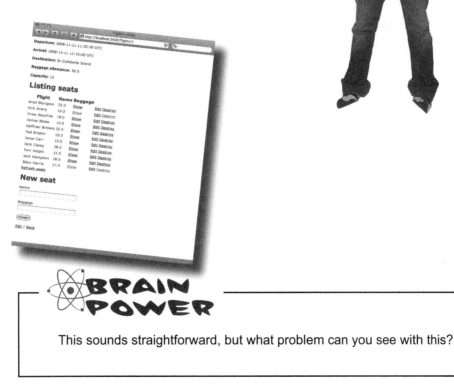

⚛ BRAIN POWER

This sounds straightforward, but what problem can you see with this?

We only know how to update one part of the page at a time

So far, when we've made an Ajax request, we have always updated just one part of the page with the HTML returned by the server:

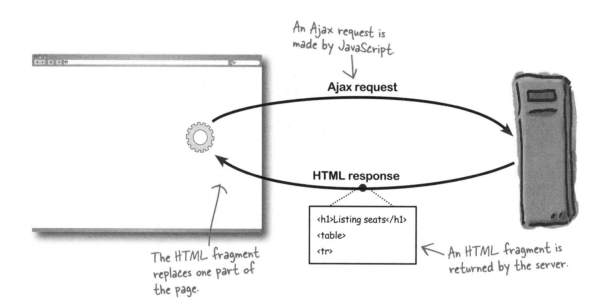

An Ajax request is made by JavaScript.

Ajax request

HTML response

```
<h1>Listing seats</h1>
<table>
<tr>
```

The HTML fragment replaces one part of the page.

An HTML fragment is returned by the server.

So what's different this time?

The difference this time is that we need to update the seat list *and* the notices section at the top of the page. That's two completely separate pieces of HTML that need to be replaced.

So how can we use a single response from the server to make multiple changes to a page? Should we make multiple requests? Or send several pieces of HTML?

There's actually a much neater way of doing several operations as the result of a single request.

The trick is to send something other than HTML back in the response.

The controller needs to return JavaScript instead of HTML

If the controller sends HTML data back to the browser, then JavaScript will normally do something simple with it, like use it to replace part of the page. But if the controller sends JavaScript code back to the browser, that code can do as many things as the controller needs it to do.

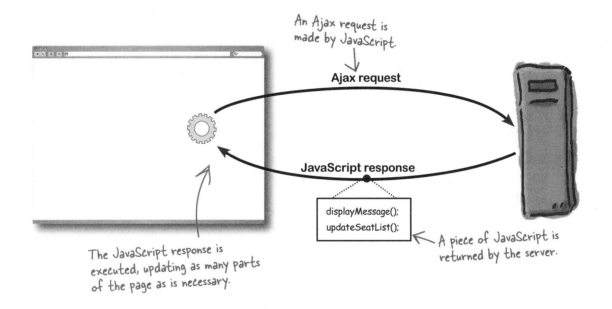

An Ajax request is made by JavaScript.

Ajax request

JavaScript response

```
displayMessage();
updateSeatList();
```

A piece of JavaScript is returned by the server.

The JavaScript response is executed, updating as many parts of the page as is necessary.

So if the controller wants to update the list of seats on the page, then display a confirmation message, then perform some sort of fancy animation that turns the entire page upside down, all it needs to do is send back the appropriate JavaScript code. Whatever is in the JavaScript will get executed.

[Note from the Good Taste police: You really don't want to do this]

> Oh great. So we just send back JavaScript do we? But I don't **know** JavaScript. Are you telling me I have to learn an **entire language** just so that I can perform a couple of changes on a **page**???

You can let Rails write the JavaScript for you.

If the controller needs to send back JavaScript instead of HTML, you might expect that you will need to how to write JavaScript code. But actually you don't.

Rails provides an object called a ***JavaScript generator*** which does exactly what the name suggests—it ***generates JavaScript***.

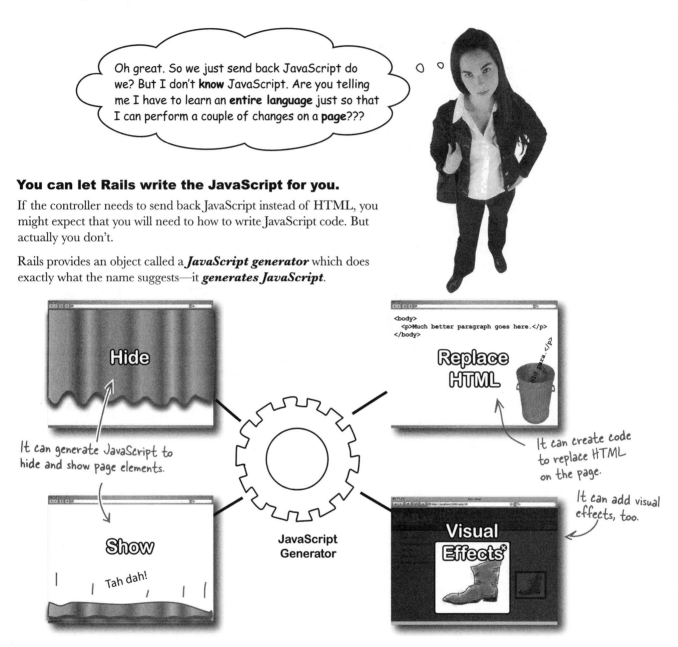

It can generate JavaScript to hide and show page elements.

Tah dah!

JavaScript Generator

It can create code to replace HTML on the page.

It can add visual effects, too.

The thing is, that while knowing JavaScript can be an advantage, most of the time, the JavaScript code you will be sending back to the browser will be doing some fairly standard things, like replacing a piece of HTML, or hiding part of the page, or calling some JavaScript library function to do an animation. And a JavaScript generator can write the code to do each of those things for you.

All you need to do is call it the right way.

Code Magnets

Complete the controller code to generate JavaScript to replace the
HTML in the 'notices' <div/> to say that the seat was booked.

```ruby
def create

  @seat = Seat.new(params[:seat])

  render :update do |page|

    if ........................

      page. ......................................., ...................................................

    else

      page. ......................................., ...................................................

    end

  end

end
```

app

controllers

seats_controller.rb

'Sorry - the seat could not be booked'

replace_html

'notices'

@seat.save

'notice'

replace_html

'Seat was successfully booked'

Code Magnets Solution

Complete the controller code to generate JavaScript to replace the
HTML in the 'notices' <div/> to say that the seat was booked.

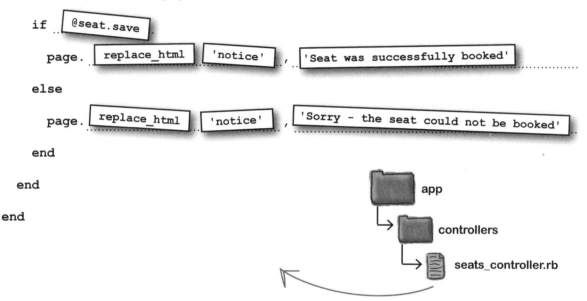

```
def create

  @seat = Seat.new(params[:seat])

  render :update do |page|

    if @seat.save

      page. replace_html  'notice' , 'Seat was successfully booked'

    else

      page. replace_html  'notice' , 'Sorry - the seat could not be booked'

    end

  end

end
```

app
→ controllers
  → seats_controller.rb

The controller code generates JavaScript to update a section of the web
page with id='notice'. So which part of the web page will that be? Well -
the layout for the flights pages contains a special output area at the top of
each page for notices. You need to edit the flights layout and add an id to
the <p> element like this:

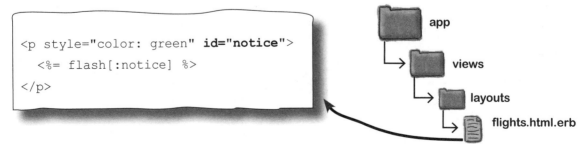

```
<p style="color: green" id="notice">
  <%= flash[:notice] %>
</p>
```

app
→ views
  → layouts
    → flights.html.erb

So what does Rails generate?

The page JavaScript generator creates the following JavaScript:

There's *no way* you want to write this yourself...

```
try {
Element.update("notice", "Seat was successfully booked");

Element.update("seats", "<h1>Listing seats</h1>\n\n<table>\n
<tr>\n    <th>Flight</th>\n    <th>Name</th>\n    <th>Baggage</
th>\n  </tr>\n\n\n  <tr>\n    <td>Brad Sturgeon</td>\n    <td>22.0</
td>\n    <td><a href=\"/seats/1\">Show</a></td>\n    <td><a href=\"/
seats/1/edit\">Edit</a></td>\n    <td><a href=\"/seats/1\" onclick=\"if
(confirm('Are you sure?')) { var f = document.createElement('form');
f.style.display = 'none'; this.parentNode.appendChild(f); f.method =
'POST'; f.action = this.href;var m = document.createElement('input');
m.setAttribute('type', 'hidden'); m.setAttribute('name', '_
method'); m.setAttribute('value', 'delete'); f.appendChild(m);var s
= document.createElement('input'); s.setAttribute('type', 'hidden');
s.setAttribute('name', 'authenticity_token'); s.setAttribute('value',
'aec87b235224924109e33b3207d464c64207e733'); f.appendChild(s);f.
submit(); };return false;\">Destroy</a></td>\n  </tr>\n\n  <tr>\n
<td>Kirk Avery</td>\n    <td>15.0</td>\n    <td><a href=\"/
seats/2\">Show</a></td>\n    <td><a href=\"/seats/2/edit\">Edit</
a></td>\n    <td><a href=\"/seats/2\" onclick=\"if (confirm('Are
you sure?')) { var f = document.createElement('form'); f.style.
display = 'none'; this.parentNode.appendChild(f); f.method = 'POST';
f.action = this.href;var m = document.createElement('input');
m.setAttribute('type', 'hidden'); m.setAttribute('name', '_
method'); m.setAttribute('value', 'delete'); f.appendChild(m);var s
= document.createElement('input'); s.setAttribute('type', 'hidden');
s.setAttribute('name', 'authenticity_token'); s.setAttribute('value',
```

This will be returned to the browser when the Ajax booking form is submitted to the controller. Previously, the browser would take the contents of the controller response and use it to replace some part of the page. But now, we want the browser to *execute* the response. We want it to run our generated JavaScript.

But how do we tell the form to execute the JavaScript response?

If you don't say where to put the response, it will be executed

Let's look at the Embedded Ruby code that generates the Ajax form:

```erb
<% remote_form_for(seat, :update=>'seats') do |f| %>
  <%= f.error_messages %>

  <%= f.hidden_field :flight_id %>
  <p>
    <%= f.label :name %><br />
    <%= f.text_field :name %>
  </p>
  <p>
    <%= f.label :baggage %><br />
    <%= f.text_field :baggage %>
  </p>
  <p>
    <%= f.submit "Create" %>
  </p>
<% end %>
```

This code creates all of the JavaScript that's necessary to fire off an Ajax request when the form's Create button is pressed. The form then takes whatever is returned by the server and uses it to replace the part of the page labeled with id = 'seats'.

Now that was fine when the server was sending HTML back to the browser. But now it's sending JavaScript and we don't want the form to put that just anywhere. We want it to execute it, and that's a very different deal.

The change we actually need to make to the page template is very small. All we need to do to make the form execute the code is remove the update parameter:

The update parameter has been removed.

```erb
<% remote_form_for(seat) do |f| %>
```

TEST DRIVE

Now, when a seat is booked, the form displays a success or failure message.

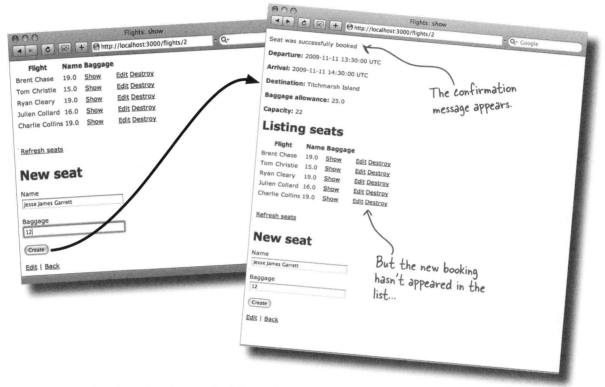

The confirmation message appears.

But the new booking hasn't appeared in the list...

But the page doesn't update the seat list. We need to generate extra JavaScript to update the seat list.

Sharpen your pencil

You need to write an extra call to update the seat list with the contents of the appropriate partial.

```
page.replace_html ' ............... ', :partial => ' ....................... ',
        :locals => { ................ => ........................................... }
```

Sharpen your pencil
Solution

You need to write an extra call to update the seat list with the contents of the appropriate partial.

This is the <div> we are updating

This will use the app/view/flights/_seat_list.html.erb partial

```
page.replace_html ' ...seats... ', :partial => 'flights/seat_list '
      :locals => { :seats => @seat.flight.seats }
```

The array of seats in the flight

The completed code can will now do several things

Here's what the completed code should look like:

```
def create
  @seat = Seat.new(params[:seat])
  render :update do |page|
    if @seat.save
      page.replace_html 'notice', 'Seat was successfully booked'
    else
      page.replace_html 'notice', 'Sorry - the seat could not be booked'
    end
    page.replace_html 'seats', :partial => 'flights/seat_list',
      :locals => {:seats =>  @seat.flight.seats }
  end
end
```

We can call methods on the page JavaScript generator as often as we like. So if the seat is saved correctly, the page object will generate code to updates the notice and it creates JavaScript to update the seat list.

TEST DRIVE

Now when a new seat is booked, not only does the confirmation message appear, but the seat list gets updated too:

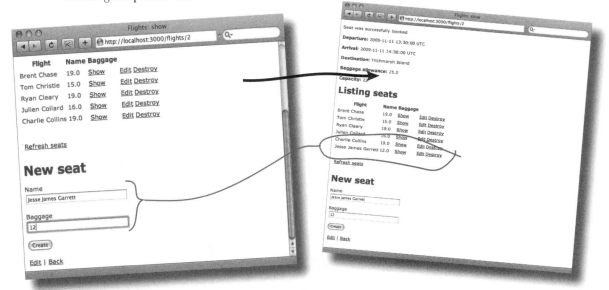

The system goes live and people are able to quickly book multiple seats.

> Multiple seats means multiple stags in my bar... better get some more rum in!

Head First **Lounge:** Titchmarsh Island

Tools for your Rails Toolbox

You've got Chapter 7 under your belt, and now you've added the ability to add Ajax to your applications.

Rails Tools

Ajax applications make background requests using JavaScript

The Protoype library provides you with most of the functions to do Ajax

There are several Ajax helpers provided by Rails:

<%= link_to_remote %> will create an Ajax link.

<%= periodically_call_remote %> starts an Ajax timer

<%= remote_form_for %> creates an Ajax form

If the Ajax helpers are given :update parameters, they will replace the part of the web page with a matching id.

If the :update parameter is omitted, they will execute the JavaScript the controller returns.

8 XML and multiple representations

It all looks different now...

Heavens - you've really changed, Dorothy.

You can't please everyone all of the time. Or can you?

So far we've looked at how you can use Rails to quickly and easily develop web apps that **perfectly fit one set of requirements**. But what do you do when **other requirements come along**? What should you do if some people want **basic web pages**, others want a **Google mashup**, and yet more want your app available as an **RSS feed**? In this chapter you'll create **multiple representations** of the same basic data, giving you the **maximum flexibility** with **minimum effort**.

Climbing all over the world

Head First Climbers is a web site for mountaineers all over the world. Climbers report back from expeditions to record the locations and times of mountains they have climbed, and also to report dangerous features they've discovered, like rock slides and avalanches.

The information is obviously very important for the safety of other climbers, and many climbers use mobile phones and GPS receivers to read and record information straight from the rock face. Used in the right way, the system will save lives and yet—somehow—the web site's not getting a lot of traffic.

So why isn't it popular?

The application is very basic. It's simply a scaffolded version of this data structure:

Incident	
mountain	*string*
latitude	*decimal*
longitude	*decimal*
when	*datetime*
title	*string*
description	*text*

id	mountain	latitude	longitude	when	title	description
1	Mount Rushless	63.04348055...	-150.993963...	2009-11-21 11:...	Rock slide	Rubble on the ...
2	Mount Rushless	63.07805277...	-150.977869...	2009-11-21 17:...	Hidden crev...	Ice layer cove...
3	Mount Lotopaxo	-0.683975	-78.4365055...	2009-06-07 12:...	Ascent	Living only on...
4	High Kanuklima	11.123925	72.72135833...	2009-05-12 18:...	Altitude si...	Overcome by th...

As you've noticed by now, scaffolding is a great way to *start* an application, but you'll almost always need to modify the code to change the generic scaffolding code into something that's more appropriate for the problems your users are trying to solve.

So what needs to change about this application?

Do this!

> Create a scaffolded application that matches this data structure.

The users hate the interface!

It doesn't take too long to find out why the web site isn't popular: **the user interface**.

The system is used to manage ***spatial*** data—it records incidents that happen at particular places and times around the world. The location information is recorded using two numbers:

 The ***latitude***. This is how far North or South the location is.

The ***longitude***. This is a measure of how far West or East a location is.

The users can record their data OK: they just read the latitude and longitude from GPS receivers. But they have a lot of trouble *reading* and *interpreting* the information from other climbers.

> I'm sure that dangerous rock slide is supposed to be some place near here...

HighPhone

So people can add data to the application, but they can't understand the data they get from it. That's cutting the number of visitors, and the fewer visitors there are the less information is getting added... which causes even less people to use the app. It's a real downward spiral.

Something needs to be done or the web site will lose so much business it has to close down.

Think about the data that the application needs to display. How would **you** display the information? What would be the best format to make the information easily comprehensible for the climbers who need it?

The data needs to be on a map

The system records geographic data and it should be displayed on a map.

The correct data is being stored, and the basic functions (create, read, update, and delete) are all available. The problem is **presentation**. The location is *stored* as two numbers—the latitude and longitude—but that doesn't mean it has to be *displayed* that way.

Instead of seeing this...

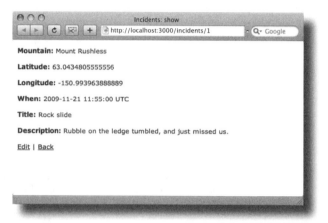

...climbers need to see something like this:

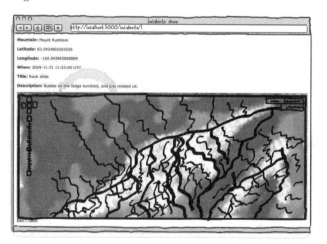

Now this is obviously going to be a pretty big change to the interface, so the web site guys have decided that rather than change the whole application, they are going to run a small pilot project to create a version of the page that displays an incident and get it to display a map. But they have no idea what to do, and need your help.

What's the first thing YOU would do?

We need to create a new action

We don't want to *change* the existing code—we only want to *add* to it. Until we are sure that the new interface works, we don't want to upset any of the existing users. After all, there aren't that many left...

So we'll add a new action called `show_with_map`. At the moment, someone can see one of the incidents using a URL like this:

```
http://localhost:3000/incidents/1
```

We'll create a new version of the page at:

```
http://localhost:3000/incidents/map/1
```

This way, the pilot users only need to add /map to get the new version of the page. We'll use this for the route:

Remember to add this as the first route in your config/ routes.rb file.

```
map.connect 'incidents/map/:id', :action=>'show_with_map', :controller=>'incidents'
```

Sharpen your pencil

We can create the page template by copying the `app/views/incidents/show.html.erb` file. What will the new file be called?

....

The incidents controller will need a new method to read the appropriate `Incident` model object and store it in an instance variable called `@incident`. Write the new method below:

....
....
....
....
....

Sharpen your pencil
Solution

We can create the page template by copying the `app/views/incidents/show.html.erb` file. What will the new file be called?

.... **app/views/incidents/show_with_map.html.erb** ....

The incidents controller will need a new method to read the appropriate `Incident` model object and store it in an instance variable called `@incident`. Write the new method below:

.... show_with_map is the ——→ **def show_with_map**
.... name of the action.
                                 @incident = Incident.find(params[:id]) ←— This will be the id
                                                            number from the URL.
                              end

The new action seems to work...

If you now look at the two versions of the incidents page, we see that they both display the correct data. What do you notice?

Do this!

Create the page template and the new controller method now.

Mountain: Mount Rushless

Latitude: 63.0434805555556

Longitude: -150.993963888889

When: 2009-11-21 11:55:00 UTC

Title: Rock slide

Description: Rubble on the ledge tumbled, and just missed us.

Edit | Back

← This is the original scaffolded page.

This version has a different URL.

Incidents: show_with_map — http://localhost:3000/incidents/map/1

Mountain: Mount Rushless

Latitude: 63.0434805555556

Longitude: -150.993963888889

When: 2009-11-21 11:55:00 UTC

Title: Rock slide

Description: Rubble on the ledge tumbled, and just missed us.

Edit | Back

← This is the version that calls the new show_with_map action.

Both versions show the same data.

Both versions of the incidents page look identical—and that's a problem.

The new page needs a map... that's the point!

But of course we *don't* want the new version of the page to look the same. We want to add a map.

So how will we do that? There's no way we're going to build our own mapping system. Instead we'll create a **mashup**. A mashup is a web application that integrates data and services from other places on the web.

Most of the mapping services allow you to embed maps inside your own web application, but we'll use the one provided by Google. Google Maps give you a lot of flexibility. Not only can you embed a map in a web page, but you can also, without too much work, add your own data onto the map and program how the user interacts with the map and data.

Here's a high-level view of how it will work:

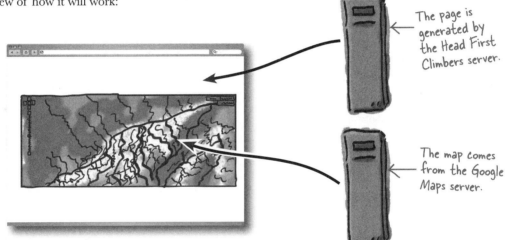

The page is generated by the Head First Climbers server.

The map comes from the Google Maps server.

The map will be displayed at the approximate location of the recorded incident, and a symbol mark the exact point.

The Head First Climbers application will generate the code to call the map, and the data to display on it, but the map itself, and the bulk of the code that allows the user to do things like drag the map or zoom in and out, will come from the Google Maps server. Even though Google will provide the bulk of the code, we still need to provide two things:

 The HTML and JavaScript to call the map. This will be a little complex, so we will put the HTML and JavaScript we need in a separate partial that we can call from our page template.

 The data we need to display on the map. To begin with we will use an example data file to make sure the map's working.

So what will the map code look like?

So what code do we need?

We need to have the following code in a partial called `_map.html.erb`:

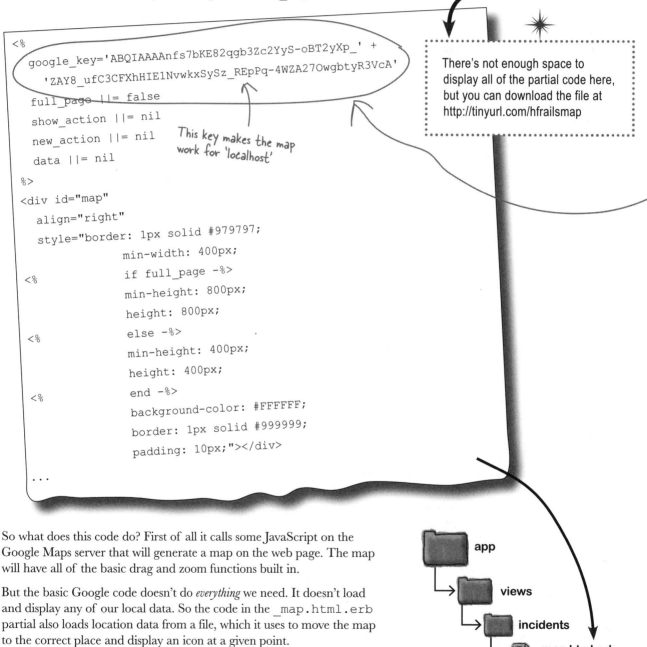

Download It!

There's not enough space to display all of the partial code here, but you can download the file at http://tinyurl.com/hfrailsmap

```
<%
  google_key='ABQIAAAAnfs7bKE82qgb3Zc2YyS-oBT2yXp_' +
    'ZAY8_ufC3CFXhHIE1NvwkxSySz_REpPq-4WZA27OwgbtyR3VcA'
  full_page ||= false
  show_action ||= nil
  new_action ||= nil
  data ||= nil
%>
<div id="map"
  align="right"
  style="border: 1px solid #979797;
                min-width: 400px;
<%              if full_page -%>
                min-height: 800px;
                height: 800px;
<%              else -%>
                min-height: 400px;
                height: 400px;
<%              end -%>
                background-color: #FFFFFF;
                border: 1px solid #999999;
                padding: 10px;"></div>
...
```

This key makes the map work for 'localhost'

So what does this code do? First of all it calls some JavaScript on the Google Maps server that will generate a map on the web page. The map will have all of the basic drag and zoom functions built in.

But the basic Google code doesn't do *everything* we need. It doesn't load and display any of our local data. So the code in the `_map.html.erb` partial also loads location data from a file, which it uses to move the map to the correct place and display an icon at a given point.

But there's a little complication with the code...

app
views
incidents
_map.html.erb

The code will only work for <u>localhost</u>

Google places a restriction on the use of the code. They insist that you say which host you're going to use it on. That means before you can use it on www.yourowndomain.com, you need to tell Google about it. In order to make sure that people comply with this condition, the code will only run if you provide it with a **Google Maps key**. The key is generated for a particular host name, and if you try to embed a Google map into a page coming from anywhere else, the map will refuse to run.

But for now, there's not a problem. The **_map.html.erb** partial we're going to use has the Google Maps key for localhost—so as long as you run the code on your own machine it will be fine. But remember, you'll need to apply for your own key before running the code anywhere else.

Geek Bits

If you want to embed Google Maps in your own web apps, you need to sign up with Google. To do this, visit the following URL: http://tinyurl.com/mapreg

Sharpen your pencil

You need to include the map partial in the `show_with_map.html.erb` template. We need to pass a local variable called `data` containing the path to the map data. We'll use a test file for this at `/test.xml`.

Write the code to call the partial.

....

....

....

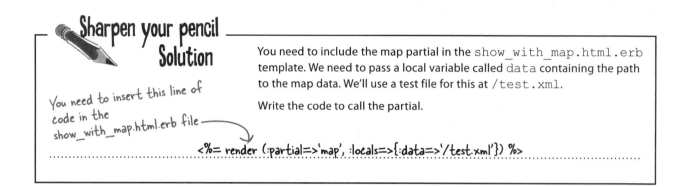

Sharpen your pencil
                        Solution

You need to include the map partial in the show_with_map.html.erb template. We need to pass a local variable called data containing the path to the map data. We'll use a test file for this at /test.xml.

Write the code to call the partial.

You need to insert this line of code in the show_with_map.html.erb file

```
<%= render (:partial=>'map', :locals=>{:data=>'/test.xml'}) %>
```

Now we need the map data

Before we can try out the embedded map, we need to provide it with map data. To begin with we will just use the test.xml test file. This is what it looks like:

Download It!

To save you typing in the long numbers, you can download the test.xml file from http://tinyurl.com/maptest

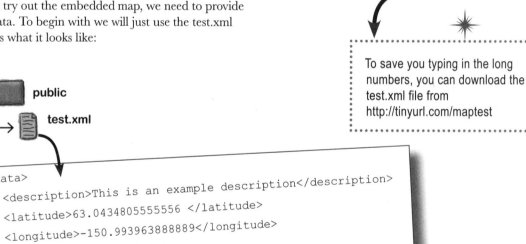

public

test.xml

```
<data>
    <description>This is an example description</description>
    <latitude>63.0434805555556 </latitude>
    <longitude>-150.993963888889</longitude>
    <title>Test Data</title>
</data>
```

The mapping data provides the latitude and longitude of the test incident. When the Google map loads, our map partial will pass it the contents of this file and the incident should be displayed and centered.

Test Drive

So what happens if we go to a URL like:

```
http://localhost:3000/incidents/map/1
```

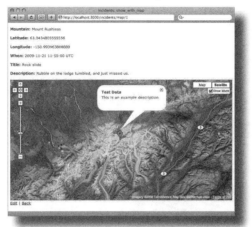

The map works! But what if we go to a different URL?

Every map looks exactly the same, regardless of the data. That's because each map is using the same data: the contents of the test.xml file.

In order to make the map display the location of a given incident, we need to generate a data file for each page.

What do we need to generate?

We're passing XML data to the map, and the XML data describes the location of a single incident. The location is given by the latitude, the longitude, the title, and the description. We need to generate XML like this for *each* incident.

So the system will work something like this:

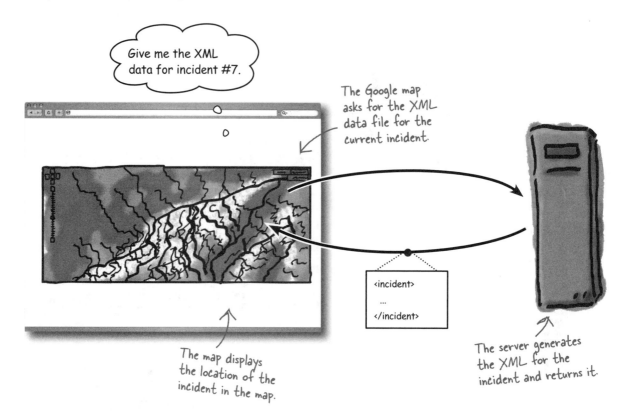

If this is starting to feel familiar, good! The Google Map is actually using Ajax to work. Remember how we used Ajax to download new version of the seat list in the previous chapter? In the same way, the Google Map will request XML data for the location of an incident.

So the next thing is to generate the data. Where will we get the data from?

We'll generate XML from the model

The data for the generated XML will come from the Incident model. We'll be using just four of the attributes, the latitude, longitude, title, and description.

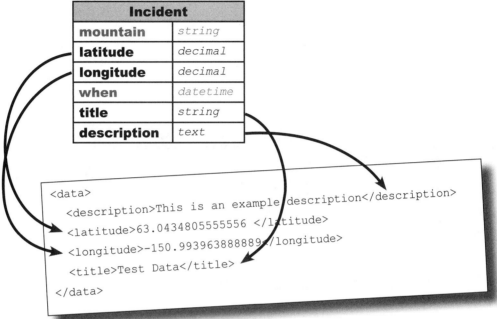

But how do we generate the XML? In a way, this is a little like generating a web page. After all, XML and HTML are very similar. And just as web pages contain data from the model, our XML files will also contain data from the model.

So one option would be to create a page template containing XML tags instead of HTML tags:

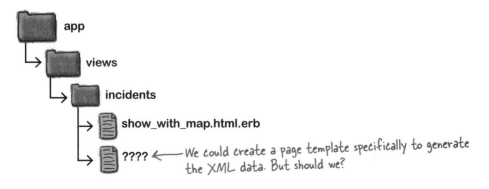

That way *would* work, but there's a better way...

A model object can generate XML

Model objects contain data. XML files contain data. So it kind of makes sense that model objects can generate XML versions of themselves. Each model object has a method `to_xml` that returns an XML string:

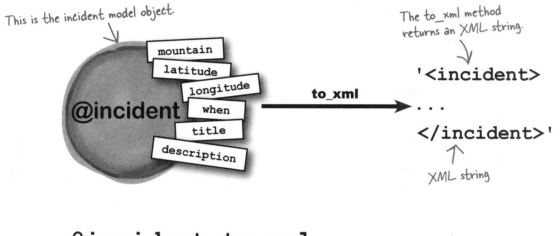

This is the incident model object.

mountain
latitude
longitude
when
title
description

@incident

to_xml

The to_xml method returns an XML string.

'<incident>
...
</incident>'

XML string

@incident.to_xml

The to_xml method returns an XML string representing the model object.

But creating the XML is only half the story. The other half is returning that XML to the browser. We're not using a page template, so the whole job will have to be handled by the controller rendering the XML...

What will the controller code look like

We can amend the show_with_map method to output the XML:

This is the incident object we were already reading. →

The render method returns the XML.

```
def show_with_map
  @incident = Incident.find(params[:id])
  render :text=>@incident.to_xml
end
```

The text parameter says what we'll be returning to the browser.

→ This will create an XML string that describes the incident object.

The render method returns the XML to the browser. We've seen the render method before, but this is a slightly different version. Most of the time you use render to generate a web page from a template or partial. But you can also just pass it a string object—and that's what we're doing here.

Geek Bits

To make your life simpler, the Rails folks also allow you to pass a parameter to the render method called :xml

```
render :xml=>@incident
```

If the render method is passed an object using the :xml parameter, it will call the to_xml method on the object and send that back to the browser. The :xml version of the render command will generate the same content as the render command in our controller, but it will also set the mime-type of the response to text/xml. But for now, we will use the :text version above.

there are no
Dumb Questions

Q: Remind me, what does the render method do again?

A: render generates a response for the browser. When your browser asks for a page, that's a request. render generates what gets sent back.

So what do we get now if we go to:

```
http://localhost:3000/incidents/map/1
```

```
Source of: http://localhost:3000/incidents/map/1
```

```xml
<?xml version="1.0" encoding="UTF-8"?>
<incident>
  <created-at type="datetime">2009-11-21T11:59:31Z</created-at>
  <description>Rubble on the ledge tumbled, and just missed us.</description>
  <id type="integer">1</id>
  <latitude type="decimal">63.0434805555556</latitude>
  <longitude type="decimal">-150.993963888889</longitude>
  <mountain>Mount Rushless</mountain>
  <title>Rock slide</title>
  <updated-at type="datetime">2009-11-21T11:59:31Z</updated-at>
  <when type="datetime">2009-11-21T11:55:00Z</when>
</incident>
```

The controller is now returning XML containing the data from the incident object with id = 1.

But is there a problem? The XML we're generating looks *sort* of the same as the example XML, but there are a few differences:

- We're generating too many attributes. The example data file only contained information about the latitude, longitude, title, and description. But this piece of XML contains **everything** about an incident, even the date and time that the incident record was created.

- The root of the XML file has the wrong name. The generated XML takes its root name from the variable we were using, `<incident>`. But we need the XML to have a root named `<data>`.

```xml
<data>
  <description>This is an example
    description</description>
  <latitude>63.0434805555556 </latitude>
  <longitude>-150.993963888889</longitude>
  <title>Test Data</title>
</data>
```

The XML is *almost* in the right format, but *not quite*.

We need to modify the XML that `to_xml` produces.

Code Magnets

The `to_xml` method has some optional parameters that let us modify the XML that it returns. See if you can work out what the values of the parameters should be:

```
def show_with_map

  @incident = Incident.find(params[:id])

  render :text=>@incident.to_xml(

    ................ =>[............... ,............... ,............... ,............... ],

    ................ => ...............  )

end
```

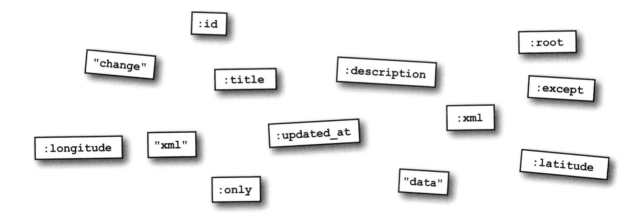

:id

:root

"change"

:title

:description

:except

:xml

:longitude

"xml"

:updated_at

:latitude

:only

"data"

Code Magnets Solution

The `to_xml` method has some optional parameters that let us modify the XML that it returns. See if you can work out what the values of the parameters should be:

```
def show_with_map

  @incident = Incident.find(params[:id])

  render :text=>@incident.to_xml(

    :only =>[ :latitude , :longitude , :title , :description ],

    :root => "data" )

end
```

Because we're using the render :text=>... version of the render command we can use the options in to_xml and modify the output.

:id

"change"

:except

:xml

"xml"   :updated_at

there are no
Dumb Questions

Q: Shouldn't we generate the XML in the model?

A: You could, but it's not a good idea. You may need to generate different XML in different situations. If you added code to the model for each of those XML formats, the model would quickly become overloaded.

TEST DRIVE

Now when we go to:

`http://localhost:3000/incidents/map/1`

we get XML that looks a little different.

```
○ ○ ○                  Source of: http://localhost:3000/incidents/map/1
<?xml version="1.0" encoding="UTF-8"?>
<data>
  <description>Rubble on the ledge tumbled, and just missed us.</description>
  <latitude type="decimal">63.0434805555556</latitude>
  <longitude type="decimal">-150.993963888889</longitude>
  <title>Rock slide</title>
</data>
```

You've managed to modify the XML so that it only displays the data we need and has a properly named root element. It looks a lot closer to the example XML file.

The `to_xml` method doesn't allow you to make a lot of changes to the XML it produces, but it's good enough for most purposes... including sending the XML to Google for some custom mapping.

With very little work, `to_xml` gave us exactly the XML we wanted.

Meanwhile, at 20,000 feet...

Hey! Where did
my web page go?!!!

HighPhone

Some people on the pilot program have a problem.

The web pages have disappeared! Before the last amendment a URL like:

```
http://localhost:3000/incidents/map/1
```

generated a web page. The trouble is, now that URL just returns XML,
instead of a nice Google map.

Before your latest changes:

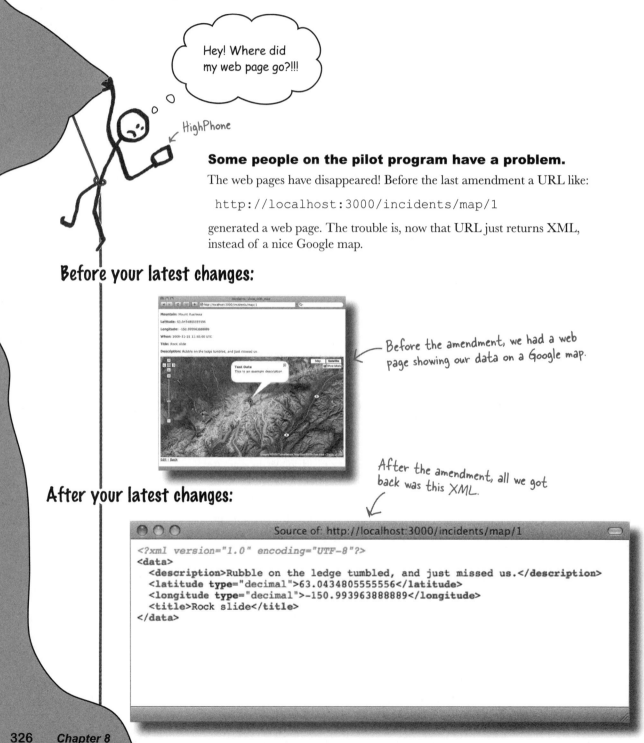

Before the amendment, we had a web
page showing our data on a Google map.

After the amendment, all we got
back was this XML.

After your latest changes:

```
○ ○ ○                    Source of: http://localhost:3000/incidents/map/1
<?xml version="1.0" encoding="UTF-8"?>
<data>
  <description>Rubble on the ledge tumbled, and just missed us.</description>
  <latitude type="decimal">63.0434805555556</latitude>
  <longitude type="decimal">-150.993963888889</longitude>
  <title>Rock slide</title>
</data>
```

We need to generate XML **and** HTML

The `show_with_map` action originally generated a web page with
the `show_with_map.html.erb` page template. But once we
added a `render` call to the controller method, Rails ignored the
template and just generated the XML:

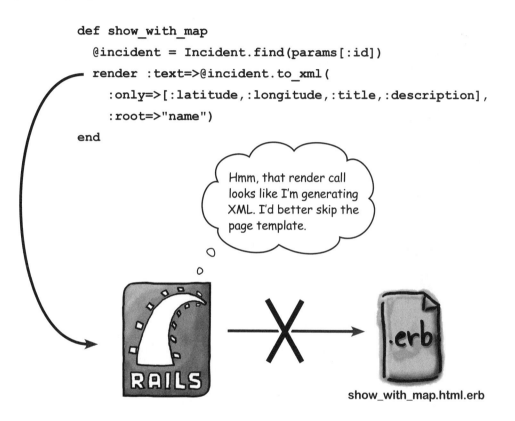

```
def show_with_map
   @incident = Incident.find(params[:id])
   render :text=>@incident.to_xml(
      :only=>[:latitude,:longitude,:title,:description],
      :root=>"name")
end
```

Hmm, that render call
looks like I'm generating
XML. I'd better skip the
page template.

show_with_map.html.erb

Of course, that makes sense, because there's no way an action can
generate XML and HTML *at the same time*.

But we still need a web page to display the map, and the map still
needs XML map data. So what do we do?

**We need some way of calling the controller in one
way to generate HTML, and calling the controller in
another way to generate XML.**

Generating XML and HTML should be easy. We just create another action.

Mark: Another action?

Bob: Sure. One to generate XML and another to generate HTML.

Laura: Well that's not a great idea.

Bob: Why not?

Laura: That would mean duplicating code. Both methods would have code to read an incident object.

Bob: Whatever. It's only one line.

Laura: Well now it is. But what if we change things in the future?

Mark: You mean like if the model changes?

Laura: Or if it we get the data from somewhere else, like a web service.

Bob: It's not such a big deal. Let's worry about the problems we have right now, okay?

Mark: I don't know. Laura, what would you do?

Laura: Simple. I'd pass a parameter to the action. Tell it what format we want.

Mark: That might work.

Bob: Come on, too much work.

Laura: Less work than creating another action.

Mark: But one thing...

Laura: Yes?

Mark: Doesn't the URL identify the information we want?

Laura: So?

Mark: Shouldn't we use the same URL for both formats?

XML and HTML are just <u>representations</u>

Although the HTML and XML look very different, they are really visual representations of the *same thing*. Both the HTML web page and the XML map data are both describing the same Incident object data. That incident is the core data, and it's sometimes called the **resource**.

A **resource** is the data being presented by the web page. And the web page is called a **representation** of the resource. Take an Incident object as an example. The Incident object is the resource. The incident web page and the map data XML file are both representations of the resource.

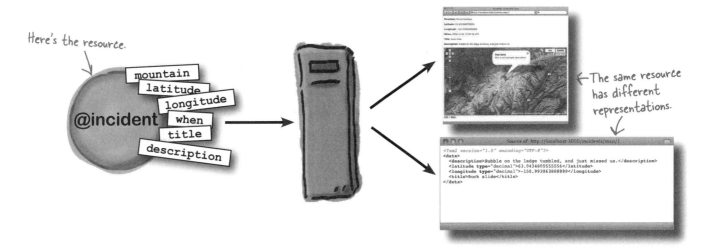

Here's the resource.

@incident — mountain, latitude, longitude, when, title, description

←The same resource has different representations.

Thinking about the web as a set of resources and representations is part of a design architecture called **REST**. REST is the **architecture of Rails**. And the more RESTful your application is, the better it will run on Rails.

But how does this help us? Well, to be strictly RESTful, both the XML data and the web page should have the same URL (Uniform *Resource* Locator) because they both represent the same resource. Something like this:

> **http://localhost:3000/incidents/maps/1**

But to simplify things, we can compromise the REST design (a little bit) and use these URLs for the two representations:

> **http://localhost:3000/incidents/maps/1.xml**
> **http://localhost:3000/incidents/maps/1.html**

One URL returns the XML data; the other returns the HTML.

How should we decide which format to use?

If we add an extra route that includes the format in the path:

```
map.connect 'incidents/map/:id.:format', :action=>'show_with_map',
  :controller=>'incidents'
```

This will record the format from the extension.

we will be able to read the requested format from the XML and then make decisions in the code like this:

```
if params[:format] == 'html'
  # Generate the HTML representation
else
  # Generate the XML representation
end
```

http://localhost:3000/incidents/map/1.html

This extension will be stored in the :format field.

http://localhost:3000/incidents/map/1.xml

But that's not how most Rails applications choose the format to generate. Instead they call a method called respond_to do and an object called a **responder**:

```
respond_to do |format|
  format.html {

    _____

  }
  format.xml {

    _____

  }
end
```

format is a 'responder' object.

The code to generate a web page goes here.

The code to generate the XML goes here.

This code does more or less the same thing. The format object is a responder. A responder can decide whether or not to run code, dependent upon the format required by the request. So if the user asks for HTML, the code above will run the code passed to format.html. If the user asks for XML, the responder will run the code passed to format.xml.

So why don't Rails programmers just use an if statement? After all, wouldn't that be simpler code? Well, the responder has **hidden powers**. For example, it sets the mime type of the response. The mime type tells the browser what data-type the response is. In general, it is much better practice to use respond_to do to decide what representation format to generate.

Exercise

The `show_with_map` method in the controller needs to choose whether it should generate XML or HTML. Write a new version of the method that uses a responder to generate the correct representation.

Hint: If you need to generate HTML, other than reading a model object, what else does the controller need to do?

....

....

....

....

....

....

....

....

....

....

....

....

....

....

....

The `show_with_map.html.erb` page template currently calls the map partial and passes it the `/test.xml` file. What will the partial call look like if it is going to call the generated XML file?

....

....

Exercise Solution

The `show_with_map` method in the controller needs to choose whether it should generate XML or HTML. Write a new version of the method that uses a responder to generate the the correct representation.

Hint: If you need to generate HTML, other than reading a model object, <u>what else does the controller need to do?</u>

Nothing! When generating HTML we can leave Rails to call the show_with_map.html.erb template

```
def show_with_map
    @incident = Incident.find(params[:id])
    respond_to do |format|
        format.html {

        }
        format.xml {
            render :text=>@incident.to_xml(
                :only=>[:latitude, :longitude, :title, :description],
                :root=>"name")
        }
    end
end
```

We can leave this empty – Rails will call the template for us

The `show_with_map.html.erb` page template currently calls the map partial and passes it the `/test.xml` file. What will the partial call look like if it is going to call the generated XML file?

```
<%= render(:partial=>'map', :locals=>{:data=>"#{@incident.id}.xml"}) %>
```

there are no
Dumb Questions

Q: If the format.html section doesn't need any code, can we just skip it?

A: No. You still need to include format.html, or Rails won't realize that it needs to respond to requests for HTML output.

TEST DRIVE

If we look at the XML version of the page at:

```
http://localhost:3000/incidents/map/1.xml
```

we get an XML version of the incident:

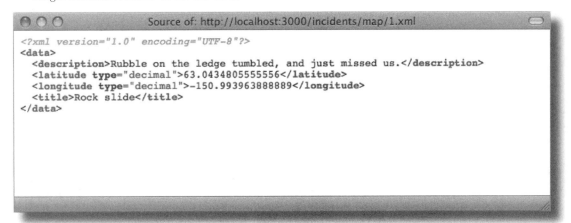

```
Source of: http://localhost:3000/incidents/map/1.xml
<?xml version="1.0" encoding="UTF-8"?>
<data>
  <description>Rubble on the ledge tumbled, and just missed us.</description>
  <latitude type="decimal">63.0434805555556</latitude>
  <longitude type="decimal">-150.993963888889</longitude>
  <title>Rock slide</title>
</data>
```

So what about the HTML version:

http://localhost:3000/incidents/map/1.html

http://localhost:3000/incidents/map/3.html

It works. Now different incidents show different maps. But before we
replace the live version of the code, we better make sure we understand
exactly how the code works.

So what really went on here?

How does the map page work?

Let's take a deeper look at what just happened and how the HTML page
is rendered.

 The controller spots that an HTML page is needed.
The browser points to the HTML version of the page. The controller realizes
that HTML rather than XML is required, and so calls
`show_with_map.html.erb`. HTML is sent back to the client browser.

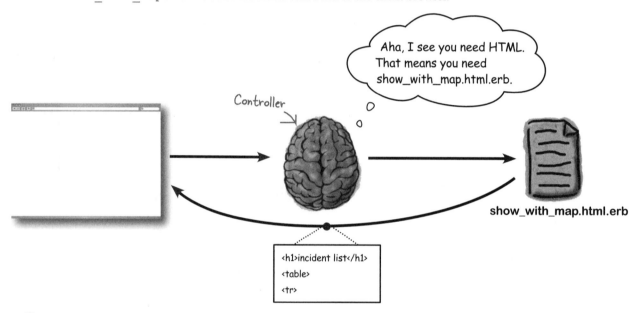

> Aha, I see you need HTML.
> That means you need
> show_with_map.html.erb.

Controller

show_with_map.html.erb

```
<h1>incident list</h1>
<table>
<tr>
```

2 **JavaScript requests the Google Map.**
JavaScript within the web page requests map data from the Google Maps
server. The Google Maps server returns it.

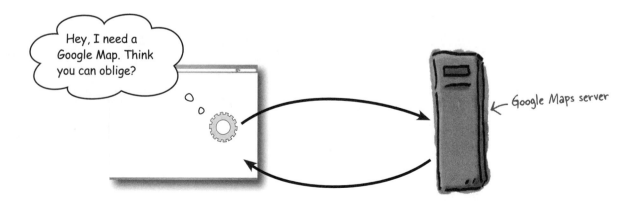

> Hey, I need a
> Google Map. Think
> you can oblige?

← Google Maps server

3 **JavaScript requests the incident XML.**
JavaScript within the page requests XML for the incident from the controller. It then displays it on the map.

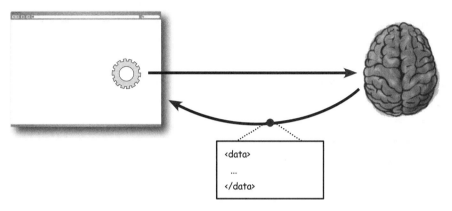

```
<data>
  ...
</data>
```

there are no
Dumb Questions

Q: **You say that a resource should always have the same URL. Why is that?**

A: It doesn't *have to*, but REST—Rails' main design principle—says it should.

Q: **But if the format is in the URL, doesn't that mean that different URLs are used for the same resource?**

A: Yes, sure does. Adding the format to the URL compromises the RESTfulness of the design... a little bit. But it's a common trick. It's simple, and works well.

Q: **So there's no way to use the same URL for different formats?**

A: There is a way to do it. If the request contains an "Accepts:" header say—for example—that the request is for "text/xml", the responder will run the code for the XML format.

Q: **Is there a way of listing the attributes you *don't* want to include in to_xml output?**

A: Yes. Instead of using the `:only` parameter, you can use the `:except` parameter. Rails is remarkably consistent and you will found several places where calls in Rails have optional `:only` parameters. In all cases you can switch them for `:except` parameters to say which things you *don't* want.

Q: **Is there some way that the controller can tell the difference between an Ajax request from JavaScript and a browser request?**

A: Sort of. The expression `request.xhr?` usually returns 'true' for Ajax requests and 'false' for simple browser requests. The problem is that while it works for the requests generated by the Prototype library, it doesn't work with *all* Ajax libraries.

Q: **Why do I have to call render sometimes and not others?**

A: If you are happy to run the default template (the one whose name matches the action), you can omit the `render` call.

Q: **You say that the generated XML and the HTML are different representations, but they don't contain the same information, do they?**

A: That's true—they don't. The XML generated for a single incident contains a smaller amount of data than the HTML representation. But they both present information about the same resource, so they are both representations of the same thing.

The code is ready to go live

Our new version of the location page works well, so let's replace the scaffolded show action with the `show_with_map` code.

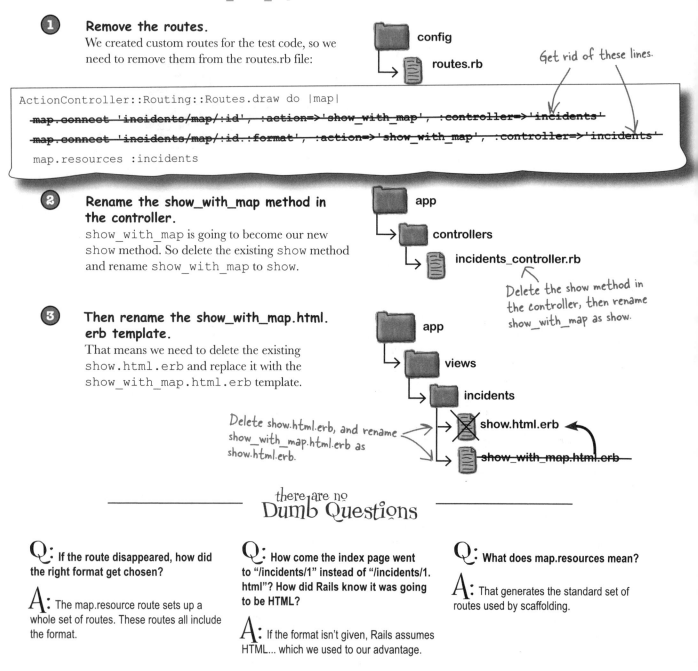

1 Remove the routes.

We created custom routes for the test code, so we need to remove them from the routes.rb file:

config

routes.rb

Get rid of these lines.

```
ActionController::Routing::Routes.draw do |map|
  map.connect 'incidents/map/:id', :action=>'show_with_map', :controller=>'incidents'
  map.connect 'incidents/map/:id.:format', :action=>'show_with_map', :controller=>'incidents'
  map.resources :incidents
```

2 Rename the show_with_map method in the controller.

`show_with_map` is going to become our new `show` method. So delete the existing `show` method and rename `show_with_map` to `show`.

app

controllers

incidents_controller.rb

Delete the show method in the controller, then rename show_with_map as show.

3 Then rename the show_with_map.html.erb template.

That means we need to delete the existing `show.html.erb` and replace it with the `show_with_map.html.erb` template.

app

views

incidents

Delete show.html.erb, and rename show_with_map.html.erb as show.html.erb.

show.html.erb

show_with_map.html.erb

there are no
Dumb Questions

Q: If the route disappeared, how did the right format get chosen?

A: The map.resource route sets up a whole set of routes. These routes all include the format.

Q: How come the index page went to "/incidents/1" instead of "/incidents/1.html"? How did Rails know it was going to be HTML?

A: If the format isn't given, Rails assumes HTML... which we used to our advantage.

Q: What does map.resources mean?

A: That generates the standard set of routes used by scaffolding.

TEST DRIVE

Now the the mapped pages have replaced the default "show" action. So now the main index page links to the mapping pages, not the text versions.

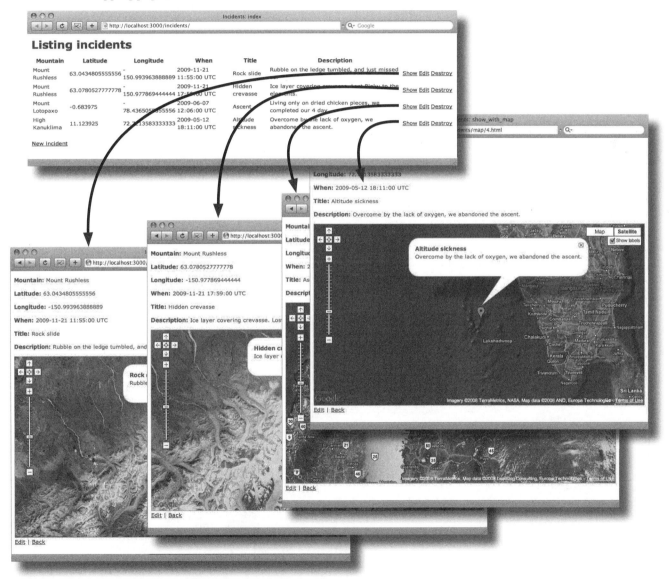

One thing though - isn't that index page kind of... boring? Especially compared to all those nice visual map pages!

🏃 **LoNg ExeRcise** ────────────────────────────────

The users have asked if the index page can display a whole set of all the incidents that have been recorded, and fortunately the `_map.html.erb` partial can generate multiple points if it is given the correct XML data.

This is the existing index method in the incidents controller. Rewrite the method to generate XML from the array of all incidents. You only need to change the root element to "data".

```
def index
  @incidents = Incident.find(:all)

  respond_to do |format|
    format.html # index.html.erb
    format.xml  { render :xml => @incidents }
  end
end
```

....

....

....

....

....

....

....

....

....

....

📁 **app**

↳ 📁 **controllers**

↳ 📄 **incidents_controller.rb**

The index page will need to include a map. Write the code to insert the map at the given point. You will need to pass the path of the XML version of the index page as data for the map.

```erb
<h1>Listing incidents</h1>

<table>
  <tr>
    <th>Mountain</th>
    <th>Latitude</th>
    <th>Longitude</th>
    <th>When</th>
    <th>Title</th>
    <th>Description</th>
  </tr>

<% for incident in @incidents %>
  <tr>
    <td><%=h incident.mountain %></td>
    <td><%=h incident.latitude %></td>
    <td><%=h incident.longitude %></td>
    <td><%=h incident.when %></td>
    <td><%=h incident.title %></td>
    <td><%=h incident.description %></td>
    <td><%= link_to 'Show', incident %></td>
    <td><%= link_to 'Edit', edit_incident_path(incident) %></td>
    <td><%= link_to 'Destroy', incident, :confirm => 'Are you sure?',
            :method => :delete %></td>
  </tr>
<% end %>
</table>


.......................................................................................................


<br />
<%= link_to 'New incident', new_incident_path %>
```

app

views

incidents

index.html.erb

Long Exercise Solution

The users have asked if the index page can display a whole set of all the incidents that have been recorded and fortunately the `_map.html.erb` partial can generate multiple points if it is given the correct XML data.

This is the existing index method in the incidents controller. Rewrite the method to generate XML from the array of all incidents. You only need to change the root element to "data".

```
def index
  @incidents = Incident.find(:all)

  respond_to do |format|
    format.html # index.html.erb
    format.xml  { render :xml => @incidents }
  end
end
```

```
def index
  @incidents = Incident.find(:all)


  respond_to do |format|
    format.html # index.html.erb
    format.xml {

      render :text=>@incidents.to_xml(:root=>"data")

    }
  end
end
```

app

controllers

incidents_controller.rb

The index page will need to include a map. Write the code to insert the map at the given point.
You will need to pass the path of the XML version of the index page as data for the map.

```erb
<h1>Listing incidents</h1>

<table>
  <tr>
    <th>Mountain</th>
    <th>Latitude</th>
    <th>Longitude</th>
    <th>When</th>
    <th>Title</th>
    <th>Description</th>
  </tr>

<% for incident in @incidents %>
  <tr>
    <td><%=h incident.mountain %></td>
    <td><%=h incident.latitude %></td>
    <td><%=h incident.longitude %></td>
    <td><%=h incident.when %></td>
    <td><%=h incident.title %></td>
    <td><%=h incident.description %></td>
    <td><%= link_to 'Show', incident %></td>
    <td><%= link_to 'Edit', edit_incident_path(incident) %></td>
    <td><%= link_to 'Destroy', incident, :confirm => 'Are you sure?',
              :method => :delete %></td>
  </tr>
<% end %>
</table>
```

`<%= render (:partial=>'map', :locals=>{:data=>"/incidents.xml"}) %>`

```erb
<br />
<%= link_to 'New incident', new_incident_path %>
```

app
→ views
→ incidents
→ index.html.erb

Test Drive

Now when users go to the front page, they see the incidents in a list and on the map. When an incident is clicked, the details are displayed, as well as a link to the incident's own page.

All of the incidents are now plotted on the map.

The information window contains a link to the incident's own "show" page.

The map uses the XML generated by the index method of the controller to create the points.

Hey, there's so much data now! I'd really like to know about the incidents that have been posted in the last 24 hours. How about a news feed?

Most web sites now provide **RSS news feeds** to provide easy links to the main resources on a site.

But what does an RSS news feed look like?

RSS feeds are just XML

This is what an RSS feed file would look like for the climbing site:

```
<rss version="2.0">
  <channel>
    <title>Head First Climbers News</title>
    <link>http://localhost:3000/incidents/</link>
    <item>
      <title>Rock slide</title>
      <description>Rubble on the ledge tumbled, and just missed us.</description>

      <link>http://localhost:3000/incidents/1</link>
    </item>
    <item>
```

This is just an XML file. If you use an RSS news reader, or if your browser can subscribe to RSS news feeds, they will download a file just like this, which contains a list of links and descriptions to news stories.

So how can WE generate an RSS feed like this?

Do any of the tags in the RSS look particularly surprising or unclear? What do you think channel does? What about link?

We'll create an action called news

Let's create a new route as follows:

```
map.connect '/incidents/news', :action=>'news', :controller=>'incidents', :format=>'xml'
```

Sharpen your pencil

Write the controller method for the new action. It needs to find all incidents with `updated_at` in the last 24 hours. It should then render the default XML by calling `to_xml` on the array of matching incidents.

Hint: The Ruby expression `Time.now.yesterday` returns a date-time value from exactly 24 hours ago.

....

....

....

....

....

....

....

....

....

....

....

....

....

....

....

Sharpen your pencil
Solution

Write the controller method for the new action. It needs to find all incidents with `updated_at` in the last 24 hours. It should then render the default XML by calling `to_xml` on the array of matching incidents.

Hint: The Ruby expression `Time.now.yesterday` returns a date-time value from exactly 24 hours ago.

```
def news
  @incidents = Incident.find(:all, :conditions=>['updated_at > ?', Time.now.yesterday])
  render :xml=>@incidents
end
```

You could have also used `:text=>@incidents.to_xml`.

TEST DRIVE

This is the XML that is generated by the `news` action:

We've generated XML for the correct data, but it's not the sort of XML we need for an RSS news feed. That's OK though, we had that problem before. When we were generating XML data for the location data it was in the wrong format, and we were able to adjust it then.

Remember – this is time dependent so incidents will only appear if they've been modified in the last 24 hours

We just need to modify this XML in the same way... don't we?

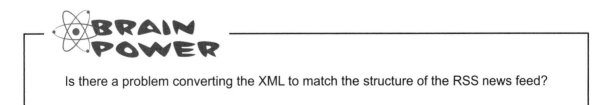

Is there a problem converting the XML to match the structure of the RSS news feed?

We have to change the structure of the XML

The `to_xml` method allows us to make a few simple changes to the
XML it produces. We can swap names and choose which data items to
include. But will it give us enough power to turn the XML we *have* into
the XML we *want?*

This is what we have...

```xml
<?xml version="1.0" encoding="UTF-8"?>
<incidents type="array">
  <incident>
    <created-at type="datetime">2008-11-21T11:59:31Z</created-at>
    <description>Rubble on the ledge tumbled, and just missed us.</description>
    <id type="integer">1</id>
    <latitude type="decimal">63.0434805555556</latitude>
    <longitude type="decimal">-150.993963888889</longitude>
    <mountain>Mount Rushless</mountain>
    <title>Rock slide</title>
```

```xml
<rss version="2.0">
  <channel>
    <title>Head First Climbers News</title>
    <link>http://localhost:3000/incidents/</link>
    <item>
      <title>Rock slide</title>
      <description>Rubble on the ledge tumbled, and just missed us.</description>
      <link>http://localhost:3000/incidents/1</link>
    </item>
    <item>
```

... but this is what we want.

We need more XML POWER

The news feed XML can't be generated by the `to_xml` method. While
`to_xml` can modify XML output slightly, it can't radically change XML
structure. For instance, `to_xml` can't move elements between levels. It
can't group elements within other elements. `to_xml` is designed to be
quick and easy to use, but that also makes it a bit inflexible.

For true XML power, we need something more...

So we'll use a new kind of template: an XML builder

If we created another HTML page template, we could generate whatever
XML output we like. After all, HTML is similar to XML:

This actually looks a whole
lot like HTML...

```
<rss version="2.0">
  <channel>
    <title>Head First Climbers News</title>
    <link>http://localhost:3000/incidents/</link>
    <% for incident in @incidents %>
    <item>
      <title><%= h incident.title %></title>
      <description><%= h incident.description %></description>
```

But Rails provides a special type of template that is specifically designed to
generate XML; it's called an **XML Builder Template**.

XML Builders live in the same directory as page templates, and they are
used in a similar way. If someone has requested an XML response (by
adding .xml to the end of the URL), the controller only needs to read the
data from the model, and Rails will automatically call the XML builder
template. That means we can lose a line from the **news** action:

This is the "new" method
from the incidents
controller.

```
def news
  @incidents = Incident.find(:all, :conditions=>['updated_at > ?', Time.now.yesterday])
  render :xml=>@incidents
end
```

This code will now just read the data from the model and the XML bulder
template will do the rest.

So what does an XML builder look like?

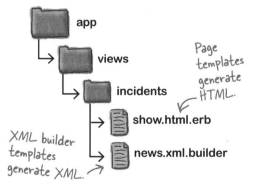

app

views

Page
templates
generate
HTML.

incidents

show.html.erb

XML builder
templates
generate XML.

news.xml.builder

XML Builders Up Close

Page templates are designed to look like HTML files with a little Ruby sprinkled in. XML builders are different. They are pure Ruby but are designed to have a structure similar to XML. For example, this:

```ruby
xml.sentence(:language=>'English') {
  for word in @words do
    xml.word(word)
  end
}
```

might generate something that looks like this:

```xml
<sentence language="English">  ← Attribute
  <word>XML</word>
  <word>Builders</word>
  <word>Kick</word>  ← Elements
  <word>Ass!</word>
</sentence>
```

So why did the Rails folks make a different kind of template? Why doesn't XML Builder work just like a Page Template? Why doesn't it use Embedded Ruby?

Even though XML and HTML are very similar—and in the case of XHTML, they are technically equal—the ways in which people use HTML and XML are subtly different.

  Web pages usually contain a lot of **HTML** markup to make the page look nice, and just a *little* data from the database.

  Most of the content of the **XML**, on the other hand, is likely to come from the data and conditional logic and far less from the XML markup.

Using Ruby—instead of XML—as the main language, makes XML Builders more concise and easier to maintain.

Pool Puzzle

Your **job** is to take code snippets from
the pool and place them into the
blank lines in the code. You may
not use the same snippet more
than once, and you won't need
to use all the snippets. Your **goal**
is to complete the XML builder
template that will generate RSS.

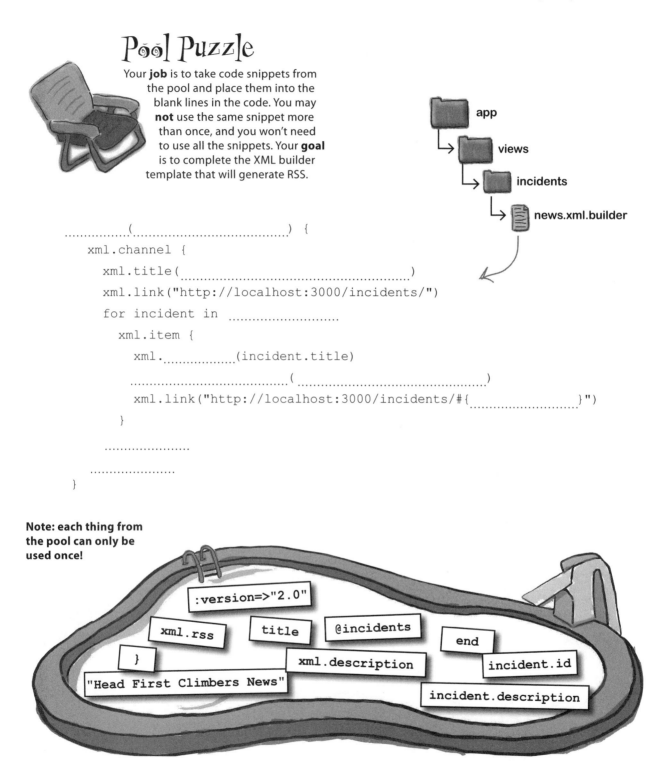

app
→ views
→ incidents
→ news.xml.builder

```
..............(...........................) {
  xml.channel {
    xml.title(...........................................)
    xml.link("http://localhost:3000/incidents/")
    for incident in ...........................
      xml.item {
        xml.................(incident.title)
        ..........................(..............................)
        xml.link("http://localhost:3000/incidents/#{...................}")
      }
      ....................
    ....................
  }
```

**Note: each thing from
the pool can only be
used once!**

:version=>"2.0"

xml.rss   title   @incidents

}   end

xml.description   incident.id

"Head First Climbers News"

incident.description

Pool Puzzle Solution

Your **job** is to take code snippets from the pool and place them into the blank lines in the code. You may **not** use the same snippet more than once, and you won't need to use all the snippets. Your **goal** is to complete the XML builder template that will generate RSS.

app
→ views
→ incidents
→ news.xml.builder

```
xml.rss( :version=>"2.0" ) {
  xml.channel {
    xml.title( "Head First Climbers News" )
    xml.link("http://localhost:3000/incidents/")
    for incident in @incidents
      xml.item {
        xml. title (incident.title)
        xml.description ( incident.description )
        xml.link("http://localhost:3000/incidents/#{ incident.id }")
      }
    end
  }
}
```

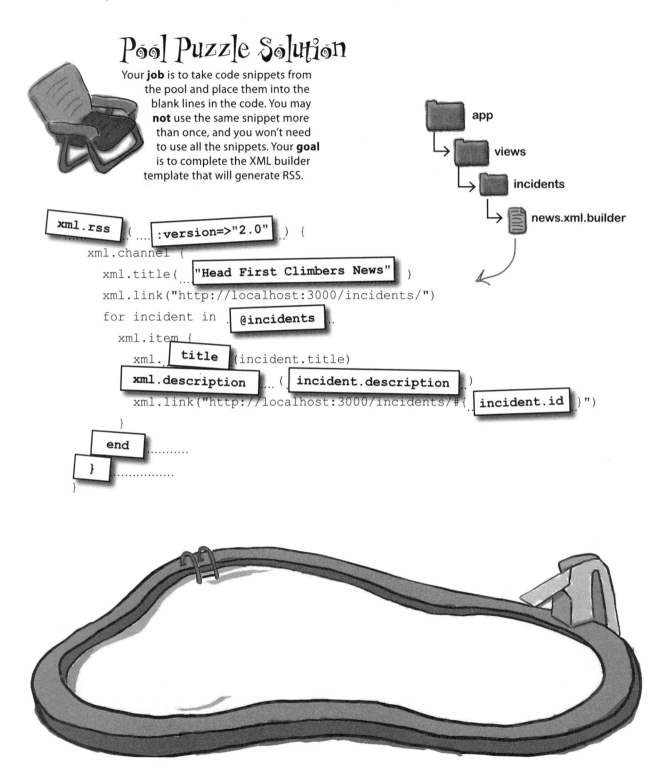

Now let's add the feed to the pages

But how will users find the feed? Browsers sense the presence of a news feed by looking for a `<link... />` reference within a page.

The folks at Head First Climbers want the news feed to appear on every page, so we will add a reference to the RSS feed in the `incidents` layout file, using the `auto_discovery_link` helper:

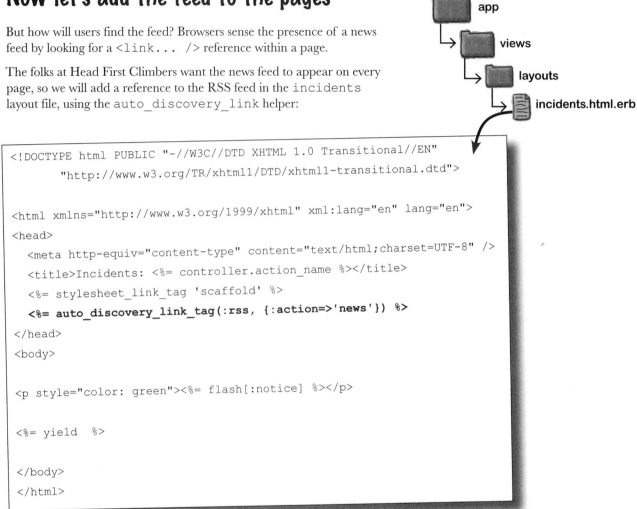

app
views
layouts
incidents.html.erb

```
<!DOCTYPE html PUBLIC "-//W3C//DTD XHTML 1.0 Transitional//EN"
        "http://www.w3.org/TR/xhtml1/DTD/xhtml1-transitional.dtd">

<html xmlns="http://www.w3.org/1999/xhtml" xml:lang="en" lang="en">
<head>
  <meta http-equiv="content-type" content="text/html;charset=UTF-8" />
  <title>Incidents: <%= controller.action_name %></title>
  <%= stylesheet_link_tag 'scaffold' %>
  <%= auto_discovery_link_tag(:rss, {:action=>'news'}) %>
</head>
<body>

<p style="color: green"><%= flash[:notice] %></p>

<%= yield  %>

</body>
</html>
```

This should create a link like this:

```
<link href="http://localhost:3000/incidents/news.xml"
   rel="alternate" title="RSS" type="application/rss+xml" />
```

But to see if it works, we need to fire up our web browser again.

Test Drive

Now, when a user goes to the web site, an RSS feed icon appears in their browser:

Different browsers have different ways of showing they have found a news feed.

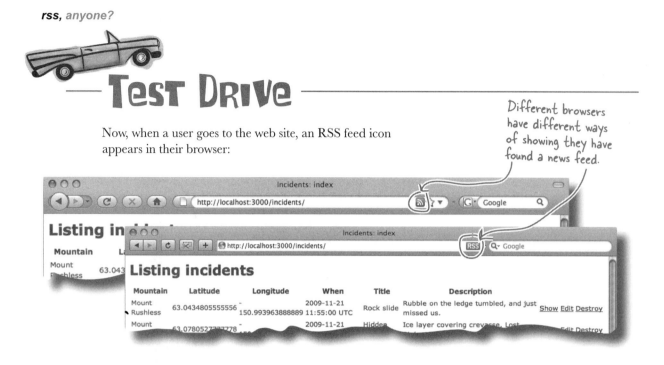

And if they subscribe to the feed, or simply read it, they will see links to incidents that have been posted in the previous 24 hours.

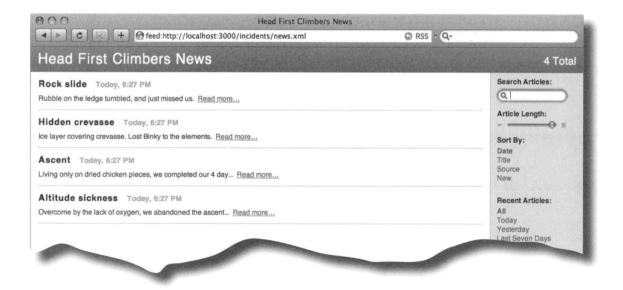

On top of the world!

One of the first news items on the web site is posted by our intrepid climber, and thousands of climbers hear of the good news.

Tools for your Rails Toolbox

You've got Chapter 8 under your belt, and now you've added the ability to use XML to represent your pages in multiple ways.

Rails Tools

to_xml generates an XML for any model object

:only and :root parameters allow you to modify the to_xml format

respond_to creates a _responder_ object that will help you generate multiple representations for a resource

XML builder templates are like page templates for creating XML

XML builder templates give you more flexibility than by simply using to_xml

responders set the response mime-type and also decide whether to call page templates or XML builder templates

9 REST and Ajax

Taking things further

This is such a
RESTful route...

It's time to consolidate your mash-up skills.

So far you've seen how you can add **Google Maps** to your web apps to clearly show
spatial data. But what if you want to **extend the functionality that's already there**? Keep
reading, and we'll show you how you can add more **advanced Ajax goodness** to your
mash-ups. And what's more, you'll learn a bit more about **REST** along the way.

Too many incidents!

With the improved user interface, the number of visitors to the Head
First Climbers site has soared. The trouble is, so many incidents are being
logged that there are too many for people to easily read through them.

There are so many
incidents! I need to
scroll past them all to get
to the map, and that's
tricky while I'm hanging.

**The index page of the site displays the information in
two ways.**

  At the top of the page is a detailed list of incidents with latitudes and
longitudes. The trouble is, lots of people scroll past this to get to the map at
the end of the page.

  On a map showing a cut-down amount of detail when you click on an
incident. The problem here is not all the data is shown on the map.

Neither of these are entirely satisfactory. It's hard to locate the incidents
from the list, and that's why we added a map. But the map doesn't display
all of the data available. So what should we do?

The map could show more details

The ideal solution would be to make the map *do more*. If it could be changed to display more useful information about the incidents, we could probably just remove the the list of incidents and make the front page one big multi-functional map. That would mean we wouldn't need to go to separate pages in order to enter more data, for example.

We could show all the data on one big multi-functional map like this.

There's just one problem: the map partial was *downloaded*. It's simple enough to *use*, but should we really change the code? Fortunately, there's a development technique the map partial uses that means we don't need to touch the downloaded code itself. But what is it?

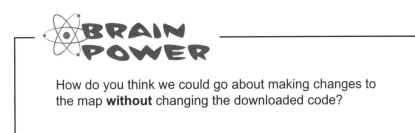

BRAIN POWER

How do you think we could go about making changes to the map **without** changing the downloaded code?

We can extend the map using Ajax

The people who wrote the map partial figured that pretty soon people would want to extend the way the map worked. And because the map partial calls Google Maps, and Google Maps is built using Ajax, it made sense that the way to extend the map is with Ajax.

At the moment, the map works by making a request back to the server asking for an XML file containing the details of all of the mountaineering incidents recorded on the system. By default, the map displays the title and description contained in the XML.

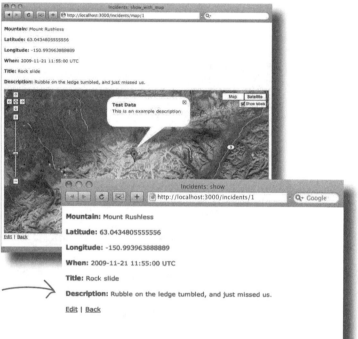

But the map partial also allows you to pass it the name of an **action** that will display the information for an incident. And that action can be whatever you like, so if you wanted, you could generate something that looked like the original version of the incident show page.

We need to display this output in the information window on the map. ⟶

We need the _map.html.erb partial to make Ajax requests, so this means it will need access to the Prototype library. We can allow this in the same way we did before, by adding a reference to the JavaScript library in the layout file like this:

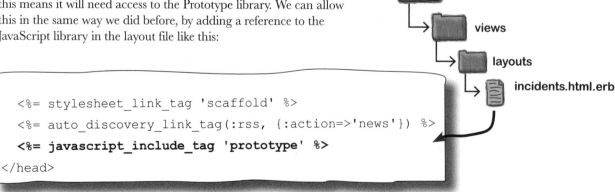

```erb
<%= stylesheet_link_tag 'scaffold' %>
<%= auto_discovery_link_tag(:rss, {:action=>'news'}) %>
<%= javascript_include_tag 'prototype' %>
</head>
```

But how do we convert the index page?

The first thing we need to do to change the front page is remove the list of incidents and make the map larger:

— We need to remove the list of incidents.

← We need to make the map <u>way</u> bigger.

We also need to tell the map partial the name of the action that will display the incident information. That's quite a few changes, but it will actually make the index.html.erb template a lot simpler than it was before.

In fact, this is all we'll be left with:

This means we will generate a larger map to fill the page.

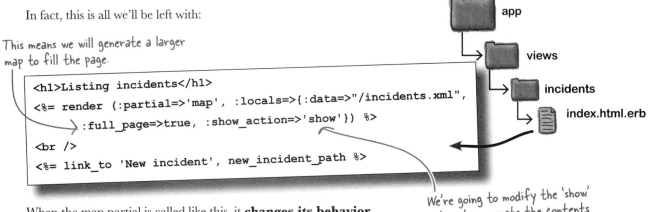

app

views

incidents

index.html.erb

```
<h1>Listing incidents</h1>
<%= render (:partial=>'map', :locals=>{:data=>"/incidents.xml",
       :full_page=>true, :show_action=>'show'}) %>
<br />
<%= link_to 'New incident', new_incident_path %>
```

We're going to modify the 'show' action to generate the contents of the information window.

When the map partial is called like this, it **changes its behavior**. Before, when an incident was clicked, the partial ran a piece of default JavaScript that displayed the title and description in the pop-up information window. Making this change means that when an incident is clicked on the map, the partial calls the show action and displays the action's response in the window.

Or at least it will, once we make the show action generate the correct output.

What will the "show" action need to generate?

We already have a show action, and this generates a web page containing the details of an incident and a map with the incident's location.

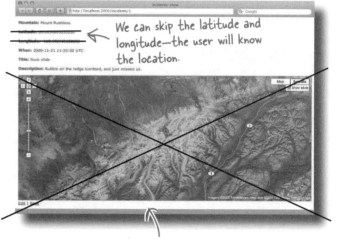

We can skip the latitude and longitude—the user will know the location.

But that's *way more* than we need now. The show action only needs to generate the text details of an incident, and because the information is going to be displayed next to a point on a map, we won't need to display the latitude and longitude either.

There's one other thing that's different: we only need a **page fragment**. We don't want the standard HTML boilerplate that will be produced by a *page template*. So this means our action will need to generated from a partial template. We'll call this _show.html.erb.

We don't need the map.

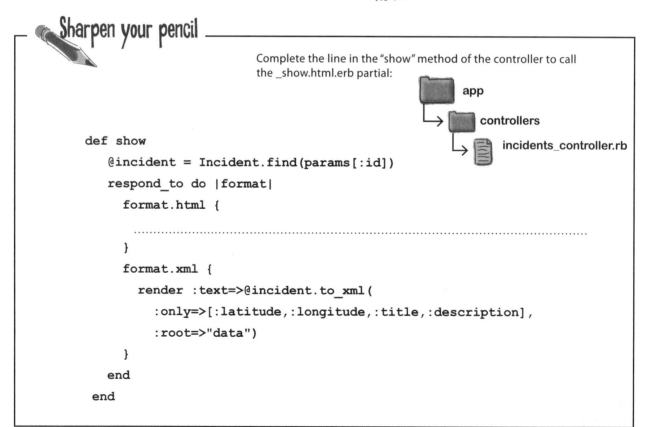

───

✏️ Sharpen your pencil

Complete the line in the "show" method of the controller to call the _show.html.erb partial:

app
→ controllers
→ incidents_controller.rb

```
def show
    @incident = Incident.find(params[:id])
    respond_to do |format|
      format.html {

        ..................................................................................

      }
      format.xml {
        render :text=>@incident.to_xml(
          :only=>[:latitude,:longitude,:title,:description],
          :root=>"data")
      }
    end
end
```

Code Magnets

Complete the code for the new _show.html.erb partial. Remember - you won't need to display all of the information.

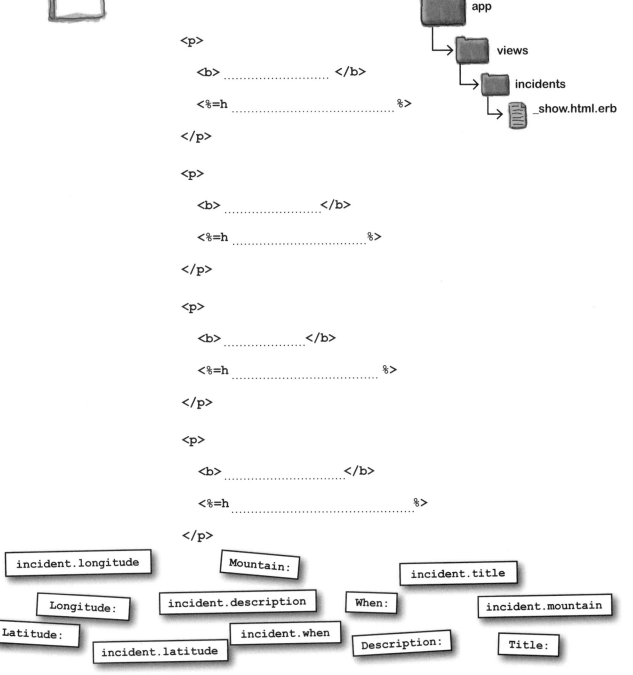

```
<p>
    <b> ......................... </b>
    <%=h ................................. %>
</p>

<p>
    <b> ....................... </b>
    <%=h ............................ %>
</p>

<p>
    <b> ................... </b>
    <%=h ................................ %>
</p>

<p>
    <b> ............................. </b>
    <%=h ................................... %>
</p>
```

app
→ views
→ incidents
→ _show.html.erb

incident.longitude

Mountain:

incident.title

Longitude:

incident.description

When:

incident.mountain

Latitude:

incident.when

Description:

Title:

incident.latitude

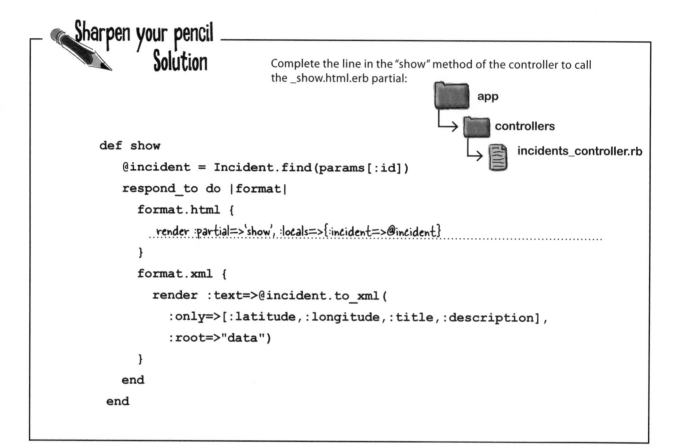

Sharpen your pencil
Solution

Complete the line in the "show" method of the controller to call the _show.html.erb partial:

```
def show
    @incident = Incident.find(params[:id])
    respond_to do |format|
      format.html {
        render :partial=>'show', :locals=>{:incident=>@incident}
      }
      format.xml {
        render :text=>@incident.to_xml(
          :only=>[:latitude,:longitude,:title,:description],
          :root=>"data")
      }
    end
end
```

app
controllers
incidents_controller.rb

Code Magnets Solution

Complete the code for the new _show.html.erb partial. Remember -
you won't need to display all of the information.

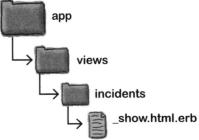

app
→ views
→ incidents
→ _show.html.erb

```
<p>
    <b> Mountain: </b>
    <%=h  incident.mountain  %>
</p>

<p>
    <b> When: </b>
    <%=h  incident.when  %>
</p>

<p>
    <b> Title: </b>
    <%=h  incident.title  %>
</p>

<p>
    <b> Description: </b>
    <%=h  incident.description  %>
</p>
```

```
incident.longitude          Latitude:          Longitude:          incident.latitude
```

TEST DRIVE

Now if we go along to the index page, sure enough—the list of incidents has disappeared and the map is much larger. But more important is what happens when the user clicks on one of the incidents on the map:

When the map detects a mouse click on an incident, it generates an Ajax request to the show action, and this generates the details in HTML for the incident. The map receives the HTML and uses it to replace the content of the incident's information window. This then gets displayed to the user.

The new map functionality is a success!

The new map functionality is greeted enthusiastically by the climbers. They no longer need to scroll past a long list of incidents to get to the map. Now they can get all the information they need direct from the map itself. There's just one thing...

> If only I could enter new incidents on the map itself, rather than go through all these pages...

Climbers want to report new incidents using the map.

They can use GPS units to find their latitude and longitude and type that in, but the site would be a lot easier for them if they could simply plot a point on the map and fill in the other details right there. That would make data-entry quicker for the climbers.

So how does entering data on the map compare with what we're currently doing?

We need to create requests using Ajax, too

If someone wants to create a new incident report, they currently have to go through the following steps:

 Click on the New Incident link on the front page.
You can't enter data directly on the front page, you need to follow a link to the "new" page instead.

Here's the link to create a new incident...

 Manually enter the latitude and longitude on the New page.
There's no map on this page, so you need to enter the latitude and longitude manually and save the record.

New incident

Mountain

Latitude ← Users have to enter the latitude and longitude manually.

Longitude

When
2008 ▼ November ▼ 24 ▼ — 17 ▼ : 00 ▼

Title

Description

(Create)
Back

3 **The incident you've created is displayed.**

Once you've clicked on the save button, you're to the cut-down "show" page we've just created. And if you need to create a second incident or get back to the main map, you need to hit the back button a couple of times to the front page—where you begin all over again.

> **○ ○ ○**
>
> ◀ ▶ ↻ ⊠ + ⊕ http://localhost:3000/incidents/5/edit
>
> Mountain `K9`
>
> When `2009 ⬍` `November ⬍` `26 ⬍` — `15 ⬍` : `24 ⬍`
>
> Title `Yeti spotted`
>
> Description
> `Dropped by camp looking for food. Played cards for a`
> `while. Lost $4 to him.`
>
> (Update)

So what needs to change?

Rather than go through all these steps, the users want the interface to be much simpler. They just want to click on the map and fill in the details using a form in the pop-up window.

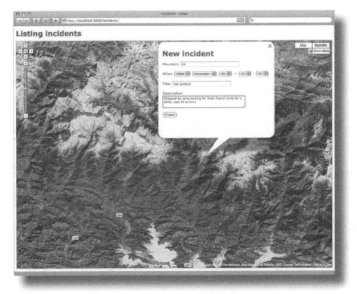

To make that change, we need to generate the "new" form using Ajax. We also need the map to call the form when someone clicks on a new spot. But how?

The map partial lets us specify a "new" action

So far we've looked at showing the incident details on the map. But how do we go about creating new incidents?

The `_map.html.erb` partial lets us specify an action to handle new incidents, in the same way it lets us specify an action for showing incident details. This means that we can add a "new" action to the `index.html.erb` file like this:

```
<h1>Listing incidents</h1>
<%= render (:partial=>'map', :locals=>{:data=>"/incidents.xml",
    :full_page=>true, :show_action=>'show', :new_action=>'new' }) %>

<br />

<%= link_to 'New incident', new_incident_path %>
```

We're going to use the "new" action to generate a form on the map.

We won't need a link on the front page to create new incidents, so we can ditch these lines.

If someone clicks a new spot on the map, the `_map.html.erb` will create a new marker and pop up an information window containing whatever is returned by the "new" action.

We already have a "new" action defined for the application, but it's generating a full web page. Rather than display a full web page, we need the "new" action to create a page fragment that will be displayed inside the pop-up information window. Also, we need to make sure that when the user submits the "new" form, it stays on the map.

So we'll create a partial called `_new.html.erb` that generates an Ajax form.

Exercise

You need to create a _new.html.erb partial for the form. Complete the code for the form. Remember - people won't need to enter values for the latitude and longitude, but the form will still need to record them.

```
<h1>New incident</h1>
<% remote_form_for(incident) do |f| %>
```

....

....

....

....

....

....

....

....

....

....

....

....

....

....

....

....

```
  <p>
    <%= f.submit "Create" %>
  </p>
<% end %>
```

When the map calls the "new" action, it sends the location of the new incident as request parameters. Complete the code in the incidents_controller.rb `new` method so that it calls the partial correctly:

```
format.html {
  @incident.latitude=params['latitude']
  @incident.longitude=params['longitude']
  ............................................................
}
```

app
views
incidents
_new.html.erb

app
controllers
incidents_controller.rb

![Exercise Solution]

You need to create a _new.html.erb partial for the form. Complete the code for the form. Remember - people won't need to enter values for the latitude and longitude, but the form will still need to record them.

```
<h1>New incident</h1>
<% remote_form_for(incident) do |f| %>
    <p>
      <%= f.label :mountain %> <%= f.text_field :mountain %>
    </p>
    <%= f.hidden_field :latitude %>
    <%= f.hidden_field :longitude %>
    <p>
      <%= f.label :when %> <%= f.datetime_select :when %>
    </p>
    <p>
      <%= f.label :title %> <%= f.text_field :title %>
    </p>
    <p>
      <%= f.label :description %><br/>
      <%= f.text_area :description, :rows=>3 %>
    </p>
  <p>
    <%= f.submit "Create" %>
  </p>
<% end %>
```

> We still need to record the latitude and longitude in the form, but only as hidden fields.

> Your code might look a little different.

app → views → incidents → _new.html.erb

When the map calls the "new" action is sends the location of the new incident as request parameters. Complete the code in the incidents_controller.rb `new` method so that it calls the partial correctly:

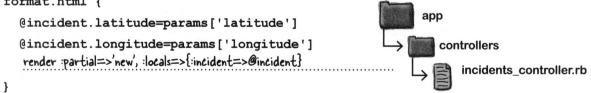

```
format.html {
  @incident.latitude=params['latitude']
  @incident.longitude=params['longitude']
  render :partial=>'new', :locals=>{:incident=>@incident}
}
```

app → controllers → incidents_controller.rb

TEST DRIVE

Now if a user goes to the front page and clicks on a fresh point on the map, they can enter details for the incident using a pop-up form. When the "Create" button is clicked, the form remains on the screen, but a new record is displayed on the database.

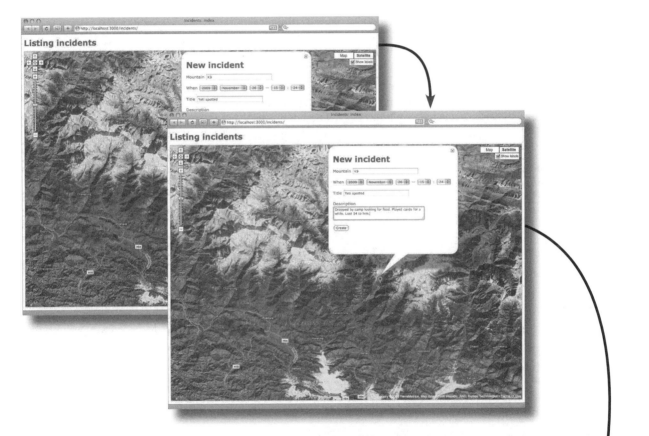

id	mountain	latitude	longitude	when	title	description
1	Mount Rushless	63.04348055...	-150.993963...	2009-11-21 11:...	Rock slide	Rubble on the ...
2	Mount Rushless	63.07805277...	-150.977869...	2009-11-21 17:...	Hidden crev...	Ice layer cove...
3	Mount Lotopaxo	-0.683975	-78.4365055...	2009-06-07 12:...	Ascent	Living only on...
4	High Kanuklima	11.123925	72.72135833...	2009-05-12 18:...	Altitude si...	Overcome by th...
5	K9	28.38535964...	84.48623657...	2009-11-26 15:...	Yeti spotted	Dropped by cam...

So is everything OK?

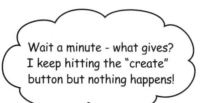

Wait a minute - what gives?
I keep hitting the "create"
button but nothing happens!

The climbers are confused.

Even though the form works fine and incidents are being saved to the
database, it actually *looks* like nothing is happening. When the user clicks
on the "Create" button, there's no feedback indicating the record was
saved. This means that the users are repeatedly hitting the Create button,
and the database is starting to get lots of duplicate records.

Something needs to be done. Back in the old days when we just had
scaffolding, when a user reported an incident with the "new" page, the
browser would immediately switch to the "show" page. This confirmed
that the data was saved to the database.

← *The original "new" form.*

The system displayed the → *"show" page to confirm the record was saved.*

Could we have something like that in the Ajax app?

How do we PROVE an incident was saved?

The system really needs to show the created record in the pop-up window using the "show" action. So if someone enters details of an incident, the pop-up should change to show a *read-only* version of the incident.

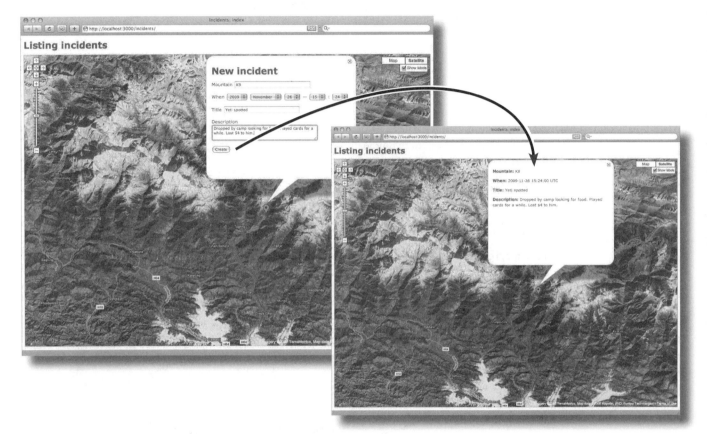

That way, the pop-up information window will work like a little browser, forwarding to the new information. Except of course, our code can't just *forward* the browser to the new information. We need to keep climbers on the same page... just with new information showing.

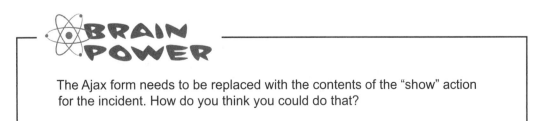

The Ajax form needs to be replaced with the contents of the "show" action for the incident. How do you think you could do that?

The form needs to update the contents of the pop-up's <div>

Even though it looks almost like a desktop application, Google Maps basically boils down to just HTML and JavaScript. It's just a web page. That means that the pop-up information window—and everything else—are just pieces of HTML.

The contents of the pop-up window are defined in a <div> element with:

```
id='map_info'
```

This is important because we're using an Ajax form to create a new incident report, and Ajax forms can be used to dynamically update parts of a web page **using their ids**.

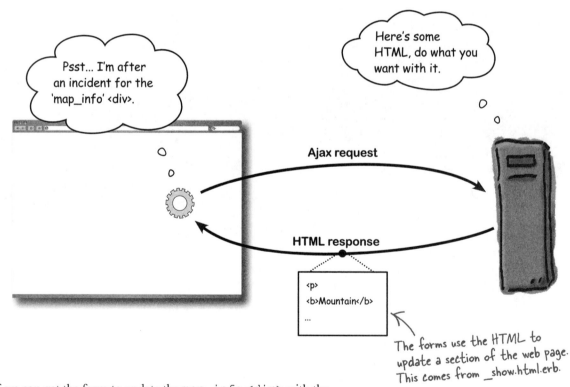

So if we can get the form to update the map_info <div> with the contents of the "show" action for the incident, it should give the users the feedback they need.

Sharpen your pencil

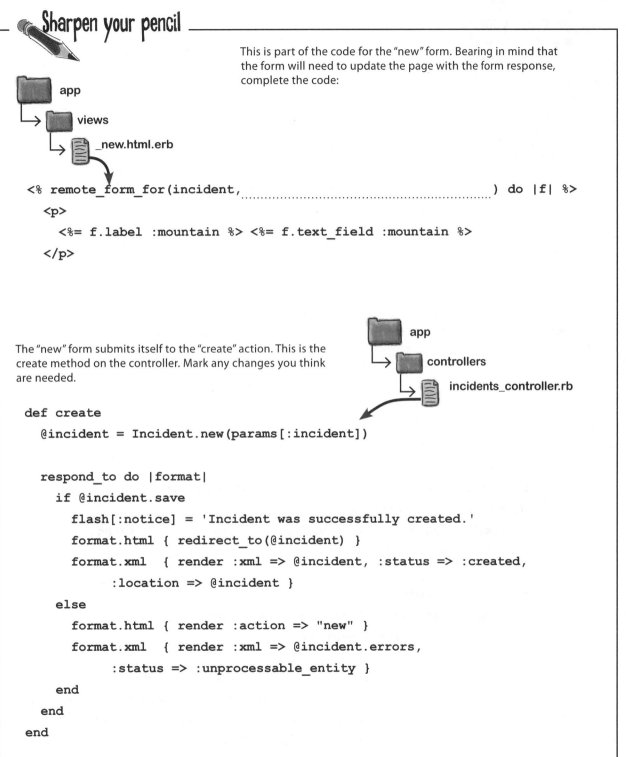

This is part of the code for the "new" form. Bearing in mind that the form will need to update the page with the form response, complete the code:

app

→ **views**

→ **_new.html.erb**

```
<% remote_form_for(incident, ...................................... ) do |f| %>
  <p>
    <%= f.label :mountain %> <%= f.text_field :mountain %>
  </p>
```

The "new" form submits itself to the "create" action. This is the create method on the controller. Mark any changes you think are needed.

app

→ **controllers**

→ **incidents_controller.rb**

```
def create
  @incident = Incident.new(params[:incident])

  respond_to do |format|
    if @incident.save
      flash[:notice] = 'Incident was successfully created.'
      format.html { redirect_to(@incident) }
      format.xml  { render :xml => @incident, :status => :created,
            :location => @incident }
    else
      format.html { render :action => "new" }
      format.xml  { render :xml => @incident.errors,
            :status => :unprocessable_entity }
    end
  end
end
```

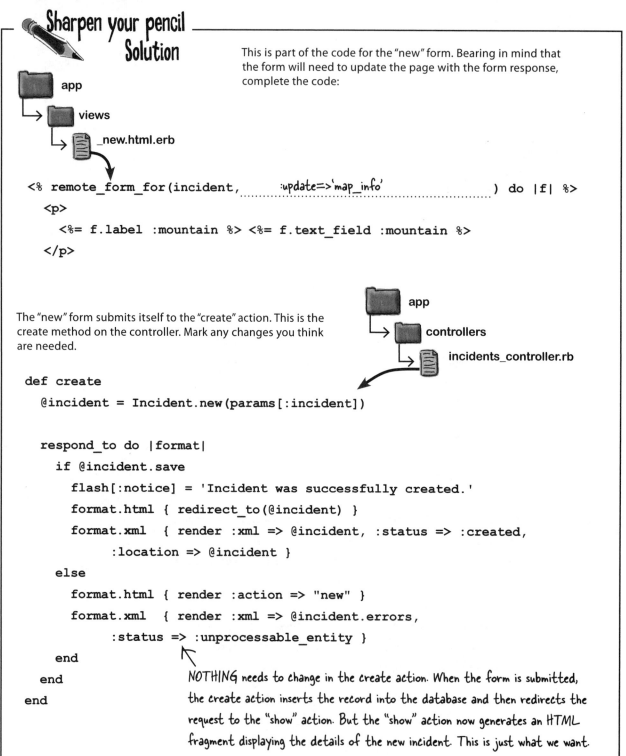

Sharpen your pencil
Solution

app
→ views
→ _new.html.erb

This is part of the code for the "new" form. Bearing in mind that the form will need to update the page with the form response, complete the code:

```erb
<% remote_form_for(incident, :update=>'map_info' ) do |f| %>
  <p>
    <%= f.label :mountain %> <%= f.text_field :mountain %>
  </p>
```

The "new" form submits itself to the "create" action. This is the create method on the controller. Mark any changes you think are needed.

app
→ controllers
→ incidents_controller.rb

```ruby
def create
  @incident = Incident.new(params[:incident])

  respond_to do |format|
    if @incident.save
      flash[:notice] = 'Incident was successfully created.'
      format.html { redirect_to(@incident) }
      format.xml  { render :xml => @incident, :status => :created,
          :location => @incident }
    else
      format.html { render :action => "new" }
      format.xml  { render :xml => @incident.errors,
          :status => :unprocessable_entity }
    end
  end
end
```

NOTHING needs to change in the create action. When the form is submitted, the create action inserts the record into the database and then redirects the request to the "show" action. But the "show" action now generates an HTML fragment displaying the details of the new incident. This is just what we want.

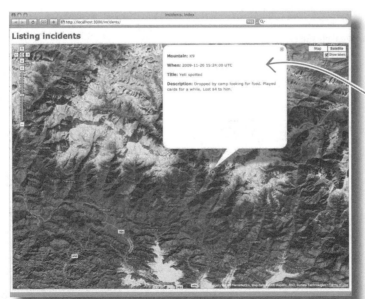

TEST DRIVE

So now what happens when the user creates an incident?

Clicking on a new point on the map displays the Ajax form, just like before:

But when they hit the "Create" button, not only does the system save the record to the database, it also returns a page fragment containing the incident details, which the Ajax form now uses to update the `map_info <div>` inside the pop-up window.

The 'map_info' <div> inside the pop-up window gets updated.

there are no
Dumb Questions

Q: **What happens if the user's browser doesn't have JavaScript enabled?**

A: The application map won't run. Ajax applications, like Google Maps, require JavaScript.

Q: **If Google Maps is an Ajax application, how come we didn't have to include the Prototype library in the last chapter?**

A: Google Maps calls all of it's own Ajax libraries from the Google servers, so it doesn't need the Prototype library.

Q: **So why do we have to pull the Prototype library in this time?**

A: If you pass action names to the map partial, the partial will need to make Ajax requests to the server. For that it needs the Prototype library... independent of what Google Maps is doing.

Q: **Is there a way of making the application work without the map if someone's disabled JavaScript?**

A: You could if you modified your controller. The controller decides which views to display, so it could run different templates and partials if there was no JavaScript.

Q: **I still don't get how respond_to works. If format. html is some kind of method call, how come there's code between {...} following it?**

A: In Ruby, methods can accept pieces of code between {...} (or do...end) as parameters. So the code between { and } is passed for format.html, and it decides whether or not to run it.

Q: **How does the map partial work?**

A: It's not that complicated, but it's mostly JavaScript, so we don't get into much detail here. You could check out *Head First JavaScript* for a lot more on those sorts of details, though!

Q: **But I really want to know how it works!**

A: It's worth looking through the _map.html.erb file. If you want to know more about JavaScript did we mention, *Head First JavaScript* is a great book :-)

Avalanche!

So far we've allowed users to see more detailed information on the map, and also create new incidents onto it direct. But what about edits?

How things works now...

There are two places where scaffolding gives you an edit option.

On the original scaffolded version of the "index" page, you could click the "Edit" link next to any of the records and jump to the edit form. But we can't do anything like that now because the list of incidents on the index page has been replaced by the map. And we know that the map partial doesn't have any "Edit" functions built in.

So where else could we edit things in the original scaffolding? Well, another place is in the incident "show" page. In the scaffolded version of the application, there was an "Edit" link on the "show" page.

So could we do something like that? How about if we add an "Edit" link to the set of details that are displayed in the pop-up window.

Would that work?

We could have an "Edit" link in the pop-up

We need to add an "edit" link to the details that appear when someone selects an incident from the map. When someone clicks on the "edit" link, we switch the contents of map_info <div> to display an edit form and then use that to amend the record.

We already have the "show" function built. The "edit" form should be similar to the "new" form, and we already have the back-end code in the controller to amend the record.

How hard can it be?

We'll start by modifying the "edit" action

We need some way of generating an edit form that will appear in the pop-up window. We'll create a partial called **_edit.html.erb**. The partial looks pretty similar to the _new.html.erb:

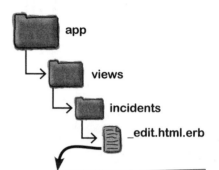

app

views

incidents

_edit.html.erb

```
<% remote_form_for(incident, :update=>'map_info') do |f| %>
  <p><%= f.label :mountain %> <%= f.text_field :mountain %></p>
  <%= f.hidden_field :latitude %>
  <%= f.hidden_field :longitude %>
  <p><%= f.label :when %> <%= f.datetime_select :when %></p>
  <p><%= f.label :title %> <%= f.text_field :title %></p>
  <p><%= f.label :description %><br/><%= f.text_area :description, :rows=>3 %></p>
  <p>
    <%= f.submit "Update" %>
  </p>
<% end %>
```

The code in _edit.html.erb and _new.html.erb are the same, but in this case we'll keep them in separate files.

So why have two partials?

The two partials are basically the same code, but it's a good idea to keep them separate. At the moment they both look the same, but that might not always be the case.

As an example, we might want to change what functionality is available through the "new" and "edit" pages. We might decide that we need users to insert the date of an incident, but we may want to stop them editing it afterwards. Another possibility is that we might want to make the two pages look different from each other.

If the two forms look the same, I wonder how one will insert a record into the database and the other will update a record?

Rails knows if the form's model object has been previously saved to the database.

So the code that the `form_for` helper generates changes depending upon whether it is dealing with an unsaved object (in which case, the form will call the "create" action) or an object that's already been saved in the past (in which case, the form will call the "update" action).

Talking of actions, as well as creating the partial, we need to modify the "edit" action method in the controller to return the "edit" partial when it's called:

```
def edit
    @incident = Incident.find(params[:id])
    render :partial=>'edit', :locals=>{:incident=>@incident}
end
```

there are no
Dumb Questions

Q: How does Rails know if an object has already been saved?

A: It calls a method called "new_record?". That return true if the object has never been saved.

Q: Why does "new_record?" have a question mark at the end?

A: It's a Ruby convention. Most methods returning true or false, have a question-mark in their name.

Q: Why do we have to have hidden fields for latitude and longitude?

A: We don't want people to edit them.

Q: Yeah - I know that. But why even mention them at all?

A: The form object gets converted into the fields in the form. If they weren't mentioned in the form fields, they would disappear.

Q: But we don't have fields for id, created_at and updated_at fields?

A: No - but Rails knows that they're needed, so the form_for helper will create them for you.

And we'll also need a new link on the show page

We should now be able to generate an edit form, but how will the user get to it? We need an "Edit" link to appear when the user looks at the details of the incident. The link will need to be added to the `_show.html.erb` partial.

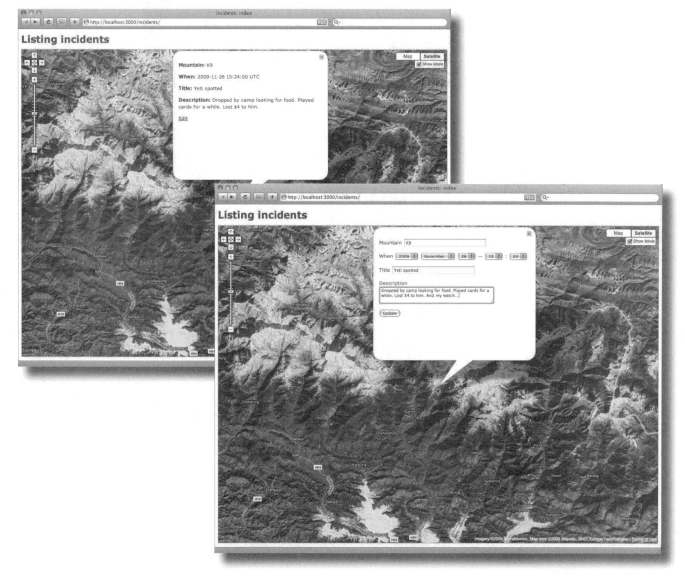

To generate the link, we'll use the `link_to` helper.

So how do we use the link_to helper?

The `link_to` helper takes two parameters: the name of the text in the link and the place we're going to.

```
<p><%= link_to "Edit", "/incidents/#{incident.id}/edit" %></p>
```

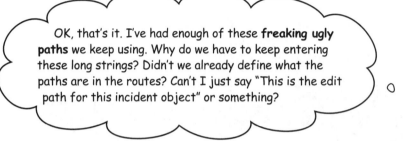

OK, that's it. I've had enough of these **freaking ugly paths** we keep using. Why do we have to keep entering these long strings? Didn't we already define what the paths are in the routes? Can't I just say "This is the edit path for this incident object" or something?

That's a very good point.

So far we have created lots of paths and URLs using strings. But what if we change the format of the links in the future? We can fix things in the routes pretty quickly, but we will have a lot of redundant strings in the code containing paths.

Having the same sort of information in two places is bad because it breaks an important Rails principle:

Don't Repeat Yourself ← Didn't we say this before?

But if the routes already record the structure of the paths and URLs, maybe it's worth looking at routes in a little more detail.

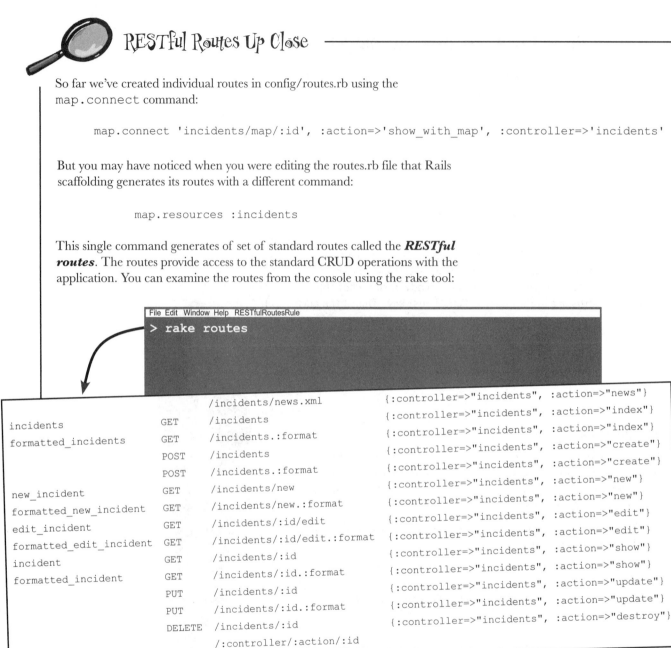

RESTful Routes Up Close

So far we've created individual routes in config/routes.rb using the `map.connect` command:

```
map.connect 'incidents/map/:id', :action=>'show_with_map', :controller=>'incidents'
```

But you may have noticed when you were editing the routes.rb file that Rails scaffolding generates its routes with a different command:

```
map.resources :incidents
```

This single command generates of set of standard routes called the ***RESTful routes***. The routes provide access to the standard CRUD operations with the application. You can examine the routes from the console using the rake tool:

File Edit Window Help RESTfulRoutesRule

```
> rake routes
```

		/incidents/news.xml	{:controller=>"incidents", :action=>"news"}
incidents	GET	/incidents	{:controller=>"incidents", :action=>"index"}
formatted_incidents	GET	/incidents.:format	{:controller=>"incidents", :action=>"index"}
	POST	/incidents	{:controller=>"incidents", :action=>"create"}
	POST	/incidents.:format	{:controller=>"incidents", :action=>"create"}
new_incident	GET	/incidents/new	{:controller=>"incidents", :action=>"new"}
formatted_new_incident	GET	/incidents/new.:format	{:controller=>"incidents", :action=>"new"}
edit_incident	GET	/incidents/:id/edit	{:controller=>"incidents", :action=>"edit"}
formatted_edit_incident	GET	/incidents/:id/edit.:format	{:controller=>"incidents", :action=>"edit"}
incident	GET	/incidents/:id	{:controller=>"incidents", :action=>"show"}
formatted_incident	GET	/incidents/:id.:format	{:controller=>"incidents", :action=>"show"}
	PUT	/incidents/:id	{:controller=>"incidents", :action=>"update"}
	PUT	/incidents/:id.:format	{:controller=>"incidents", :action=>"update"}
	DELETE	/incidents/:id	{:controller=>"incidents", :action=>"destroy"}
		/:controller/:action/:id	

Each of these lines is a single route, and in some cases, the routes are named. So `edit_incident` is the name of the "/incidents/:id/edit" route.

But how does that help us tidy the path in the code?

Rails provides helpers for each named route

Those RESTful route names are important, because they help you refer to a route **from inside your code**. They let you turn this:

```
"/incidents/#{incident.id}/edit"
```

into this:

```
edit_incident_path(@incident)
```

For every named route, Rails gives you helpers to generate paths on the local server and complete URLs.

Paths on the local server

`edit_incident_`**path**`(@incident)` returns `/incidents/3/edit` if `@incident` has id = 3

Complete URLs

`edit_incident_`**url**`(@incident)` returns `http://localhost:3000/incidents/3/edit`

They're called ***RESTful*** route helpers because they can accept ***resources***, or model objects, as parameters. Remember - one of the principles of REST design is to think of web applications as containers for resources.

The helpers for `incidents` and `new_incident` are called without resources—for example, as `incidents_url` or `incidents_path`.

The route helpers will not only remove redundant path formats from your code, but they are also easier to read and reduce the chances of you making an error in a path description.

So what does that do to our code? It changes from this:

```
<p><%= link_to "Edit", "/incidents/#{incident.id}/edit" %></p>
```

into this:

```
<p><%= link_to "Edit", edit_incident_url(incident) %></p>
```

Test Drive

So once the "Edit" link has been added to the "show" partial, what happens when we click on an existing incident on the map?

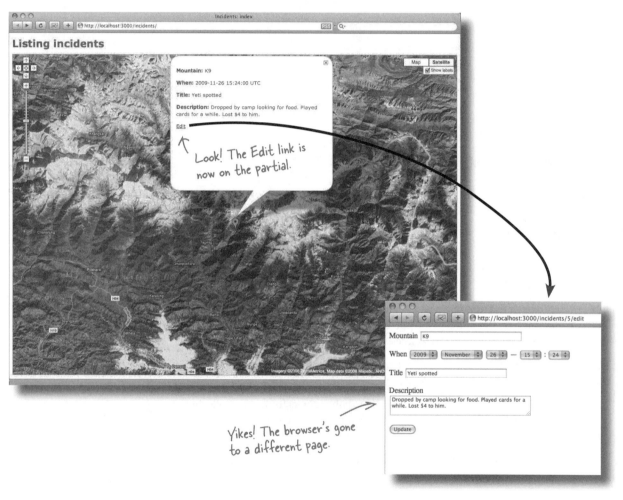

Look! The Edit link is now on the partial.

Yikes! The browser's gone to a different page.

The link simply took the browser to:

```
http://localhost:3000/incidents/5/edit
```

The trouble is, this now sends the contents of the _edit.html.erb partial back to the browser like it was another page.

We really need to stay on the same page in the browser, so how do we fix it?

Ajax links to the rescue

The "new" form we created earlier was able to replace the contents of the pop-up information window because it made an Ajax call to the server. It used the server response to replace the contents of the `map_info <div>`.

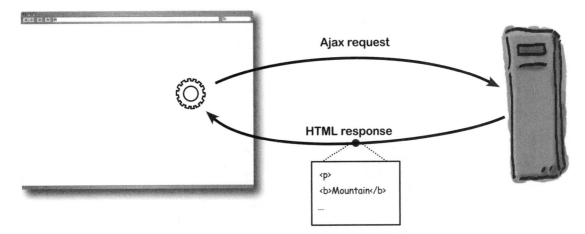

But the link we just added didn't do that. It just told the browser to link to another page. If we create an Ajax link instead of a browser link, we can get around the problem.

An Ajax link works a lot like an Ajax form. When you click on an Ajax link, it doesn't tell the browser to go to a different page, instead it generates an Ajax request to the server and uses the response to update part of the page. If this sounds familiar, it's because Ajax links are almost identical to the Ajax buttons we used earlier on to refresh the seating list at Coconut Airways.

To convert the link into an Ajax link, we have to change this:

```
<p><%= link_to "Edit", edit_incident_url(incident) %></p>
```

to this:

```
<p><%= link_to_remote "Edit", :update => "map_info",
       :url=>edit_incident_url(incident) %></p>
```

— This is the part of the page we want the link to update.

— This is the URL that will generate the HTML for the update.

The link should now generate an edit form from the server and display it in the pop-up window. Let's see how it works now.

TEST DRIVE

When we click on an incident, the information window looks exactly the same as before.

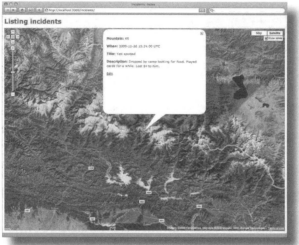

The link looks the same, but remember that behind the scenes, it's no longer a simple link. Instead there's a whole lot of JavaScript mojo going on, waiting to generate an Ajax request when the link is clicked. So what happens when we click it?

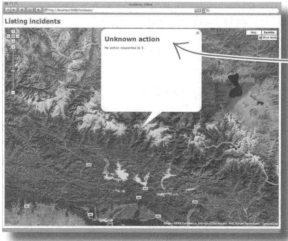

Uh oh. That doesn't look good...

Instead of displaying the edit form, we get this weird "Unknown action" error. So what the heck happened?

We need to dig a little deeper into the routes...

We're using the wrong route!

When Rails receives the Ajax request from the link, the Ajax link sends out a request correctly to:

```
http://localhost:3000/incidents/5/edit
```

Instead of matching the request to the `edit_incident` route, it matches to one of the default routes:

```
                               /incidents/news.xml         {:controller=>"incidents", :action=>"news"}
                                                           {:controller=>"incidents", :action=>"index"}
incidents              GET     /incidents                  {:controller=>"incidents", :action=>"index"}
formatted_incidents    GET     /incidents.:format          {:controller=>"incidents", :action=>"create"}
                       POST    /incidents                  {:controller=>"incidents", :action=>"create"}
                       POST    /incidents.:format          {:controller=>"incidents", :action=>"new"}
new_incident           GET     /incidents/new              {:controller=>"incidents", :action=>"new"}
formatted_new_incident GET     /incidents/new.:format      {:controller=>"incidents", :action=>"edit"}
edit_incident          GET     /incidents/:id/edit         {:controller=>"incidents", :action=>"edit"}
formatted_edit_incident GET    /incidents/:id/edit.:format {:controller=>"incidents", :action=>"edit"}
incident               GET     /incidents/:id              {:controller=>"incidents", :action=>"show"}
formatted_incident     GET     /incidents/:id.:format      {:controller=>"incidents", :action=>"show"}
                       PUT     /incidents/:id              {:controller=>"incidents", :action=>"update"}
                       PUT     /incidents/:id.:format      {:controller=>"incidents", :action=>"update"}
                       DELETE  /incidents/:id              {:controller=>"incidents", :action=>"destroy"}
                               /:controller/:action/:id
```

Routing matches it to this route here, and not the edit_incident route further up.

Rails tries to match it to the default route near the bottom, and it sets the :action parameter to '5' and the :id parameter to 'edit'. There's no action called '5', so it fails.

But how can that be? Our URL (http://localhost:3000/incidents/5/edit) is the same path format as the `edit_incident` route (/incidents/:id/edit). So why didn't it match? After all, the link worked fine before we converted it to Ajax.

BRAIN POWER

Look at the list of routes again. The original link and the Ajax link are both going to the same URL. Why do you think the Ajax link was matched to the wrong route?

The HTTP method affects the route that's chosen

There's one column in the routes that we've not really looked at:

Look what's here...

		/incidents/news.xml	{:controller=>"incidents", :action=>"news"}
incidents	GET	/incidents	{:controller=>"incidents", :action=>"index"}
formatted_incidents	GET	/incidents.:format	{:controller=>"incidents", :action=>"index"}
	POST	/incidents	{:controller=>"incidents", :action=>"create"}
	POST	/incidents.:format	{:controller=>"incidents", :action=>"create"}
new_incident	GET	/incidents/new	{:controller=>"incidents", :action=>"new"}
formatted_new_incident	GET	/incidents/new.:format	{:controller=>"incidents", :action=>"new"}
edit_incident	GET	/incidents/:id/edit	{:controller=>"incidents", :action=>"edit"}
formatted_edit_incident	GET	/incidents/:id/edit.:format	{:controller=>"incidents", :action=>"edit"}
incident	GET	/incidents/:id	{:controller=>"incidents", :action=>"show"}
formatted_incident	GET	/incidents/:id.:format	{:controller=>"incidents", :action=>"show"}
	PUT	/incidents/:id	{:controller=>"incidents", :action=>"update"}
	PUT	/incidents/:id.:format	{:controller=>"incidents", :action=>"update"}
	DELETE	/incidents/:id	{:controller=>"incidents", :action=>"destroy"}
		/:controller/:action/:id	

So what are those GET, POST, PUT and DELETE words about?

They are the ***HTTP methods***—also called the ***HTTP verbs***. Every request uses a particular HTTP method, and Rails uses the method as well as the path to decide *which* route to use.

But what exactly are they?

So what's an HTTP method?

Despite the name, HTTP methods are really nothing like the Ruby
methods you find in, say, a controller. Instead, an HTTP method is
mentioned in the low-level HTTP-talk that happens when a client
contacts the server:

With the GET method

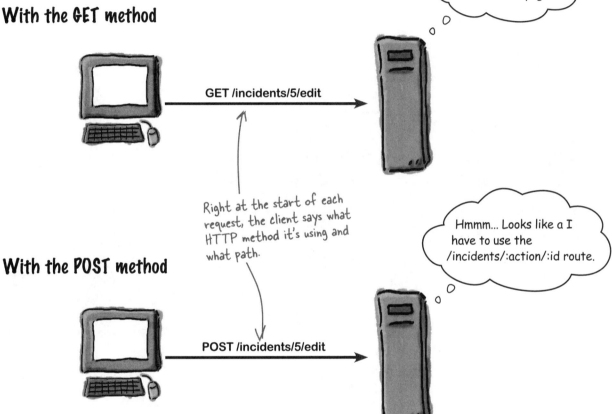

Ah - so you want to see the Edit page...

GET /incidents/5/edit

Right at the start of each request, the client says what HTTP method it's using and what path.

With the POST method

Hmmm... Looks like a I have to use the /incidents/:action/:id route.

POST /incidents/5/edit

So why did the two versions of the link do different things? Well -
ordinary HTML hyperlinks send **GET** requests to the server. But, by
default, Ajax links send **POST** requests.

So to make the link work, we *also* need to tell the link what HTTP
method to use like this:

```
<p><%= link_to_remote "Edit", :update => "map_info",
      :url=>edit_incident_url(incident), :method=>'get' %></p>
```

TEST DRIVE

It works!

When we click on an incident link, we see the information displayed with an "Edit" link. When we click on the link, it creates an Ajax request for the edit form, which is used to replace the contents of the pop-up.

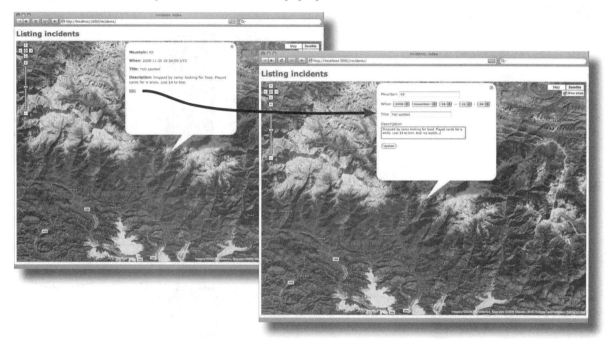

And what about the form? Well that works pretty like the "new" form did. It updates the incident and then redisplays it:

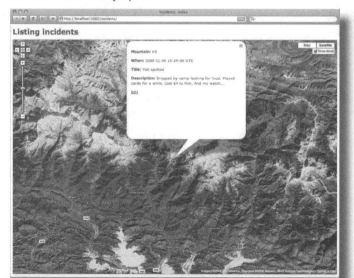

Q: Is it really that bad to use strings as paths?

A: Strings will work, but they will be harder to reader and more prone to errors than using the helpers.

Q: Why more prone to errors?

A: If you mis-type the name of a route helper, Rails will create an error and tell you. If you mis-type a path in a string, the system will either not report an error, or report some other error caused by the bad path.

Q: Why does link_to_remote create a POST request, but link_to just creates a GET?

A: link_to creates a simple HTML hyperlink. Browsers always use GET for simple hyperlinks. But link_to_remote creates an Ajax request and Ajax requests are always submitted as POSTs by default.

Q: Why does HTTP even bother having GET and POST? What good do they do?

A: GET requests are designed to be repeatable. So it shouldn't matter how many times you make the same GET request. GETs are commonly used for request that just read information. But POST requests are used for requests that might change the data on the server each time, so they're normally used for requests that update the database.

Q: So what about PUT and DELETE?

A: PUT is used for requests that will create new records in the database. And DELETE is used for database deletes.

Q: Is that true for all web applications?

A: It's true for Rails apps. Using the correct HTTP method is very important part of RESTful design.

Q: So is this how form_for is able to use the same code to generate forms that can update or insert?

A: Yes. If the object has already been saved, then form_for generates a form that will use the POST action. If the object is new, then it will generate a form that uses PUT.

Q: Someone told me that browsers can't use PUT and DELETE. Is that true?

A: Very few browsers support PUT and DELETE. So to make sure that things still work, Rails adds another hidden field called "_method" which stores the name of the HTTP action. If a request is received with _method="PUT", Rails will treat it as a PUT request, even if it was actually submitted with a POST.

Q: But what is RESTful design?

A: It's a way of designing web applications that tries to stay truer to the original design of the web. You can find out more about it at http://tinyurl.com/28nguu.

Head First Climbers needs you!

The mountaineers are loving the application. But we think you can do a better job.

It's time to lay your thing down and seriously pimp this application. Add more details, add more widgets, add more eye candy. Here are some ideas:

> Why can't people post extra files? Photos, links, videos, commentaries?

> How about connecting the incidents together with some sort of expedition object?

> They can create, they can read and they can update the incidents. But what — no delete??? How about fixing that?

> How about mashing up the mash-up with another Web 2.0 application? Why can't we Twitter straight from the top of K2?

> How about letting people drag the points around on the map? (You may need to learn a little of the Google Maps API for this one. See http://tinyurl.com/2bfbm2)

> How about animating the incidents from the expedition?

> How about... something else?

Build your best version of the Head First Climbers app, then submit your URL in the Head First Labs "Head First Rails" forum. You stand the chance of winning a bunch of O'Reilly goodness and the World Wide Fame of being featured on Head First Labs!

Visti us here for details on how to enter the contest.

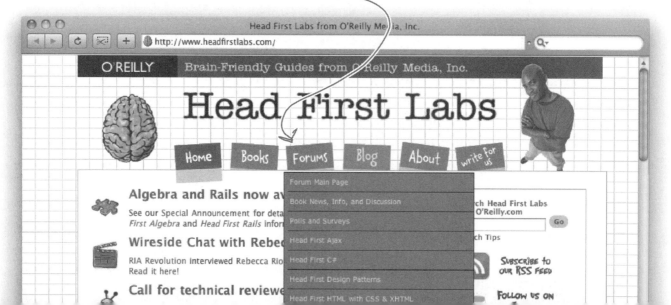

Tools for your Rails Toolbox

You've got Chapter 9 under your belt, and now you've added the ability to add more advanced Rails functionality to your web apps.

Rails Tools

rake routes displays the routes for the application

<route name>_path(object) returns the path for the given named path, using the id from the given object

edit_<model_name>_path(object) returns the path to the editor for the object

new_<model_name>_path returns the path to the new editor

Changing "_path" to "_url" returns a full URL instead of just the local path

Rails in the real world

He's all grown up now. I hope he doesn't go off the Rails.

You've learned a lot about Ruby on Rails.

But to apply your knowledge to **the real world**, there are a number of things you need to think about. How do you connect your application to **another database**? How do you **test** Rails apps? How do you make the most out the Rails and the **Ruby language**? And where do you find out the latest on **what's happening** with Rails? Keep reading, and we'll put you on the inside track that will take your development skills to the next level.

I can see we've covered a lot of ground for building Rails web apps, but that's just been in the book. What about in the real world? You can't tell me that everything goes like this when you're out there developing in the wild...

All of the techniques you've learned so far ARE useful... but there's more to learn.

Yes, it's true. Things out in the world don't always go the way they should. Not only that, but Rails is a pretty big framework. There's more than this book, or any other book less than a few zillion pages, could ever hope to cover.

But there's no reason to assume you're not prepared! Skim through these last few pages to see what you know, and even pick up a few more tips on things you don't.

WHAT'S MY PURPOSE?

We only covered a handful of the many helpers that are available in Rails, but there are plenty more to choose from. See if you can match each of the helpers below to what it actually does.

`number_to_phone`   Lets browsers autodetect an RSS feed.

`number_to_percentage`   Allows you to time how long bits of template code take to run.

`error_message_on`   Formats a number as a US phone number.

`auto_discovery_link_tag`   Formats a number as a percentage.

`image_tag`   Returns a set of select tags for year, month and day.

`benchmark`   Helps you to format your error messages.

`date_select`   Returns an image tag that you can use in a template.

WHAT'S MY PURPOSE? SOLUTION

We only covered a handful of the many helpers that are available in Rails, but there are plenty more to choose from. See if you can match each of the helpers below to what it actually does.

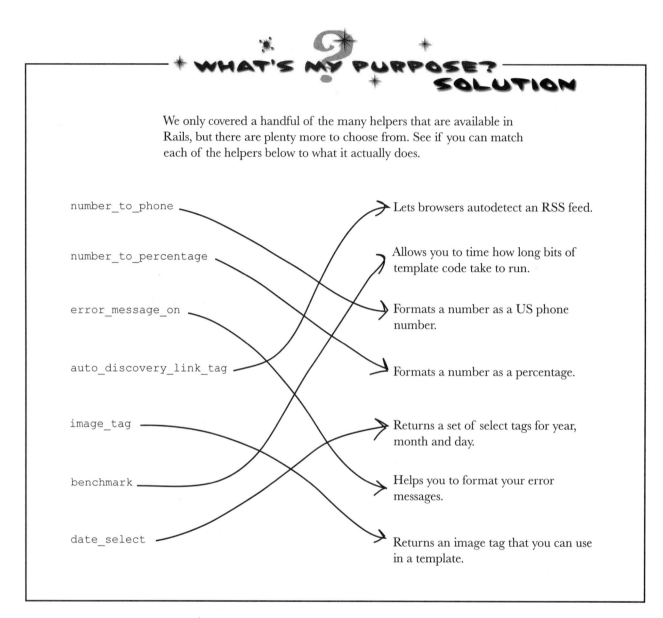

number_to_phone — Lets browsers autodetect an RSS feed.

number_to_percentage — Allows you to time how long bits of template code take to run.

error_message_on — Formats a number as a US phone number.

auto_discovery_link_tag — Formats a number as a percentage.

image_tag — Returns a set of select tags for year, month and day.

benchmark — Helps you to format your error messages.

date_select — Returns an image tag that you can use in a template.

Geek Bits

To find out more about the helpers that are available in the current version of Rails see **http://tinyurl.com/railshelpers**

Look! It's a big Ruby "Try this" page

Did you notice how little Ruby you had to know in order to develop
cool Rails web apps? Even so, knowing a bit more Ruby can sometimes
be useful. Here are some sample bits of Ruby you might want to
experiment with. Just type them in and see what happens...

Try this!

Read the lines of a file into an array called "a"

```
a=File.readlines("filename.txt")
```

Sort an array

```
a.sort
```

Reverse a string

```
"Bass ackwards".reverse!
```

Return a copy of a string that is reversed

```
"Bass ackwards".reverse
```

Does the String s contain "Waldo"?

```
/Waldo/ =~ s
```

Is the String a zip code?

```
/^\d{5}$/ =~ "90210"
```

Converting a string to a Fixnum

```
"12345".to_i
```

Convert a String to a float

```
"3.1415".to_f
```

Convert an object to a string

```
a.to_s
```

Pretty-print the contents of an array

```
[1, 2, 3, 4, 5].inspect
```

Pretty-print the contents of an array

```
{:a=>1, :b=>"c"}.inspect
```

Create a string with 50 =-signs

```
"=" * 50
```

Get an array of words from a string

```
"to be or not to be".split
```

Return the class (datatype) of an object

```
o.class
```

Round a Float to the nearest whole number

```
(3.14).round
```

Find a square-root

```
Math.sqrt(16)
```

Delete a file

```
File.delete("filename.txt")
```

The current date and time

```
Time.now
```

The current year

```
Time.now.year
```

Give a method another name

```
alias my_method
```

Return an array of files in a directory

```
Dir.entries("directoryName")
```

Web apps need testing too

Automated testing is one of the most important parts of software development, and yet until now, we haven't mentioned it. So why not? Testing a piece of software relies on a thorough understanding of the tools you are using, and designing tests can be far more difficult (and enjoyable) than writing the code itself. That's why this book has concentrated on giving you the skills to understand how Rails works and thinks. Only once you understand that can you start to think about how you will test applications.

But that doesn't mean that you do testing long after you have finished writing a system. Far from it. The best tests are written **before** you write ← your main code.

For more information, see "Extreme Programming Explained," ISBN-13: 978-0321278654.

Rails comes with a ton of testing support, far more than almost any other framework. Every application contains a set of test scripts (in the test directory), and every time you generate scaffolding, Rails also generates a set of standard tests for you. So, if you go into the folder where you wrote the scaffolded tickets application in chapter 1 and type:

```
File Edit Window Help TestsAreGood
> rake test
```

Rails will run a whole suite of tests for you. Does that mean that you never need to write your own? Actually, no. A lot of your time as a Rails developer will be spent writing and maintaining tests.

So what kinds of tests are available?

There are three main types of test:

Unit tests

Rails sometimes uses terms that are not quite the same as you'll find elsewhere. In most systems, a "unit test" is a test of any standalone piece of code. But Rails is more specific than that. In Rails, a "unit test" means a test of a model class. Rails creates standard unit tests for you in the `test/unit` directory whenever you generate a model either directly, or via scaffolding.

Functional tests

What Rails means by a functional test is a test of an individual controller. Functional tests check that if you make a particular kind of request, you get a particular kind of response. You can find functional tests in `test/functional`. Again, Rails creates functional tests whenever you generate controllers, either directly or via scaffolding.

Integration tests

This are high-level tests that read a little like the sort of test-scripts that manual testers use. Integration tests test the system as a whole. So they automate the set of actions that a typical user might perform on your system. There is a special folder for integration tests (`test/integration`), but they are not generated automatically. They are very specific to what you need your system to do and so you need to create them yourself.

Finally, the test data for all of these tests is stored in data files in `test/fixtures`. A fixture is just a fancy name for a set of test data. Rails will store the data from the fixtures in a special, separate test database to make sure that your development (or live data) does not get mixed up with data required for your tests.

For more information on testing in rails see **http://tinyurl.com/railstest**

Going live

Your application won't stay in development all its life, and at some point, you'll need to send it live. So what do you do then? It's not a good idea if your application has code in it that specifies the location of the database and so on. After all, you don't want the live and test versions of the code to do different things. You just want them to use different databases.

That why Rails lets you specify ***environments***. An environment sets the location and type of your database as well as a few other settings, such as how log messages will be recorded.

By default, an application is set up to use three different environments:

 development
This is the environment that is used by default. It's the environment that we have been using all the way through the book. The development environment uses the db/development.sqlite3 database.

 test
This environment is set aside for the use of the automated testing scripts.

 production
This is your live environment.

But how do you switch between environments?

When you start the server, Rails looks for an environment variable called RAILS_ENV. This will tell it which environment to run. If you want to switch from the development enviroment to the production environment, you need to set the RAILS_ENV variable:

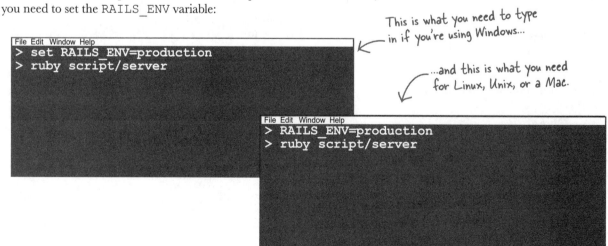

This is what you need to type in if you're using Windows...

```
File Edit Window Help
> set RAILS_ENV=production
> ruby script/server
```

...and this is what you need for Linux, Unix, or a Mac.

```
File Edit Window Help
> RAILS_ENV=production
> ruby script/server
```

So how do you change the database?

If you look at the `config/database.yml` file, you will find the database details for each environment.

For example, your original **SQLite** production environment might be set like this:

```
development:
  adapter: sqlite3
  database: db/development.sqlite3
  timeout: 5000
```

SQLite

But if you wanted to change the production environment to use an **Oracle** database, it would probably look something like this:

```
development:
  adapter: oracle
  host: mydatabaseserver
  username: scott
  password: tiger
```

Oracle

Or, if you want the live environment to use a **MySQL** database hosted on the same machine as Rails, you would change it to:

```
production:
  adapter: mysql
  database: my_db_name
  username: root
  password:
  host: localhost
```

MySQL

What's REST?

We've heard a lot in this book about REST. How Rails uses REST. How REST design is the new guiding principle of Rails. How if you use REST, your teeth will be brighter, your life will be happier, and all will be goodness and sunshine with the world.

Let's start with the basics. **REST** stands for **Representational State Transfer**, and it's a way of structuring how people work with computer systems. Obviously, the most important computer system around is the World Wide Web, and it's significant that the guy who came up with REST—Roy Fielding—was also one of the authors of the HTTP spec.

So why does it matter that the HTTP guy is also the REST guy? Well, because RESTful design really means designing your applications to work the way the web was originally meant to look.

So what are the main principles of REST?

 All the important stuff is a resource.
What this means is that all the important data in your system is separately identifiable things that you can do stuff to. If you have a web site that sells donuts, then the donuts are resources.

 Every resource has a proper name.
On the web, this means that everything has a URL.

 You can perform a standard set of operations on the resources.
The CRUD (Create, Read, Update and Delete) operations are a fairly typical set of operations, and they are supported by Rails and the web.

4 **The client and server talk to each other statelessly**
This means that when a client (like a browser) talks to a RESTful application, it is as a distinct set of requests and responses. The client talks to the server. The server answers. Then the conversation ends.

All of these things seem pretty obvious, don't they? They are a pretty good description of how the web works.

And they were a good description of how the web worked. Before it went wrong...

The web application that went astray

Imagine there was a web application that allowed somebody to sell spare parts for rockets:

They might create a system that displays a rocket component like this:

> http://www.boosters-r-us.com/airframes/472

The web site is about rocket components and this is a URL that can be used as the name of the component.

But look at what happens when someone updates the details of the component, like—say—its price. The web form in the system submits the details to this URL:

> http://www.boosters-r-us.com/airframes/472/update

The trouble with this is it's not RESTful. Why? Well URLs in a RESTful system are supposed to be names of resources. And this second URL doesn't represent a **thing** it represents an **action**.

Why is not being RESTful a problem?

Have you ever revisited a URL in your browser and been asked if you want to **repost data**? The browser history is just a list of URLs and that should mean that it is a list of names. But if a web application uses URLs that represent activities then when you go back through your history, the browser won't know whether you intend to redo the actions.

HTTP verbs are the only verbs you need

But how do we get around this problem? The third principle of REST says that there should a well defined list of actions available. A RESTful application uses HTTP methods to define the activity and leaves the URL to name the resource:

These are the used in the RESTful routes in a scaffolded application.

CRUD operation	HTTP method	URL
Create a component	POST	http://www.boosters-r-us.com/airframes/
Read a component	GET	http://www.boosters-r-us.com/airframes/472
Update a component	PUT	http://www.boosters-r-us.com/airframes/472
Delete a component	DELETE	http://www.boosters-r-us.com/airframes/472

Living on the Edge

Rails is changing all the time, but how will you stay up with all the latest and greatest features that have been added? One way is to run on the **Edge**.

Rails make it really easy to run on the very latest build of Rails (called Edge Rails) by downloading and installing the latest version of the framework directly into your application.

Now in some other application frameworks, changing to the latest version of the framework would be incredible difficult. You would have go to a web browser. Download the files. Read the latest install instructions. Play with paths Set up the configuration so that it matches your system. And so on. It would be so complicated that very few people would bother.

But lots of people run on Edge Rails. Why? Well it's not just because they want to use the latest features. Rails is in furious development all the time, and you may find that even a small upgrade might break some piece of your application. So to make sure that their apps will keep working as Rails evolves, they don't wait for weeks or months to upgrade, some of them update to the Edge every day.

But how do you install Edge Rails in your application? It's simple. You do this:

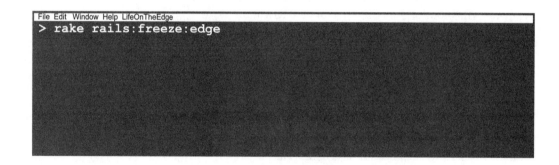

```
File Edit Window Help LifeOnTheEdge
> rake rails:freeze:edge
```

That single command is all you need. The rake tool will connect to the Rails development servers and download the latest version of the rails scripts and install them in the vendor/plugins directory of your application. Every time you start the Rails server, the code in the vendor directory is used before going to the main Rails install on the machine. That means that Edge Rails will be used for that single application.

Life can be pretty hairy on the Edge. But sometimes it's better to find version compatibility issues, one at a time...

Getting more information

Even though Rails allows you to create fully-functional web applications fast and safely, there's no doubt that to really master Rails can take a really long time. There's simply so much of it.

This means you need a pretty good reference. And the best references are online. Rails is changing all the time. Every day new things are checked into the Rails source code, and the only way to keep up with it is to go online. Here are some great web sites to get you started:

 http://www.rubyonrails.org/
The home of Rails itself. It's not only the place for software but also presentations, screencasts and links for further reading.

 http://wiki.rubyonrails.org/rails
This gives detailed instructions on installation and troubleshooting, as well as providing links to further online resources.

 http://ryandaigle.com/
Ryan's blog contains a wealth of information on the latest cool tricks you can do in Rails.

 http://www.ruby-lang.org/en/
The latest information on the Ruby language.

Built-in documentation

As well as a plethora of online material, your Ruby on Rails contains most of the things you'll need, right out of the box. The two most important command line tools are:

```
ri <something>
```

Where <something> is a Ruby class that you need to know more about. For example, "ri Array" will tell you all about the Array class.

Another source of useful information is through the gem server. Gem is the most commonly used package management tool for Ruby and it is probably the command you used to install Rails. Gem has a built in server that provides the same kind of API documentation you find at the http://api.rubyonrails.org site. To start it type:

```
gem server
```

and then open a browser at:

```
http://localhost:8808/
```

A little light reading...

Of course, here at Head First Labs, we're book people. And it's doesn't matter how great the online material is, there's nothing to beat having an actual real book with pages and everything to help you absorb the material. Now that you've got to the end of this book, and your brain is feeling fit and full of new Ruby on Rails expertise, you might want to take the chance to try out these other tripendicular tomes:

The Ruby Way

We love this book at Head First. It's a big, meaty work, but it's beautifully written by Hal Fulton. This is a book that will take you on a deep journey into the Ruby language. The great thing is that it doesn't just give you the details of the language, but it also explains the philosophy behind the language design. Many of the things that make Rails so great come directly from Ruby. And many of those things are mentioned in this book.

Agile Web Development with Rails

This is a great book to take you further into Rails development. An interesting thing about it is that it is written like a development project. So a few months before a new version is released, a beta version is released online for people to try out and comment on.

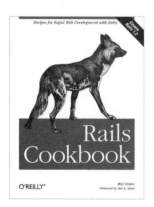

Rails Cookbook

Once you get up and running with Rails, you will probably need to solve the same kinds of problems that many, many other people have had to deal with before you. Fear not! *Rails Cookbook* gives a you a delicious set of pre-written pieces of code to get you through your difficulties.

Head First books on related topics

Now, as well as books on Ruby and Rails, you might find it useful to read up on the related topics. And what's the best way to bootstrap your brain in a new subject? With Head First books, of course!

Head First Ajax

Rails comes with a ton of built in support for Ajax development, but to really make the most out of it, you need to get to grips with how Ajax really works. And what better way than with *Head First Ajax*?

Head First JavaScript

Ajax is built on JavaScript, and if you know in detail how to hack JavaScript, you'll really make your application sing. *Head First JavaScript* is a great way into the language.

Head First Software Development

In this book, you've learned about how to program in the Ruby on Rails framework. If you want to move from *programming* to *development*, then pick up this book. It will teach you how the real pros do it, from how to run the planning in your project, to automated testing and continuous integration.

Tools for your Rails Toolbox

You've got Chapter 10 under your belt, and now you've added some real world things you need to think about.

Rails Tools

Rails contains a bunch of extra helpers that you can use in your applications

The Ruby language is pretty powerful. While you can create cool web apps without much Ruby knowledge, knowing a bit more Ruby is useful.

rake test – runs the automated tests in your application

rake rails:freeze:edge – installs the latest version of Rails into your application

RAILS_ENV=production – runs your system against a *live* database

ri <something> – gives you information about the methods of a Ruby object

gem server – starts the Ruby documentation server

Your brain – this is most powerful development tool you have

CHAPTER 10

Leaving town...

It's been great having you here in Railsville!

We're sad to see you leave, but there's nothing like taking what you've learned and putting it to use. You're just beginning your Rails journey, and we've put you in the driving seat. We're dying to hear how things go, so *drop us a line* at the Head First Labs web site, **www.headfirstlabs.com**, and let us know how Rails is paying off for **YOU**!

Index

Symbols

@ad variable 67
  default value 114

A

:action parameter 58, 59
actions 74, 107
  page templates and controller methods 117, 129
ActiveRecord 6
air reservation system (see Coconut Airways project)
Ajax 263–306, 359–400
  creating requests using 368–369
  dynamically updating parts of web page 376
  :full_page 361
  generating Ajax form 370
  helpers 306
  JavaScript generator 298–302
  libraries 272
  links 391
  "Refresh" link 273
  :show_action 361
  timer events 279–281
Ajax Exposed 284
application framework 4–6
architecture
  MVC (see MVC architecture)
  REST (see REST)
arrays 81–82
  for loops 86–87
  index 82
  partials 242
asynchronous requests 271, 275
authenticity token 275
auto_discovery_link helper 353

B

background requests 271, 292
belongs_to attribute 256, 261
browsers
  asking for updates 278–279
  JavaScript disabled 380
  updating entire page 270
Bullet Points
  background requests 292
  belongs_to attribute 256
  controllers 70
  CRUD operations 18
  displaying data 92
  form_tag helper 170
  has_many attribute 256
  JavaScript events 292
  migrations 43
  MVC architecture 43
  page sequences 170
  page templates 70
  params[:field_name] 170
  partials 256
  puts "A string" 170
  rails <app name> 18
  rake db:migrate 43
  relationships 256
  routes 70
  Ruby object 70
  ruby script/server 18
  scaffolding 18
  _tag fields 170
  validate method 256
  validators 201
  XML HTTP Requests (XHRs) 292
business logic 22

C

calling methods on a nil object 152

CamelCase 15, 52, 60

_ character 230

class file for controller 52

Coconut Airways project 220–262
  excess baggage validation 249–258
    reverse relationship 253
  partials 225
    array of seats 242
    calling with render command 231
    creating 230
    local variables 234–235
  relationships 244–248
    defining 247
  Test Drive 259, 303
    confirmation message 305
    excess baggage validation 255
    hiding flight number field 241
    initializing seat object 236
    JavaScript button 276–277
    JavaScript events 288
    page fragment 269
    relationships 248
    replacing create method 291
    seat-list array 243
    timer code 283
    viewing booking form 232
  updating only seat list 266–306
    browsers asking for updates 278–279
    JavaScript form 286–292
    updating create method 289–291
    (see also Ajax)
:conditions parameter 181

connecting models (see relationships)

controller code 21

controller create method 121

controller methods, actions 117

:controller parameter 58, 59

controllers 70
  error messages 208
  formatted data 119
  generate controller command 52, 53
  naming conventions 53
  params[:action] 59
  params[:controller] 59
  sending data to view 66–67

Convention Over Configuration principle 9, 18

create method, updating in Coconut Airways project 289–291

crossword puzzles, Scaffoldless Grid 99–100

CRUD operations 10, 18, 158

custom pages, error messages 207

D

database queries 179
  condition parameter 181
  modifying conditions 180–181

databases 74
  changing 409
  saving data 106

database system 4–6

data, converting to object before saving 120–122

DELETE requests 397, 411

deleting data 145–150

development cycle 28

Don't Repeat Yourself principle 14

Download It!
  _map.html.erb 314

duplicated code 94

E

Edge Rails 412

edit_incident route 393–394

editing front page of web site 9

edit_<model_name>_path(object) 399

environments 408

environment variables, RAILS_ENV 408

ERb (Embedded Ruby) 54–56
    assembling pages 229
    expressions 69
    generating web pages 88

ERb Files Up Close 226

error messages
    changing in validation 197
    custom pages 207
    displaying 212
    validators not displaying 204

error_messages method 212

errors.add_to_base(...) 261

expressions 69

F

f.error_messages 212, 216, 217

:field_name parameter 170

finders 80, 174–186
    attributes 173
    :conditions 181
    database queries 179
    matching this or that 178
    versus relationships 252

Finders Up Close 179

for loops 86–87

formatted data 119

form_for helper 166, 385

forms 107
    Ajax requests 286–292
    associated with model object 110
    creating object before displaying 115–116
    in relation to objects 109
    _tag fields 170

form_tag helper 166, 170

:full_page parameter 361

functional tests 407

functions, restricting access to 142–144

G

Geek Bits
    CamelCase 52
    Google Maps 315
    helpers 404
    SQLite3 14
    :xml render method 321

Gem 413

gem server 416

generate controller command 52, 53

generate model command 50, 53

GET requests 395, 397, 411

getting started 1–44
    application framework 4–6
    business logic 22
    Convention Over Configuration principle 9, 18
    CRUD operations 10, 18
    database system 4–6
    Don't Repeat Yourself principle 14
    editing front page of web site 9
    helpers 37
    migrations 14–18, 32–35, 43
        rake command 35
    modifying applications 19–20
    MVC architecture 21–28, 43
        view versus controller 22
    naming conventions 15, 34
    object-relational mapping library 4–6
        ActiveRecord 6
    page templates 26
        editing 36–37
    rails <app name> 18
    Rails architecture 20–28
    rails command 7, 18
    Rails development cycle 28
    rake command 18

getting started (*continued*)

rake db:migrate 35, 43

ruby command 18

ruby script/server 8–9, 18

Ruby versus Rails 9

scaffold command 12, 14

scaffolding 10–13, 18

symbols 27

Test Drive 8, 28, 42
> creating tables with migration 16–17
> scaffolding 13

timestamps and migrations 35

web server 4–6

Google Maps 359
> :full_page 361
> generating Ajax form 370
> key 315
> mashup 313–356
>> generating XML mapping data 318–322
>> mapping data 316
> server 313–314
> :show_action 361
> (see also Ajax)

H

has_many attribute 247, 253, 254, 256

Head First Climbers project 358–400
> converting index page 361
> edit_incident route 393–394
> editing pop-up windows 382–385
> generating Ajax form 370
> Google Maps mashup 313–356
>> generating XML mapping data 318–322
>> mapping data 316
> Google Maps server 313–314
> mapping location data 310–312
> multiple representations 326–356
>> which format gets requested 334–335
> RSS feeds 344–356
> show_with_map action 311, 327
> Test Drive 366, 396
>> Ajax links 392
>> Edit link added to the "show" partial 390

Google Maps mashup 317, 322, 325, 333, 337, 342
> map_info <div> 379
> pop-up form 373
> RSS feed 347, 354
> updating contents of pop-up's <div> 376

helpers 37, 397, 404
> Ajax 306
> auto_discovery_link 353
> form_for 166, 385
> form_tag 166, 170
> link_to 386, 387

HTML
> <link... /> reference 353
> multiple representations 327–337
>> deciding which format to use 330
>> which format gets requested 334–335

HTTP Authentication 142–143

HTTP methods 394–395, 411

HTTP requests and responses 124

I

:id parameter 60

ids, web page 376

index page
> arrays 81–82
> building 73–92
> finder methods 80
> generating hyperlinks for each element 87
> reading all records 79–80

inserting data 104–132
> forms (see forms)
> SQL insert statement 122

integration tests 407

J

JavaScript 275
> Ajax requests 286–292
> authenticity token 275

disabled 380
events 292
timer events 279–281
(see also Ajax)
JavaScript engine 271
JavaScript generator 298–302

L

layouts 94–98, 226
reference 353
link_to helper 386, 387
local variables 234–235

M

_map.html.erb 314
map partial 380
mapping data 310–312, 316
    generating XML 318–322
map.resources 336
mashups 313
MeBay project 46–102
    actions 107
    @ad variable 67
        default value 114
    building applications without scaffolding 49
    controller create method 121
    controllers, formatted data 119
    controllers sending data to view 66–67
    converting data to object before saving 120–122
    converting records to objects 68
    deleting data 145–150
    forms 107
        associated with model objects 110
        creating object before displaying 115–116
        in relation to objects 109
    generate controller command 52

index page
    arrays 81–82
    finder methods 80
    generating hyperlinks for each element 87
    reading all records 79–80
index page, building 73–92
inserting data 104–132
layouts 94–98
migration 51
model-generator command 50
MVC architecture 49
page templates 54–56
    adding loops with scriptlets 89
    converting into Ruby code 88–90
    matching controller method 117
    reusing 128
    single template that controls other templates 94–98
rake db:migrate command 51
redirects 130–131
routes 57–60
    priority 76
Ruby expressions 69
saving data 106
securing applications, restricting access to functions 142–144
sending data to view 64–67
Test Drive 56
    blank ads 63
    controller code 118
    create.html.erb page template 127
    custom page control 211
    deleting ads from site 150
    edit.html.erb page template 140
    layouts
    new index page 92
    page template for the "new" form 113
    records converted to objects 70
    redirects 132
    security code 144
    updating controller's create method 123
    validation 213
updating data 133–143

MeBay project (*continued*)

    validation 203–218

        displaying error messages 212

        error messages and controllers 208

        validators not displaying errors 204

methods returning true or false 385

migrations 14–18, 32–35, 43

    MeBay project 51

    rake command 35

    timestamps 35

model code 21

model form 162, 166

model objects 81

    forms associated with 110

    generating XML 319–320

    skipping validation 197

models

    connecting (see relationships)

    generate model command 50, 53

    naming conventions 53

    validating in 190

modifying applications 19–20

multiple representations 326–356

    deciding which format to use 330

    resources 329

    which format gets requested 334–335

MVC architecture 21–28, 43

    MeBay project 49

    view versus controller 22

MySQL databases 409

N

naming conventions 15, 34

    controllers 53

    models 53

    tables 53

new_<model_name>_path 399

nil 114

    calling methods on a nil object 152

No Dumb Questions

    actions 74

    Ajax forms 292

    arrays 82

    asynchronous requests 275

    authenticity token 275

    business logic 22

    calling render 335

    CamelCase 60

    Convention over Configuration principle 18

    databases 74

    editing front page of web site 9

    examining tables 53

    form_tag versus form_for 170

    generate controller command 53

    generate model command 53

    GET and POST requests 397

    Google Maps 380

    helpers 37, 397

    :id 60

    JavaScript 275

    JavaScript disabled 380

    local variables 235

    map partial 380

    map.resources 336

    methods returning true or false 385

    migration 33

    model form 162

    non-model form 162

    page templates 74

    partials 235, 256

    primitives 74

    PUT and DELETE requests 397

    rails command 18

    rake command 18

    rake db:migrate command 53

    redirects 131

    render method 321

    requests 60

    responses 60

    REST 335

    RESTful design 397

route configuration 60
ruby command 18
ruby script/server 9
Ruby versus Rails 9
saved objects 385
scaffolding 60, 162
strings as paths 397
symbols 27
timer events 281
validation
    asking model object to skip 197
    changing error messages 197
validators 197
view versus controller 22
non-model form 162, 166

O

object-relational mapping library 4–6
    ActiveRecord 6
objects 70
    attributes 68
    converting records to 68
    in relation to forms 109
    model objects 81
    saved 385
Oracle databases 409

P

page fragments 269, 362
page sequences 170
page templates 26, 70, 74, 226
    actions 129
    adding loops with scriptlets 89
    converting into Ruby code 88–90
    editing 36–37
    Embedded Ruby (ERb) 54–56
    matching controller method 117
    partial (see partials)
    reusing 128
    single template that controls other templates 94–98

partials 225, 226, 256
    arrays 242
    calling with render command 231
    creating 230
    local variables 234–235
    passing variable to 261
passwords 142
_path 399
Pool Puzzle
    Coconut Airways project 239–240
    getting started 5–6
    MeBay project 71–72
    validation 209–210
    XML builder template 351–352
pop-up windows, updating contents 376
POST requests 395, 397, 411
primitives 74
Prototype library 272
    Google Maps 380
Protoype library 306
PUT requests 397, 411
puts <string> 170, 186

Q

queries 179
    condition parameter 181
    modifying conditions 180–181

R

Rails
    architecture 20–28
    development cycle 28
    environments 408
    helpers 37, 404
    JavaScript generator 298–302
    primitives 74
    versus Ruby 9
rails <app name> 18

rails command 18
    file generation 7
RAILS_ENV=production 416
RAILS_ENV variable 408
Rails Exposed 22
Rails principles
    Convention Over Configuration 9, 18
    Don't Repeat Yourself 14
Rails resources
    books 414–415
    built-in documentation 413
    web sites 413
Rails Toolbox
    Rails Tools
        @ad.save 152
        @ad.update_attributes 152
        Ajax applications 306
        Ajax helpers 306
        changing "_path" to "_url" 399
        edit_<model_name>_path(object) 399
        errors.add_to_base(...) 261
        f.error_messages 217
        find(:all, :conditions=>[...]) 186
        form_tag 186
        gem server 416
        helpers 416
        http_authentication 152
        new_<model_name>_path 399
        :only parameter 356
        passing variable to partial 261
        Protoype library 306
        rails app-name 44
        RAILS_ENV=production 416
        rake db:migrate 44
        rake rails:freeze:edge 416
        rake routes 399
        redirect_to 152
        render :action=>'new' 217
        render :partial=>"name" 261
        render :template=>"a/template" 217
        responder object 356
        responders 356
        respond_to 356

ri <something> 416
:root parameter 356
<route name>_path(object) 399
Ruby language 416
ruby script/generate controller 101
ruby script/generate migration 44
ruby script/generate model 101
ruby script/generate scaffold 44
ruby script/server 44
save method 217
to_xml 356
update_attributes method 217
validates_format_of 217
validates_inclusion_of 217
validates_length_of 217
validates_uniqueness_of 217
XML builder templates 356
    Ruby Tools
        "#{" and "}" 152
        arrays 101
        arrays, looping through 101
        calling methods on a nil object 152
        nil 152
        params[...] 152
        puts <string> 186
rake command 18
    migrations 35
rake db:migrate command 15, 35, 43, 51, 53
rake rails:freeze:edge 416
rake routes 399
Ready Bake Code, layout file for Rubyville Health Club
    project 164
Ready Bake Sign-In Code 143
Ready Bake Super-Template Code 95
records
    converting to objects 68
    finding client records in Rubyville Health Club project
        171–172
redirects 130–131
relationships 244–248
    defining 247
    excess baggage validation 249–258
    reverse 253
    versus finders 252

Relationships Up Close 246

render command
    calling 335
    calling partial 231

render method 321
    :xml 321

requests 60, 124, 278
    Ajax 286–292
    asynchronous 271, 275
    background 271, 292
    JavaScript 271
    XML HTTP Requests (XHRs) 292

required fields, validating 196–198

reservation system (see Coconut Airways project)

resources 329

responder object 356

responders 356

respond_to 356

respond_to do method 330

responses 60, 124, 278

REST 329, 335, 410–411

RESTful design 397

RESTful Routes Up Close 388–389

reusing existing page template 128

ri <something> 413, 416

:root parameter 356

<route name>_path(object) 399

routes 57–60, 70
    :action 58
    configuration 60
    :controller 58
    params[:action] 59
    params[:controller] 59
    priority 76

Routing Exposed 77

RSS feeds 344–356

Ruby
    ERb (see ERb (Embedded Ruby))
    expressions 69
    for loop 86
    methods returning true or false 385
    objects 70
    primitives 74
    Try this! 405
    versus Rails 9

ruby command 18

Ruby language 416

ruby script/server 8–9, 18

Rubyville Health Club project 154–186
    CRUD operations 158
    database queries, modifying conditions 180–181
    determining to fix scaffolding or write new code 156–161
    finders 174–186
        attributes 173
        :conditions 181
        database queries 179
        matching this or that 178
    finding client records 171–172
    layout file 164
    search function 159–186
        adding to interface 163–165
        building form 160
    Test Drive 156, 177
        layout including search functionality 165
        search functionality 169
        updating finder code 182
        validators 195, 198
    validating data 188–202
        in model 190
        simple validation (see validators)
    validating required fields 196–198

S

save method 217

saving data 106

scaffold command 12, 14

scaffolding 10–13, 18, 60, 162
    building applications without 49
    determining to fix or write new code 156–161
    editing pop-up windows 382–385

scriptlets 89

search function
    finder method (see finders)
    Rubyville Health Club project 159–186
        adding to interface 163–165
        building form 160

securing applications
    HTTP Authentication 142–144
    restricting access to functions 142–144
    username and password 142–144

:show_action parameter 361

show_with_map action 311, 327

SQL insert statement 122

SQLite3 14

SQL queries 180–181
    condition parameter 181

strings as paths 397

symbols 27

T

tables
    examining 53
    naming conventions 53

_tag fields 170

templates (see page templates)

testing applications 406–407
    functional tests 407
        integration tests 407
        unit test 407

timer events 279–281

timestamps 15
    migrations 35

to_xml method 348, 356

Try this! Ruby 405

U

underscores 15

unit test 407

update_attributes method 217

updating data 133–143

_url 399

username and password 142–143

V

validate method 250, 256, 261

validates_format_of 199, 200, 217

validates_inclusion_of 199, 200, 217

validates_length_of 199, 200, 217

validates_numericality_of 194

validates_presence_of 197

validates_uniqueness_of 199, 200, 217

validation 187–218
    asking model object to skip 197
    error messages
        changing 197
        custom pages 207
        displaying 212
    excess baggage (Coconut Airways project) 249–258
    MeBay project 203–218
        displaying error messages 212
        error messages and controllers 208
    Rubyville Health Club project 188–202
    simple (see validators)
    validating in model 190

validators
> checking if number 194
> how validators work 192–193
> not displaying errors 204
> required fields 196–198
> validates_numericality_of 194
> validates_presence_of 197

variables
> local 234–235
> passing variable to partial 261

view code 21
> editing 26–27
> page templates (see page templates)

views
> controllers sending data to 66–67
> sending data to 64–67
> versus controllers 22

W

Watch it!
> arrays 82
> naming conventions 15
> render calls 231

web pages, browsers updating entire page 270

web server 4–6

X

XML 307–356
> generating from model object 319–320
> generating mapping data 318–322
> multiple representations 326–356
>> deciding which format to use 330
>> which format gets requested 334–335
> RSS feeds 344–356
> to_xml method 348

XML Builders Up Close 350

XML builder templates 349–350, 356

XML HTTP Requests (XHRs) 292

:xml render method 321